# Chester County, South Carolina

# DEED ABSTRACTS

## VOLUME I
## 1785–1799 [1768–1799]
### Deed Books A-F

By

## Brent H. Holcomb

SCMAR
2005

HERITAGE BOOKS
2021

# HERITAGE BOOKS

*AN IMPRINT OF HERITAGE BOOKS, INC.*

**Books, CDs, and more—Worldwide**

For our listing of thousands of titles see our website
at
www.HeritageBooks.com

Published 2021 by
HERITAGE BOOKS, INC.
Publishing Division
5810 Ruatan Street
Berwyn Heights, Md. 20740

Copyright © 2005 Brent H. Holcomb
SCMAR
Columbia, South Carolina

Library of Congress Catalog Card Number: 2004098732

International Standard Book Numbers
Paperbound: 978-0-7884-1496-1

# INTRODUCTION

Chester County was formed in 1785 as a county of Camden District. It was included in Pinckney District 1791-1799. In the year 1800 with the end of the county court system, it became Chester District. In the colonial period the area of Chester County was considered part of Craven County in South Carolina as well as part of St. Mark's Parish. Prior to the border surveys of 1764 and 1772, the area was included in the North Carolina counties of Anson, Mecklenburg, and Tryon. For this reason many grants and deeds from North Carolina are referenced in the Chester County deeds. Land grants from North Carolina are frequently referred to as "north patents." The South Carolina deeds prior to 1785 were recorded in Charleston and in some cases a few years later. The Charleston deeds have been abstracted and published through the year 1788, those from 1773-1788 by the writer. The deeds of the aforementioned North Carolina counties have also been abstracted and published. The deeds in this volume were recorded 1785 - 1799. As is common, there are deeds recorded from a much earlier time period. The earliest deed included in this work dates from 17 November 1768 (C, 5-7). Therefore, with this work, the deed abstracts for the Chester County area are now in print from the beginning to the year 1799. With the beginning of county courts in South Carolina, deeds were required to be either acknowlededged or proved by the oaths of two witnesses until 1788. Deeds which had been proved prior to 1785 before a Justice of the Peace were frequently accepted on that proof and recorded. Beginning in 1788 only one witness was required to prove a deed before recording. The deeds in this volume have been abstracted from South Carolina Archives microfilm, Rolls C2268, C2269, and C2270.

Chester County bordered on the counties of York, Fairfield, Union, Kershaw, and Lancaster. Like other counties in South Carolina, Chester County became a district in the year 1800. Pinckney Judicial District, of which Chester County had been a part, was discontinued at that time. The term *county* was resumed in 1868. There are curious references to the area as "Sumpter County" (Deed Book A, pages 161-165; 282-286; and pages 296-298). Sumter District did not exist until the year 1800, being formed from the counties of Clarendon, Claremont, and Salem. It became Sumter County in 1868. It has nothing to do with Chester County, South Carolina.

My thanks to Mr. James D. McKain for preparing the excellent index.

Brent H. Holcomb
October 27, 2004

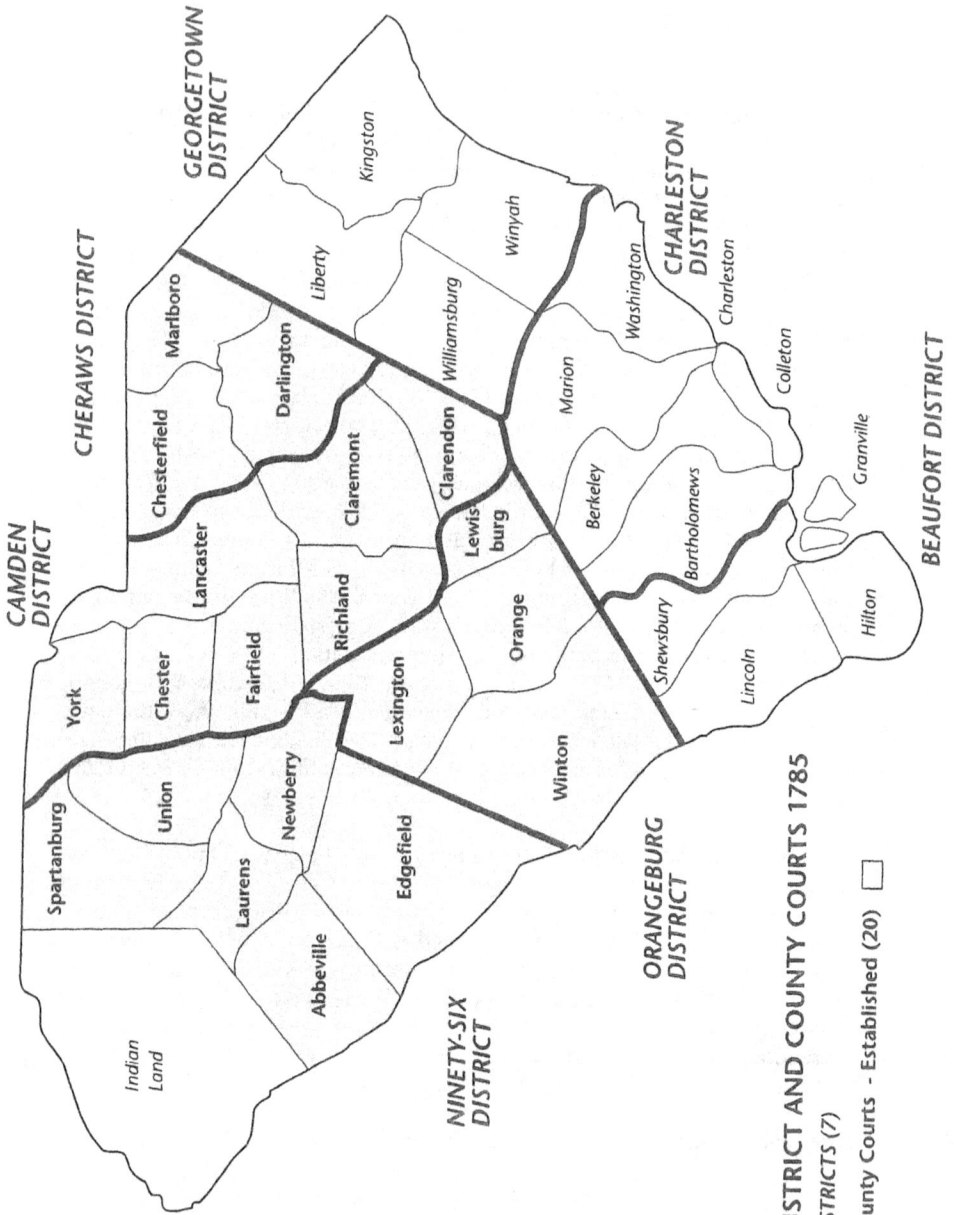

Map courtesy of the South Carolina Archives and History Center.

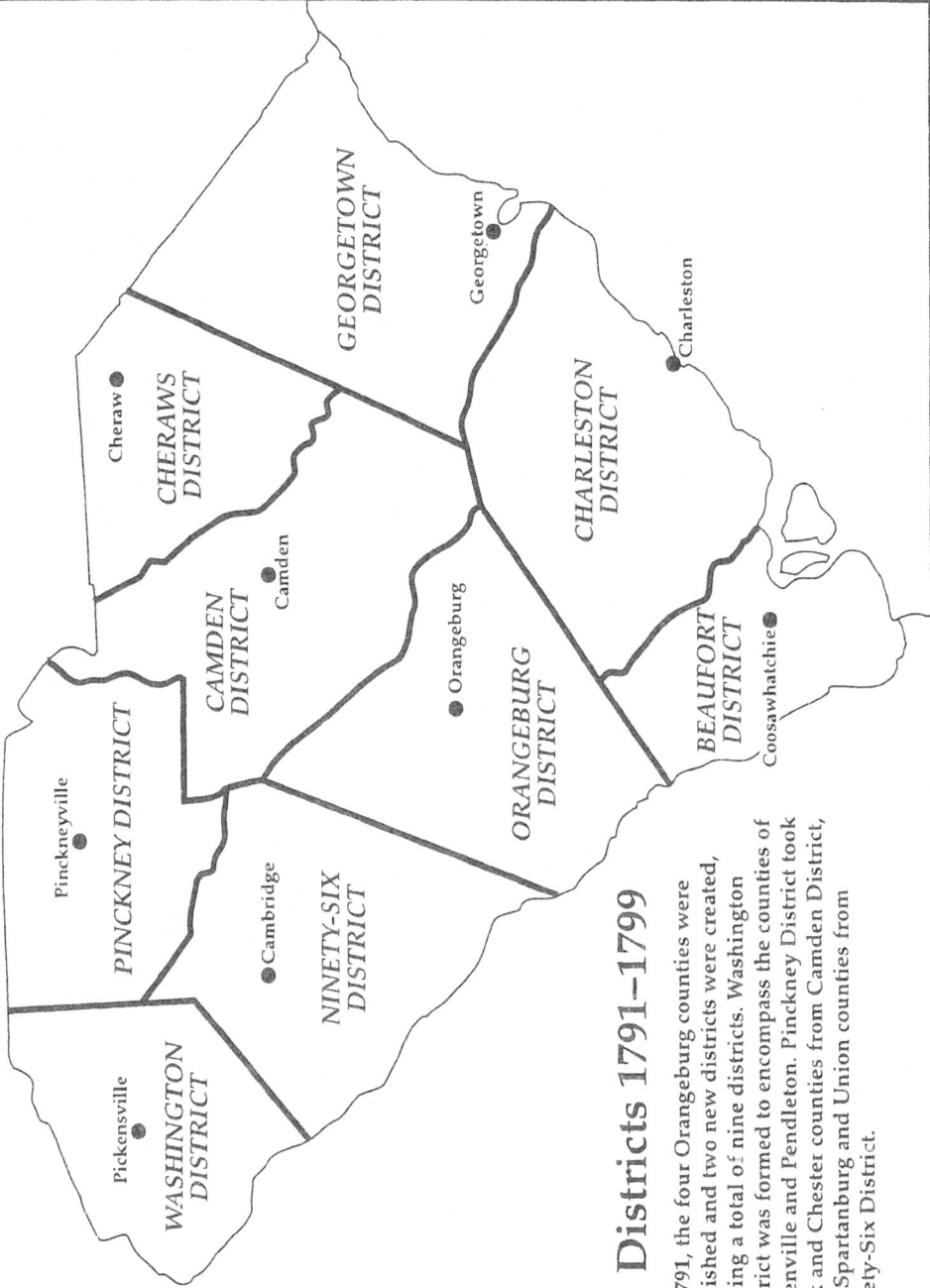

# Districts 1791–1799

In 1791, the four Orangeburg counties were abolished and two new districts were created, making a total of nine districts. Washington District was formed to encompass the counties of Greenville and Pendleton. Pinckney District took York and Chester counties from Camden District, and Spartanburg and Union counties from Ninety-Six District.

# CHESTER COUNTY SOUTH CAROLINA
## DEED ABSTRACTS

**A, 1-4**: 19 Nov 1786 [*sic*], Micheal Dickson of Camden District, Craven County, Province of SC, planter, and wife Sarah, to John Service of same, for £62, weaver, 50 acres, part of tract granted 23 Jan 1773 to Micheal Dixon, 150 acres on waters of Bull run in Craven County. Micheal Dickson (LS), Sarah Dickson (X) (LS), Wit: Wm Boyd, John Miller, James McQuistion. Acknowledged by Micheal Dickson at court held for Chester County at the House of John Walker 20 July 1785.

**A, 4-7**: 16 May 1781, John Walker & Jane his wife of Camden District, Craven County, SC, to John Service of same, weaver, for £200, 100 acres granted to John Walker 19 Nov 1772 to John Walker, 100 acres on a small branch of Hickory Creek, adj. land surveyed for Micheal Dickson, John Walker. John Walker (X) (LS), Jane Walker (X) (LS), Wit: Wm. Boyd, John Campbell, John McLilley. Acknowledged by John Walker at court held for Chester County at the House of John Walker 20 July 1785.

**A, 7-12**: Lease and release. 7 & 8 Aug 1779, Peter Wiley of parish of St. Marks, SC, weaver, to Francis Wiley of same parish, planter, for £2000, tract granted 13 May 1768 to Peter Wiley, 250 acres on a small branch of Rockey Creek in Craven County adj. Phillip Walker. Peter Wylie (LS), Wit: Alex Gaston, William Wylie. Acknowledged by Peter Wylie at court held for Chester County at the House of John Walker 21 July 1785.

**A, 12-17**: Lease and release. 6 & 7 June 1783, Francis Wylie of Parish of St. Mark, SC, planter, to William Wylie, yeoman of same parish, for £200, tract granted to Francis Wylie, 100 acres on a small branch of Rockey Creek adj. Robert McClary. Francis Wylie (LS), Wit: David Morrow, James Wylie. Acknowledged by Francis Wylie at court held for Chester County at the House of John Walker 21 July 1785.

**A, 17-18**: William Gaston, James Gaston, Joseph Gaston & Martha Gaston, Joseph Gaston Junr, John Gaston, Alexander Walker & Easther Walker, all of Chester County, SC, planter, appoint Hugh Gaston of said county, saddle, our true & lawful attorney for us, to sell two tracts of land in the state of Georgia, Washington County, the warrants of survey granted unto Alexander Gaston & David Gaston, 8 Oct 1785. William Gaston (LS), John Gaston (LS), James Gaston (LS), Joseph Gaston Junr (LS), Joseph Gaston (I S), Martha Gaston (LS), Alexr Walker, Easther Walker. Acknowledged 18 Oct 1785.

**A, 18-22**: 26 Feb 1780, David Morrow & Mary his wife of Camden District, SC, to John Green of same, for £3000 current money of said state, tract on both sides of south fork of Fishing Creek, 100 acres granted to said David Morrow by patent from SC, 30 June 1766. David Morrow (X) (LS), Mary Morrow (X) (LS), Wit: Wm Jones, John Mills, Jonathan Jones. Acknowledged by David Morrow at court held for Chester County at the House of John Walker 20 Oct 1785.

**A, 18-22**: 19 Jan 1785, John Green & Mary his wife of Craven County, SC, to James Langsbey, merchant, of same place, 50 acres, being a moiety of tract of land granted to David Morrow & by him conveyed to John Green 26 Feb 1780. John Green (LS), Mary Green (m) (LS), Wit: John Simpson, William Jones, Jonathan Jones. Acknowledged by John Green at court held for Chester County at the House of John Walker 20 Oct 1785.

**A, 25-27**: 19 Jan 1785, Jonathan Jones & Barsheba his wife of Parish of St. Mark, SC, yeoman, to James Langbey of same parish, merchant, for £150, tract granted 10 May 1768 to Robert Glover, 250 acres on James McClure's spring branch, being conveyed to Henry Culp by an indenture 21 Sept 1768, memorial entered in the Auditor's Office in Book I. No. 9, 20 Oct 1768, and again conveyed by said Culp to Jonathan Jones 6 June 1772, memorial entered 29 April 1772 in Book W. No 4, pages 407-409. Jonathan Jones (LS), Bersheba Jones (B) (LS), Wit: William Jones, John Green, John Simpson. Proved at a court held for Chester County at the house of John Walker 209 Oct 1785 by the oath of John Green.

**A, 27-29**: 7 Sept 1785, Isaac Eoff of Chester County, SC, planter, to James Langsbey of said county, merchant, for £8 sterling, 200 acres on south fork of Fishing Creek, adj. Samuel Morrow, Miller, granted to John McEllilly by patent 9 April 1770, and registered in Book No 6, No Carolina, Tryon County, and conveyed from McEllilly to John Penny 17 Oct 1772 and from said Penny to Moses Alexander by deed 18 Oct 1771 and registered in Tryon County 11 Nov 1771 in Book N. 6,and left by said Moses Alexander by his will to Nathaniel Alexander Do'r, his son & Heir, which said Natha'l Alexander conveyed to Isaac Eoff, 26 March 1784. Isaac Eoff (LS), Wit :John Mills, Wm. Jones, Bersheba Jones (B). Proved by the oath of John Mills and William Jones 20 Oct 1785.

**A, 30-32**: 23 Oct 1784, Col. Edward Lacey & Jane his wife of District of Camden, SC, to James McNeel of same, for £105 SC money, 440 acres with a Dwelling House & about 40 acres of Cleared Ground thereon, on Susey Branch, being a fork of Turkey Creek of Broad River, adj. land laid out for George Saddler, Col. Patrick McGriff, granted by patent to said Edward Lacey by Gov. Tryon of North Carolina, 29 April 1768. Edw'd Lacey (LS), Jane Lacy (LS), Wit: Pat McGriff, Abraham Pearce. Acknowledged by Edward Lacy and Jane his wife 10 Oct 1785.

**A, 32-33**: 24 Dec 1784, Joseph Brown and wife Sarah of Camden District, to Thomas Roden of same, planter, for £50 sterling, 200 acres granted to said Joseph Brown by patent 16 Jan 1772 from SC. Joseph Brown (LS), Sarah Brown (LS), Wit: William Roden, James Brown, Sarah Brown. Acknowledged by Joseph Brown 17 Jan 1786 at a court held at the house of John Walker.

**A, 33-35**: South Carolina, Chester County. 15 Dec 1785, Archabald Elliott, planter, to William Elliott, son of the said Archabald Elliott, both of said county and state, for natural love & affection, 152 acres on both sides of the south fork of Fishing Creek, adj. said Archebald Elliott, Robert Gill, Rev. John Simpson, Alexander & Samuel Brown, George Craig, part of tract granted to David Leeves and conveyed to said Archb'd Elliott by lease & release, and the other part a part of tract granted to said Arch'd Elliott. Archabald Elliott (E) (LS), Wit: Hugh Dods, William Farie. Acknowledged by Archebald Elliott 17 Jan 1786.

**A, 35-37**: 13 Jan 1783, Alexander Brown of Camden District, planter, to Samuel Brown of same, son to said Alexander Brown, for natural love & affection, tract on south side of South fork of Fishing Creek, between lands of said Alexr Brown, William Elliott, George Craig, Jonathan Jones & John Mills, 130 acres. Alexander Brown (LS), Wit: Alexr Brown Junr, J. McFarlin. Proved by the oath of John McFarlin 18 Jan 1786.

**A, 37-40**: 11 June 1785, James Forguson Sr. of Chester County, planter, to Robert Forguson of said county, yeoman, for £200 lawful money of said state, land granted 10 May 1768 to James Forguson Senr, part of 500 [sic, for 200?] acres on SW side Cataba River between Fishing Creek and Rocky Creek, 100 acres, half of 200 acres, viz the north end or side of the same granted on which said James Forguson now lives, reserving to the said James Forguson the privilege of enjoying the same during his life, or his wife Agnes's life time. James Forguson (LS), Wit: Wm Wiley, Abr'm Forguson. Proved by the oaths of William Wiley and Abraham Forguson 17 Jan 1786.

**A, 40-43**: 11 June 1785, James Forguson Senr of Chester county, to Abraham Forguson, shoemaker, of same, for £400, 100 acres, half of 200 acres granted to said James Forguson Senr 10 May 1768, on SW side Cataba River between Fishing Creek... James Forguson (LS), Wit: Wm Wiley, Robert Ferguson. Proved by the oaths of William Wiley and Robert Forguson 17 Jan 1786.

**A, 43-46**: 1 Oct 1785, William McFaden of Chester County to George Lewis of same, for £500 lawful money of SC, tract granted 24 Jan[?] 1770 by SC, to William McFadin, 200 acres in Craven County now Chester, on west side of Fishing Creek, vacant on all sides. Wm McFaden (LS), Ann McFaden (X) (LS), Wit: William Wiley, Thos Dugan, Robert Forguson. Proved 17 Jan 1786 by the oath of William Wiley and Robert Forguson.

**A, 46-47**: George Morris for £30 sterling to John Morris, one red cow & Calf marked with a Crop in Each Ear & also a split in each ear and an under peace taken out of the right ear, also another Red Cow & yearling, the cow marked with a Crop & a hold in the right Ear & a crop & split in the left ear, also a brown cow & yearling marked with a crop & under peace in the right and a Crop & split in the left ear, also a red heiffer marked with a crop & split in each ear, also ten head of geese, three bee hives, also one black horse about eleven years old, about thirteen hands three inches high, his brand is unknown as this time & has a crop of his left ear, also a black mare six years old & about thirteen hands high, & branded on the near shoulder & Buttock supposed to be thus S, also two featherbeds & furniture & three bed steads, as also two basons, two dishes, four plates, three pots & one frying pan, 21 Dec 1785. George Morris (LS), Wit: John McCown, Thos Stroud (X), Andrew Hemphill. Acknowledged by said George Morress 17 Jan 1786.

**A, 47-48**: Peter Petree, planter, of Chester County, appoint Col. Archabald Little of Orrange Co., NC, my lawful attorney, to sue for, recover & receive of Amos Tims, planter, of Granville county, NC, all such sums of money, debts, etc., due me, 17 Jan 1786. Peter Petree (LS), Wit: James Stewart, Hazel Hardwick. Acknowledged at a court held for Chester County at the house of John Walker 18 Jan 1786. Present: Joseph Brown, David Hopkins, James Knox, Andrew Hemphill, Gentlemen Justices.

**A, 49-53**: Lease and release. 30 & 31 Oct 1777, Archabald Elliott of Parish of St. Marks, SC, yeoman, to Joseph Walker of same, planter, for £___, land granted 31 Aug 1753 by North Carolina to James McCullough, 400 acres in the county of Anson, North Carolina, but now by the continuation of the Boundry Line in South Carolina and Craven County on the south side of Fishing Creek upon a great ranch thereof between the middle path & the second path including the Old Indian Camps & a tree marked IMG, and said James McCullogh being dec'd Alexander McCullough, eldest son & Executor of the will & heir at law of the estate of the s'd James McCullough, hath sold 400 acres by lease and release 24 Nov 1762, now conveys 10 acres of said tract to Joseph Walker, Archabald Elliott (A) (LS), Wit: Hugh Whiteside, Saml Lard, John Gaston. Acknowledged 10 Jan 1786 by Archabald Elliott.

**A, 54-59**: Lease and release. 27 & 28 May 1776, John Combest & Agnes his wife, planter, of St. Marks Parish, to Peter Culp of same, for £---, land granted 19 Aug 1774 by SC to John Combest, 50 acres in Craven County on both sides of Fishing Creek, adj. Peter Culp. John Combest (LS), Ann Combest (X) (LS), Wit: Nicholas Bishop, John Carter. Proved by the oath of John Carter 28 Dec 1785 before James Knox, J.P. Proved in court by the oath of Nicholas Bishop 3 July 1786.

**A, 59-61**: 10 Jan 1785, John Moultrey of Craven County, SC, planter, to William Shaw of Gilford County, North Carolina, for £100 sterling, 250 acres on east side Broad River on a branch called Sandy Run, adj. John Walker, Hazel Haderdge, Amos Tims, granted to said John Moultrey 19 March 1773. Wit: Charles McClure, James Houston, Tho Dick. Proved by the oath of Charles McClure & James Houston 18 Jan 1786.

**A, 61-62**: South Carolina, Camden District. Nathaniel Sample appoints Phillip Walker, Esqr., of said district, lawful attorney to receive from all persons whatever & particularly of John McGlamery, all sums of money, debts, demands, etc., 5 April 1783. Nathaniel Sample (LS), Wit: Robert Cooper. Proved in Camden District by the oath of Capt. Robert Cooper 17 July 1785 before Joseph Palmer, J.P. Proved in court 18 Jan 1786 by the oath of Robert Cooper.

**A, 62-66**: 22 Oct 1783, Archibald Elliott & Sarah his wife, planter, to the Rev. John Simpson, V. D. M., for £200 sterling, 169 acres on south fork of Fishing Creek, adj. lands of said Archabald Elliott, John Simpson, Alexr Brown, the same being originally granted to said Archabald Elliott by patent A. D. 1772. Archabald Elliott (AE) (LS), Wit: William Elliott, Daniel Cooke. Proved in Camden District by the oath of Daniel Cooke 15 Nov 1783 before Wm Tate, J.P. Acknowledged by Archabald Elliott and wife Sarah in court 18 Jan 1786.

**A, 66-68**: 15 Feb 1785, Isaac Smith and Mary his wife of Camden District, SC, to David Carr of same district, for £200 proclamation money paid to William Terrell, tract granted 1767 by NC, 250 acres, surveyed to Isaac Smith 9 Jan 1767, in Craven County on both sides Fishing Creek, adj. Phillip Walker, John Latta. Isaac Smith (LS), Mary Smith (O) (LS), Wit: David Hunter, Robt Scott. Proved 18 Jan 1786 by the oath of David Hunter and order to lie for further proof.

**A, 69-71**: 5 Aug 1782, John Miles of Camden District, to Charles Miles of same, for £2000 current money of SC, 138 acres in Craven County on north side of Broad River on a branch thereof called Turkey Creek, part of 200 acres granted to James Miles by patent 20 April 1763 by SC, & now by the decease of said James Miles hath descended to John Miles, who is the eldest son & heir to said James Miles. John Miles (LS), Wit: William Given, Wm Miles, Rich'd Miles. Proved by the oath of Wm Given 15 Aug 178 before Jo. Brown, J. P. Acknowledged by John Miles in court for Chester county at the house of John Walker.

**A, 71-73**: 16 Aug 1785, John Henderson of Camden District, SC, planter, to Archabald McQuestion of same, for £20 sterling, 200 granted 7 May 1771 by SC to said John Henderson, in Craven County & branch of Rockey Creek called Bull run. John Henderson (LS), Wit: David McQuestion, Hugh McQuestion, James Wilson (mark). Proved by the oath of David McQuestion & Hugh McQuestion 18 Jan 1786.

**A, 74-75**: 4 May 1785, David Hopkins of Camden District to James Tims of same, for £100 old currency, 100 acres according to the platt surveyed 10 April 1773 on a warrent granted to me 6 April 1773, on waters of Sandy River, adj. land laid out to Moses Bond, plat certified 1 Aug 1785 and granted to ____ Mitchell 10 Oct 1784. D'd Hopkins (LS), Wit: Jeremiah Kingley, Jas Doughtrey, Thos Humpres. Acknowledged by David Hopkins in court 19 Jan 1786.

**A, 75-77**: 6 Oct 1785, John Jemby of Chester county, SC, to Ann Miller (otherwise Hart), widow of said county, for £15 s5 d8 sterling, 100 acres on the dry fork of Fishing Creek in Craven otherwise Chester county on the Seludy River that goes to the Fish dam ford on Broad River, adj. Richard Berrell, the same being granted to John Jimby by patent 8 Dec 1774, recorded in Book TTT, page 586. John Jimby (X) (LS), Wit: John Miles, Wm. Boyd, Dav'd Boyd. Proved by the oaths of John Mills & David Boyd 21 Jan 1786.

**A, 77-79**: 11 June 1785, James Furguson Senior of Chester County, planter, to Robert Ferguson of same, yeoman, for £100, 100 acres, part of a tract granted 10 May 1786 to James Furguson Senior, 500 acres on SW side Catabaw River between Fishing Creek & Rockey Creek, vacant on all sides. James Forguson (LS), Wit: Wm Wiley, Abraham Forguson.

**A, 79-82**: Lease and release. 27 & 28 May 1776, John Combest & Agnes his wife of Parish of St. Mark, planter, by grant dated 19 Aug 1774 by SC to John Combest, 50 acres on both sides Fishing Creek, adj. Peter Culp, John Latta. John Combest (LS), Ann Combest (X) (LS), Wit: Nicholas Bishop, John Carter. Proved 18 Jan 1786 by the oath of Nicholas Bishop and ordered to lie for further proof, and proved 8 July 1786 by the oath of John Carter.

**A, 83-84**: 8 April 1786, Thomas Rodin of Camden District, SC, planter, for £62 sterling, to William Head, 100 acres, part of 800 acres granted to Joseph Brown 16 Jan 1772, transferred from Joseph Brown to Thomas Roden 24 Dec 1784, on east side of John Moberly's land. Thomas Rodin (LS), Mary Rodin (M). Enoch Pearson, Ezekiel Sanders, Thomas Saunders (mark). Acknowledged by Thomas Rodin 18 April 1786.

**A, 85-90**: Lease and release. 29 & 30 June 1786, David Boyd & Margret his wife of Chester County, Camden District, SC, to William Boyd of same, 100 granted 13 May 1768 to Margaret Wylie now wife of David Boyd, in Craven County now Chester County on a branch of Rockey Creek adj. land surveyed for Jane McCarlney. David Boyd, Margaret Boyd (mark), Wit: William Boyd, Samuel Boyd, John Boyd. Proved by the oaths of William Boyd & John Boyd 7 July 1785 [sic].

**A, 90-92**: 15 Apr 1786, John Miles of Chester County, to William Miles of same, for £76 sterling, tract on east side of Turkey Creek adj. Matthew Floid, James Miles, 76 acres. John Miles (LS), Wit: Jo Palmer, Jno Martin. Acknowledged by John Miles 18 April 1786.

**A, 92-95**: 5 Aug 1782, John Miles of Camden District, to Charles Miles of same, for £1000 current money, 138 acres in Craven County on north side of Broad River on a branch thereof called Turkey Creek, part of 200 acres granted to Jas Miles 20 April 1783 by SC. John Miles (LS), Wit: William Givin, Wm. Miles, Rich'd Miles. Proved by the oath of Wm Given 5 Aug 1782 before Jos Brown, J. P.

**A, 95-97**: 15 April 1786, John Miles of Chester County to William Miles of same, for £100 sterling, tract on a branch of Turkey Creek adj. Jas Miles, Wm Minter, Joseph Feamster, 100 acres by a plat annexed to the grant to said John Miles dated 19 Aug 1774. John Miles (LS), Wit: Jo Palmer, John Martin. Acknowledged by John Miles 18 April 1786.

**A, 97-98**: _____ 1786, John Miles of Chester County to William Miles of same, for £100 sterling, tract on a branch of Turkey Creek adj. Jas Miles, Wm

Minter, Joseph Feamster, 100 acres granted to James Miles by patent 20 Apr 1763. John Miles (LS), Wit: Jo Palmer, John Martin.

**A, 99-102**: Lease and release. 1 & 2 Nov 1785, Robt Miller of Camden District, Chester County, SC, planter, to Elizabeth Miller Senior of same, for £60 lawful money, 200 acres, one half of tract of 400 acres in Craven County now Chester on a small branch of a creek, adj. land surveyed for John Mills, and vacant land, surveyed for Josias Miller now deceased, therefore the right and title falls to his eldest son Robert Miller. Robert Miller (LS), Wit: Samuel Miller, Thomas miller (+), Archibald McQuestion. Acknowledged by Robert Miller the deed from him to his mother Elizabeth 19 April 1786.

**A, 103-105**: 11 Nov 1785, John McFadin of Chester county to Thomas Dugan of same, for £200 lawful current money of SC, 50 acres, part of 331 acres granted 18 May 1771 to John McFaddin on Fishing Creek in Craven County now Chester, adj. John Mathies, Jacob Beechley, Robt Martin, Andrew & Thomas Martin. John McFaddin (Seal), Wit: William Wiley, Robert Furguson. Proved 19 April 1786 by the oaths of William Wiley & Robert Forguson.

**A, 105-108**: 3 Jan 1786, John Gill & Sarah his wife of Chester County, planter, to Josiah Porter, planter, of same, for £62 s10 sterling, 200 acres on Crofts Branch on the So fork of Fishing Creek, adj. Edward Crofts,Samuel Porter, being on the east end of 500 acres formerly in the County of Mecklingburg, NC, but by the extention of the boundary line, now in the State of South Carolina, Chester County adj. Johnston & Corners line, granted 25 April 1767 by Gov Tryon of NC to John Gill. John Gill (LS), Sarah Gill (LS), Wit: Samuel Porter, James Gill, Robt Gill. Proved 19 April 1786 by the oaths of Samuel Porter and James Gill.

**A, 108-112**: Lease and release. 11 & 12 April 1786, Thomas Franklyn and Persilla his wife of Chester County, planter, to William Trussell of same, for £22 sterling, tract granted 21 Jan 1785 by SC to Thomas Franklyn Senior, 138 acres on waters of Sandy River, adj. said Trussell's own line. Thomas Franklyn (LS), Percilla Franklyn (LS), Wit: Rich'd Evans, John Franklyn, James Trussell (X). Acknowledged by Thomas Franklyn 18 April 1786 and Persley Franklyn relinquished dower 3 July 1786.

**A, 113-114**: 15 Oct 1784, Isaac Kelough, planter, of Camden District, SC, and Mary his wife, to Daniel Williams, gentleman, of same, for £71 s8 d6 sterling, 150 acres on Turkey Creek including the plantation whereon the said Isaac Kelough doth dwell, granted to Moses McCarta by patent 4 May 1769, near John McKnitt Alexander's land [later says 270 acres]. Isaac Kelough (LS), Mary Kelough (X) (LS), Wit: James McNeel, William Burress. Proved by the oath of James McNell 20 Oct 1785 and further proved by the oath of William Burress.

**A, 114-116**: 3 June 1774, William McClure of Parish of St. Marks, SC, student, to John McClure of said province, planter, tract granted 8 Feb 1768 to James

aforesaid, for £5, 50 acres, being part of land belonging to William Wilson deceased husband to said Jean and father to the said James Wilson, on north side of Rockey Creek, adj. Thomas Dye, James Morriss. Jean Wilson (I) (LS), James Wilson (X) (LS), Wit: Robert Robison, Samuel Strange (mark), Mary Wilson (L). Proved 1 Oct 1786 by the oaths of Robert Robinson and Samuel Strange.

A, 147-151: 20 March 1784, Archibald Elliott and Sarah his wife of Craven County, SC, planter, to Robert Gill of same, planter, for £300 lawful money of SC, 80 acres, part of 150 acres on both sides of the south fork of Fishing Creek adj. said Archibald Elliott, Rev. Mr. Simpson, William Elliott, Elizabeth Wilson, granted by NC 31 Aug 1753 to James McCulloch and sold by Alexander McCulloch acting executor of the will of said James McCulloch deceased to Archibald Elliott 24 Nov 1762, and part of a tract granted to said Archibald Elliott by SC 2 March 1764, and 21 acres being part of 150 acres granted to David Lewis of Mecklinburgh County NC, and conveyed 11 Feb 1772 by said David Lewis [different grants mentioned are confusing]. Archibald Elliott (AE) (LS), Sarah Elliott (O) (LS), Wit: Jas McFarlan, Saml Kelsey.

A, 151-152: 20 March 1784, William Elliott of Craven County, planter, to Robert Gill of same, planter, for ten shillings, 9 acres on south fork of Fishing Creek adj. said William Elliott, part of 150 acres conveyed to said Robert by Archibald Elliott father to the said William Elliott. William Elliott (LS), Wit: Jas McFarlan, Saml Kelsey. Proved 3 Oct 1786 by the oath of Jas McFarlan & Saml Kelsey and also lease and release from Archibald Elliott to Robert Gill proved by the same witnesses at the same time.

A, 153-156: 29 Jan 1780, Saml McKenney of Parish of St. Marks, SC, yeoman, to George Kelsey of same, yeoman, for £2000 current money, 200 acres granted 29 April 1768 by NC to James Smith, now in Craven County, SC, on west side Catawba River on the north side of the main Fishing Creek on both sides of the Cain Run, and both sides of the Waggon Road. Samuel McKinsey [sic] (LS), Wit: Hugh Whiteside, John Mills, Samuel Kelsey. Proved by the oaths of Hugh Whiteside and Samuel Kelsey 2 Oct 1786.

A, 156-160: Lease and release. 9 & 10 Dec 1782, Arthur Hicklin of Camden District, Craven County, SC, for £4000 current money, to John Smith of Camden District, 150 acres granted 1 Aug 1758 by SC to Casper Sleger, and said Casper Sleger did convey to Andrew Rogers and to his son Arthur Rogers, and said Arthur Rogers did convey to Arthur Hicklin. Arthur Hicklin (X) (LS), Wit: William Hicklin, James Paden, Alexander Kinney. Proved by the oaths of William Hick and James Paden 2 Oct 1786.

A, 161-165: Lease and release. 2 & 3 Nov 1784, John Evans of Sumpter county, SC, planter, to Richard Evans of Sumter County, planter, for £50 sterling, 100 acres granted to Owin Evans now deceased, in Craven County (now Sumter County) on a branch of Sandy Run waters of Broad River, and said Owin Evans deceased did buy the good will of the said plantation from John Cob, it being relapsed, and said Owin Evans by his will to his son John Evans. John Evans (LS), Wit: Thomas Chambers, Owin Evans, William Boyd. Acknowledged by John Evans 2 Oct 1786.

**A, 166-168**: 3 Oct 1786, James Knox and Elizabeth his wife of Camden District, Chester County, SC, to Robert Cherry, hatter, for thirty English guineas, tract granted 6 April 1768, memorial entered in Book H. No. 8, page 499, 27 July 1786, and recorded in the Secretaries Office, Book CCC, page 473, 450 acres surveyed to him by John Gaston, Deputy Survey, by virtue of a warrant dated 28 May 1767, on waters of Rockey Creek. James Knox (LS), Elizabeth Knox (LS), Wit: William Knox, David Hunter.

**A, 169-171**: South Carolina, Camden District, Chester County. 3 Sept 1786, Hazel Hardwick and Mary Hardwick for £200[?] sterling, to Richard Taliaferro of same county, planter, 442 acres on waters of Sandy River adj. William Britain, Christopher Loving, some person unknown, granted to said Hazel Hardwick by SC 3 April 1786. Hazel Hardwick (LS), Mary Hardwick (LS). No wit. Acknowledged by Hazel Hardwick and wife Mary 1 Oct 1787 [*sic*].

**A, 171-173**: South Carolina, Camden District, Chester County. 13 Sept 1786, Hazel Hardwick and Mary Hardwick for £100 sterling, to Richard Taliaferro of same county, planter, 390 acres granted to said Hazel Hardwick by SC 3 April 1786. Hazel Hardwick (LS), Mary Hardwick (LS). No wit. Acknowledged by Hazel Hardwick and wife Mary 1 Oct 1786.

**A, 173-174**: 15 July 1786, James Langsby & Elizabeth his wife of Chester County, merchant, to William Jones, blacksmith, of same, for £50 sterling, tract granted to David Morrow[?] and conveyed by him to John Green 26 Feb 1780 and by said Green to James Langsbee 19 Jan 1785, recorded in Book A in Chester County, on so fork of Fishing Creek. James Langsbee (LS), Elizabeth Langsbee (X) (LS), Wit: John Simpson, Jonathan Jones. Proved by the oaths of John Simpson and Jonathan Jones 2 Oct 1786.

**A, 175-177**: 15 July 1786, James Langsby & Elizabeth his wife of Chester County, merchant, to William Jones, blacksmith, of same, for £100 sterling, tract granted to Robert Glover, 250 acres on James McClure's spring branch, waters of So fork of Fishing Creek, Craven County, and conveyed to Henry Culp 21 Sept 1768, a memorial entered in the Auditors Office in Book I, No. 9, 20 Oct 1768, and said land conveyed to Jonathan Jones by said Culp 6 June 1772, memorial of which is entered in the Registers office 29 April 1778, W V 4, page 207, conveyed by Jones to James Langsbey 19 Jan 1785, memorial entered in the office of Chester County in Book A. James Langsbee (LS), Elizabeth Langsbee (X) (LS), Wit: John Simpson, Jonathan Jones. Proved by the oaths of John Simpson and Jonathan Jones 2 Oct 1786.

**A, 178-180**: 15 July 1786, James Langsby & Elizabeth his wife of Chester County, merchant, to William Jones, blacksmith, of same, for £80 sterling, two acres on waters of So Fork of Fishing Creek in Chester county, adj. Samuel Morrow, Miller, granted to John McLilly by patent 9 April 17-- and registered in Book No. 6, in Tryon County, NC, and by him conveyed to John Penny by writing dated Oct 1771 and from Penny to Moses Alexander 18 Oct 1772, and entered in Tryon, 11 Nov 1771, and by Moses Alexander by his will to Nathaniel Alexander and by said Alexander to Isaac Eoff by deed 26 March 1784, and Isaac Eoff conveyed to James Langsby, 7 Sept 1785, and recorded in Chester County in Book A. James Langsbee (LS), Wit: John Simpson, Jonathan Jones. Proved by the oaths of John Simpson and Jonathan Jones 2 Oct 1786.

**A, 181-183**: 5 May 1786, William Jones of Chester county, Blacksmith, and wife Catherine, to Jonathan Jones his son of same, for £50 sterling, 150 acres granted 26 July 1774 to John Brown on south side of the south fork of Fishing Creek in Craven County adj. John McLillies, John Miller, Augusteen Culp, conveyed by said John Brown 9 March 1779 to William Jones. Wm Jones (LS), Catharine Jones (LS), Wit: John Hays, Saml Knox. Acknowledged by William Jones and Catherine his wife 2 Oct 1786.

**A, 184-187**: Lease and release. South Carolina, Camden District. 6 & 7 Dec 1784, Daniel Prince Snr of said state and district, to Walthal Burton of same, for £50 sterling, 200 acres on Flinthams Creek adj. William Stone, Mr. Collins, granted 16 Dec 1786 to George Flinn and conveyed to Daniel Price by lease & release. Daniel Price. Wit: James Huey, John Pratt.

**A, 187-189**: 4 Oct 1786, Walthal Burton of Camden District, planter, to George Head, planter, for £200 sterling, tract on a branch of road River called Flinthams Creek adj. William Stone, Collins, 400 acres granted 3 June 1766 by SC to Daniel Price and George Flinn & conveyed to Walthal Burton by special deed. Walthal Burton, Wit: William Head, John Wade.

**A, 189-190**: South Carolina, Camden District. 7 Nov 1786, Allin Burton of district aforesaid, plant, to John Collin of same, planter, for £100 sterling, 150 acres in Camden District on waters of Sandy River granted 21 Jan 1785. Allen Burton (LS), Wit: Thomas Jinkins, James Coxson (I), Benjamin Burton.

**A, 191-197**: Lease and release. 18 & 19 Feb 1777, Daniel McDonald, planter, of Camden District, SC, to William McDonald, planter, for £500 current money, 250 acres on Wateree River in Craven County, adj. John Gipson, first surveyed for Thomas Haynes 22 Sept 1749 and granted by SC to Samuel Waggoner 8 April 1756, and recorded in Book RR, page 9, and conveyed from Samuel Waggoner to Daniel McDonald 24 Feb 1761. Daniel McDonald (Seal), Wit: Glass Caston, Jesse Tilman, William Wood (X).

**A, 198-205**: Lease and release. 18 & 19 Feb 1777, Daniel McDonald, planter, of Camden District, SC, to William McDonald, planter, for £500 current money, 150 acres on Wateree River in Craven County, adj. John Gipson, Thomas Haynes, surveyed for John Gipson 7 Sept 1749 and granted by SC 4

April 1753 and recorded in Book OO, page 183, conveyed from John Gipson to Daniel McDonald 25 March 1754. Daniel McDonald (Seal), Wit: Glass Caston, Jesse Tilman, William Wood (X).

A, 205-210: Lease and release. 17 & 18 July 1785, John Bell of Craven County, Camden District, for £150 south currency, to Charles Arterbury of same, 100 acres in Craven County in a place called Welches fork, a small branch of Sandy River, granted 30 Sept 1774. John Bell (LS), Wit: Jas Knox, John Adair.

A, 210-213: 20 Jan 1784, Turner Kendrick of Camden District, planter, to George Bishop Jr. of same, for £50 current money, tract granted 4 May 1775 to David McCriett, on north side of Broad River on Susey Bowls branch, branch of Turkey Creek adj. said Turner Kendrick. Turner Kendrick (LS), wIt: George Bishop, William Bishop.

A, 213-214: South Carolina, Chester County. 2 Jan 1786, Elizabeth Strain of county aforesaid for natural love and affection to Agness Brown and for the better maintenance of the said Agness Brown, a young negro wench about 11 years of age named Phillis, likewise a cow & calf. Elizabeth Strain (LS), Wit: David Strain, Samuel Brown.

A, 215-216: South Carolina, Camden District. 9 Nov 1786, Allen Burton of district aforesaid, planter, to Thomas Jenkins of same, for £100 sterling, 78 acres in Camden District on waters of Sandy River as appears by grant 21 Jan 1785. Allen Burton (LS), Wit: James Coxson (I), John Colvin, Benjamin Burton.

A, 216-218: 2 Jan 1787, William Young of Chester county to Robert Smith of same, for £5, 23 acres, part of a tract laid out for Mannin Gore and releast to William Young 21 Jan 1785. William Young (X). [no wit]

A, 218-219: 14 Nov 1786, Leonard Pratt and John Pratt with Sarah Pratt, said John's wife, of Chester county, Camden District, to Hazel Hardwick of same, for £35 s13 d4 sterling, tract on waters of Sandy River, 250 acres. Leonard Pratt (LS), John Pratt (LS), Sarah Pratt (LS), Wit: Richd Taliaferro, John Colvin, James Gore.

A, 220-221: 2 Jan 1787, John Humphres of Chester County to Robert Smith of same, for £40 Virginia money, part of tract laid out for Ambros Nix adj. land laid out for Thomas Roden, laid land out to Charles Humphris, land laid out for Ferguson, 100 acres. John Humpris (X).

A, 222-227: Lease and release. 9 & 10 Feb 1786, Thomas Rivess living in the State of Georgia, on Brier Creek, planter, to John Findley of the Waxsaws, Lancaster county, planter, for £84 s14 sterling, 140 acres on a branch of Wateree River called Fishing Creek, which grant was to Alexander McCown, recorded in Book FFF, page 375, on which said Thomas Reaves formerly lived, adj. land laid off by William Carson, 140 part of tract of 300 acres

13

granted 21 April 1775. Thomas Reaves (X) (LS), Wit: John McCown, Robert Robinson, Robert Thompson.

A, 228-233: Lease and release. 15 & 16 July 1786, David McCall & Mary his wife of Chester County, yeoman, to William Lewis of same, for £100 lawful money, 125 acres on a branch of Rockey Creek granted 3 April 1786 to David McColla adj. John Burns, William Milling, Mary Bigham. David McColla (LS), Mary McColla (LS), Wit: Michael Dickson, William Morray, Samuel Adams.

A, 234-235: 1 April 1787, David McCall of Chester County, to Peter Coonrod of same, for £10 sterling, 308 acres on waters of Sandy River, adj. Douglas, William Ferguson, John Adair, and granted to James Neilson 2 April last past. David McColla (LS), Wit: Edw'd Lacey, Patrick McGriff, John Mills. Proved 3 July 1787 by the oaths of Patk McGriff and John Mills.

A, 235-238: 7 April 1787, Joseph McKinney of Chester County, yeoman, to Samuel Lusk of York County, for £40 sterling, 100 acres granted 18 May 1773 to Joseph McKinney in Chester county on Neely's branch of Fishing Creek, adj. William Neely. Joseph McKinney (I), Wit: Hugh Whiteside, John McGlamery (X), Patrick McKinney (X).

A, 238-243: Lease and release. 4 & 5 Oct 1786, Michael Dickson, planter, of Camden District, to David McDill of same, for £450 current money, 300 acres between Catawba River & Broad River on both sides of Rockey Creek at the ford of the Saludy Road, being land that was surveyed for John Fondren, granted 16 April 1765 by NC to Michael Dickson. Michael Dickson (LS), Wit: Charles Miller, Samuel H. Dickson, John McDill.

A, 244-245: 3 April 1787, David Pruit of Union County, Ninety Six District, to Owen Evans of Chester County, Camden District, for £300 SC money, part of 400 acres granted to Richard Warin 23 Dec 1771, which contains 200 acres on a branch of Sandy River called the Cany Fork, adj. Benjamin Carter, Edmond Russel, William Boyd. David Pruit (mark), Wit: Will Boyd, John Eves, Richard Evans.

A, 245-247: 10 April 1787, John Evins of Chester county to James McCarter of Abeville County, for £40 lawful money, 196 acres in Camden District on a branch of Sandy River adj. John Evins, James Wilkey, James Ferguson, part of tract of 532 acres laid out to said John Evins the grant dated 5 June 1786, recorded in Grant Book MMMM, page 108. John Evins (LS), Wit: Richard Evins, Owen Evins, Agness Evans (X).

A, 247-248: South Carolina, Camden District, Chester County. 13 March 1787, John Gresham, planter in Chester County, to David Grisham, planter, of same, for one sixpence sterling, 100 acres on the waters of Flintams Creek of Sandy River, by a plat granted to said John Gresham 45 Dec 1785, platt certified 15 Sept 1784, and recorded in Book GGGG, page 153, per Peter Freneau with the great seal of the state, part of above grant as specified. John

Gresham (mark), Elinor Gresham (X), Wit: Robert Lemons, Jeremiah Gresham (mark), Alexander Johnston.

**A, 249-250**: South Carolina, Camden District, Chester County. 13 March 1787, Robert Lemmon, planter of county aforesaid, to Jeremiah Gresham of same, for £10 sterling, tract on a branch of Broad River called Sandy Creek alias Stone Creek, part of 155 acres granted to said Robert Lemmon 2 Oct 1786, recorded in Book OOOO, page 100, per John Vanderhorst, secretary. Robert Lemmond, Unity Lemmond (mark), Wit: David Gresham (mark), Alexander Johnston.

**A, 251**: William Miller & Ann Heart of Chester County for £77 s10 sterling to John Latta of same, a negro woman slave named Dolly, 24 Feb 1787. William Miller (LS), Ann Heart (O) (LS), Wit: John Mills Junr, Nicholas Bishop, John Mills Snr.

**A, 252-254**: 1786, Hampton Stroud of Rockey Creek, Chester County, planter, to Edward Stedman of Fishing Creek, same county, for £14 s4 d8, tract on Rockey Creek adj. Thomas Dye, John Smyth. Hampton Stroud (mark), Mary Stroud (X). Wit: Elijah Bankston, Samuel Ferguson, Thomas Stroud (X).

**A, 255-259**: Lease and release. 28 & 29 Nov 1786, John Wall, being the heir of Bird Wall deceased, of State of SC, for £--- to William Wall and Charles Wall of Chester County, tract granted 12 July 1771 to Bird Wall, 100 acres on Rockey Creek, south side of Catawba River adj. Benjamin Street, William Nettles, Abraham Stover, William Wall. John Wall (X) (LS), Wit: Elijah Gibson (X), Abram Gibson (A), Isom Lowry.

**A, 259-263**: Lease and release. 28 & 29 Nov 1786, John Wall of SC, heir of William Wall deceased, to William Wall and Charles Wall of Chester County, for £100 sterling, tract granted 27 Sept 1769 by SC to William Wall and Charles Wall, 150 acres on the Catawba River in Craven County adj. Abraham Stover. John Wall (X), Wit: Elijah Gibson (X), Abraham Gibson (A), Isom Lowry. [lease not completed]

**A, 264-266**: 11 April 1780, Philip Walker & Martha Walker his wife of Rocky Creek, Camden District, planter, for £10,000 lawful money, to Thomas Morrison of same, tract granted 1 June 1767 to Philip Walker, 100 acres on a branch of Catawba River called Rockey Creek, adj. John McDonald. Philip Walker (O), Martha Walker, Wit: Robert Morrison, Samuel Weere, Alexander Rosborough.

**A, 266-269**: 11 Sept 1786, John Culp of Mecklanburgh County, North Carolina, to Benjamin Culp of Chester County, SC, for £100 sterling, 150 acres granted to John Culp on waters of Fishing Creek adj. Archibald Ellott. John Culp (K) (LS), Wit: William Wiley, Andrew Lockhard, John Wiley Junr.

A, **269-273**: Lease and release. 30 & 31 March 1787, William Hicklin, planter, of Lancaster County, SC, to James Burns of Chester County, for 40 shillings sterling, 100 acres on Bull Run adj. John McLilly, Benjamin Ellis, James Burns, the same being obtained by a bounty warrent dated 12 Jan 1768 to John Waugh, sold to John Nichols 1 Feb 1768 by said John Waugh, conveyed by James Nichols to said William Hicklin, the patent to John Waugh dated 16 June 1768[?]. William Hicklin, Wit: James Paden, Robert Boyd.

A, **274-277**: Lease and release. 11 Nov 1785, Isaac Evins of Craven County, Camden District, to William Boyd of same, planter, for £100 sterling, 100 acres granted to Isaac Evins 1 Dec 1769 on a branch of Rockey Creek adj. land surveyed for Richard Storey, entered in the auditor's office in Book I No 9, page 83, recorded in Book DDD, page 568. Isaac Evins, Wit: John Bell, John Burns, Susanna Glover (mark)

A, **277-282**: Lease and release. 9 & 10 Oct 1785, John Carter of Chester County, planter, to James Bishop, planter, for £22 sterling, 111 acres part of tract granted 2 May 1770 to Jacob Carter now deceased for 200 acres between Catawba River and Broad River on Rockey Creek, where the road from the south fork of Catawba River to Charles Town crosses it, part of said tract was bequeathed to the said John Carter by the will of Jacob Carter deceased 3 Dec 1780[?]. John Carter (LS), Wit: John Dickson, Charles Miller, William Miller.

A, **282-286**: Lease and release. 1 & 2 Sept 1784, Wm Lard & Sarah his wife of Sumpter County, SC, to Ann Herbison of same, for £14 s5 d8½, 150 acres granted 7 April 1770 by SC to Abraham Dey 300 acres in Craven County now Sumpter County on a branch of Rockey Creek, adj. Samson, John Carson, Mary Herbison, Alexander Campbell. William Lard (LS), Sarah Lard (mark), Wit: William Boyd, Patrick Herbison (mark), Robert Martin.

A, **287-291**: Lease and release. 27 Aug 1787, Benjamin Street of Campden District, Chester County, Doctor, and Mary his wife, to Abner Wilks of same, for £42 sterling, 150 acres, part of 300 acres granted 15 Feb 1769 by SC to John Rennels adj. William Sandefur, James Montgomery, on north side of Hogs branch conveyed 9 Sept 1769. Benjamin Street, Mary Street (X), Wit: Francis Wilks, Jonathan Hand, David Eakens. Proved by the oaths of Francis Wilkes and Jonathan Hand 1 Oct 1787.

A, **291-295**: Lease and release. 28 June 1787, William Hogan of Chester County to James Dillard of same, for £00, 160 acres, pat of tract on south side of Sandy River granted to John Davis by grant 1 June 1767 and to said Hogan 1 Dec 1784. William Hogan, Wit: T. Lewis, William Hall, James Dillard Junr. Proved by the oath of William Hall and James Dillard Junior 1 Oct 1787.

A, **295-296**: 24 May 1787, David Hopkins of Chester County, to Edward Grimes, a free Negro of same, for £13 lawful money, said Edward agrees to serve the said David Hopkins for twelve months and said Hopkins will supply said Edward with sufficient cloaths, meat, drink, washing & lodging during that time. Edward Grimes (X), D'd Hopkins, Wit: Jas Glenn Junr, John Harper (X).

**A, 296-298**: 3 Sept 1783, Elisha Dye & Richard Dye of Sumpter County, State of South Carolina, planters, to Robert Jameson of county & state aforesaid, by a grant bearing date 7 April 1770 from William Bull, Gov. of Province of SC, to Abram Dye now deceased, 300 acres on Bullskin run, waters of Rocky Creek, recorded in Book EEE, page 230, now for £225 lawful money of said state paid by Robt Jameson, convey 150 acres of the above mentioned tract adj. Adam Eager, Widow Harbinson, Archibald Henderson. Elisha Dye, Richard Dye (R), Wit: James Hanna, William McCullock.

**A, 299-301**: 3 Sept 1787, Philip Walker of Chester County, yeoman, to John McGlamary of same, for £100 sterling, 300 acres granted 21 Dec 1764 to Mary Smith widow, said tract then in Macklenburg County, NC, but by the continuation of the boundary line now in the State of SC, Chester County on the north side of Fishing Creek, conveyed by said Mary Smith alias Morris and her husband Robert Morris 6 Jan 1767 to Nathaniel Sample and said Nathaniel Sample by power of atty empowered Philip Walker to convey said tract to John McGlamary. Philip Walker. Acknowledged in open court 3 Oct 1787 by Philip Walker.

**A, 301-302**: South Carolina, County of Chester. John Redford of Mecklenburg County, NC, confesses that he spoke "serten fallce and scandos words" concerning Isaac Pritchart and Jean his wife, which he never had any reason to suspect their being guilty of anything, 15 Aug 1787. John Redford (mark) (Seal), Wit: J. Mills, Arch'd Davie.

I John Redford deliver to Isaac Prichard a bay horse of four years of age in full settlement of all debts 15 Aug 1787. John Redford (mark), Test: J. Mills.

I assign my rite and title to the above gill of sale to William Arbuckle, 18 Aug 1787. Isaac Prichard, Wit: Robert Gill.

**A, 302-304**: 4 Nov 1786, William Boyd, surveyor of District of Camden, to John Servis, weaver, of same, for £10 lawful money of SC, 100 acres on a branch of Rockey Creek adj. Jain McCartney, John Combest, including the forks of the grassy runs below the waggon road between Cuttoba and Broad River in Chester county. Will: Boyd (Seal), Wit: Hugh Stuart, Samuel Crook, George Kennedy. Acknowledged in open court 2 Oct 1788.

**A, 304-308**: Lease and release. 7 & 8 May 1787, John Jaggers of State of SC to William Hall of same, for £50 sterling, 474 acres granted to said John Jaggers on NW side of Sandy River adj. Anderson Thomas, Robert Alcorn. John Jaggors (Seal), Wit: T. Lewis, Nathan Jaggers, James Minis (mark). Acknowledged in open court 2 Oct 1787.

**A, 308-310**: 17 Sept 1787, James Burns of Chester County, planter, to Robert Boyd of same, for £50 sterling, 100 acres on a branch of Rockey Creek called Bubrun adj. John McAlily, Benjamin Ellis, James Burns, obtained by warrant dated 12 Jan 1768 to John Waugh then sold to James Nichols and by his bonds dated 1 Feb 1768 conveyed by James Nichols to William Hicklin, and then by William Hicklin to James Burns. James Burns (Seal) (Seal), Wit: James Williamson, Robert Morrison.

**A, 311-312**: South Carolina, Chester County. 26 March 1787, Ferdinand Hopkins of state aforesaid to Alexander Donald of same, for £100 sterling, 86 acres to a plat and grant dated 9 Oct 1784 in the south fork of Sandy River on the north side of the Old Saludie Road adj. James Fletchall, Thos Jenkins, which being the dividing line that separates Watson's hundred acres from the remaining part of the survey of 186 acres. F. Hopkins (Seal), Wit W. Cason, Jeremiah Kingsley. Acknowledged in open court 3 Oct 1787.

**A, 312-313**: 2 Jan 1780, William McCaw and Anne his wife of Camden District, SC, planter, to Samuel Weir of same, for £60 lawful money, 100 acres, part of 450 acres granted 14 Sept 1771 to William McCaw, on waters of Rockey Creek in Camden District adj. Philip Walker, Peter Wylie, Thomas Huston. William McCaw (LS), Anne McCaw (O), Wit: James Greer, James Bankhead. Acknowledged in open court 3 Oct 1788.

**A, 315-316**: Mary Hambleton of Chester county for £100 sterling to John McGlamary of same, mortgage of one sorrel horse, one black mare, one bay mare, and two year old filley, ten head of neat cattle, two head of sheep, twelve head of hogs, one womans saddle, one case of bottles, one pannel'd chest, four pots, one bed stead, three beds and bed cloths, pewter, one plow and gears, two spinning wheels and other household furniture, one Riffle gun, one saddle, one cheek reel, one hand saw, one gown pratton, two axes, about seven acres of corn, 8 Sept 1787. Mary Hambleton (mark), Wit: Daniel Cooke, Thomas White. Proved by the oaths of Daniel Cook & Thos White 3 Oct 1787.

**A, 316-317**: South Carolina, Camden District. 25 June 1787, John Gresham of district aforesaid, planter, to Isaac Taylor, planter, for £350 old south currency, tract on a branch of Broad River called Creek otherwise Stones Creek adj. Lucey Collins, 100 acres by grant dated 1 May 1772. John Grissom (mark) (LS), Wit: Thos Baker Franklin, William Grissom (T). Proved 4 Oct 1787 by the oath of John Bell and Thos B. Franklin.

**A, 318-319**: South Carolina, Chester County. 3 Oct 1787, Col. Partrick McGriff, planter, to James Lay, both of state and district aforesaid, 100 acres granted by patent to Pat McGriff 2 Oct 1786. Pat: McGriff (LS). Acknowledged in open court 4 Oct 1788.

**A, 319-321**: 22 Sept 17-- Alexander Brown and Samuel Brown his son of Chester County, planter, to George Gill of same, for £106 sterling, 130 acres on the south side of the south fork of Fishing Creek adj. Alexr Brown, George Craig, Henry Culp, William Millin, part of 290 acres granted to said Alexr Brown 29 April 1768 by NC, conveyed by deed of gift by said Alexr Brown to Samuel Brown 13 Jan 1783 and recorded in the records of said county. Alexander Brown (Seal), Samuel Brown (Seal), Wit: Willey S. Brown, William Wylie, Saml H. Dickson. Proved 4 Oct 1787 by the oaths of William White [*sic*] and Saml Dickson.

**A, 321-323**: 2 Jan 1780, Thomas Huston and Agness his wife of Camden District, SC, planter, to Samuel Weir of same, planter, for £100 lawful money, 150 acres granted 13 Aug 1762 by SC to Hugh McDonald, on both sides Rockey Creek in Craven County, conveyed from said Hugh McDonald to George Weir 31 March 1764, and from George Weir to Thomas Huston 7 & 8 Jan 1773. Thomas Huston (LS), Agnes Huston (mark) (LS), Wit: William McCaa, James Greer, Elenor Huston. Acknowledged in open court 4 Oct 1788.

**A, 325-326**: South Carolina, Camden District. 31 Aug 17--, Patrick McGriff to Thomas McGriff, both of state and district aforesaid, for £50 sterling, 100 acres, granted to Mr. Kirkpatrick in 1768. Pat. McGriff (LS), Wit: Edw'd Lacey, Rich'd Miles, Hugh Stuart. Acknowledged 4 Oct 1788.

**A, 327-328**: 10 Dec 1783, Katharine Brown of Camden District, widow, to William Brown of same, for £100 current money, 116 acres, part of a tract of 350 acres granted to said Katharine Brown by patent 23 Jan 1773, the said 116 acres being laid off the west end of the above said tract of 350 acres. Katharine Brown (mark), (LS), Wit: James Adare, John Walker, Turner Kendrick. Acknowledged 4 Oct 1787.

**A, 328-329**: 5 Jan 1788, Rich'd Taliaferro of Chester county, to William Britain of same, for 20 shilling sterling, one acre of land whereon the said Britain griss mill stands. Rich'd Taliaferro (LS).

**A, 329-330**: 3 Jan 1788, Thomas Crosby of Chester County, planter, to Thomas Lewis of Greenville County, for £50 acres in the District of Camden, part in Chester County and part in Fairfield County, on the south side of Sandy River adj. James Dillard, heirs of Amos Davis deceased, Richard Crosby, granted to said Thomas Crosby 21 Jan 1785. Thos Crosby (LS), Wit: Allen deGraffenreid.

**A, 331-335**: Lease and release. 5 & 7 Jan 1788, Richard Davis of Chester county planter, to Allen DeGraffeenreidt of same, for £100 sterling, 300 acres on Sandy River, half of a tract of 6700 acres granted to John Hitchcock by NC, 3 Feb 1754, recorded in the Auditor Genls Office 23 Fe 1754, and from said John Hitchcock to Ann Davis, wife of said Richard Davis, desired by his last will and testament the one half of said 600 acres. Richard Davis (X) (LS), Ann Davis (X) (LS), Wit: John Pratt, Thos Crosby.

# CHESTER COUNTY SC DEED ABSTRACTS

**A, 336-338**: 3 Jan 1788, James Neely of Chester County, yeoman, to Thomas Neely of same, yeoman, for £10, tract granted 26 May 1774 to James Neely, 220 acres in Craven County on a branch of Fishing Creek adj. Wm McKiney. James Neely (LS).

**A, 339-340**: 16 Aug 1787, Mager Grisham of Chester County, and wife Fanny, to Thomas Baker Franklin of same, for £10 sterling, 50 acres granted to said Grisham 20 Aug 1786 by SC, on a branch of Sandy River adj. Thomas Franklin, James Huey, James Dougherty, Nolly Catser. Mager Grisham (mark), Fannay Grisham (mark), Wit: Pat McGriff, Edm'd Nunn, James Nunn.

**A, 341-343**: 16 Aug 1787, Mager Grisham of Chester County, and wife Fanny, to Thomas Baker Franklin of same, for £10 sterling, 100 acres granted to said Grisham 2 Oct 1786 by SC, on a branch of Sandy River adj. Thomas Franklin. Mager Grisham (mark), Fannay Grisham (mark), Wit: Pat McGriff, Edm'd Nunn, James Nunn.

**A, 344-346**: 2 Jan 178, Hugh Kelsey of Chester County, shoe maker, to Robert Kelsey of same, waggon maker, for £20 sterling, 100 acres granted 6 Feb 1773 to Thomas Kelsey in Craven County on a branch of Rockey Creek adj. Henry Smith, the above named Thomas Kelsey deceased intestate and Hugh Kelsey above mentioned is his Elder Brother and heir to the aforesaid tract. Hugh Kelso (LS).

**A, 347-348**: 3 Aug 1787, John Dougharty of Chester county to Thomas Baker Franklin of same, for £10 sterling, 100 acres granted 3 April 1786 on a branch of Sandy River, adj. Mager Grissim, Thomas Franklin, William Trusell. John Dougharty (LS), Wit: John Pratt, James Gore, John Franklin.

**A, 349-353**: 15 Sept 1787, Thomas Franklin of Camden District to Robert Dunlap of same, farmer, for £17 s10 sterling, 100 acres on waters of Sandy River granted 3 April 1786 conveyed from John Dougharty to said Thomas Franklin. Thomas Bak'r Franklin.

**A, 354-356**: 15 May 1777, Mary Hannah of St. Marks Parish, Craven County, young woman, to William Miller of same, for £200 current money, 100 acres granted to Mary Hannah 8 Dec 1774 in Craven County on waters of Rockey Creek adj. Nicholas Bishop, William Miller. Mary Hannah (O) (LS), Wit: Will Boyd, John McQueston, Agness Hannah (mark).

**A, 357-358**: 20 Aug 1787, Thomas Humphries and wife Mary of Chester county to George Blessit of same, for £50, 100 acres part of tract granted to Thomas Humphrey 6 Feb 1786, adj. William Nunn, Washington Hopkins, John Terry. Thomas Humphreys (LS), Mary Humphres (X) (LS), Wit: Francis Nunn, Alex'r Donald, Thomas Jenkins.

**A, 359-361**: 9 Jan 1788, David Boyd and Margaret his wife of Chester county, SC, to William Boyd of same, young man, for £200 sterling, 250 acres, part of tract granted 15 Nov 1774 to David Boyd, 350 acres, on Stamps branch between the main and south forks of Fishing Creek then in Craven County, now Chester County, adj. James Gill. David Boyd (LS), Margaret Boyd (X) (LS), Wit: Will Boyd, John Boyd, Ann Boyd.

**A, 362-363**: 4 Jan 1788, Samuel McCance of Chester County, SC, blacksmith, to John Simpson, minister, of same, for £30 proc. money, 32 acres in Camden District on waters of the South fork of Fishing Creek joining and between the lands of Jno Simpson, Christopher Strong, and Alexander Brown, part of tract granted to said Samuel McCance by plat dated 23 Oct 1764. Saml McCance (LS).

**A, 364**: 4 Jan 1788, Col. David Hopkins of Chester County for £100 lawful money to Caleb Davis, 371 acres granted to Col. David hopkins 45 Feb 1787 and certified 6 Jan 1787 including the plantation whereon the said Caleb Davis is now living. D'd Hopkins (LS), Wit: James Traver, Jeremiah Davis.

**A, 365-367**: 8 June 1780, David Hopkins, Esquire, & Mary his wife of Camden District to Ferdinand Hopkins of the state of Virginia, County of Cumberland, for £5000 current money, two tracts of land: one tract in Camden District on north side of Broad River granted by NC 28 June 1752 to John Smith and conveyed by said Smith to Mark Edwards Senr then by Mark Edwards Senr to David Hopkins Esq., 300 acres; a tract granted to David Hopkins Esqr by SC 19 Nov 1772 in Camden District on north side Broad River adj. the tract above mentions, 300 acres. D'd Hopkins (LS), Mary Hopkins (LS), Wit: Nathl Abney, James Jarrard.

**A, 368-370**: 3 Jan 1788, James McClure and Jane his wife of Chester County, planter, to Richard Gladney of Fairfield County, for £12 sterling, 100 acres, part of 200 acres surveyed for David Hunter 7 Oct 1767 in Chester County on waters of Fishing Creek and waters of Rockey Creek and said James McClure Senior did purchase said tract from David Hunter and said James McClure Senior by his will bequeathed to his son said James McClure Junr said 200 acres. James McClure (LS).

**A, 370-374**: Lease and release. 10 Nov 1787, John Turner of Fairfield County to John Holman for £50 SC money, 100 acres granted 19 Feb 1767 to James Cobb adj.land surveyed for John Lee. John Turner (LS), Wit: Rich'd Taliaferro, John Bell.

**A, 375-376**: 25 Jan 1785, John Owen of Craven County, SC, to James Gill of same, for £150 sterling, two tracts of land: the first of 100 acres between Rocky Creek and the south fork of Fishing Creek in Craven County adj. Robert Knox, Richard Kerrel, granted to Joseph Galbreth 12 Aug 1768; the other tract of 82 acres on Carrels branch of Fishing Creek adj. Richard Carrell, granted to John Anthony by patent 15 March 1771, which tracts were conveyed by Joseph Galbreath and John Anthony to said John Owen. John Owen (LS), Wit: Elijah Brown, Willey S. Brown, Josiah Porter.

A, 377-382: Lease and release. 19 & 20 Oct 1783, John Stone, Moses Stone & Jacob Stone of Craven County, SC, planters, with the consent of their mother Ruth Stone, to Daniel Carril & William Stone of same, planters, for £200 current money, 202 acres on Sandy Creek, a branch of Broad River adj. John Colvin, Daniel Price, granted 17 June 1763. John Stone (X) (LS), Moses Stone (mark) (LS), Jacob Stone (X) (LS), Wit: Cain Carrell, Willis Carrell, Thomas Franklin (N).

A, 382-387: Lease and release. 11 April 1772, Richard Carrell of Parish of St. Mark, SC, planter, to John Walker of same, planter, for £200 lawful currency, 150 acres granted 16 June 1763 by SC to Richard Carrell on a branch of Fishing Creek. Richard Carrel (mark), Wit: William Dickson, Wm. Brown, Wm Dickson Junr, William Berry.

A, 387-389: 12 Nov 1787, William Adair & Mary his wife of Camden District, Chester County, to Claudias Charvin of same, for £235 sterling, tract on south fork of Fishing Creek, 280 acres, being the lowest half of a tract of 560 acres granted 29 March 1753 to Abraham Kirkendall and conveyed to said William Adair 15 May 1754. Wm Adair (LS), Mary Adair (LS), Wit: Jo Palmer, Jno Williams, Edward Lacey, James McNeil.

A, 390-394: Lease and release. 1 & 2 June 1780, Michael Dickson of Camden District, planter, to William Millin of same, yeoman, for £5000 money of SC, 150 acres on Rocky Creek, part of 300 acres granted by NC 16 April 1765 to Michael Dickson, then in Mecklinburg County between Catawba River & Broad River at the Foard of the Saluda Road. Michael Dickson (LS), Wit: Thomas Camron, Charles Miler, James McCaw.

A, 395-396: 3 Feb 1783, John Pugh of Camden District for £500 to Thomas Wallace of same, tract on the head of Sandy River granted to John Pugh by NC, 100 acres, part of 300 acres on Gibeses path, including the Improvement where Wm Banks formerly lived. Jno Pugh (LS), Wit: Jas Pegan, Jn. Week (I).

A, 397-398: 1 Dec 1787, James McCluer of Chester County, to Robert Miller & Mary Miller & Henry Miller, planters & spinner, for £15 sterling, 25 acres in Chester County on waters of Rocky Creek, part of tract formerly containing 150 acres lately surveyed for William Miller adj. land surveyed for Al'xr Rosborough, granted to Robert Miller 16 Feb 1773. Robert Miller (LS), Henry Miller (LS), Henry Miller (LS), Mary Miller (O) (LS), Wit: Saml Lowry, Andrew Miller.

A, 399-403: 9 Nov 1787, John Turner of Fairfield County to John Holman, for £50, tract granted 18 June 1763 by SC, 50 acres on waters of Rocky Creek. Jno Turner (LS), Wit: Rich'd Taliaferro, John Bell.

**A, 403-404**: 3 Jan 1788, James McClure & Jean his wife of Chester County, planter, to Richard Gladney of Fairfield County, for 200 acres in Chester County on waters of Fishing Creek and Rockey Creek. James McClure (LS).

**A, 405-406**: 29 Aug 1787, William Humphress of Camden District, Chester county to John Hais of same, for £80 sterling, 100 acres, part of 200 acres granted to Joseph Brown on a small branch leading into Sandy River surveyed 22 March 1767 P John Wilkeson. Wm. Humphris (LS), Lucy[?] Humphres. Wit: Abner Wilks, Daniel Jaggers, Nathan Jaggers.

**A, 407-408**: 10 Jan 1788, Doctor Cladias Charvin of Chester County, to Daniel Williams of York County, whereas the said Daniel Williams hath become bound with said Claudious Charvin to William Adair by several bonds dated 12 Nov 1787 for the payment of several sums of money in the whole £258 s5 d4 sterling, now to secure payment 260 acres, part of 520 acres granted to Abraham Kuykendall on south fork of Fishing Creek. Claudious Chervin (LS).

**A, 408-409**: John Smith of Chester County, for natural love and affection to my son Moses Smith, the negro man named Fortune & the negro boy named Tom, the mare & Colt that I bought from Richard Quinn, two cows & calves, and a small negro girl named Dinna, 4 May 1787. John Smith (Seal), Wit: Sm Boyd, And'w Hemphill.

**A, 409-410**: John Smith of Chester County, for natural love and affection to my son Joshua Smith, the negro man named Abram & the negro boy named Cupit, the negro girl named Sibbina, & The young negro boy named Jack, the mare called Liberty, the young grey horse, eight head of cattle, the bed & its furniture, 4 May 1787. John Smith (Seal), Wit: Sm Boyd, And'w Hemphill.

**A, 411-415**: Lease and release. 4 & 5 April 1788, William Armour of Camden District, to John Heren of same, for £50 sterling, 150 acres on waters of Sandy River, granted to said William Armour 3 July 1786. Wm Armour (A), Mary Armour (X), Wit: Robert Collins Senr, Robert Collins Junr (R).

**A, 416-417**: 13 Aug 1785, Thomas Roden and wife Mary of Camden District to John Moberly of same, planter, for £44 s5 sterling, 88½ acres, part of 200 acres granted to Joseph Brown 16 Jan 1772, transferred from Joseph Brown to said Thomas Roden, on a small branch leading into Sandy River called Stamp branch, adj. John Hitchcock, Mannin Goar. Thomas Roden (LS), Mary Roden (M) (LS), Wit: Moses Hill, Wm. Roden, Lewis Robert (X).

**A, 418-422**: Lease and release. 24 & 5 Feb 1787, John Dougherty of Camden District to Thomas Roden of same, for £44 sterling, tract of 100 acres on Welshes fork, waters of Sandy River granted to said John Dougherty 21 Jan 1785. John Dougharty (LS), Agey Dougharty (X) (LS), Wit: Wm Armor (A), Moses Stone (X) Wm Grisham (W).

**A, 423-428**: Lease and release. 25 & 6 Feb 1787, John Dougharty of Camden District to Thomas Roden for £10 sterling, 100 acres on waters of Sandy River adj. Dougharty, Isaac Taylor, granted to said John Dougharty 3 April 1786. John Dougharty (LS), Agey Dougharty (X) (LS), Wit: Wm Armor (A), Moses Stone (X) Wm Grisham (W).

**A, 428-433**: Lease and release. 8 & 9 Feb 1788, Peter Wiley of Chester County [lease says Fairfield County] to George Agnes of Chester County, for £100, tract granted 26 Sept 1772 to Caleb Smith, 100 acres and by him for £100 to David Nickels and by David Nickels for £240 1 Jan 1783 to Peter Wiley, on both sides Big Rockey Creek adj. Hugh Nellson. Peter Wiley (X) (Seal), Wit: Jas Stinson, Edward Steedman.

**A, 433-434**: 20 Nov 1787, Edmund Franklin and Rachel his wife of Camden District, Chester County to Anderson Thomas of same, for £1000 sterling, 200 acres on Sandy River a branch of Broad River granted to Edward Franklin though a mistaken in stead of Edmond Franklin 29 April 1769, entered in the Auditor's Office in Book H No. 8, page 457, 4 July 1768, recorded in the Secretarys office in Book CCC, page 88. Edmund Franklin (mark) (LS), Rachel Franklin (LS), Wit: John Doyle, William Doyle (R), Owen Franklin (X).

**A, 435**: Thomas Fletchall of Ninety Six District bound to Ambros Nix of Camden District in the sum of £1000 currency of SC, 18 Feb 1778, to make titles for 200 acres of land on Little Sandy River. Tho Fletchal (LS),Wit: John Davis, Thomas Crosby.

**A, 436-437**: 11 April 1785, William Irving of Camden District to Alexander Moor of same, for £9 sterling, 150 acres on Rockey Creek adj. Philip Walker, Peter Nantes. William Irving (mark), Wit: James Brice, James Gill, Robert Cresswell.

**A, 437-438**: 7 April 1788, Jeremiah Thomas of Chester county to Wm Raney of same, for £100 sterling, 100 acres, part of a tract of land granted to Moses Bond and by him conveyed to John Jenkins and from said Jenkins to Jonathan Thomas deceased and from the said deceased it devolved on the aforesaid Jeremiah Thomas as heir at law. Jeremiah Thomas (Seal).

**A, 439-440**: 5 April 1788, Robert Gorrel and Agness his wife of Chester County to Reuben Lacey of same, for £22 sterling, 50 acres known by the name of Gorrells old fields on the road leading from Loves ford on Broad River to the nation ford on Cataba River on the waters of Turkey Creek. Robert Gorrell (LS), Agness Gorrell (LS), Wit: Wm. Miles, Will Gorrell, Edw'd Lacey.

**A, 441-442**: 9 April 1788, William Brown of York County ,SC, to John Walker, late of the County of Chester, for £60 sterling, 116 acres on waters of Turkey Creek in the County of Chester being part of a tract granted to Katharine

Brown 23 Jan 1773 for 100 acres, conveyed to the said William Brown from said Catharine Brown 10 Dec 1783. Wm. Brown (LS), Wit: Edw'd Lacey, John Bell, Pat McGriff.

A, 443-447: Lease and release. 12 & 13 April 1776, John Land of Parish of St. Mark, Craven County, SC, to Saml Griffin of same, for £125, 100 acres granted 16 Jan 1772 to John Land, recorded in the Secretarys office of said prince in Book KKK, page 349. John Land (Seal), Wit: Ralph Griffin (H), George Morris, Andrew Hemphill.

A, 448-450: 9 April 1788, John Mills Esq, coroner of Chester County, to James Norton of same, whereas James Norton in the county court of Chester did implead John Allan admr. of the estate of Thomas Burns decd on an action of debt and in July Court in 1787 did obtain judgment in the same court for his debt & costs of suit to be levied off the goods and chattles, lands and tenements of said John Allan, in the sum of £43 s1 d1 sterling, now for £35 sterling sold to James Norton, 100 acres on Rockey Creek granted to Thomas Burns by patent 19 Sept 1758 by SC. John Mills Cor Ches't Coy (Seal), Wit: David Hunter, William Moore. Acknowledged by John Mills in Court 10 April 1788.

A, 450-451: 9 April 1788, William Young of Camden District, Chester County to Ezekiel Landers of same, for £50 sterling, 377 acres adj. Ferguson. William Young (+) (LS), Elender Young (+), Wit: W. Emery, Thomas Sanders (mark), Char's Degraffenreidt.

A, 452-453: 19 April 1788, William Young of Camden District, Chester County to Christopher Degraffenreidt of same, for £70 sterling, 250 acres on Strans branch acres. William Young (+) (LS), Elender Young (+), Wit: W. Embry, Thomas Sanders (mark), Ezekl Sanders (X).

A, 453-459: Lease and release. 9 & 10 April 1780, Nathan Jaggers of Chester county to John Jaggers of same, for £100 sterling, 100 acres on north side of Rockey Creek granted to Benjamin Street 15 July 1765 by SC, 200 acres. Nathan Jaggers (Seal), Wit: Peter Seely, Elender Seely (X).

A, 459-460: 9 April 1788, William Young of Camden District, Chester County, to John Young of same, for £23 sterling, 100 acres. William Young (+) (LS), Elender Young (+), Wit: W. Embry, Thomas Sanders (mark), Chr's Degraffenreidt, Ezekiel Sanders.

A, 461-466: Lease and release. 5 & 6 March 1788, John Morris & wife Mary of Chester county to Benjamin Morris of same, for £100 sterling, 350 acres granted 18 May 1773 to Thomas Morriss on waters of Rockey Creek then Craven County adj. Wm Stroud, Alexander Ratteree, recorded in Book PPP, page 93, said John Morriss & Mary his wife being in the right of lawfull heirs of Thomas Morris decd. John Morriss (X) (LS), Mary Morriss (X) (LS), Wit: Andw Hemphill, Benjamin Smith, John Furguson.

**A, 467-472**: Lease and release. 25 & 26 Jan 1788, James Jack & wife Margaret, planters, to John Hays, blacksmith, for £15 sterling, 100 acres originally given to Joseph Mitchell of Mcklnburg in NC by a grant 26 Oct 1767, formerly in the county of Mecklenburg, N Carolina, now in the County of Craven County, SC, on a branch of the south fork of Fishing Creek, between lands of Brown & Miller, by said Mitchell conveyed to James Jack 28 Aug 1778, recorded in the Secretarys Office in Charleston in Book T No. 5, page 399. James Jack (LS), Wit: John Downing, Robert Lusk. [For the deed referred to, see *South Carolina Deed Abstracts 1783-1788*, page 273, by Brent H. Holcomb.]

**A, 473-475**: 6 May 1780, James Burcham, Blacksmith, of Camden District, SC, to Jas Blair of same, for £5000 lawful money, 350 acres granted 26 July 1774 to Robert McFaddin in Craven County on a small branch of Fishing Creek adj. Jas Ferguson, John Ferguson, conveyed to Jas Burcham by Isaac McFaddin, "prior air" of the said Robert McFaddin, 26 Aug 1779. Jas Burcham (Seal), Wit: Wm Wiley, William Hadden.

**A, 476**: 21 April 1786, John Bell and Ann his wife of Chester County, planter, to John Walker of same [deed not completed].

**A, 477**: blank

**A, 478-481**: 25 Dec 1787, Robert Patton, Esqr., and wife Sarah of SC to William Richardson Davie, Esqr., of State of North Carolina, for £450 current money of SC, 400 acres of land formerly in North Carolina, Anson County, on the west side of Cattawba River granted unto and surveyed for James Patton, near his own land. Robert Patton (LS), Sarah Patton (LS), Wit: Saml Lowrie, Willey S. Brown, Joseph Davie.

**A, 481-483**: 25 Dec 1787, Robert Patton, Esqr., and wife Sarah of SC to William Richardson Davie, Esqr., of State of North Carolina, for £100 current money of SC, 100 acres of land formerly in Craven County, on the west side of Catawba River joining all lands on north patent lands belonging to James Patton & Robert Patton as appears by a grant obtained by Prudence Patton from SC. Robert Patton (LS), Sarah Patton (LS), Wit: Saml Lowrie, Willey S. Brown, Joseph Davie.

**A, 484-486**: 25 Dec 1787, Robert Patton Esqr & Sarah his wife of Camden District to William R. Davie, Esqr., of NC, for £3000 current money of SC, tract on west side of the Catabaw River originally granted to Matthew Patton by NC, 558 ares, adj. Jas & Robert Patton, Robert Patton, Robert Morrison, Isaac Taylor, and the Cataba River, 378 acres as appears by a grant from SC to Robert Patton, heir of the above mentioned Matthew Patton. Robert Patton (LS), Sarah Patton (LS), Wit: Saml Lowrie, Willey S. Brown, Joseph Davie.

**A, 487-488**: 25 Dec 1787, Robert Patton Esqr & Sarah his wife of Camden District to William R. Davie, Esqr., of NC, for £100 current money of SC, 190 acres, part of 568 acres granted to Matthew Patton by patent by NC, and devolved to the above named Robert Patton by Heirship, for 378 acres from SC. Robert Patton (LS), Sarah Patton (LS), Wit: Saml Lowrie, Willey S. Brown, Joseph Davie.

**A, 489-491**: 5 Jan 1788, Pleasant William Farguson & Mary Farguson widow of James Farguson decd, both of Chester county, to John Farguson of same, for £500 current money of SC, tract granted 10 May 1768 to Jas Farguson Junr decd, 200 acres in Craven County now Chester on SW side Catawba River on the hand of two small branches of Rockey Creek. Pleasant Wm. Farguson (Seal), Mary Farguson (X) (LS), Wit: William Wyley, James Adams.

**A, 492-493**: 15 Feb 1788, Wm Ford Senior of Chester County for £10 sterling and natural love to William Ford his son, 200 acres late the property of William Storment, on waters of Little Rockey Creek &U in the occupation of Ginens Allen. William Ford Senr (LS), Wit: James Morris (X), Mary Ford (X).

**A, 494**: Samuel Hughey of Chester County for £100 sterling to Mark Edwards, one sorrel mare and two bay geldings, one iron grey gelding and five head of cattle, eight head of hogs, one feather bed & Furniture, parcel of pewter, four geese. Saml Hughey, Wit: Ezekiel Sanders, William Sharpe, James Edwards.

**A, 495**: 16 April 17788, David Hopkins Esqr. of Chester County, to Nathan Sims of same, for £200 sterling, tract of 160½ acres, part of tract of land of 321 acres granted to David Hopkins in the District of Camden on waters of Sandy River, granted 5 Feb 1787. Dd. Hopkins (Seal), Wit: James Glenn, Thomas Glenn.

**A, 496-498**: 24 Aug 1787, Wm Arnold & Agness his wife of York County, to John Feares of Chester County, blacksmith, for £70 sterling, tract in the County of Chester, on waters of Fishing Creek adj. lands of David Hunter, Saml Hambleton, granted to John McKinney 30 Oct 1766, memorial entered in Book H. No. 8, page 368, 7 Dec 1767, and recorded in the secretarys office in Book BBB, conveyed by said John McKenney to John Harris 13 Dec 1778, and by said John Heares & Jane his wife to William Arnold by deed 9 April 1784. William Arnold (LS), Agness Arnold (X) (LS), Wit: David Hunter, Elijah Browne, Lewis Thompson.

**A, 499-501**: 24 Aug 1787, Wm Arnold & Agness his wife of York County, to John Phares (Farress) of Chester County, for £70 sterling, tract in the County of Chester, on waters of Fishing Creek adj. lands he now lives on, formerly John McKinneys land, 150 acres n the platt annexed to the original grant the same bearing date 20 May 1773, memorial entered in the Auditor Generals office in Book M. No. 12, page 410, 13 Aug 1773, granted to Saml McKinney and conveyed to John Heares 29 Aug 1778, and by John Hearis to said Wm Arnold. William Arnold (LS), Agness Arnold (X) (LS), Wit: David Hunter, Elijah Browne, Lewis Thompson.

A, 502-505: 5 Feb 1788, Christopher Morgan & Martha his wife, planters, of Chester County, for £26 to George Morris of same county, planter, 50 acres adj. George Morriss, David Powell, Blackley Shewmake. Christopher Morgan (X) (Seal), Martha Morgan (Seal), Wit: Andrew Hemphill, Robert Hemphill.

A, 505-508: 8 July 1788, John Couper Senr of Mclenburg County, NC, to Thomas Gerrit of Rockey Creek in Chester County, SC, for £20 sterling, 200 acres granted 14 Oct 1774 by SC to Jno Couper, adj. lands of Charles Kitchings, John Weir, Thomas Morton. John Cooper (mark) (LS), Wit: John Mills, James Kell, Robert Jamison.

A, 509-510: South Carolina, Camden District. 16 June 1788, Robert Lemonds of District aforesaid, planter, to George Head, planter, for £100, tract granted 6 Feb 1786. Robert Lemons (Seal), Wit: Jas Huey, Joseph Timms, Jas Goo McLoan.

A, 511: John Mills Junr, Edw'd Lacey & John Walker bound to the Treasurers of the State of SC in the sum of £1000 sterling in John Mills making default, 8 July 1788, condition that John Mills shall perform his duty as a Genl Tax Collector for Chester County as provided 27 Feb last by law. John Mills (Seal), Edward Lacey (Seal), John Walker (J) (Seal).

A, 512-517: Lease and release. 14 & 15 May 1787, Saml Carter of Camden District and wife Elizabeth to Randel Carter of same, for £50 sterling money of SC, 107 acres on waters of Sandy River, part of tract granted to said Saml Carter 17 May 1785. Samuel Carter (Seal), Elizabeth Carter (X) (Seal), Wit: William Carter, Moses Hill, Jose Scot[?].

A, 518-519: 9 July 1788, James Ramsey of Chester County, planter, to James McClihena of same, for £5 current money, 20 acres on south fork of Fishing Creek adj. and between lands granted to William Jones and John Price, part of a grant conveyed by John Price to James Ramsey adj. James Ramsey, William Jones, granted to John Price by NC 25 April ---- and conveyed by John Price, entered in the Auditor Generals office in 1767. James Ramsey (LS), Wit: John Price, Tho Moore.

[N. B. There is an error in numbering: the next page is numbered 529.]

A, 529-531: 9 July 1788, John McClehena & William McClehena of Chester County, SC, planters, to James Ramsey of same, planter, for £5 current money, 20 acres on south fork of Fishing Creek, between lands granted to Wm Jones and John Price, part of tract granted to Wm Jones by NC 23 Feb 1754 and conveyed to James Johnson and James Johnson conveyed the same to us James & Wm. McClehena, entered in the Auditor Generals office of SC 2 Dec 1767. James McClehena (LS), William McClehena (LS), Wit: John Price, Thos Moore.

**A, 531-533**: 7 Sept 1787, John Carson of Rockey Creek in Chester county, planter, to Andrew Stinson (Stevenson) of same, planter, for £60 sterling, 100 acres granted 13 May 1768 by SC to John Carson in Craven County, on a small branch of Rockey Creek adj. land surveyed for Dugall Ballantine, Mary Herbeson, grant recorded in Book DDD, page 137. John Carson (LS), Elizabeth Carson (LS), Wit: James McLonan, James Kell, Sarah Miskelly (X).

**A, 534-537**: 16 April 1788, John Carson of Rockey Creek in Chester county, planter, to Andrew Stinson (Stevenson) of same, planter, for £25 sterling, 50 acres granted 5 Nov 1787 to John Carson on waters of Rockey Creek adj. land surveyed for Dugall Ballantine, Mary Herbeson, grant recorded in Book DDD, page 137. John Carson (LS), Elizabeth Carson (LS), Wit: James McLonan, James Kell, Sarah Miskelly (X).

**A, 537-538**: 4 July 1788, Peter Lemby of Fairfield County, SC, to James Mannin Gore of Chester County, for £20, tract on deep lick creek of Sandy River granted to said Peter Lemby 5 Sept 1785, recorded in Book EEEE, page 436. Peter Lemby (X) (LS), Wit: T. Lewis, Elijah Major.

**A, 539-540**: 28 June 1788, David Hopkins of Chester County to John Richardson of Fairfield County, for £20 sterling, tract on branches of Jones Creek adj. lands of David Hopkins Esqr., surveyed 6 July 1773 on a warrant granted to Ephraim Mitchell 15 Oct 1784, 100 acres. David Hopkins (LS), Wit: Paul C. Abney, H. Watson.

**A, 540-542**: South Carolina, Camden District. 5 Feb 1787, John Wilkison of Orange Burg District, to Jas Adair of Camden District, for £---, 200 acres on heads of Sandy River in Chester County, granted 13 Oct 1772 to John Hitchcock. John Wilkison (Seal), Wit: John Prescout, Enoch L. Seal. James Fowler.

**A, 542-543**: 4 Oct 1788, James Shepherd of Wilks County, Georgia, to John Terry of Chester County, for £500 sterling, 450 acres in Chester county granted to David Morrow and by him conveyed to William Rey & by said Rey to John Warren and from said Warren to James Shepperd. James Shepperd (LS), Wit: Wm. Gassaway, W. Morrow, George Blissett (X).

**A, 544-546**: 6 Aug 1788, Patrick Hambleton of Chester county, yeoman, to Daniel Cook of same, for £100 sterling, 300 acres granted 1 Sept 1768 to Patrick Hambleton on waters of Fishing Creek adj. Saml Hambleton. Patrick Hambleton (X) (LS), Wit: Thos Whiteside, Anthony McMeans.

**A, 547-548**: John Love of Camden District bound to Adam McCool, Wm. Gaston & James Love, in the sum of £5000, John Love to make to Adam McCool a sufficient rite for a piece of land on Turkey Creek between lands of Wm. Gaston & John Love, 100 acres on which John Love Senr now dwells, and also to Wm Gaston for 600 acres on a fork of Turkey Creek on which Jas

Gill now lives. John Love (LS), Wit: Margrat Davis (O), Jane Love. Proved by the oath of James Yancey 11 Oct 1788.

**A, 548-549**: 17 July 1788, James Dougharty of Orange Burg District, SC, to John Colsen of Chester county, for £50 sterling, tract on Welshes fork of Sandy River, 500 acres adj. Jas Sharp, Jno Dougharty, granted to said James Dougharty 6 Feb 1786. James Dougharty (Seal), Wit: Thos Jinkins, John Colvin Junr (X).

**A, 549-550**: Alexander Brown of Fishing Creek, SC, planter, appointed friend John Mills Junr of said county my attorney to receive any sums of money or other property due me in the name of Alexander Brown Senr decd, 15 Sept 1788. Alexander Brown (Seal), Wit: Michael Dickson, Joseph Lynn.

**A, 551-553**: 2 Oct 1779, Danl Cook of Camden District, Craven County, taylor, to Joseph Booth of same, for £600 lawful currency, 100 acres granted 25 July 1774 to Danl Cook on waters of Fishing Creek adj. Wm McFaddin, Charles Strong. Danl Cook (Seal), Wit: Robert Martin, William Lard.

**A, 554-556**: __ Sept 1788, Hugh Gaston and wife Martha of Chester County, planter, to Jerred Edwards of same, for £100 current money, 100 acres granted 16 Sept 1774 to Hugh Gaston. Hugh Gaston (Seal), Martha Gaston (Seal).

**A, 556-557**: South Carolina. 22 Sept 1788, John Sadler to John Owin, both of state aforesaid, for £40 sterling, tract granted to the said John Sadler by William Tryon, Gov. of NC, 300 acres (except 200 acres made over to John Pugh by a deed where he now lives), 100 acres with a small improvement where William Banks formerly lived, in Chester County, on the head branch of Sandy River, plat dated 1769 including the creek on both sides. John Sadler (LS), Mary Sadler (LS), Wit: David Owin, William Sadler.

## END OF DEED BOOK A

**B, 1-2**: 21 March 1785, William Collins of Rockey Creek, Craven County, Camden District, St. Marks Parish, Blacksmith, to James Kell of same county, district, and parish, for £28 s11 d5 current money of SC, 50 acres, granted 18 Aug 1763 by SC to John Walker, on Rockey Creek, which is a branch of the Cataba River falling in on the west thereof, transferred to William Collins by lease and release in 1776. William Collins (LS), Wit: John Bell, Elijah Davis, John Kell.

**B, 3**: 18 Sept 1788, Adam Williamson of Chester County to Hannah Evans of same, for £55 sterling, 227 acres in Camden District on the waters of Sandy River, east side of Broad River adj. land granted to Owen Evans adj. land granted to James Forgesson, James McCarter, part of tract of 532 acres laid out unto John Evans the grant dated 5 June 1786, recorded in Book MMMM, page 108. Adam Williamson (Seal), Wit: Mary Evans, Owen Evans, Elizabeth Evans.

**B, 4**: 24 March 1787, John Evans of Chester County to Adam Williamson of same, for £50 sterling, 220 acres on waters of Sandy River adj. land granted to Owin Evans, James Ferguson, James McCarter, part of 532 acres laid out to said John Evans, grant dated 5 June 1786, recorded in Book MMMM, page 108. John Evans (LS), Wit: Owen Evans, Elizabeth Evans, Agnes Evans (X).

**B, 5**: 6 Oct 1788, James Huey of Chester County to Major Gresham of same, for £200, 100 acres granted to Edward Wilson by SC and transferred from said Wilson to Dennis Carroll and from Carrell to John Wood Junr and from him to James Huey, tract on waters of Sandy River. James Huey (S), Sarah Huey (LS), Wit: Elijah Nunn, John Franklin, John Rogers (R).

**B, 6**: 12 July 1788, John Hays of Chester county to James Hays of same, for £100, 100 acres, part of 200 acres granted to Joseph Brown on a small branch known by the name of Rockey Branch running into Sandy River surveyed 25 March 1767 by John Wilkinson. John Hays (N) (Seal), Wit: Edmond Lea, Jacob Dungan, Tho's Gore.

**B, 7**: 17 Sept 1788, John Love of Chester County to James Love Junr of same, for £5 sterling, tract on Broad River and Turkey Creek, part of three tracts of land granted to John Love 4 Dec 1771, 5 June 1786, and 29 April 1768 by SC, 138 acres at the mouth of Turkey Creek. John Love (LS), Wit: Wm Gaston, Caleb Baldwin, Wm. Love.

**B, 8-9**: 17 Sept 1788, John Love of Chester County to James Love Junr of same, for £5 sterling, tract on waters of Turkey Creek, part of two tracts of land granted to John Love, one by NC 15 Feb 1764, and the other by SC for 84 acres 29 April 1768 by SC. John Love (LS), Wit: Wm Gaston, Caleb Baldwin, James Love.

**B, 9-10**: 31 March 1788, Robert Harper & Margaret his wife of Chester County, silver smith, to John Hays of same, for £10 sterling, 15 acres on south fork of Fishing Creek adj. Mills, part of tract of 142 acres granted to the said Robert Harper 1 Sept 1785. Robert Harper (Seal).

**B, 10-11**: 31 March 1788, Robert Harper & Margaret his wife of Chester County, silver smith, to John Hays of same, for £10 sterling, 14½ acres on south fork of Fishing Creek adj. Mitchell, part of tract of 142 acres granted to the said Robert Harper 1 Sept 1785. Robert Harper (Seal).

**B, 12-13**: 27 April 1788, John Hayes, Blacksmith of Chester county, to Robert Harper of same, cooper, for ten shillings. 51 acres on waters of south fork of Fishing Creek on north side of said Creek, part of 100 acres granted to Joseph Mitchell of Macklenburg, NC, by a grant from NC 26 Oct 1767, conveyed by said Mitchell 28 Aug 1778 recorded in Charleston in Book T No. 5, page 398, to James Jack, and by James Jack to John Hayes. John Hays (Seal), Wit: John Mills, Mary Mills.

**B, 14**: 18 Dec 1779, James Fletchall of Camden District to Joseph Davis of same, for £406 s5 SC money, tract on south side of south fork of Sandy River, granted to James Fletchall 22 Oct 1768, 15 acres. James Fletchall (LS), Wit: Robert Saunders (X), Thos Gore (X).

**B, 15**: John Rast of Orrange Burgh District, planter, to John Franklyn in Charleston District, a negro man named Abram[?], 6 May 1788. John Rast. Proved by the oath of Thomas Rast (X) in Chester County 10 May 1788 before John Pratt, J.P.

**B, 15-16**: Manuel Powel of Camden District, planter, bound to Isom and Joseph Powell in the sum of £5000 current money of SC, 8 Dec 1777, to make title to Isom & Joseph Powell for a tract on so side of Rockey Creek on branch sides of the Turkey branch, adj. Moses Reaves, late the property of David Powell deceased. Manuel Powell (X), Wit: Hugh Montgomery, William Hasden, John Montgomery. Ordered to be recorded in July Court 1788.

**B, 16-17**: South Carolina, Chester County. 16 July 1788, Martha Lamands and Robert Lamands of county aforesaid to Samuel Lacey of same, for £30 sterling, 300 acres in Chester County on waters of Sealeys fork on Sandy River granted by patent to James Lamands 5 May 1773, recorded in Book OOO, page 569, a memorial entered in Book M N page 389 20 Aug 1773. Martha Lamands (mark) (LS), Robert Lamonds (LS), Wit: James Fowler, John Gill, Agness Gill.

**B, 17-18**: Chester County. John Carson of county aforesaid appoint Philip Walker of said county my lawful attorney to receive from all persons, especially £10 s9 due from Andrew Stevenson on bond now int he hands of William Archer, 4 June 1788. John Carson (Seal), Wit: John MCDonald, L. R. Isbell.

**B, 18-19**: 9 Oct 1786, Thomas Baker Franklin of Chester county, CS, to John hayes of same, for £50 sterling, 150 acres on east and north and west sides of said plantation, adj. David Morrow, James Trussel, Major Gresham, John Franklin, part of 300 acres granted to Thomas Baker Franklin by patton 2 Oct 1786 by SC, on bear branch, a branch of Sandy River. Thomas Baker Franklin (Seal), Wit: Will Boyd, John Franklin, Abraham Miller (A).

**B, 20**: South Carolina, Chester County. Edward Lacey, Sheriff of Chester County by virtue of two executions put into my hands at the suits of Fielden Woodroof & John Ewart vs Thomas Moore have leveyd on and agreeable to law by publick sale, 10 July last, sold to John Walker Junr a negro boy named Prince taken as the property of said Moore for £30 sterling, 8 Oct 1788. Edward Lacey (LS).

To Col. Edward Lacey, Sheriff of Chester County. Sir, you will please to execute titles to Joseph Brown, Daniel Brown, James Adair & Reuben Lacey for the land purchased by me at Sheriff sale late the property of John Walker (miller), 10 Oct 1788. James McNeal (LS).

**B, 21-22**: 2 Dec 1788, Zacheriah Roberts of Chester county, Camden District, SC ,to Allen Degraffenreid of same, for £100 sterling, 300 acres, half of a tract of 600 acres granted to John Hitchcock by NC 3 Feb 1754 and recorded in the Auditor Generals office 23 Feb 1754. Zacheriah Robert (LS), Mary Roberts (LS), Wit: Wm Embrie, Rich'd Davis, Zeph Roberts.

**B, 23-24**: South Carolina, Chester County. 6 Jan 1789, Thomas Huston of county aforesaid to Elliot Lee of same, for £200 sterling, 150 acres on Saluda Road & on the dry fork of Saluda Creek in Craven County (now Chester County). Thomas Huston (Seal), Wit: Jas Yancy. Saml Brown.

**B, 24-26**: 28 Dec 1788, Michael Hart of Lincoln County, North Carolina, yoman, to Wm Sleeker Junr, son of George Sleeker deceased, & to Edward White & Agness Sleeker exors of said George Sleeker to their care, for £300, tract granted 12 Feb 1773 by SC to Michael Hart, 200 acres in Craven County on drafts of the N fork of Fishing [Creek]. Michal Hart (X) (LS), Wit: Robert White, Thomas Neely. Proved by the oath of Thomas Neely 6 Jan 1788 before Hugh Knox, J.P.

**B, 26-28**: 17 March 1786, Margaret Barnett widow & Exrx of John Barnett decd of SC, Camden District, to Stith Fennall of same, planter, for £500 sterling, 150 acres, part of tract granted 25 Sept 1754 by NC to Casper Sleager, 778 acres, conveyed to Archer Elliot 1 Sept 1768 and by him to Wm McKinney, 150 acres of said tract, 2 May 1771, and said McKinney sold said 150 acres to John Barnett decd 22 April 1774, and said tract being sold by John Barnett to Rebekkah Barnett decd by bond or obligation to make a right, and said Rebeckah Barnett willed said land to her son Wm Barnett who sold the same to Stith Fennall, the deed made by Wm. McKinney to John Barnett recorded in SC Book L No. 5, page 240 and 242 30 July 1784.

Margaret Barnet (LS), Wit: William Wiley, Benjamin Rives, John Studm't (IS).

**B, 29-30**: South Carolina, Chester County. 6 Jan 1789, Thomas Jenkins of said county to John Sealy of same, for £85 sterling, 100 acres adj. John Seely, granted 3 June 1766 by SC. Thomas Jenkins (LS).

**B, 30-31**: South Carolina, Chester County. 20 Dec 1899. George Bishop of county aforesaid to John Abernathy, late of York County, SC, for £45 sterling, 79 acres granted to David McCreight 4 May 1775. George Bishop (+) (LS), Wit: Wm Liles, Edward Lacey, George Sadler.

**B, 31-33**: 6 Dec 1788, John McCooll of Union County, SC, planter, to Benjamin Love of Chester County, planter, for ten shillings, 150 acres adj. Jno Anderson, Stewart Brown, Samuel Femster, Clelan Rodgers, Benja'n Love. John McCooll (LS), Wit: William Love, Richard Love, Gardn'r Jamison.

**B, 33-34**: South Carolina, Chester County. 9 Nov 1788, John Nunn of county aforesaid to Major Gresham of same, for £10 sterling, tract on waters of Stones Creek of Sandy River, 41 acres, adj. John Pratt, Daniel Price, granted 3 April 1786. John Nunn (LS), Eliz'a Nunn (LS), Wit: Jas Hardwick, Sarah Pratt[?], Ann Kitchens (X). Proved by the oath of James Hardwick 5 Jan 1789 before John Pratt, J.P.

**B, 35-37**: Lease and release. 28 June 1787, William Hogan of Chester county ot James Dillard of same, for £100, 160 acres on south side of Sandy River originally granted to John Davis 1 June 1767 for 200 acres conveyed from said Davis to said Hogan 1 Dec 1784. William Hogans (LS), Wit: T. Lewis, William Hall James Dillard Junr.

**B, 38-39**: 6 Oct 1785, James Neely & his wife Martha of Chester County, Camden District, planter, to Isom Fielding of same, for £500 current money, tract granted 1 Sept 1768 to Wm Gaston, late of said province now state, 100 acres adj. Elizabeth Craig, conveyed to James Neely 18 Jan 1769 recorded in the Office of said province in Book D-4, page 61, 16 April 1773. James Neely (LS), Wit: Thomas Farrell, Stith Fennell, William Wiley.

**B, 40-41**: 22 Oct 1788, James Hays of Chester County to John Roden of same, for £100 sterling, 100 acres, part of 200 acres granted to Joseph Brown on a small branch leading into Sandy River surveyed 28 March 1767 P John Wilkeson. James Hays (LS), Penneso [Pennelope?] Hays (mark) (LS), Wit: Francis Wilks, Greenberry Roden, Abart Lee. Proved by the oath of Greenberry Roden 5 Jan 1789 before John Pratt, J.P.

**B, 41-43**: 5 Sept 1788, Alexander Brown, attorney for Alexander Brown Senr, late of this place, Chester County, yeoman, to Joseph Lyon of same, school-master, for £100, sterling, 160 acres, part of tract granted 29 April 1768 by NC to Alexander Brown Senr, 290 acres in Mecklenburg County, NC, at the time of survey but now in the state of SC, Chester County on both sides of the south fork of Fishing Creek adj. and between the lines of George Craig, Henry Culp, William Miller, John Boyd & David Lewis, including his plantation, and by power of attorney from Alexander Brown Senr to his son Alexander Brown Junr 20 Sept 1787. Alexander Brown (LS), Wit: John Simpson, William Elliott.

South Carolina, Camden District. Alexander Brown of district aforesaid appoints Alexander Brown Junr his attorney to sell tract whereon I formerly lived, 20 Sept 1787. Alexander Brown (LS), Wit: William Moore. Proved by the oath of William Moore 11 Sept 1788 before Hugh Whiteside, J.P.

**B, 44-45**: 21 Aug 1777, Alexander Porter of Mecklenburg County, NC, to John Bell of Craven County, SC, planter, for £100 current money, 200 acres granted 4 May 1775 by SC to Alexander Porter, on north fork of Rockey Creek in Craven County adj. land surveyed for William Stroud, Margaret Campbell, James Bigham. Alexander Porter (LS), Wit: James Bigham, Samuel Bigham.

**B, 46-50**: Lease and release. 8 & 9 Sept 1776, Elizabeth Steen of Craven County, Parish of St. Marks, SC, spinner, to William Millen of same, for £50 current money, 100 acres in Parish of St. Marks, Craven County, on a branch of Rockey Creek, granted 1 March 1775. Elizabeth Steen (mark) (LS), Wit: Michael Dickson, Charles Miller, John Combest. Proved in Camden District by the oath of Charles Miller 27 Nov 1779 before Wm. Brown, J.P.

**B, 50**: Robert Gorrell, Edward Lacey & John Pratt bound to the justices of Chester county in the sum of £100 current money of SC, 6 Jan 1789, tavern license to Robt Gorrell to keep tavern at his house in said county for one year.

**B, 51**: South Carolina, Chester County. We the under named subscribers free holders being duly summoned as appraisers to appraise a certain gray horse now astray in the possession of Wm Magarity and bounded thus WE on the near shoulder, which we do appraise to £5 sterling, 10 Aug 1788. John Bell, William Gaston, James Kell. Andrew Hemphill, J.P.

**B, 51**: South Carolina, Chester County. We the under named subscribers free holders being duly summoned as appraisers to appraise a certain brown bay coloured mare now astray in the possession of Moses Smith no brand to be seen at this time. She has three small white spots in her fore head the one below the other which said mare we doth appraise to £3 s11 d6, 3 Jan 1789. Robert McCollough, Jas Hemphill, Joshua Smith. Andrew Hemphill, J.P.

**B, 51-52**: Thomas B. Franklyn, Patrick McGriff & James Gore bound to the justices of Chester County in the sum of £100 current money, 6 Jan 1789, said Thomas B. Franklin hath obtained license to keep tavern at his house for one year. Thomas B. Franklin (LS), Patrick McGriff (LS), James Gore (LS).

**B, 52**: John Hayes & James Trussell of Chester County bound to Thomas B. Franklin of same, 1 Dec 1788, to relinquish all title, claim or right to a certain parcel of land sold by said Franklin to John hayes, part of tract now the property of John Terry for £5 paid by said Thos Franklin to John Hays and James Trussell. John Hayes (mark) (LS), James Trussell (mark) (LS), Wit: H. V. Cason, John Franklin.

**B, 53**: Thomas Jinkins, Edward Lacey & Richard Taliaferro bound to the justices of Chester county in the sum of £100 current money, 7 Jan 1789, whereas Thos Jinkins hath obtained license to keep tavern at his house for the space of one year. Thomas Jinkins (LS), Edward Lacey (LS), R. Taliaferro (LS).

**B, 53-54**: Samuel Morriss of Ninety Six District quit claim to Edward Lacey of Camden District to a negro wench named Jude about 24 years of age, yellow complected, has lots part of the fore finger off her right hand, as also the child who is named Isaac, 22 Nov 1788. Samuel Morriss, Wit: Wm. Miles, James McNeale.

**B, 54**: Thomas Bragg, Edward Lacey & Richard Taliaferro bound to the justices of Chester county in the sum of £100 current money, 7 Jan 1789, whereas Thos Bragg obtained license to keep tavern at his house for the space of one year. Thomas Bragg (LS), Edw'd Lacey (LS), R. Taliaferro (LS).

**B, 55**: South Carolina, Chester County. Sampson Noling was attached to answer Alexander Walker of a plea of Trespass on the case for which the said Alex on 7 Oct 1787 account with the said Sampson concerning several accounts & sums of money that the said Sampson to said Alexander then due, and said Sampson was then found in arrears in the sum of £30 sterling, and said Sampson then assumed and faithfully promised to pay, and said Sampson tho after requested hath not paid. John Walker, Plff Attorney. We find verdict for the Defendant. Thos Jinkins, foreman.

**B, 55-56**: 3 July 1784, Patrick Hamilton of Craven County, SC, weaver, to Peter Robinson of same, for 50 guineas sterling, 300 acres on waters of Fishing Creek adj. Samuel Hamilton, granted as Bounty to Patrick Hamilton 1 Sept 1768. Wit: Michael Stedman, William Smith.

**B, 57-58**: 25 Oct 1788, John Hayes of Chester county to James Trussell of same, for £100, 150 acres adj. David Morrow, James Trussell, Major Gresham, John Franklin. John Hayes (mark) (LS), Wit: John Trussell, Absalom Humphrys, John Ramsey (+).

**B, 58-60**: 22 March 1789, Samuel Neely of Chester County, yeoman, to John Chambers of York County, for £50, one half of tract granted 21 Oct 1758 by NC to William Neely, 400 acres in Anson County but now in the State of SC, Chester County, on both sides Fishing Creek on west side Cataba River, said tract conveyed to Samuel Neely 26 Feb 1778, adj. Archibald Elliott, Neeley, Hugh Whiteside, 200 acres. Samuel Neely (LS).

**B, 60-61**: 28 Oct 1787, Leonard Pratt of Chester County to William Watson of same, for £10 sterling, 100 acres granted 9 Sept 1774 on Martins branch of Sandy River. Leonard Pratt (X) (LS), Wit: John Pratt, John Watson.

**B, 61-62**: 24 March 1789, George Kelsey of Chester county, planter, to William Whiteside of same, wheelwright, for £16 sterling, tract granted 29 April 1768 by NC to James Smith, 200 acres in Mecklenburg County, NC, but now in Chester County, on west side Cataba River and north side of main Fishing Creek on both sides of the Kairney Run & on both sides of the Waggon Road adj. William Neely, conveyed to Samuel McKinney by James Smith and Lillies his wife 21 June 1774 and by Samuel McKinney to George Kelsey 29 Jan 1780. George Kelsey (LS), Wit: Hugh Whiteside, Wm. Neely, Jas Neely.

**B, 62-67**: Lease and release. 16 & 17 May 1788, Thomas Leonard of Chester County, planter, to William Crook of same, planter, for £40 lawful money, 114½ acres, part of 346 acres on waters of Fishing Creek in Chester county, granted to Davice Leonard, adj. said Davice Leonard, Casper Sleeker, Archibald Clark, Doct. Emer, and the said Davice Leonard dying intestate, the said Thomas Leonard being his oldest & only son,. Thomas Leonard (LS), Wit: John McCreary, John Steel.

**B, 67-69**: 1 Jan 1789, Edward Lacey, Esqr., High Sheriff of Chester County, to William McKinney of same, whereas the said William McKinney in the county court of Fairfield did implead Peter Robison of a plea of debt in 1787 did obtain judgment, and on the lands, chattels, etc., of said Peter Robeson to levy the sum of £21 s1 d11 sterling, exposed to public sale on 8 October last, sold 300 acres on waters of Fishing Creek adj. David Hunter, John Robeson, granted 1 Sept 1768 from SC, now sold for £9 s9 sterling to William McKinney. Edward Lacey Shff C Cy (LS).

**B, 69-70**: 1 July 1788, John Long of Camden District, SC, to Drury Going of same, for £50 sterling, tract on waters of Turkey Creek adj. James KirkPatrick, 100 acres. John Long (Seal), Wit: Alexander Tomb, David Tomb, Job Goin.

**B, 70-71**: 8 Jan 1789, William Barrow of Fairfield County, executor of the estate of Willm Barrow decd, to Alexander Stevenson of the county of York, for £60 current money, 200 acres, a tract granted to Wm. Barrow now decd, by NC 23 May 1772 on both sides of Owens branch of Sandy River adj. Edward Craft. William Barrow executor (LS), Wit: Edward Lacey, Jane Lacey, Robert Conley (X).

**B, 71-72**: 14 Feb 1789, Elijah Nunn of Chester County to Edmund Lee of same, for £85 sterling, 100 acres granted to Joseph Brown 16 Jan 1772 & to Jno Moberley in 1787, transfer'd from Moberly to Elijah Nunn, adj. Ezekiel

Sanders, Degraffenreid, Hitchcock. Elijah Nunn (LS), Wit: John Wright, John Jaggers.

**B, 73**: _____ 1789, William Gaston of Chester County to Drury Going of same, for £3 s14 sterling, tract on Mill Creek, part of tract granted to William Gaston 3 Sept 1787 by SC, 200 acres. William Gaston (LS).

**B, 74**: Hugh Cooper of Chester County have appointed friend Robert Cooper of same, blacksmith, attorney to receive from Robert Barrow of the state of North Carolina the full damages sustained by me by said Borrow taking and detaining two of my horses from July 1780, 9 July 1789. Hugh Cooper (LS) before Hugh Whiteside, J.P.

**B, 74-77**: Lease and release. 27 & 27 Dec 1782, Daniel Collson of Camden District, Craven County, SC, miller, to William McDonald of same place, planter, for £300 current money, 100 acres granted to Arthur Hicklin Junr by SC 23 Oct 1765 and transferred by him to said Daniel Collson by deed of gift, recorded in the public register's office of said state 30 May 1774. Daniel Collson (LS), Wit: W. Howell, Thos Howell.

**B, 77-78**: Robert Gorrell of Chester County appointed friend Ralph Gorrell of Guilford County, North Carolina, his attorney and also John Cunningham of the Kingdom of Ireland, and City of Londonderry, merchant, attorneys to receive from John Calhoun, late of Charleston, SC, the sum of £159 Irish money, 17 Dec 1789. Robt Gorrell (LS).

**B, 78-80**: 16 Dec 1788, Christopher Straight of Chester County, blacksmith, to George Straight of same, planter, for £30 sterling, 300 acres granted 28 Oct 1763 to James Moore by NC in Mecklenburg County, but now in York County, SC, on waters of the south fork of Fishing Creek on the crabtree branch including a large meadow on the waggon Road adj. Wm Taylor, conveyed to Christopher Straight by James Moore 24 Feb 1772, a memorial entered in Book M No 12, page 52, 24 Dec 1772. Christopher Straight (LS).

**B, 80-81**: 22 Aug 1786, William Henry of Mecklenburg County, NC, yeoman, to William Farriss of Chester County, SC, for £50, 150 acres, part of 190 acres granted 22 April 1767 by NC to William Henry, between the south and north fork of Fishing Creek adj. Samuel McCance, Samuel Neely, Hugh Whiteside, Wm Neely, Archibald Elliott. William Henry (LS), Wit: Hugh Whiteside, William Whiteside, Thomas Whiteside.

[two apparent loose pages between 80 and 81]: John McEwen the younger and Margaret McEwen of the District of Fairfield for love and affection to our children John McEwen, Joseph McEwen, and Ann McEwen, and for one dollar to us paid by James Barber of district aforesaid, one certain female slave named Doll about the age of 16 years, to said James Barber until the youngest child of said John and Margaret shall attain the age of 21, 15 June 1805. Jno McEwen Junr (LS), Margaret McEwen (mark) LS), Wit: Jos Evans.

Proved in Fairfield District by the oath of Joseph Evans 17 March 1809 before D. R. Evans, J.P. Q.U.

**B, 82-83**: 23 March 1789, Samuel Neely of Chester County to John Latta of same, for £50 sterling, 200 acres granted 21 Oct 1758 to William Neely by NC, at the time in Anson County, but now in Chester County on both sides of Fishing Creek on the NW side of Cataba River, tract conveyed by Wm Neely to Samuel Neely 26 Feb 1778. Samuel Neely (LS).

**B, 83-84**: 23 Feb 1789, Cladius Charvin of Chester County to Daniel Williams of York County, for £260, that said William stands security for said Charvin unto Wm Adair in three different bonds, the first one payable 1 Jan 1789, the second same day 1709 and the third the same day 1791, mortgage of one negro wench named Jimm, one Road & one black mare, one sorrel gelding colt three years old next spring, one gray Phillis two years old next spring, one last springs brown colt & one old grey horse, three cows,two yearling heifers, and one young bull calf, one eight day clock with her case, four pewter dishes, twelve plates ditto, a parcel of household furniture, two metal pots, one Dutch oven, 6 chairs, two tables, one bed steads & earthing ware, two sheets, 6 blankett & a parcel of medicines and books, four light body cots, three shirts, 12 pair stockings, 6 stocks, 6 cambrick handkerchiefs, 3 pair breeches, 6 jackets, and sundry other cloathing, 200 bushels of Indian corn, etc. Claudius Charvin (LS), Wit: Geo Purvis, Josephus Fraultman[?], David Adrian.

**B, 85-86**: 10 June 1789, Isaac McFaddin and wife Elizabeth of Chester County to John Ferguson of same, for £50, 246 acres, part of tract granted 26 July 1774 by SC to Robert McFadden deceased, 350 acres, on a small branch of Fishing Creek in Craven County, now Chester, adj. Jas Ferguson Junr, John Ferguson, 104 being formerly sold to Jas Blair 6 May 1780. Isaac McFadden (LS), Elizabeth McFadden (X) (LS), Wit: David Hunter, Ralph McFadden, Cander McFadden.

**B, 87**: 19 May 1789, James Harp of Newberry County, to William Embry of Chester County, for £50 sterling, tract in Chester County on the dividing line between Woods & Harp, part of tract granted to Richard Whitaker 21 Jan 1785, 125 acres. James Harp (H) (LS), Wit: Allen Robison, Tobias Harp (mark), William Collom (+).

**B, 88-89**: 25 June 1789, Adam McCool of Chester County to Wm. Love of same place, for £30 sterling, tract granted 1 Dec 1772 for 250 acres on both sides of Little Turkey Creek, north side Broad River. Adam McCool (LS), Wit: Thomas Brandon, James Barron, Adam McCool.

**B, 89**: 30 Jan 1788, David Hopkins, Esqr., of Chester county to William Britain of same, for £50 sterling, 100 acres on branches of Sandy River adj. Thomas Gore, granted 15 Oct 1784. David Hopkins (LS), Wit: Fer'd Hopkins, James Fraser.

**B, 90-94**: Lease and release. 25 Jan 1786, Richard Whitaker of York County, SC, to James Harp of Ninety Six District, SC, for £200 sterling, 125 acres on waters of Broad River adj. John Woods, Herculous, near to McCool road, part of tract granted to Richard Whitaker 25 Jan 1785. Richard Whitaker (R) (LS), Wit: David Patrick, William Patrick.

**B, 94-95**: 5 July 1785, Richard Whitaker of York County, SC, to John Woods of Lincoln County, NC, for £50 sterling, 125 acres on Brushy fork of Sandy River adj. Love's corner, 225 acres including Mreses [sic] Mill seat on Brushey fork Creek, part of tract granted to Richard Whitaker 25 Jan 1785. Richard Whitaker (R) (LS), Wit: Alexd'r Ekans, Thomas Barnett, John Fearis.

**B, 95-96**: 17 June 1789, William Roberson of Guilford County, NC, to William Massey of Lancaster County, SC, for £20 sterling, 59 acres in Chester County on north side Fishing Creek adj. Lawrence Galaker, Bradley, John McCown, by certain indentures first from Alexander McCown to John McCown and from Jno McCown to Joshua Edwards and Joshua Edwards has authorized me, William Roberson, by power of attorney. William Robertson (LS), Wit: James Massey, William Massey, William Hunt.

**B, 97**: 8 June 1789, Wilson Henderson of Chester County to Wm. Britain of same, for £10 sterling, 10 acres on waters of Sandy River adj. Capt. Taliaferro's line, Wilson Henderson, John Thomas. Wilson Henderson (LS), Wit: Richard Taliaferro.

**B, 98-100**: Lease and release. 1 July 1789, Josiah Hill of Chester County to James Adare of same, for £10, 250 acres on waters of Mill Creek, part of 12,700 acres granted to said Josiah Hill 7 July 1786, adj. William Minter, Young. Josiah Hill (LS), Wit: W. Palmer, Rich'd Miles.

**B, 101-102**: 4 July 1789, Wm Gaston, Esquire, and John Low, both of Chester County to Adam McCool of same, for £5 sterling, tract on waters of Turkey Creek, pat of tract granted to Wm Love 3 Sept 1753 by NC for 800 acres, 438 acres of which being since granted to said Wm Gaston by SC, and this present grant being part of the latter, 100 acres adj. Wm. Gaston, William Love. William Gaston (LS), John Love (LS), Wit: James Bell, James Barron, John Brandon.

**B, 102-103**: South Carolina, Chester County. 5 Oct 1789, William Clark to James Mitchell, both of said county, for £100 sterling, 300 acres on a branch of Broad River called Wm Wilsons Creek, granted to Jeremiah McDaniel in 1772 and conveyed by said McDaniel to said Clark, 29 Dec 1772. William Clark (X) (LS), Wit: Alexander Stevenson, Saml Lacey.

**B, 104-105**: 22 April 1780, John Sadler & Mary his wife of Camden District, SC, to John Pugh of same, for £10,000 current money, 200 acres, part of 300 acres granted to John Sadler by NC, adj. Thomas Brown, William Banks. John

Sadler (Seal), Mary Sadler (O) (LS), Wit: Robert Collins, Isaac Sadler, John Gilliam.

**B, 105**: 27 Dec 1788, John Richardson of Fairfield County to Robert Collins of Chester county, for £35 sterling, tract on the branch of Jones's Creek adj. David Hopkins Esqr., surveyed 6 July 1773 on a warrant granted to Ephraim Mitchell, Esqr., 6 April 1733, and granted to said Ephraim Mitchell 15 Oct 1784, 100 acres. John Richardson (mark) (LS), Jean Richardson (mark), Wit: Edward Watts, Saml McMillan, Robert Collins Senr.

**B, 106-107**: South Carolina, Chester County. 3 Oct 1789, Thomas Jinkins of county aforesaid to William Mobberly of same, for £80 sterling, 100 acres on Sandy Creek, granted 6 June 1766 by SC. Thomas Jinkins (LS), Wit: Wm. Jinkins, Barnett Allen, Pat. McGriff.

"All writing in this Book following is done since April Court 1790 by Peter Corbell, D. C. C. C."

**B, 107-111**: Lease and release. 4 & 5 July 1784, Moses McCown and Frank his wife of Camden District, planters, to James McCown Junr & Mary McCown, planter, of same, for £1200 sterling, 200 acres on the conjunction of the Catawba River & the mouth of Fishing Creek adj. lands granted formerly to James Bradley, conveyed to said Moses McCown by James McCown Senr, and also 200 acres two miles up Fishing Creek from the aforesaid described tract of 200 acres adj. lands of Alexander McCown, which the said Moses McCown now lives on, granted to Robert Swan by SC and conveyed by Robt Swan to said Moses McCown. Moses McCown (Seal), Frank (X) (LS), Wit: David Hunter, Hugh McWaters. Proved by the oath of Hugh McWaters 5 July 1785 before Charles Picket, J.P.

**B, 112-113**: 4 Sept 1789, Josiah Hill of Chester County to John Pew of same, for £10 sterling, 100 acres, part of tract of 12,700 acres granted to said Josiah Hill 6 Nov 1786 adj. John Pew, Josiah Hill, John Parker. Josiah Hill (LS), Wit: Edw'd Lacey, Samuel Lacey, Samuel Lacey Junr.

**B, 113-114**: 12 May 1776, James Thomas of Ninety Six District, to William Embry of Craven County, SC, for £125 current money, tract in Craven County on NE side Broad River adj. John Hitchcock, 150 acres granted to James Thomas 3 Aug 1774. James Thomas (LS), Wit: John Starn, Thos Hughes, Richard Hughes[?]. [See **B, 124-126**, on page 42, apparently a lease and release.]

**B, 114-116**: Lease and release. 9 & 10 June 1789, John Steel of Chester County to Thomas Steel of same, that said John Steel, he being the heir of Catharine Steel widow deceased for £100 sterling, sells 200 acres, part of a tract of 400 acres granted to Catharine Steel on both sides of Fishing Creek adj. Catharine Steel, John Lennard, William Gaston. John Steel (seal), Wit: George Morris, Thomas Bell.

**B, 117-118**: 27 Nov 1788, Robert Tindel, Thomas Akin, both planters, of Chester County, to John Caldwell of same, for £15 lawful money, tract on waters of Jack Loves branch, 100 acres adj. Thomas Akins, Love's Road, Sandy River Road which goes from Benjamin Love's called the new Great Road, granted to Robert Tindall and Thos Akins 5 Sept 1785, Robert Tindall's grant recorded in Book LLL, page 430, and Thomas Akins' grant dated 5 June 1786. Robert Tindall (LS), Thomas Eakins (LS), Wit: James Johnson, James McCalla, Staff'd Curry.

**B, 119**: Hannah Bishop of Chester County, widow, appoints friend John Carter of same, planter, attorney to receive from the will of my father Thomas Braiken, late of the State of Pennsylvania, deceased, all such legacies to me, 6 April 1790. Hannah Bishop (LS), Wit: William Hughes, Jo. Brown.

**B, 119-122**: Lease and release. 22 & 23 Sept 1789, Jonathan Jones and Bathsheba his wife of Chester county to James Langsby, late of same, for £17 sterling, 114 acres on south side of the Cataba River on McClures branch, which runs into the south fork of Fishing Creek, granted to Jonathan Jones 2 Oct 1786. Jonathan Jones (LS), Bethsheba Jones (B) (LS), Wit: John Hardin, Joseph Jones (O).

**B, 123**: 18 July 1789, Christopher Degraffenreid of York County to Ambrose Nix of Chester County, for £100 sterling, 250 acres in Chester County on Starns branch. Christopher Degraffenreid (LS),Wit: William Embry, John Nix (X), Thos Saunders (P).

**B, 124-126**: 13 May 1776, James Thomas of Ninety Six District, SC, to William Embry of Craven County, SC, for £125 current money of said province, tract on NE side Broad river adj. John Hitchcock, granted to James Thomas 11 Aug 1774. James Thomas (LS), Wit: John Starn, Thos Hughes, Richard Huse. [See **B, 113-114**, on page 41, apparently a lease and release.]

**B, 126-128**: Lease and release. 23 Sept 1789, James Sharp of Orangeburg District, planter, to William Sharp of Camden District, planter, for £200 sterling, 200 acres in Camden District, Chester County, on Sandy Creek. James Sharp (LS), Wit: Edward Bowlin (B), Thomas C. Warner.

**B, 129-133**: Lease and release. 14 & 15 July 1787, John Daugherty of SC to Hugh McKown of same, for £10 current money, 100 acres in Chester County on the head waters of Sandy River adj. Amos Davis. John Dougharty (LS), Wit: James Corry, David Grissom (X), James McKown.

**B, 134**: 11 Nov 1789, William Britain and wife Jean of Chester County for £100 sterling, to Ambrose Lee of same, tract on waters of Sandy River, 100 acres. William Brittain (LS), Wit: Richard Taliaferro, William Shaw.

**B, 135-136**: 2 Nov 1789, John Colvin of Chester County, planter, to Martin Elom of same, for £70 sterling, tract on Welshs fork of Sandy River, 500 acres adj. James Sharp, John Dougherty, granted to James Dougherty 6 Feb 1786 and conveyed from said James Dougherty to said John Colvin 11 July 1788. John Colvin (LS), Wit: John Pratt, William Sharp, Ann Kitchings (+).

**B, 136-137**: 27 Nov 1789, Joseph Davis of Camden District, Chester County, to Allen Degraffenreid of same, for £50 sterling, 20 acres on the south fork of Sandy River, part of 100 acres originally granted to James Fletchall, William Head, said Degraffenreid. Joseph Davis (LS), Wit: Thomas Wilks (+), John Nix (+), Wm. Hughes.

**B, 138-139**: Amos Timms for £60 sterling to James Allison, 200 acres granted to Amos Timms in 1773, in Chester County, dated 17 Oct 1789. Amos Timms (Seal), Wit: Joseph Timms, John Timms, James Gilchrist (+).

**B, 139-140**: South Carolina, Chester County. 7 Sept 1789, Thomas Baker Franklin of Chester County, planter, to John Franklin of same, for £50 sterling, 271 acres, part of four different grants, one granted to Thomas Franklin 24 Nov 1767 100 acres, part of one granted 24 Dec 1772 for 200 acres, part of one granted to Major Gresham in October 1786 for 100 acres, and part of one granted to Thomas Baker Franklin 5 Feb 1787. Thomas Bak: Franklin (LS), Wit: Pat'k McGriff, Alex'r Johnson, James Gore.

**B, 141-142**: 21 Aug 1789, John McFadden & Mary McFadden his wife of Chester County, to William McDonald of same, for £30 sterling, tract on waters of Fishing Creek on the north side adj. John White, Catharine Steel, 100 acres granted to said John McFadden 22 Nov 1771. John McFadden (LS), Mary McFadden (LS), Wit: William Crook, Andrew Lockart, John Gordon.

**B, 143-144**: 26 July 1789, Major Gresham of Chester County to John Raney of same, for £50 sterling, 100 acres, a tract granted to Major Gresham 5 Dec 1785. Major Gresham (LS), Wit: Elijah Nunn, Thos Bak'r Franklin, William Raney.

**B, 144-145**: 15 Dec 1789, Richard Evans of Chester County, to Mary Evans of same, for £20 sterling, 100 acres in Camden District on a branch of Sandy River. Rich'd Evans (LS), Wit: Adam Williamson, Elizabeth Evans.

**B, 145-146**: 26 July 1789, Major Gresham of Chester County to John Raney of same, for £50 sterling, 50 acres granted to Major Gresham on a branch leaving into the Bear Branch adj. John Hopkins. Major Gresham (LS), Wit: Elijah Nunn, Thos Bak'r Franklin, William Raney.

**B, 147-148**: 14 Nov 1789, James Brown and Ann his wife of Chester county, to Joseph Feemster of York County, for £50 sterling, 91 acres, part of tract on waters of Boles branch, 200 acres granted to James Brown 7 Nov 1785, adj. John Belton, James Miller, William Minter. Ja's Brown (LS), Ann Brown (LS), Wit: James Feemster, Jean Brown, James Adare.

**B, 148**: 13 March 1790, James Timms & Patty his wife, both in Camden District, Chester County, to James Frasier of same, for £40 current money, 231 acres, part of 335 acres granted to James Timms 6 Nov 1786 on Sealeys Creek, a branch of Sandy River, adj. Christopher Loving, James Clark, Robert Frost, Col. Patrick McGriff. James Timms (LS), Patty Timms (X) (LS),Wit: Jeremiah Kingsley, Ambrose Lee (mark).

**B, 149-154**: 10 May 1790, Joseph Brevard, Esq., Sheriff of Camden District, SC, to Capt. Edward Allen of Town of Salem in Commonwealth of Massachusetts, whereas David Hopkins of Chester County, Esqr., was seized of certain tracts of land on NE side Broad River, one tract of 650 acres comprehending two different tracts or surveys, one of 350 acres originally granted to James Moore 4 Nov 1762, and other of 300 acres granted to said David Hopkins 19 Nov 1772 adj. Mark Edwards, John Hitchcock; second 640 acres granted to said David Hopkins 15 Oct 1784 on waters of Little River and Broad River adj. John Richardson, Nathaniel Harbin, David Hopkins, William Tucker, Mobley; third 640 acres granted to Daniel Colville 1 Aug 1785 on waters of Little River adj. Thomas Shannon, surveyed 28 Dec 1784; fourth 640 acres granted to Edward Colville 4 Sept 1785 on waters of Broad River adj. said David Hopkins, William Thomas, surveyed 4 April 1785; fifth, 322 acres granted to Littlebury Colville 1 Aug 1785 on waters of Little River adj. said David Hopkins, Hampton, John Winn, Thomas Addison, surveyed 30 Dec 1784; said David Hopkins together with John Winn being indebted to John Manson and Thomas Manson of Charleston, merchants, and they did commence in action for debt in the sum of £906 sterling and £7 d18 like money, sheriff sells tracts for £177 s15 sterling to Edward Allen. Joseph Brevard (Seal), Wit: John Egleston, Rich'd Lloyd Champion. Also included an inventory of other property including slaves Cato, Jack, Phebe, Hannah, Edy, Amy and child, Tintany and child, Nancy, Commadore Bobb, Sarah & her child.

**B, 155**: 19 Feb 1790, William Kirkland Junr of Camden District to John Taylor of Chester County, for ten shillings sterling, 277 acres according to grant to said William Kirkland certified for 25 Nov 1785 on a branch of the waters of Sandy River, waters of Broad River in Chester or Camden District adj. Thos Crosbey, John McCalpin. William Kirkland (LS), Wit: Ezekiel Sanders, Eleazer Gore.

**B, 156-157**: 15 Sept 1789, Rich'd Taliaferro & Milley his wife of Chester county to John Wright of same, for 92 English guineas, 162 acres adj. Mr. Christopher Loving. Richard Taliaferro (LS), Milley Taliaferro (LS), Wit: Will Boyd, Edmund Lee.

**B, 157-159**: 1 April 1790, Robert Cherry & Lettuce his wife of Chester county to Hugh McClure of same, for £40, tract granted 6 April 1768 by SC to James Knox, memorial entered in the Auditors Office in Book N. No. 8, page 499, 27 July 1768, and recorded in the Secretaries Book CCC, page 473, 450 acres surveyed to him by John Gaston, Deputy Surveyor, by virtue of a warrant dated 28 May 1767 on waters of Rockey Creek adj. David Hunter, conveyed by James Knox to Robert Cherry 3 Oct 1786. Robert Cherry (LS), Lettuce Cherry (m) (LS), Wit: John McCollough, Thomas Porter, John Cherry.

**B, 159-162**: Lease and release. 14 & 15 Sept 1789, Moses Duke of Fairfield County to William Dunavant of Lancaster County, for 16,403 pounds of neat & inspected tobacco, 320 acres on south side Wateree River granted to Joseph Bradley 4 Nov 1762, recorded in the Secretary's Office in Book EEE, page 382. Moses Duke (LS), Wit: A. Dunavant, J.P., William Wilson.

**B, 162-164**: 25 Jan 1790, John Franklin of Chester County to William Shaw of same, for £100 sterling, 17 acres, part of tract granted to John Franklin 24 Dec 1772, also part of another pattent dated 20 Jan 1785 to John Franklin, 106 acres in Camden District on waters of Sandy River. John Franklin (L)S, Wit: Samuel Craig, William Rainey (X).

**B, 164-165**: 15 Sept 1789, Richard Taliaferro & Milley his wife for 92 english guineas, tract granted to Hazel Hardwick and by him conveyed to Richard Taliaferro. Richard Taliaferro (LS), Milley Taliaferro (LS), Wit: Will Boyd John Wright.

**B, 165-167**: 26 Nov 1782, Samuel Caldwell and his wife Margaret of District of Camden, planter, to Thomas Morrison of same, weaver, for £100 lawful money, tract granted 1 Sept 1768 to Samuel Caldwell, 100 acres on waters of Rocky Creek in Craven County adj. Edward Henderson. Samuel Caldwell (LS), Margaret Caldwell (X) (LS), Wit: William McClintock, James Stuart (mark).

**B, 167-170**: Lease and release. 6 & 7 April 1788, John Yarbrough Senr of State of SC to Littleton Randolph Isbell of Chester County, for £100 sterling part of grant to John Land for 250 acres on north side Rockey Creek adj. Lewis Yarborough, dated 16 July 1765, recorded in Book ZZ[?], page 161 and sold to said John Yarborough Senr. John Yarbrough Senr (LS), Wit: Jno'a Hemphill, Daniel Muse Senr, William Yarbrough.

**B, 170-171**: 18 May 1789, James Hemphill Senr of Chester County to Andw Hemphill of same, for £32 s12 d6, 150 acres in Chester County on a tract called the big tract adj. William Forguson. James Hemphill, Wit: Chas Wall, William Wall (mark), Jesse Bandy.

**B, 172-175**: Lease and release. 25 & 26 Feb 1790, Daniel Comer & Elizabeth his wife of Union County to Allen Degraffenreid of Chester county, for £100 sterling, 200 acres in Chester county on waters of Sandy River, 100 acres granted to Samuel Wells & Conveyed from him to Col. Thomas Fletchall, the other 200 acres granted to said Fletchall and by virtue of an act of the Assembly of this State the same is vested in Daniel Comer. Daniel Comer (Seal), Elizabeth Comer (X) (Seal), Wit: W. Embry, Thos Brandon, Archibald

Riddle. Elizabeth Comer relinquished dower in Union County before Thos Brandon, J.P.

B, 175-177: 3 July 1789, James Potts of Charleston, Cooper, to William Anderson of Chester County, planter, for £50 sterling, 100 acres on east side of Broad River near a creek called Turkey Creek, waters of said Broad River. James Potts (2) (LS), Wit: Geo: Leslie, James Mitchell.

B, 177-178: South Carolina, Chester County. 24 March 1790, John Seely of county aforesaid to Peter Seely of same, for one shilling sterling, 200 acres on the north branch of Sandy River by a grant dated 19 Sept 1758. John Seely (Seal), Jane Seely (X) (LS), Wit: Asa Darby, Sarah Seely, Samuel Seely.

B, 178-179: South Carolina, Chester County. 13 Oct 1789, Alexander Brown to James Brown, both of county aforesaid, for £100, tract on which he now lives, 116 acres on waters of Turkey Creek, part of tract laid out for & granted to Catharine Brown 23 Jan 1773, being transfer'd by will of said Catharine Brown at her decease. Alexd'r Brown (LS), Wit: William Given, David Patterson, C. Brackfield.

B, 179-182: 2 Jan 1778, Robert Laird of Craven County ,Camden District. St. Marks Parish, planter, and Elizabeth his wife to Reese Hughes of same, planter, for £200, 100 acres, part of tract granted to Micam Fisher in the province of North Carolina in 1752 285 acres in Craven County SC on both sides of Rockey Creek in Camden District, said Fisher having sold the said tract to Stephen White blacksmith in 1759, and by said Stephen White & Agness his wife sold to Lodowick Laird 24 Aug 1764 and by said Lodowick Laird said platt was recorded in South Carolina and said Lodowick having sold to Robert Laird his son 100 acres of said plantation on east side of Rockey Creek in 1774, and a memorial entered in SC 25 Aug 1774 in Book M, page 133. Robert Laird (Seal), Eliza's Laird (X) (Seal), Wit: John Kell, William Laird, Josiah Hughes.

B, 182-185: 6 April 1790, James McGaughey & Jean his wife of Chester County, planter, to John Mills Junr of same, planter, for £58 s6 d8 sterling, tract granted 10 Sept 1765 by SC to Saml Morrow, 100 acres on south fork of Fishing Creek in Craven County (now Chester), and Samuel Morrow sold to James McGaughey 27 April 1771, memorial entered in Book L. No. 11, page 100, 6 Jan 1772. James McGaughey (LS), Jennet McGaughey (+) (LS), Wit: James Pegan, James Graham.

B, 185-188: Lease and release. 12 & 13 Nov 1788, Thomas Stroud of Chester County to John Barber of Fairfield County, for £50 sterling, 100 acres granted to James Jack & Jean Jack, released by them to Arthur Scott & Jean Scott 6 Dec 1772 and by Arthur Scott & Jean Scott to Thomas Stroud 16 Jan 1779, on big Rockey Creek, then Craven County now Chester County. Thomas Stroud (X) (LS), Wit: Samuel Forguson, George Eggnew (mark), Andw Hemphill.

**B, 188-190**: 26 Nov 1789, Alexander McCown Senr of Chester County, Camden District, to John McCown of same, for £150 sterling, 100 acres, part of two separate grants, one part for 30 acres being part of 340 acres granted to Joseph Bradley 4 Nov 1762 by SC, and said Joseph Bradley conveyed 30 acres to Alexander McCown 5 Dec 1772; the other part being 70 acres, part of 300 acres granted to Alexander McCown 25 April 1774, on south side of Fishing Creek in the bent of said creek. Alexander McKown (Seal), Wit: Andw Hemphill, John Steel.

**B, 190-192**: South Carolina, Chester County. 30 Dec 1789, Alexander McKown Senr for £150 sterling to James McKown, 100 acres, parts of three sundry grants: 100 acres on south side Fishing Creek adj. Archibald McDowel, recorded in Book FFF, page 374 and Laurence Gallaher released to Alexander McKown Senr 3 Oct 1771; 100 acres being a part of 300 acres granted to said Alexr McKown 21 April 1774 on SW side Wateree River on Fishing Creek, recorded in Book PPP, page 221 adj. John McKown; also 609 acres on south side Fishing Creek, part of 100 acres granted to Alexander McKown 19 Aug 1774. Alexander McKown (LS), Wit: Andw Hemphill, John Steel.

**B, 193**: Daniel Comer & Thomas Brandon of Union County bound to Thomas Jenkins of Chester County in the sum of £4000 sterling, 28 May 1789, the said Daniel Comer to keep indemnified Thomas Jenkins & others the heirs of Richard Jenkins decd, against the penalty of a bond which said Richard Jenkins signed in his lifetime as security for Thomas Fletchall that he the said Thomas Fletchall should administered the estate of Edward Flenthem deceased. Daniel Comer (LS), Thos Brandon (LS), Wit: Edward Lacey J. P., John Pratt J. P.

**B, 194**: South Carolina, Pendleton County. 16 April 1790, personally appeared before us Andrew Pickens and Robert Anderson, Esqrs., two of the justices of said county, Mary Roberts, wife of Zechariah Roberts, who being by us friendly and separately examined apart and out of the hearing & presents of her husband, relinquished dower to tract sold to Allen DeGraffenreid. Mary Roberts (LS), Wit: W. Embry, Rt Maxwell. Andw Pickens J.P., Robert Anderson J.P. Proved in Chester County by the oath of W. Embry 22 April 1790 before D. Hopkins, J.P.

**B, 195-196**: South Carolina, Pendleton County. 16 April 1790, personally appeared before us Andrew Pickens and Robert Anderson, Esqrs., two of the justices of said county, Ann Davis, wife of Richard Davis, who being by us friendly and separately examined apart and out of the hearing & presents of her husband, relinquished dower to tract sold to Allen DeGraffenreid. Ann Davis (X) (LS), Wit: W. Embry, Rt Maxwell. Andw Pickens J.P., Robert Anderson J.P. Proved in Chester County by the oath of W. Embry 22 April 1790 before David Hopkins, J.P.

**B, 196-197**: 1 July 1790, Robert Miller of Chester County to James McClure of same, for £5 sterling, 56 acres in Chester county on waters of Rocky Creek, a corner of a tract which formerly contained 150 acres adj. land surveyed for William Miller and land surveyed for Alexander Roseborough, John McKown, Robert Miller, granted to said Robert Miller by patent 6 Feb 1773. Robert Miller (Seal), Wit; Hugh McCluer, David Dvs [Davis?].

**B, 198-199**: 6 April 1790, Thomas Morrison & Elizabeth his wife of Chester county to Alexander Roseborough & Robert Millen of same, for five shillings, tract granted 1 Sept 1768 by SC to Samuel Caldwell, 100 acres on waters of Rockey Creek adj. land granted to Edward Henderson, sold by said Saml Caldwell to said Thomas morrison 26 Nov 1782. Thomas Morrison (M) (LS), Elizabeth Morrison (mark) (LS), Wit: Christopher Strong, William Elliott.

**B, 200**: James Fletchall of Camden District bound to Capt. David Hopkins of same, in the sum of $1000, 2 April 1779, said James Fletchall to make right to two certain tracts of land on the south fork of Sandy River, 100 acres granted to said James Fletchall and well known by the plantation whereon the said James Fletchall now lives, and another 100 acres well known by the plantation whereon old Mrs. Davis now lives and rented to her the said Mary Davis by said James Fletchall, adj. Ambrose Nix, sold by said Ambrose Nix by Thomas Fletchall, on or before 8 April 1780. James Fletchall (LS), Wit: Levy Smith, Jas Garratte. Proved by the oath of Levy Smith 28 __ 1789 before Charles Sims, J.P.

**B, 201-202**: 21 Oct 1789, William Miles of Camden District, Chester County, to Benjamin Waring of Camden District, for five shillings, 100 acres granted to John Miles 19 Aug 1774 adj. Wm Minter, Joseph Feemster & Jas Miles, and one other tract of 100 acres granted to Daniel Harshaw 21 March 1768 adj. William Givins, John Miles, Richard Miles & Hugh Simpson, and one other tract of 400 acres granted to Thos Robins 4 May 1775 adj. Col. Lacey, Robert Gorrell, and another 400 acres adj. the last tract and Robt Gorrell granted to Josiah Hill. William Miles (LS), Wit: Nancy Anderson, John Winn.

**B, 202-203**: 22 Oct 1789, William Miles of Camden District, Chester County, and Benjamin Waring of Camden District, Claremont County, of the other part, whereas said Benjamin Waring at the express request of said Wm. Miles did enter into a joint bond with him & Daniel Huger & John Winn, whereby they were bound unto Smith, Desaussure & Darrell in the sum of £6910 for the payment of £3455, as security said William Miles mortgages five tracts mentioned in previous instrument [see above]. William Miles (LS), Wit: Nancy Anderson, John Winn. Proved in Claremont County by the oath of Nancy Anderson 22 Oct 1789 before J. S. Guignard, mag. C. C.

**B, 204-205**: William Armer of Chester County, South Carolina, appoints friend Thomas Lewis of state aforesaid his attorney to ask, recover, etc., all belonging to said William Armer within the state of North Carolina, 5 Aug 1789. Wm Armer (A) (LS), Wit: Pat McGriff, Rich'd Taliaferro.

**B, 205**: South Carolina, Chester County. Daniel Cook of Chester County, taylor, for £60 sterling, to John McGlamery, a negro boy Sank about 16 years of age, 29 Dec 1789. Daniel Cook (LS), Wit: Hugh Whiteside Senr, Hugh Whiteside.

**B, 206**: Petter Robeson of Chester county for £17 sterling to John Latta Senr and James Smith, of both same place, one bay mare branded on the left buttock DH and on the left shoulder, the same on the cushion, also one young mare two years old just branded on the left shoulder, also one horse year old a dark bay branded on the left shoulder and buttock, three head of black cattle, one dark brindle cow with sum white spots about her flanks, also one steer calf black with a white face, one heir of a redish brindle color, also beds and their furniture, one chest and two post and one dutch over, 28 Dec 1789. Peter Robeson (LS), Wit: Hugh Whiteside, Daniel Cook.

**B, 207-208**: David Hopkins of Camden District bound to James Glenn of Cumberland County, Virginia, in the sum of £1000 sterling, 12 April 1783, to make title to 150 acres of land known by the plantation where George Vaughn now lives adj. Wm Crosby, John Crosby on Broad River, and another tract of 150 acres on south side of the river adj. Eli's Hollingsworth, Thomas Shockley, Wm. Seaster. David Hopkins (LS), Wit: Ber'd Glenn, Ferdinand Hopkins, Unis Lion. Proved in Union County by the oath of Bernard Glenn 4 June 1790 before Charles Sims, J.P.

**B, 208-209**: South Carolina, Chester County. Alexander Johnson, Wm. Boyd and Philip Pearson, surveyor, and John Winn, James Crage, Joseph Brown and Edwards Lacey, Esquires, of Camden District, where as there is divers controversies and disputes arisen between James Bingham and Rua[?] Hughes, both of Chester County, planters, concerning certain lands in dispute on Rocky Creek and whereas for the puting an end to the said difference and disputes they, they said James Bingham and Rua Hughes, by their bonds dated 1 Aug 1789, in the penal sum of £500 sterling, do make Alexander Johnson, Wm. Boyd, Philip Pearson, John Winn, James Crage, Joseph Brown and Edward Lacey arbitrators, 2 Oct 1789.

**B, 210**: South Carolina, Chester county. 21 Dec 1789, this may survive to certify the 300 acres of land sold by execution at the suit of Philip Walker (viz) John Campbell which I purchased at said sale from Edward Lacy, I do relinquish all claims, I having received full satisfaction from the said Campbell for the debt for which the said land was sold. Alexander Campbell.

**B, 210-212**: South Carolina, Chester County. 17 Nov 1787, Littleton Isbell of Chester County to Hugh Randolph of same, for £50 sterling, 150 acres on heages branes near Little Rocky Creek adj. land formerly John Morton's, Peter Sandefur, Isaik Grimmes, John Bishop. Littleton Isbell (LS), Wit: Sera Fetherston (X), Andw. Hemphill, Thomas Land. Proved by the oath of Thomas Land 29 Aug 1789 before Andw Hemphill.

**B, 212-213**: South Carolina, Chester County. William Whiteside of Chester County for £16 sterling to George Relsey of same, mortgage of 100 acres in Chester County adj. said George Relsey with three horse creators, one back horse six years old about 13 hands high and branded 3 R on the left shoulder, one bay mare with a star in her face branded W on the let shoulder, one sorrel mare about 9 years old with a large blaze in her face the branded unknown, likewise three cows (marks given). William Whiteside (LS), Wit: Hugh Whiteside.

**B, 214-215**: South Carolina, Chester County. Alexander McCown Senr of Chester County for £20 sterling to Sarah McCown Junr, one negro boy named Derry about five years old, two cows and calves, 1 Oct 1789. Alexander McCown (LS), Wit: Andw Hemphill, John Steel. Proved by the oath of John Steel before James Knox, J.P.

**B, 215-217**: South Carolina, Chester County. Alexander McCown Senr of Chester County for £60 sterling to James McCown, one negro man named Buster, 1 Oct 1789. Alexander McCown (LS), Wit: Andw Hemphill, John Steel. Proved by the oath of John Steel 6 April 1790 before James Knox, J.P.

**B, 217-219**: South Carolina, Chester County. Alexander McCown Senr of Chester County for £20 sterling to Nancy McCown, one negro girl named Dina about nine years old, two cows and calves, 1 Oct 1789. Alexander McCown (LS), Wit: Andw Hemphill, John Steel. Proved by the oath of John Steel 6 April 1790 before James Knox, J.P.

**B, 219-220**: South Carolina, Chester County. Alexander McCown Senr of Chester County for £20 sterling to Elisabeth McCown Junr, one negro girl named Patty about seven years old, two cows and calves, 1 Oct 1789. Alexander McCown (LS), Wit: Andw Hemphill, John Steel. Proved by the oath of John Steel before James Knox, J.P.

**B, 220-222**: South Carolina, Chester County. Alexander McCown Senr of Chester County for £60 sterling to Elisabeth McCown Junr, one negro woman named Phillis, 1 Oct 1789. Alexander McCown (LS), Wit: Andw Hemphill, John Steel. Proved by the oath of John Steel before James Knox, J.P.

**B, 222-224**: 7 July 1790, Mary Gaston alias McClure of Chester County to Samuel Lowery of same, for £5 sterling, tract on drafts of the south fork of Fishing Creek adj. Jonathan Jones, John McCluers, James Knox, estate of James McClure deceased, said lands being granted to said Mary Gaston alias McCluer 1 Dec 1772. Mary McClure (LS), Wit: Samuel Lowry, John McCreary.

**B, 224-226**: 7 Oct 1790, Owen Evans of Pendleton County, Ninety Six District, to Joshua Ripault of county and district unknown, for £85 sterling, whereof £50 in hand paid by said Joshua Ripault, part of 400 acres granted to Richard Waring/Woring 23 Dec 1771, which part contains 200 acres on a branch of

Sandy River called Cany fork, adj. Benjamin Carter, Edmund Russell, William Boyd. Owen Evans (LS), Wit: George Wear, Adam Williamson. Proved in Chester County by the oath of Adam Williamson 2 Oct 1790 before Hugh Knox, J.P.

**B, 226-228**: 21 May 1790, Elijah Nunn of Chester County to John Wright of same, for £45, tract on waters of Sandy River, 90 acres, recorded in book KKKK, page 70. Elijah Nunn (LS), Wit: Francis Willks, Greenbery Roaden, Hezekiah Ponder.

**B, 228-230**: 21 May 1790, Elijah Nunn and wife Frances of Chester County to John Wright of same, for £200, tract on waters of Sandy River, 245 acres, recorded in book XXXX, page 369. Elijah Nunn (LS), Frances Nunn (LS), Wit: Francis Willks, Greenbery Roaden, Hezekiah Ponder.

**B, 230-232**: 29 Dec 1789, William Head Senr of Barrene[?] County to William Watson, planter, for £100, tract on Martins branch and fish hole branch adj. Ashford Jenkins, on the south side of Sandy River, 900 acres granted 5 March 1787. Wm Head Senr (LS), Wit: John Watson, Eli Cornwell, Robert Watson (+). Proved in Chester County by the oath of John Watson 3 April 1790 before John Pratt, J.P.

**B, 232-234**: 1 March 1773, Gasper Sleeker and Elizabeth his wife to George Sleeker , all of Craven County, SC, for £140 current money, 150 acres, being part of a tract of 300 acres granted to Gasper Sleeker 23 Jan 1773 on the drafts of Fishing Creek adj. Gasper Sleeker. Gasper Sleeker (LS), Elizabeth Sleeker (X) (LS), Wit: Abraham Adams (A), William Slegar (X). Proved 22 Nov 1774 in Camden District by the oath of Abraham Adams before James Simpson, J.P.

**B, 234-238**: 4 Aug 1790, William Wall of Chester County to Charles Wall of same, for £100 sterling, part of tract of land granted by John Wall the heir of William Wall deceased 29 Nov 1786 and granted to William Wall deceased, 150 acres on SW side Cataba River in Chester county adj. land of Abraham Stover, Benjamin Street, William Nettles, William Wall, 100 acres, which the two grants adjoining including 250 acres both grants by SC and by said John Wall heir of said Bird Wall and conveyed 19 Nov 1786, both grants recorded in Book A, page 255. William Wall (LS), Wit: An'dw Hemphill, Hardy Stroud (mark). Proved by the oath of Andw Hemphill 5 Oct 1790 before James Knox, J.P.

**B, 238-240**: 30 Sept 1790, Anderson Thomas & Susannah his wife of Fairfield County, Camden District, to Edward Mahan of Chester County, Camden District, for £10 lawful money of SC, 50 acres on waters of Sandy River adj. Captain Thomas, McDonald, adj. lands laid out to Thomas Low, granted to said Anderson Thomas 21 Jan 1785. Anderson Thomas (LS), Susannah Thomas (+) (LS), Wit: William Johnson (X), Edward Holsey (X). Proved by the oath of William Johnson 4 Oct 1790 before John Pratt, J.P.

**B, 240-241**: George Kennedy of Chester County for £21 s6 sterling to John Servise, one dun horse four years old, nine head of black cattle marred with the mark of John Combest decd, puter two pots, two ovens, a big wheel, one trunk, 10 Jan 1789. George Kenedy (LS), Wit: John Mills Junr, John Gill Junr.

**B, 241-242**: Peter Johnson of Mecklingburg County, North Carolina, bound to Edward Lacey Junr of Chester County, in the sum of £500 SC to make title to two tracts of land titled in the name of John Kirkconnell by patent from NC, one of 200 acres on Owens branch of Sandy River, the other containing the same and on Susey branch of Turkey Creek, 6 Aug 1785. Peter Johnson (LS), Wit: Pat McGriff, Edwd Bland.

**B, 242-244**: 5 Aug 1790, Elizabeth Henderson, a poor girl of Chester County, with the consent and approbation of James Pagen and Thomas Garrrel, two overseers of the poor for Chester County, and Philip Walker, planter, of said county, Elizabeth Henderson hath bound her self to be an apprentice with said Philip Walker until she shall come to the age of eighteen years or day of marriage. Elizabeth Henderson (mark) (LS), Philip Walker (LS). James Pagen, Thomas Garrel & Walter Brown, overseers of the poor do declare our approbation to the binding of the said Elizabeth Henderson, 5 Aug 1790. This is to certify that the within named Elizabeth Henderson is taken & received by the within Philip Walker for the age of four years and four months, 5 Aug 1790 before John Mills, J.P.

**B, 245**: Jeremiah Jaggars of Granby town, Orangeburgh District, SC, planter, appoints loving brother Nathan Jaggers of Chester County, his attorney to make title to a tract on north side of big Rocky Creek originally granted to Benjamin Street, dated at Granby, 20 March 1788. Jeremiah Jaggers (LS), Wit: Thomas Hughes.

**B, 245-246**: Elizabeth McColpin for love and good will to my granddaughter Mary Watson of Chester County, one brown bay mare about thirteen hands & a half high branded ont he near shoulder EM, has a little piece out of one of her ears, six years old last spring, and a coult of the same colour about fourteen weeks old, 5 Aug 1790. Elizabeth McColpin (mark), Wit: Joshua Gore, Joseph Watson. Proved by the oath of Joseph Watson 30 Sept 1709 before John Pratt, J.P.

**B, 246-247**: 16 Dec 1786, George Sleeker and wife Agnes of Chester County to Suffiah Adams of same, for £20 sterling, 150 acres on waters of Fishing Creek between Casper Slekar. George Sleger (X) (LS), Agnes Sleger (O) (LS), Wit: Caspar Sleger, Elizabeth Slegar (mark). Proved by the oath of Casper Sleger 28 Sept 1790 before James Knox, J.P.

**B, 248-249**: 27 Aug 1790, Edward Lacey, Esqr., high Sheriff of Chester County to James Adair, Saddler of same, whereas Joseph Brown in the county court of Chester did implead John Walker of a plea of damage in July term 1788 did obtain judgment and a fieri facias issued to said sheriff to levy of the estate of said John Walker £20 with costs, now sells 590 acres on Boles branch, waters of Turkey Creek, which surveys containing 100 acres granted to Mark Lockert and by several deeds of conveyance became vested in said John Walker, the other survey said to be 590 acres granted to said John Walker, on 7 Oct 1788 did sell to said James Adair. Edward Lacey (LS), Wit Jo Brown, Jo Palmer, Thos Hail.

**B, 249-252**: 4 Sept 1790, Robert Kelsey of Chester County, yeoman, to Hugh Kelsey of same, for £20 sterling, 100 acres, part of 450 acres granted 17 March 1775 to Robert Kelsey on a small branch of Rockey Creek adj. Jacob Carter. Robert Kelsey (R) (LS).

**B, 252-254**: 22 March 1790, Richard Taliaferro and wife Milley of Chester county to Charles Taliaferro Junior of Amherst County, Virginia, for £80 sterling, tract on waters of Sandy River, 390 acres, granted to Hazel Hardwick and by him conveyed to said Richard Taliaferro, recorded in Chester County in Book A, page 290, adj. John McCombs, James Allison, William Shaw, and said Richard Taliaferro. Rich'd Taliaferro (LS), Milley Taliaferro (LS), Wit: Christopher Loving Junior (X), William Raney (X).

**B, 254-258**: Lease and release. 21 & 22 Sept 1790, Benjamin Streat, doctor of physic, of Chester county to Eake Brown, yeoman, of same, for £50 sterling, tract granted 3 April 1772 to William Land, 100 acres on a branch of Rocky Creek called Turkey Branch, adj. land surveyed for Benjamin Land, recorded in Secretarys office in Book KKK, page 631. Benjamin Streat (LS), Wit: Andw Hemphill, Jno Wm. Clemings.

**B, 258-259**: 15 May 1790, John McColpin of Chester County to Mannin Gore of Newberry County, for £100, tract in Chester county on waters of Sandy River, part of tract granted to James Stepp by SC 26 July 1774, conveyed by Stepp to John McColpin, on the north fork of the Rockey branch, 300 acres. John McColpin (LS), Wit: Elijah Nunn, Joseph Watson.

**B, 260-261**: 15 May 1790, Mannin Gore of Newberry County to John Humphis of Chester County for £100 sterling, tract on waters of Sandy River, part of tract granted to James Stepp 26 July 1774, conveyed from Stepp to John McColpin 29 Sept 1789 conveyed from McColpin to Mannin Gore [see previous deed]. Mannin Gore (LS), Wit: Elijah Nunn, Joseph Watson.

**B, 261-263**: South Carolina, Chester County. 4 Oct 1790, Peter Koonrod of county aforesaid to Jacob Brachfield of same, for £10 sterling, tract on waters of Sandy River, part of a tract of 308 acres granted to James Nicholson and from said Nicholson conveyed to John Adair Esqr., and from said Adair to David McCalla and from said McCalla to said Peter Koonrod. Peter Koonrod (C) (LS), Wit: Robert Owen, Henry Smith, Thomas McGriff (T).

**B, 263-264**: 16 Nov 1787, Littleton Isbell of Chester County to Hugh Randolph of same, for ten shillings, 150 acres on Hedges branch near Rocky Creek adj.

John Mortan, Peter Sandefur, Isaac Grimes, John Bishop. Littleton Isbell (LS), Wit: Thomas Land, Sarah Fetherston (X), Andw Hemphill.

**B, 264-267**: 7 April 1789, James Wylie and wife Sarah of Chester county to Ralph McFadden of same, for £50 sterling, tract granted 6 April 1768 by SC to Sarah Campbell, now wife of said James Wylie, 100 acres on waters of Fishing Creek on the roads leading from Sal & Wm. Neelys to Lands Ford on Cataba River. James Wylie (LS), Sarah Wylie (mark) (LS), Wit: Fred. Hopkins, James Knox, J. McClintock, Guy McFadden. Proved by the oath of Guy McFadden 3 Jan 1791 before Hugh Whiteside.

**B, 267-268**: 30 Nov 1790, Martin Elam of Chester County to Anderson Thomas of same, for £50 sterling, tract on Welches Fork of Sandy River, 490 acres adj. James Sharp, John Daugherty, part of 500 acres granted to James Daugherty 6 Feb 1786. Martain Elam (LS), Wit: Wm. Jinkins, Wm. Armer (A). Proved by the oath of Wm. Jenkins 2 Dec 1790 before John Pratt, J.P.

**B, 268-269**: Allen deGraffenreidt, Joseph Tims, & James Gore bound to the justices of Chester County in the sum of £100 sterling, that said Allen deGraffenreidt hath obtain license to keep tavern at his house for one year. Allen deGraffenreidt (LS), Joseph Tims (LS), James Gore (LS), Wit: Richd Taliaferro, Clerk Chester county.

**B, 269-270**: Patrick Hambleton of Chester County for £15 sterling to Daniel Cook of same, taylor, seven head of cattle, three cows one a dark brandle another a light brandle with a white face, another black and white cow and two heffers, one red the other red and white speckled and one yearling heffer black and white and one yearling bullock, two beds and furniture, two pots and one duch oven, 40 head of hogs, marked with a smooth crop in both ears, with plough and tacklings, 12 Nov 1790. Pattrick Hambleton (mark) (LS), Wit: Hugh Whiteside Senr, Hugh Whiteside.

**B, 271-274**: 10 Nov 1787, Robert Farguson and wife Elizabeth of Chester county to William Wilie, for £300 current money, 150 acres, part of a tract granted 10 Jan 1771 to Edward White, 250 acres on both sides Fishing Creek adj. John McFadden, James Forguson, Andrew Martain. Robert Fargason (LS), Elisabeth Fargeson (O) (LS), Wit: Thomas Dugon, Robert McFadden, John Neely [?]. Proved by the oath of Robert McFadden 12 Nov 1709 before John Mills, J.P.

**B, 274-277**: 5 Jan 1791, Samuel Weir & Elisabeth his wife of Chester County, farmer, to Daniel Elliot, black smith, of same, for £___, tract granted 27 Nov 1771 by SC to Benjamin Cook, 200 acres on waters of Fishing Creek, west side of Catawba River adj. Tom Caldwel, Anderson, conveyed 19 & 20 Jan 1772 from Benjamin Cook to William Furgason and from him 12 & 13 March [no year indicated] by William Ferguson and Patience his wife to Samuel Wier of said county. Samuel Wier (LS), Wit: Chas Err[?], David Sham, Ebenezer Elliott.

**B, 277-278**: 31 Oct 1785, Abraham Myers of Chester County, to Thomas Morris of same, for £500 south currency, tract on waters of Bushy fork of Sandy River, 150 acres, granted 15 Oct 1784 adj. Jonathan Mayfield. Abraham Myers (LS), Sarah Myers (X) (LS), Wit: Elisha Gore, Michael Wilkilson (X).

**B, 278-280**: 27 Oct 1790, John Smith of Richmond County, Georgia, yeoman, to Newman MiCollum of Chester county, SC, for £80 sterling, tract on Breshy fork of Sandy River granted 19 Nov 1772 and certifyed 5 Nov 1772. John Smith (LS), Elisabeth Smith (LS), Wit: William Lee, JP, Francis Wilks, James Mason. Proved 22 Nov by the oath of Francis Wilks before John Pratt, J.P.

**B, 280-281**: 18 Oct 1788, Alexander More of York County, Camden District, SC, to Isaac Pritchard of Chester county, for £30 sterling, 100 acres in the forks of big and little Rocky Creek adj. George Morrow, Peter Nants[?], Philip Walker. Alexander More (LS), Wit: John Moore, John Linn.

**B, 282**: Rice Hughes Senr of Rocky Creek, Chester County, to my son Cager Hughes of same, all my movable property (viz) negroes, horses, cows, hogs, plows & tools, all this years crop, born corn and tobacco, flax and all other produce, loom and all household furniture, pots, vessels, etc. 29 Aug 1789. Rice Hughes (LS), Wit: John Kell, Messey Laird (mark).

**B, 283-284**: 4 Dec 1782, Blakely Shoemake, late of Rocky Creek, Craven County, Camden District, shoemaker, to Robert Robinson Junr of Sawneys Creek, County and District aforesaid, planter, for £20 current money, 200 acres adj. Benjamin Strate. Blackley Shoomake (LS), Wit :John Robinson, James McCreight, Matthew McCreight. Proved by the oath of Matthew McCreight 13 Jan 1788 before Wm Simmons, J.P.

**B, 285-287**: 1 Dec 1782, Blakely Shoemake, late of Rocky Creek, Craven County, Camden District, shoemaker, to Robert Robinson Junr of Sawneys Creek, County and District aforesaid, planter, for £100 current money, 200 acres adj. Benjamin Streat. Blackley Shoòmake (LS), Wit: John Robinson, James McCreight, Matthew McCreight. Proved by the oath of Matthew McCreight 13 Jan 1788 before Wm Simmons, J.P.

**B, 287-288**: 27 Dec 1790, John Roaden of Chester County, SC, to Elijah Nunn of same, for £40, 124 acres according to a plat and grant to John Roden 15 Oct 1784. John Roden (I) (LS), Wit: Abner Wolkes, Greenbery Roden.

**B, 289-290**: 11 Oct 1790, Hannah Evans of Pendleton County, SC, to John Orr of Chester County, for £25 sterling, part of 532 acres granted to John Evans 5 June 1786, 100 acres on waters of Sandy River adj. Widow Farguson, Hugh Stuart, Archable Shell. Hannah Evans (mark), Wit: Pugh Stuart, Will Boyd, Arch. Kell.

**B, 290-292**: Robert Collins of Fairfield County for £120 sterling to John Herring of Chester County, one negro woman named Hagar, four head of horses and one mare, six head of cattle, two cows & Calves, two hefers, 13 head of hogs, one waggon & gears, an account on William Allin for £5 sterling, two notes of hand one of Wm Allen for 33 Gallons of Rum, the other on Wm Gorham for 130 tobacco, two feather beds & furniture, one womans saddle, one linen wheel, three pewter basons, one pewter, five pewter plats, six earthan plats, six earthan boles, one tea pot, one pitcher, one set of tea wear, two iron pots, one duch oven, one cooper saspan, one club ax, one broad hoe, one woolen wheel, one pair of cotton cards, one side of leather, one grindstone, one jack screw, two iron wedges, one earthan crock, one Butter pot, one earthan pan, six case bottles, twelve quarter bottles and two jin jugs, 13 July 1790. Robert Collins Senr (LS), Wit: William Malone, Aron Gose (A), Nancy Franklin (X). Proved in Chester County by the oath of William Malone 31 July 1790 before John Pratt, J.P.

**B, 292-297**: Lease and release. 26 & 27 Dec 1768, Robert Brown of Parish of St. Mark, Craven County, SC, planter, to John Adams of same, planter, for £100 lawful current money, 100 acres granted to Robert Brown on Rockey Creek in Craven County. Robert Brown (LS), Margrett Brown (M) (LS), Wit: Peter Culp, Archa Aylott (AE), Edward Crofts. Proved by the oath of Peter Culp 7 Jan 1769 before Zachary Isbell.

**B, 298-303**: Lease and release. 10 & 11 Sept 1785, John Adams of Rocky Creek, Chester County, Camden District, to James Blair of same, for £100 lawful current money, 100 acres on Sandy fork of Rocky Creek purchased of Robert Brown in 1768, granted to Robert Brown 20 Aug 1767, recorded in Book BBB, page 149. John Adams (LS), Wit: John Kell, Robert Miller.

**B, 303-306**: 24 Dec 1790, James Knox and Hugh Whitesides, both of Chester County, Esq., to Alexander Craford of same, yeoman, for £80 sterling, 450 acres granted 8 March 1763 to William Taylor (now deceased) on Catauber River, and said William Taylor by his will appointed James Knox and Hugh Whiteside executors, April term 1790. John Knox (LS), Hugh Whiteside (LS).

**B, 306-310**: 2 Jan 1791, Samuel Wier of Chester county, farmer, to Ebenezer Elliott of same, farmer, for ten shillings, 100 acres granted 25 April 1767 by NC to James Henry on the ridge between Fishing and Rocky Creek on both sides of Henrys Run. Samuel Wier (LS), Wit: Chas Orr, David Strain, Daniel Elliott.

**B, 310-312**: Martain Elam of Chester County, SC, for £57 s8 to Anderson Thomas of Fairfield County one negro woman named Sarah, one negro boy named Simon, one negro girl named Grace, one negro girl named Hannah & one negro boy named Samuel, one English sorrel mare nearly 8 years old with a white streak in her face & her left hind foot white, one dark bay mare with a grey tail, ten had of cattle one marked with a swaler fork in the right "year" & a hole in the left year, one a crop and slit in the left year and a smoothe crop in the right year, six marks with a crop & a slit in the left and a crop and a hole in the right, one red brandle with a white face, one red heffer, seven head of sheep, six marks with a crop and a alit in the left & crop and a hole in the right, 30 head of hogs, marks crop and a slit in the left and crop and a whole in the right, three feather beds and furniture, one pine chest, made out of the narraway pine painted red, one trunk covered with skin with the kever on and nailed on with brass headed nails, one womans saddle with a blue cover, one mans saddle and two bridles, one puter dish, four puter basons, five puter plats and eight puter spoons, one pot and one over, one flax wheel, two stone jugs, two stone butter pots, one rifle gun and one smooth gun, one bar shear place, one cutter plow, one shuvel plow, one trowel plow, three weading hoes, three pillings hoes, two grubing hoes, three pole axes, one broad ax, one cross cut saw, one cross cut tennant saw, one hand saw, three orgers of difference size, four chisels, one foot ads, two drawing knifes, three iron wedges, one water pail one washing tub, one smoothing iron, one box iron, dated 13 Nov 1790. Martain Elam (LS), Wit: Wm. Jinkins, Wm Armer (A). Proved by the oath of William Jenkins 2 Dec 1790 before John Pratt, J.P.

**B, 312-314**: 29 Dec 1790, Hugh Millin, Esqr., Sheriff of Camden District, to Philip Fox of Chester County, whereas John Harth in the city of Charleston did in court of common pleas of Camden District implead William Jones surety for James Longesbay on an action of debt and in April Court 1786 did obtain judgment and a writ of fieri facias did issue to levy of the goods, chattles, and real estate of said William Jones the sum of £116 (with interest from June 1784) sterling, and said sheriff did expose to sale on 14 May 1788 a tract of 200 acres and the one half of a tract containing 50 acres on the south side of the south fork of Fishing Creek, the 200 acres granted to John McAlliley & 50 acres to David Morrow, sold for £58 sterling to Philip Fox. Hugh Milling late sheriff of Camden District (LS), Wit: John Mills (X), Jno. D. Tinkler.

**B, 315-320**: Lease and release. 19 & 20 April 1790, John Franklin and Morning his wife of Chester county, planter, to Robert Kenedy of same, for £70 sterling, 200 acres granted 24 Dec 1772 to Thomas Franklin on Flenthams branch of Sandy River, recorded in the Secretarys Office in Book M. No. 12, page 191, which said tract Thomas Franklin bequeathed unto John Franklin his son, which will is recorded in Chester County, said land adj. William Trussel, Cletwin Wright, John and Thomas Baker Franklin. John Franklin (LS), Morning Franklin (mark) (LS), Wit: John Willson, Samuel Craig, John Kenedy.

**B, 321-323**: 23 Oct 1790, David Venters and wife Mary of York County, SC, to Isaac McFadden of Chester County, for £20 lawful money, 220 acres granted 2 March 1789 to said David Venters on waters of Neals Creek adj. James Robinson, James Dun, William Wiley, Isaac McFadden. David Ventures (X) (LS), Mary Ventures (X) (LS), Wit: Jno McClenahan, John Dods, David Farrel. Proved by the oath of John Dods 31 Dec 1790 before Hugh Whiteside.

**B, 324-326**: 25 Oct 1790, William Patton and Jean his wife of Union County, SC, to John Dods of Chester County, for £20, 150 acres, part of tract granted 31 March 1753 by NC to William Patton for 386 acres then in North Carolina but now in South Carolina, Chester County, near the Trading path on south side Cataba River adj. Robert Patton, Isaac McFadden, William Wiley, William Humphries. William Patton (LS), Jean Patton (mark) (LS), Wit: Alexander Eakin, Robert Patton, William Patton.

**B, 327-328**: 3 July 1790, William Britain and Jean his wife of Chester county to Owin Lee of same, for £100 sterling, 98½ acres on waters of Sandy River, recorded in the Surveyor Generals Office in Book YYYY, page 503. William Britain (LS), Wit: Richd Taliaferro.

**B, 328-329**: Leakin Dausey of State of Georgia for 55 gold guineas to Philip Walker of Chester county, SC, one negro boy about seventeen years of age named Ceaser, 6 Jan 1790. Leakin Dorsey (LS), Wit: Samuel Furguson, George Morris.

**B, 330-333**: Lease and release. 4 & 5 Feb 1791, Andrew Hemphill & Isabel his wife of Chester County to Daniel Green, stiller, of same, for 30 sterling. 150 acres in Chester County adj. Townsend, adj. a tract called the Big Track, William Farguson, granted to James Hemphill Senr, released to said Andrew Hemphill 17 May 1789. Andrew Hemphill (LS), Isbel Hemphill (mark) (LS), Wit: William Steenson, Robert Bready.

**B, 334-339**: Lease and release. 9/29 Dec 1790, James Blair of Rocky Creek, Chester County, Camden District, saddler, and wife Margret to Francis Henderson of same, planter, for £100 sterling tract I purchased of John Adams in the year 1785, 100 acres on the Sandy Fork of Rockey Creek, granted to Robert Brown, recorded in book BBB, page 149. James Blair (LS), Margret Blair (X) (LS), Wit: Frances Henderson (X), Phillip Walker, James Magers.

**B, 339-340**: Patrick McGriff, planter, of Camden District, to Edward Lacey, planter, a negro wench named Jude about 18 years of age, yellow complection, stoute and well made, country born, for £100 sterling, 20 Oct 1783. Patt McGriff (LS), Wit: John Pew (T), John Adair.

**B, 341-345**: Lease and release. 1/5 Dec 1776, John Cooper Junior of Craven County, SC, to John Morrise of same, planter, for £200 currency, 100 acres on waters of Rocky Creek between it & the Beverdam branch thereof, adj. John Dier, Thomas Morrise, granted to John Cooper on the Bounty, recorded in Book GGG, page 184. John Cooper Junr (LS), Wit: John Kell, George Morrise. Proved in Camden District 18 Feb 1778 by the oath of George Morrisse before James Simpson.

**B, 346-347**: South Carolina, York County. For £31 s9 sterling paid by Archibald Gill of Chester county, a young American born negro boy about eleven or twelve years of age named Billey, 10 Nov 1790. Daniel Williams (LS), James McNeel (LS), Wit: Samuel McNeel, James Hetherington. Proved in Chester County by the oath of Samuel McNeel 5 April 1791 before Hugh Whiteside.

**B, 347-348**: South Carolina, York County. For £31 s9 sterling paid by Archibald Gill of Chester county, a young American born negro girl about ten years of age named Amelia, 10 Nov 1790. Daniel Williams (LS), James McNeel (LS), Wit: Samuel McNeel, James Hetherington. Proved in Chester County by the oath of Samuel McNeel 5 April 1791 before Hugh Whiteside.

**B, 349-352**: 25 March 1791, Isam Fielding & his wife Elizabeth of Camden District, Chester, planter, to David Hyatt of same, for £20 sterling, tract granted 1 Sept 1768 by SC to Wm Gaston, late of aforesaid province, 100 acres on waters of Fishing Creek adj. Elizabeth Crag, released to James Neely 18 Jan 1769, and recorded in Book D-4, page 61 16 April 1773. Isam Fielding (X) (LS), Elizabeth Fielding (X) (LS), Wit: Benjamin Reives, William Pace [Peace], Williamson Harper (X). Proved by the oath of Williamson Harper 5 April 1791 before Phillip Walker, J.P.

**B, 353-355**: 29 Nov 1790, Thomas Leonard of Chesterfield County, SC, to Joshua Crook of Chester County, SC, for £75 sterling, 231½ acres in Chester County on a draft of Fishing Creek, part of tract granted to David Leonard, the said Davis Leonard dying intestate and the said Thomas Leonard his son became heir to all his lands,, granted 23 June 1774, the grant containing 146 acres and the above conveyed 231½ acres is to be cut off the south end of said tract adj. Wm Crook. Thomas Leonard (LS), Wit: John McCreary, Alexander Walker, Solomon Crook. Proved in Chester County by the oath of Solomon Crook 5 April 1791 before Phillip Walker, J.P.

**B, 355-358**: 28 Feb 1791, Peter Jones, Sheriff of Chester County, to James [sic] Wylie, whereas Abraham Wright in the County Court of Chester did implead Archibald Clerk on an action of debt and in October Court in 1790 did obtain judgment, and there should be levied £11 s10 d6 sterling, sheriff sold 22 Nov last 200 acres on Fishing Creek on the ridge between it and the Catawba River, granted 27 Nov 1770 to Archibald Clerk, sold to Francis [sic] Wylie for £7 sterling. Peter Jones sheriff (LS), Wit: Abraham Wright, James McClintock. Proved by the oath of James McClintock 6 April 1791 before John Mills, J.P.

**B, 358-360**: 15 Jan 1791, Benjamin Reives, planter, to William Harper, planter, for £5, 161 acres between Sherod Willis & Wilson Henderson, William Shadrit, Green. Benjamin Rives (LS), Wit: Wilson Henderson, Jacob Cooper, Thomas Neely. Proved by the oath of Jacob Cooper 5 April 1791 before Phillip Walker.

**B, 360-361:** 21 Jan 1788, William Roden of Chester County to Thomas Morris of same, for £50 south currency, 75 acres on Breshy fork of Sandy River on Harvey Cotrel's branch, adj. William Roaden, Thomas Morrise. William Roden (LS), Mary Roden (+) (LS), Wit: Elisha Mayfield, Jesse Obriant (X).

**B, 361-364:** 13 March 1791, Robert Gill of Chester County, planter, to Samuel Kelsey of same, for £28 sterling, 200 acres on waters of Fishing Creek, originally granted to George Glover 25 Sept 1766, recorded in the Secretaries Office in Book AAA, page 108, and said George Glover died intestate, and the full power of administration being granted unto Susannah Glover, she with Robert Glover, eldest son of George Glover deceased, did on 30 & 31 May 1770 convey to said Robert Gill, recorded in Book S No. 5, page 42 and 43. Robert Gill (LS), Wit: John Mills, Phillip Fox. Proved by the oath of John Mills 5 April 1791 before Hugh Whiteside.

**B, 365-366:** South Carolina, Chester County. Thomas Morrise of county aforesaid for £10 sterling to Hugh McClure of same, a gray mare and coult, and two cows, 3 Jan 1791. Thomas Morris (LS), Wit: John Knox, John Johnston. Proved by the oath of John Johnson 7 April 1791 before Phillip Walker, J.P.

**B, 366-369:** 28 March 1791, Jonathan Jones of Chester County, yeoman, and wife Bethsheba to William Jones of same, planter, for £50 sterling, tract granted 2 Oct 1786 to Jonathan Jones, 143 acres on Sandy River, east side of Broad River. Jonathan Jones (LS), Bethsheba Jones (mark) (LS), Wit: William Whiteside, Thomas Whiteside, Joseph Jones. Proved by the oath of Thomas Whiteside 29 March 1791 before Hugh Whiteside.

**B, 369-373:** 24 March 1791, Jonathan Jones of Chester County, yeoman, and wife Bethsheba to William Jones of same, planter, for £30 sterling, tract granted 2 Oct 1786 to Jonathan Jones, 485 acres on east side Sandy River. Jonathan Jones (LS), Bethsheba Jones (mark) (LS), Wit: William Whiteside, Thomas Whiteside, Joseph Jones. Proved by the oath of Thomas Whiteside 29 March 1791 before Hugh Whiteside.

**B, 374-375:** 25 Feb 1791, Nathan Brisco of Rutherford County, North Carolina, to John N. Bell of Camden District, SC, for 2500 weight of tobacco, 100 acres on the north side of Broad River on a branch of Turkey Creek called Susy Bells Creek granted to said Nathan Brisco 1 Aug 1785. Nathan Brisco (LS), Wit: John Mills, John Robins. Proved in Chester County by the oath of John Mills 5 April 1791 before John Pratt, J.P.

**B, 376-378:** 27 Jan 1791, Elizabeth Lowrie, a poor girl in Chester county with the consent and approbation of Thomas Garret and John Farris, overseers of the poor, and William Moore, farmer, of the other person, said Elizabeth Lowrie hath bound herself as apprentice to said William Moore until she shall come to the age of eighteen or day of marriage. Elizabeth Lowrie (mark) (LS), William Moore (LS), Wit: Thomas Whiteside, Hugh Whiteside. Thomas

Gerard (X) and John Farris gave their approbation before Hugh Whiteside, J.P., 27 Jan 1791. Elizabeth Lowrie is to receive a decent suit of clothing and a feather bed and furniture to the value or £12 sterling, likewise a good spinning wheel and to be taught to read English.

B, 379-382: 23 April 1790, Jonathan Jones Senr and Bethsheba his wife of Chester county to Jonathan Jones Junr of same, for £100 sterling, part of tract granted 8 April 1785 to Jonathan Jones Senr, 455 acres on waters of Sandy River, said part being 193 acres adj. Paul Furgason, Jonathan Jones Senr, Morrison. Jonathan Jones (LS), Bethsheba Jones (mark) (LS), Wit: William Whiteside, Thomas Whiteside, Wm Jones. Proved by the oath of William Jones 5 April 1791 before Hugh Whiteside.

B, 382-383: 15 Jan 1791, Benjamin Rives and wife Mary, planter, of State of SC, to Sharerd Willis, planter, for £5, 100 acres, being the last end of said Rives land, part of 396 acres granted to said Rives on west side Catawba River. Benjamin Rives (LS), Mary Rives (O) (LS), Wit: Wilson Henderson, Jacob Cooper, Thomas Neely. Proved by the oath of Jacob Cooper 5 April 1791 before Phillip Walker, J.P.

B, 384-386: 7 Jan 1791, Peter Jones, Esqr., Sheriff of Chester County, to Robert Walker of same, by virtue of a power of attorney from Charles Hampton of City of Charleston, in the county court of Chester, did implead Robert McCleland on an action of debt in 1789 and did obtain judgment, debt and costs to be lived of the lands and tenements of said Robert McCleland, John Mills recovered against said Robert McCleland £3 s2 d6 sterling, sells 100 acres on waters of Rocky Creek adj. lands of Peter Nance, Philip Walker, Robert Walker, Robert Miller, sold for £9 s16 sterling to Robert Walker. Peter Jones sheriff (LS), Wit: Saml Lowrie, John Walker Junr. Proved by the oath of John Walker 5 April 1791 before Phillip Walker, J.P.

B, 386-390: Lease and release. 15 Oct 1781, Robert Frost and Ruth his wife of Camden District, SC, to Edward Henderson of district aforesaid, for £200, 150 acres on a branch of Sandy River called Seeleys Creek. Robert Frost (LS), Ruth Frost (mark) (LS), Wit: Jno Mayfield, Sevillar Bond, Isam Bond. Proved by the oath of Isam Bond 23 Feb 1785 before Jo Brown, J.P.

B, 390-394: 3 May 1780, John Hitchcock of Broad River in Craven County, SC, planter, to Archabald Kell of Rocky Creek in county and province aforesaid, planter, for £160, half of tract granted 7 Nov 1770 by SC to John Hitchcock, 400 acres on a branch of Sandy Creek of Broad River, recorded in Book TTT, page 488, 200 acres adj. to land now laid off to John Hunter. John Hitchcock (LS), Wit: Zachariah Roberts, John Hunter. Proved in Camden District by the oath of John Hunter 11 Jan 1783 before Edward Lacey, J.P.

B, 395-396: 23 April 1790, Thomas Wallace of Chester County to John Pugh of same, for £500 SC currency, 100 acres granted to John Pugh by NC, part of 300 acres on Giles path, including the improvements where Wm. Banks formerly lived, adj. Thomas Wallace. Thomas Wallace (LS), Wit: Geo Gill, Patk McGriff.

**B, 397-398**: South Carolina, Camden District. Richard Smith of district aforesaid for £50 sterling, to William Moore of same, planter, tract on Rocky Creek, 100 acres adj. George Morrow, Peter Nance, Phillip Walker. Rich'd Smith (LS), Wit: Elijah Davis, John Davis, Dinah Davis.

**B, 398-400**: 9 Oct 1789, Daniel Travers and wife Sarah of Chester county to William Beck of York County, SC, for £60 sterling, tract on a branch of Turkey Creek, 150 acres granted to said Daniel Travers 1 March 1775 adj. land of James Anderson, viz the tract whereon the said Anderson now lives, land on which said Daniel Traverse now dwells. Daniel Traverse (LS), Sarah Traverse (X) (LS), Wit: James Adair, Christopher Lovin (X), James McNeel.

**B, 400**: Daniel Curry of Chester county, for love, goodwill and affection to my son David Curry of same, one negro woman named Grace, one horse valued to 15 pounds, one cow and calf, 15 June 1790. Daniel Curry (X) (LS), Wit: John Ashford Gore, Eleazer Gore.

**B, 401**: Daniel Curry of Chester county, for love, goodwill and affection to my daughter Ann Curry of same, one negro girl Mary, 15 June 1790. Daniel Curry (X) (LS), Wit: John Ashford Gore, Eleazer Gore.

**B, 401-402**: Daniel Curry of Chester county, for love, goodwill and affection to my daughter Mary Curry of same, one negro girl Silley, 15 June 1790. Daniel Curry (X) (LS), Wit: John Ashford Gore, Eleazer Gore.

**B, 402**: Daniel Curry of Chester County have given my children my negroes and one cow and calf and one horse out of the estate, and as for my stock of horse kind and cattle or hogs and household furniture, I give to my beloved wife Beston[?], 15 June 1790. Daniel Curry (X) (LS), Wit: Thomas Gore, Eleazer Gore.

**B, 402-403**: Daniel Curry of Chester county, for love, goodwill and affection to my son John Curry of same, one negro woman named Polly, 15 June 1790. Daniel Curry (X) (LS), Wit: John Ashford Gore, Eleazer Gore.

**B, 403-404**: South Carolina, Chester County. 31 March 1790, James Adair of Chester County to Herman Kolb of York County, for £20 s8 sterling, tract on waters of Sandy River, 150 acres. James Adair (LS), Anna Adair (LS), Wit: Robert Fowler, _____ Roberts, David Moffett.

**B, 405-406**: John Robinson of Newbury County, SC, appoint my trusty friend William Thomas Linton of Chester County, attorney to recover from the estate of Thomas Reavis deceased, anything belonging to me, 15 April 1790. John Robinson (+) (LS), Wit: Hugh Thomas, John Caton, Katharine Caton

(O). Proved in Union County by the oath of Hugh Thomas 1 May 1790 before Charles Sims, J.P.

**B, 407-410**: 29 June 1790, James Knox and Hugh Whiteside of Chester County, Esqrs., to Peter Culp of same, yeoman, for £12 sterling, tract granted 11 Aug 1774 to William Taylor, 100 acres on the north fork of Fishing Creek adj. Benjamin Culp, William Taylor, and said William Taylor by his will did order said plantation to be sold and did appoint Samuel Dunlap and Cornelius Anderson, Exrs., the latter being deceased and the former refusing to act and above named James Knox and Hugh Whiteside were by Chester Court appoint executors, April Term 1790. James Knox (LS), Hugh Whiteside (LS), Wit: John Mills, Hugh Knox, David Strain.

**B, 410-412**: South Carolina, Chester County. 8 May 1790, John McColpin of county aforesaid to Asa Darby of same, for £50, part of tract granted to James Stepp 26 July 1774 and conveyed from said Stepp to said John McColpin adj. John Taylor, John Humphries. John McColpin (LS), Nancy McColpin (+) (LS), Wit: Robert Frost, James Sanders. Proved by the oath of Capt. Robert Frost 5 July 1790 before John Pratt, J.P.

**B, 412-413**: John Adair of the District of Kentucky and State of Virginia appoints William Miles of Chester County his attorney to recover a small horse from John Downing, 16 March 1789. John Adair (LS), Wit: John Williams, John Miles.

**B, 413-414**: Hazel Hardwick of Chester County bound to Peter Petree of same, 10 Dec 1789, to support and maintain the possession of 50 acres adj. Joseph Timms until Hazel Petree his son shall come of the full age of 21 years. Hazel Hardwick (LS), Wit: Elijah Nunn, John Pratt, Sarah Pratt.

**B, 414-415**: David Hopkins, Ferdinand Hopkins and Newton Hopkins bound to David Pruit in the sum of £100 sterling, 10 Oct 1786, to support and maintain a good and lawful right to 300 acres on waters of Sandy River granted to Washington Hopkins 21 Jan 1785. D. Hopkins (LS), F. Hopkins (LS), N'n Hopkins (LS), Wit: Thomas Glenn, Joseph Hughey (X). David Pruit (mark), signed over his right to the bond to John Weir 5 April 1787. Wit: Will Boyd, John Dungan, Hannah Boyd.

**B, 415-416**: South Carolina, Chester County. 25 Nov 1789, John Flinthen, planter, of State of North Carolina, Orange County, to James Huey of Chester County, for £100 sterling, 100 acres per plat surveyed 27 June 1766 for Edward Flenthen on north side Broad River on Flinthen's Creek. John Flinthen (LS), Wit: John Pratt, James Gore, John Colvin.

**B, 417-418**: South Carolina, Chester County. 25 Nov 1789, John Flinthen, planter, of Orange County, NC, to James Huey of Chester County, SC, for £200 sterling, 200 acres per play surveyed 31 Oct 1765 for Daniel Prince relapsed by Edward Flinthen 2 Sept 1766 on a branch of Broad River east

Sandy River, adj. William Stone, John Lyon. John Flinthen (LS), Wit: John Pratt, James Gore, John Colvin.

**B, 418-419**: _____ 1788, John Grisham of Fairfield County, Camden District, to Jeremiah Grisham of Chester County, for £75 sterling, 100 acres on waters of Sandy River, Stones Creek, part of 200 acres granted to said John Grisham 15 Dec 1784, recorded in Book GGGG, page 153, 29 Aug 178. John Grisham (mark) (LS), Wit: John Daugharty, Isaac Wagner, Nicholas Sheets (N).

**B, 420-421**: 19 Sept 1789, James Stepp of State of Virginia, Lincoln County, planter, to John McColpin of Chester County, SC, for £100 sterling, tract on a branch of Sandy River, 600 acres adj. John Sealey, Lezerus More, Mr. Farguson, Steward Brown. James Stepp (LS), Wit: Isaac Vanmator, Edward Halsey (mark). Proved by the oath of Edward Holsey 10 April 1790 before John Pratt, J.P.

**B, 422-423**: 3 April 1790, John Starn and Mary his wife to William Young, both of Camden District, Chester, County, SC, for £10 sterling, 100 acres on Breshy fork. John Starn (LS), Mary Starn (+) (LS), Wit: W. Embry, Jarrard Young (D), John Young (D). Mary Starn, wife of John Starn, relinquished dower 3 June 1790 before D. Hopkins, J.P. Proved by the oath of Wm Embry 6 July 1790 before D. Hopkins, J.P.

**B, 424-425**: 28 June 1790, William Raney & wife Mary Raney of Chester County to Clayborn Wright of same, for £100 sterling, tract on waters of Sandy River, 100 acres, adj. Notley Coates, Samuel Craig, William Trussel, John Franklyn. William Rainey (X) (LS), Mary Rainey (mark) (LS), Wit: Owen Lee, Rich'd Wright.

**B, 426-427**: 28 June 1790, John Franklyn and wife Mourning of Chester county to William Raney of same, for £100 sterling, 100 acres on waters of Sandy River adj. Notley Coats, Samuel Craig, William Trussell, John Franklyn. John Franklyn (LS), Mourning Franklyn (mark) (LS), Wit: Peter Doran, Clayborn Wright.

**B, 428-429**: James Minnis of Chester County for £150 sterling to Nathan Jaggers, one negro woman named Jude, one sorrel horse named Ball about 1 years old nearly 15 hands high, one bay mare named Bonney about the same height nearly 15 years old, Gabrial Brown's note, my bed and furniture, all my household furniture, 20 April 1788. James Minnis (L), Wit: William Minnis (mark), Benjamin Strat.

**B, 429-434**: Lease and release. 4 Sept 1789, John McFadden and Mary his wife of Chester County to Moses Smith of same, tract granted 7 Oct 1762 by SC to John McFadden, 100 acres surveyed 16 March 1756 on Rocky Creek on south side of Wateree River. John McFadden (LS), Mary McFadden (mark), Wit: Joshua Smith, Edward Steedman.

**B, 435-436**: 8 July 1790, Richd Taliaferro & Milley his wife of Chester County to Charles Taliaferro Junior of State of Virginia, Amherst County, for £90 sterling, 390 acres on waters of Sandy River. Rich'd Taliaferro (LS), Milley Taliaferro (LS).

**B, 436-437**: South Carolina, Chester County. Patrick Finley, a singleman, of county aforesaid, hath put himself apprentice to Thomas Cabane, Tanner, of same, to learn his art, trade, and mystry, for three years, and said Cabane will prove sufficient meat, drink, washington and lodging, and to find the said apprentice in the said term six wearing shirts, three hunting shirts, six pair of over alls, a full suit of home spun cloath, one fine shirt, two felt hats at the expiration of the term, and a horse saddle, bridle & saddlebags to be valued at £15 sterling. William Finley (X) (LS), Thomas Cabeen (LS), Wit: Edw'd Lacey, Wm. Graham, Robt Kelsey, John Hutton.

**B, 438-440**: Tyger River, Mrs. Andersons, Novr the 9th 1780. Dear Sons, Last Tuesday night or rather Wednesday morning we were attacked by the British pat of Talloons Cove[?] commanded by Major Winn at the fishdam ford on Broad River, we kept the Ground with difficulty as we had a number of Tories amongst us. I am doubtfull I have lost my favorit boy Morris when the action commensed, he was lying at a ___ some distance from me & attempted to get to me & fell in with the British Cavalry when he was shot & bayoneted in such a manner that I believe there is very little hopes of his Recovery which is a Loss I particular feel as I am now destitute of servant only at will altho I have boys that are very obliging but under slender restriction the Enemy has covered the greatest part of the state. Tho I think out move to the fish dam is much in our favour as it has put it under power to remove the property taken by the Enemy and now is taken to any of the sister states, where perhaps _____ to him or them he may direct it to & as I have been so unfortunate as for all except my Lands & have now _____ my Negro I prevailed on Capt. Charles sims to take the negroes with his to Virginia & have his positive promise to deliver them to you at Mr. James Glenns in Cumberland County in the State of Virginia. I have furnished him with three valuable beast in order to convey the baggage & young negroes which I expect you will receive with the negroes there is in number seventeen a list of their names I have inclosed to you & if it is in your power to secure them from the enemy or dispose of them if you will find it advisable for I look on it to be so much dragged out of the ___... being acquainted with the cause of the world, there is Capt. Wm. Thompson, Mr. David Anderson, Mr. Mathew Sims, Mr. Nathan Glenn or Mr. James Glenn who are our near relations... from your loving father. Dd. Hopkins. Mr. Ferdinand Hopkins, Newton Hopkins. State of Virginia, Cumberland County. List of negroes Daniel, Tanner [two names illegible], Betty, Robin, Cloe, Lucey, Milley, Jacob, Isaac, Dick, Jenney, Harry, Phillis, Mingo, Morrow.

Personally appeared Charles Sims, Esqr., one of the Justices of Union County who being sworn maketh oath the during the British being in the neighbour-hood of Liles ford, Showers[?] Ferry, he being then a prisoner of war to the

British or parole he went to the Quarters of Gen. Sumpter on Tiger River and there obtained a certificate for the removal of his negroes & those of Col. David Hopkins to the State of Virginia... 6 Aug 1789, before P. Bremar, J.P.

**B, 441-443**: So Carolina, Fort Lacey, Decr 20, 1780. Letter from David Hopkins to his sons Ferdinand Hopkins and Newton Hopkins, in Cumberland County, Virginia, concerning negroes, etc.

**B, 444**: North Carolina, Orange County, March 30th 1781. Letter from David Hopkins stating that he was paroled to the plantation of Col. John Hagan[?] to his sons Ferdinand Hopkins and Newton Hopkins, in Cumberland County, Virginia.

**B, 445**: Dorothy Moore of Chester County for love, good will and affection to my daughter Dorothy More Junr of same, one negro woman named Rachel, two feather beds & furniture, one cow & calf, 4 July 1789. d. More (LS),Wit: Thos Jenkins, Wm. Jenkins, John Humphris. Proved by the oath of Thomas Jenkins.

**B, 446-447**: Rice Hughes of Craven, Camden District, SC, planter, for love, goodwill and affection to my son Josiah Hughes of same, planter, tract of land which I bought of Robt Laird, 250 acres, on north east side of Rocky Creek 16 Sept 1778. Rice Hughes (LS), Wit: John Kell, Rice Hughes Junr. Recd from Rice Hughes of Rocky Creek £482 current money 9 Nov 1778, Robt Long. Proved by the oath of John Kell 9 Nov before Philip Walker, J.P.

**B, 447-450**: 4 Nov 1789, Samuel Hambleton and Lettice his wife of Chester County to Daniel Cook of same place, taylor, for £40 sterling, tract granted 21 Jan 1785 to Samuel Hambleton, 100 acres on waters of Fishing Creek. Samuel Hambleton (H) (LS), Letties Hambleton (mark) (LS), Wit: John Mills, Chas Orr, William Miller.

**B, 450-453**: 4 Nov 1789, Samuel Hambleton and Lettice his wife of Chester County, yeoman, to Daniel Cook of same place, taylor, for £40 sterling, tract granted 21 Jan 1768 to Samuel Hambleton, 250 acres on waters of Fishing Creek, adj. Nathan Semple, John McKinney. Samuel Hambleton (H) (LS), Letties Hambleton (mark) (LS), Wit: John Mills, Chas Orr, William Miller.

**B, 454**: South Carolina, Chester County. James Thomas personally appeared before David Hopkins, Esq., one of the Justices assigned to keep the peace for said county, and being sworn, deposeth that he was the son of Daniel Thomas Senr deceased and brother to William Thomas, eldest son of Daniel Thomas deceased, and late residenter of Fairfacks County, Virginia, and that Daniel Thomas Senr deceased his father departed this life in 1780 in the month of October, leaving behind him three sons and three daughters, the eldest of which is William Thomas and that his father died intestate leaving behind him no will at all and that he very well remembers that his father in his life time and before he left the state of Virginia surveyed two tracts of land in

Hampshire County on Georges Run a branch of Patterson Creek in the state of Virginia and that never to the best of his knowledge knew of his fathers disposing of the said land in any manner whatsoever, 3 July 1790. James Thomas. D. Hopkins, J.P.

**B, 455**: South Carolina, Chester County. This day came Catharine Thomas of the County and state aforesaid former wife and now widow of Daniel Thomas Deceased before David Hopkins, Esq., one of the Justices assigned to keep the peace for and first Being Sworn on the Holy Evangelist of Almighty God Deposeth and Sayeth, that in the year 1736, she in the month of September in the same year was marryed to Daniel Thomas Senr Deceased then living in Westmorland County and State of Virginia and in the year 1737 in and upon the 25th day of May in the same year she bore a son by the said Daniel Thomas Decd whose named is called William and that she knows the said William to be the eldest son and lawfull heir of the said Daniel Thomas Snr deceased and that the said William Thomas, Eldest son of the said Daniel Thomas Senr, deceased, is now living in the County and state aforesaid on Broad River and further sayeth not, 3 July 1790. Katharine Thomas (mark. Dd. Hopkins, J.P.

**B, 456-461**: 3 Oct 1771, Laurence Gallaher of Craven County, Parish of St. Marks, planter, to Alexander McCowen of same, for £200 current money, 100 acres on a branch of Wateree River called Fishing Creek adj. land surveyed for Archabald McDowell, granted to said Laurence Gallaher by SC and recorded in the Secretarys office in Book EEE, page 375. Laurence Gallaher (mark) (LS), Wit: Thomas Jones, William Long, William Boykin. Proved in Camden District by the oath of Thomas Jones before John Newman Oglethorpe, J.P., 17 June 1774.

**B, 461-464**: 14 Oct 1789, John Hagans of Chester County to James Knox of same, practitioner of physick, whereas said John Hagans standeth justly indebted to the said James Knox in several sums of money amounting to £35 s6 d2 sterling, partly upon a Bond, partly on a note of land, for the better securing of sure payments, mortgage of 250 acres on waters of Catabaw River granted to Gasper Culp 5 Feb 1754 by North Carolina, and conveyed by Gasper Culp to John Lance[?] and by him to John Walker and by John Walker to John Hagans, and also a tract of land granted to Isaac Taylor and conveyed by said Isaac Taylor to George Heges Junior by to George Sleger and then to John Walker, and adj. land of Matthew Patton, Bever & Mill Creek, likewise one sorrel mare & col, one black mare, and other cattle, hogs, furniture, etc. John Hagans (LS), Wit: Danl Harper, Saml Herron, John Johnston. Proved by the oath of John Johnston 6 April 1790 before Hugh Knox, J.P.

**B, 464-465**: Hannah Bishop of Chester County, widow, appoint my loving friend David Porter of York County, SC, planter, in my name and for my use to demand, recover and receive from the exors of the last will and testament of my father Thomas Braken, late of the state of Pensylvania deceased, all such legacies as hath been devised to me, 25 June 1791. Hannah Bishop (LS).

**B, 465-466**: William Sharp for natural affection to give to Ann Head a sorrel horse three years old about fourteen hands high with a star in his fourhead, also a brown Ray filley two years old with a star in her fourhead, also one cow and a yearling, one feather bed and furniture, 4 April 1791. William Sharp (LS), Wit: William Colier (mark), Nicoless Colvin (X), Sarah Wood (+). Proved by the oath of Nicolas Colvin 28 June 1791 before John Pratt, J.P.

**B, 466-468**: 7 Sept 1790, Anthony McMeans and Phebee his wife of Chester County to James Lusk of same place, yeoman, for £30 sterling, tract where s'd Anthony McMeans line crosses a new road made by Samuel Lusk, adj. Alexander, Hunter, 100 acres. Anthony McMeans (A) (LS), Phebe McMeans (mark), Wit: John Feres, Samuel Lusk, Caleb Ferris. Proved by the oath of Caleb Feries 21 June 1791 before Hugh Whiteside.

**B, 468-470**: 2 Dec 1789, Elezer Gore & Elizabeth his wife of Chester County to Philip Knowling, son of Samson Knowling, of same, for £100 sterling, tract on the main Sandy River, 50 acres granted to Zachariah Isbell 8 March 1763, conveyed from said Zacheriah Isbell to James Gore; also another part of plantation of 38 acres adj. Joseph Timmons[?], granted to Zacheriah Isbell 17 Dec 1766, conveyed from him to James Gore. Eleazer Gore (LS), Elizabeth Gore (X) (LS), Wit: Joshua Gore, Sampson Noland, William Britain. Proved by the oath of Sampson Noland 6 Jan 1790 before D. Hopkins, J.P.

**B, 470-472**: 9 Sept 1782, Amos Timms of Craven County, SC, & Fanney his wife to Peter Noland of Granvilley [*sic*] County, North Carolina, for £277 s10 d9½ current money of NC, tract on Sandy Creek, north side of Broad River, 100 acres. Amos Timms (LS), Frances Timms (X) (LS), Wit: Henry Noland (X), Joseph Timms, Pearce Noland (X). Proved in Camden District by the oath of Pierce Noland 28 Oct 1782 before Joseph Brown, J.P.

**B, 472-475**: 5 Oct 1771, James Turner of Craven County, SC, weaver, and wife Susannah, to Patrick McGinty of same, taylor, for £150 current money, 200 acres granted 16 June 1768 to James Turner, on Beaverdam branch of Rockey Creek. James Turner (+) (LS), Susanah Turner (mark) (LS), Wit: Francis Henderson, Robert Gaston. Proved by the oath of Francis Henderson 4 Oct 1771 before John Gaston.

**B, 475-479**: Lease and release. 14 & 15 Sept 1788, William Paul and James Paul of Chester County, planters, to William Gaston of same, wheel right, for £7 s2 d10, 50 acres of 300 acres on waters of Beverdam Creek, or on the north fork of Rocky Creek in Chester County, granted to Henry Mcmuld[?] adj. Andrew Stevenson, Abraham Ferguson, James Bunsley[?], William Paul, being one sixth part of that plantation. William Paul (LS), James Paul (LS), Wit: Abraham Ferguson, William Fullerton. Proved by the oath of Abraham Ferguson 9 Sept 1790 before Jas. Knox, J.P.

**B, 480-484**: Lease and release. 15 Oct 1781, Edward Henderson and wife Anna of Camden District to Robert Frost of same, for £200 current money, 100 acres on a branch of Sandy River adj. John Bond's dec'd, near Seales creek. Edward Henderson (LS), Anna Henderson (X) (LS), Wit: Jn Mayfield, Seviller Bond, Isom Bond. Proved by the oath of Willson Henderson 31 May 1791 before Elijah Nunn, J.P.

**B, 484-485**: 9 Sept 1782, Amos Tims & Fanny his wife of Craven County ,SC, to Peter Noland of Granville County, NC, for £200 NC money, tract on Sandy Creek, north side o Broad River, 150 acres adj. Zachariah Isbell. Amos Tims (Seal), Fanny Tims (X) (Seal), Wit: Henry Noland (mark), Pearce Noland (+), Joseph Tims. Proved by the oath of Pearce Noland 28 Oct 1782 before Joseph Brown, J.P.

**B, 486-489**: Lease and release. 24 & 25 Nov 1786, James Nicholson of City of Charleston, SC, to David McCalla of Camden District, planter, for £50 sterling, 380 acres on waters of Sandy River adj. Douglass, John Furguson, William Furguson, Lewis, which tract was surveyed for John Adair and granted to said James Nicholson 3 April last. James Nicholson (Seal), Wit: William Wyle, John McCrory.

**B, 490-491**: 5 Oct 1782, Adam Ferguson of Camden District to Charles Humphries of same, for £500 SC currency, 100 acres in Craven County on the drafts of Sandy River adj. James Ferguson, granted 11 Feb 1773. Adam Furguson (LS), Elizabeth Furguson (X) (LS), Wit: Asa Darby, Rob't Procter (mark), Edw'd Henderson. Proved by the oath of Asa Derby 12 Jan 1784 before David Hopkins, J.P.

**B, 491-492**: 27 May 1790, Martin Elam of Chester County to Thomas Rodin of same, for £2 sterling, 10 acres, part of 500 acres adj. Roden, granted to James Daugherty 6 Feb 1786 but transferred from the said James Daugherty to John Colvin 1 July 1788 and from him to said Martin Elam 2 Nov 1789. Martin Elam (LS), Wit: Lewis Roberts (X), Abraham Paget (X). Proved by the oath of Lewis Roberts 12 June 1790 before John Pratt, J.P.

**B, 493**: In pursuant of a Resolution of the Hon. the Privy Council & an order of mine of 17 Feb last founded therein, a return having been made to me of the votes of the inhabitants of Chester County, it appears that a great majority of votes were in favor of Hugh Stewart's plantation as a proper place for fixing the public buildings of the said county, I do hereby determine that the public buildings for Chester County shall be at the plantation of Hugh Stewart on the Cross Roads formed by the Saluda Road and the Turky Creek Charleston Road, 17 May 1791. Charles Pinckney.

**B, 493-496**: 1 March 1788, Henry Hunter, Sheriff of Camden District, to John Elleson of same district, planter, whereas Moses McCown was seized in his demesne of a tract of land of 200 acres in Chester County on Fishing Creek adj. John Sinley[?], Joseph Kershaw, Esquire, John Lennard, and said Moses

McCown being indebted to Henry King, admr. of Robt King decd, and said Henry King did commence an action in the court of common pleas against said Moses McCown in April Term 1787 at Camden, and did recover against said Moses McCown £43 s10 d8 sterling, by a writ of fieri facias, sheriff sells said tract for £50. Henry Hunter, Sheriff C. D. (Seal), Wit: Jo Brevard, John McGee, John Simmison. Proved in Lancaster County by the oath of Joseph Brevard before James Kershaw, J. P., 2 March 1789.

**B, 496**: So Carolina, Chester County. Personally appeared Prisillar Franklin before me, John Pratt, J. P., and she deposeth that she saw John Franklin let Phillip Riley have a note of hand on John Colvin and that said Riley took the said note and was to run all rights and not look for Franklin for it, 27 Aug 1791.

**B, 497-498**: 4 Aug 1790, Josiah Hill of Camden District to Samuel Lowree, Esqr., of same, for £10, 100 acres in Camden District on the waters of Sandy Rive,r part of a tract of 12,700 acres granted to said Josiah Hill in 1780 [sic], adj. John Carson, John Pew, James Lemon. Josiah Hill (Seal), Wit: Patk McGriff, John Owen.

**B, 498-499**: John Hunter of Sandy River in Chester County, Camden District, SC, planter, for £3 s13 current money, to Archibald Kell of Sandy River, same county, 102 acres, being one half by equal division of 204 acres granted 5 Jan 1789, recorded in Book YYYY, page 328, on waters of Sandy River, 7 Jan 1791. John Hunter (Seal), Wit: John Kell, Alexander Kell. Proved by the oath of John Kell 5 April 1791 before John Pratt, J.P.

**B, 500**: Thomas Gore of North Carolina, Wake County, appoint James Gore of Chester County, SC, my true and lawful attorney to recover all sums of money, debts, due to me from the estate of Servis Dorre as a regular soldier in the third Ridgment commanded by Col. William Thompson, 25 May 1791. Thomas Gore (mark) (Seal), Wit: John Pratt. Proved by the oath of John Pratt 18 July 1791 before Elijah Nunn, J.P.

**B, 501-502**: 29 Aug 1791, John McFadden of Chester County, yeoman, to Thomas Walker of same, black smith, for £27 s10 sterling, 100 acres on waters of Fishing Creek adj. Cold. Irons[?] land, Robt McFadden, granted 26 July 1774 to said John McFadden. John McFadden (Seal), Mary McFadden (X) (Seal), Wit: Thos Neely, Abraham Walker, John McCreary. Proved by the oath of Abraham Walker 23 Sept 1791 before Jas Knox, J. C. C.

**B, 503-504**: 29 Aug 1791, Robert McFadden of Chester County, yeoman, to Thomas Walker of same, black smith, for £27 s10 sterling, 100 acres on waters of Fishing Creek adj. John McFadden, Casper Sleker, granted 26 July 1774 to said Robert McFadden. Robert McFadden (Seal), Esther McFadden (mark) (Seal), Wit: Thos Neely, Abraham Walker, John McCreary. Proved by the oath of Abraham Walker 23 Sept 1791 before Jas Knox, J. C. C.

**B, 505**: Tabitha Wade of Chester county appoints trust friend Jeremiah Davis of same, her attorney to recover and receive from the estate of William Munroe in Charles County, Maryland, 12 Sept 1791. Tabitha Wade (+) (LS). Acknowledged in Chester County 12 Sept 1791 before Elijah Nunn, J.,P.

**B, 506-507**: 5 June 1787, Philip Sanderfer & wife Elizabeth of York County, SC, to Samuel Irving, now of county aforesaid, for 125 guineas, tract in Chester County on Combesses fork of Rockey Creek adj. John McCown, William Wiley, Combest, John Morrow, 250 acres. Philip Sandefur (LS), Wit: Robert Greer, John Shaw, Jno Gorden Junr. Proved in Pinckney District by the oath of Robert Greer 25 Aug 1791 before Joseph Palmer, J.P.

**B, 508-509**: March 21st 1792. Indenture dated 5 Nov 1791, Thomas Baker Franklin to Magar Grisham, both of Chester county, for £50 sterling, 71 1/5 acres, part of tract granted to Thomas B. Franklin on waters of Sandy River. Thomas Baker Franklin (LS), Nancey Franklin (+) (LS), Wit: Robert Lemon, John Colvin, William Rieves.

**B, 509-511**: March 21st 1792. 15 Aug 1779, James Carr of the State of Virginia, yeoman, to John Knox of Camden District, SC, weaver, for £50 current money, 150 acres granted 11 Aug 1774 to James Carr on Beaverdam fork of Rockey Creek, Craven County adj. Thomas Lang, Jane Bigham, John Gaston Junr, John Linnin. James Carre (LS), Wit: John Gaston Junr, Ebenezer Gaston. Proved by the oath of John Gaston before Philip Walker, J.P., 6 Jan 1792.

**B, 512-514**: March 22nd 1792. 29 Oct 1791, John Knox of Kentuckey, Madison[?] County, to James McGara, minister, of Rockey Creek in Chester County, for £75 current money, 150 acres granted 11 Aug 1771 to James Carr on Beverdam fork of Rockey Creek in Chester County, adj. Thomas Land, John Gaston Junr, John Linn. John Knox (LS), Wit: James Kell, Adam Eager. Proved by the oath of James Kell 25 Jan 1792 before Philip Walker, J.P.

**B, 514-516**: March 23rd 1792. 10 Nov 1789, of Rockey Creek, Chester County, William Nesbet, planter, and wife Elizabeth to James Nisbet of same, for £90 currency, 100 acres, part of tract granted 1 Aug 1758 to Phillip Walker, 200 acres on waters of Rockey Creek, then in Craven County, now in Chester county, said grant recorded in Book SS, page 326, and said Philip Walker conveyed to William Nisbet. William Nesbet (LS), Elizabeth Nesbet (mark) (LS), Wit: Phillip Walker, John Kell, Jas Kell. Proved by the oath of James Kell 21 Jan 1792 before Phillip Walker, J.P.

**B, 516**: Charles Kitchen of Laurance County, SC, planter, for £50 to Thomas Garther of Rockey Creek in Chester County, SC, one negro woman named Ester & her two molatto boys, 31 Oct 1791. Charles Kitchen (Seal), Wit: Henry Dye, John Dye. Proved by the oath of John Dye 24 Jan 1791 before Philip Walker, J.P.

**B, 517**: March 26th 1792. Charles Kitchen of Laurance County, SC, planter, for £35 to Thomas Garther of Rockey Creek in Chester County, SC, one negro woman named Dinah, 31 Oct 1791. Charles Kitchen (Seal), Wit: Henry Dye, John Dye. Proved by the oath of John Dye 24 Jan 1791 before Philip Walker, J.P.

**B, 517-519**: Lease and release. 6 Dec 1791, Robert Williams of Camden District, Chester County, Blacksmith, to Jean Agnew of same, for £50 sterling, 100 acres, part of granted 6 July 1789 to Robt Williams for 400 acres on north side of Rockey Creek adj. Geo Agnew, Wm Stinson, Wm Higins, John Maises, John Barber[?]. Robert Williams (R) (LS), Elisabeth Williams (D) (LS), Wit: John Richmond, Thomas Stroud, John Connery. Proved by the oath of John Connery 67 Jan 1792 before Phillip Walker, J.P.

**B, 520-521**: March 27th 1792. 7 Jan 1779, Robt Duke of Parish of St. Mark, SC, yeoman, to John Leonard of same, yeoman, for £100, tract granted 23 June 1774 to Robt Duke, 300 acres on waters of Fishing Creek between it and the Catabo River adj. Thomas Steel, Benjamin Cook, Arthur Hicklin Junr, Robt Swanandum. Robert Duke (LS), Wit: Jno Duke (X), Alexander McNeail. Proved by the oath of Alexander McNeal 12 Jan 1779 before John Gaston, J.P.

**B, 522-525**: March 27th 1792. Lease and release. 31 Dec 1791, Robert Williams of Chester County, blacksmith, to Hardy Stroud of same, for £7 sterling, 100 acres, part of tract granted 6 July 1789 to Robt Williams of 400 acres on north side of Rockey Creek adj. Wm Stinson, Wm Higgins, John Maises. Robert Williams (X) (LS), Elizabeth Williams (O) (LS), Wit: John Connery, William Lenox. Proved by the oath of John Connery 6 Jan 1792 before Phillip Walker, J.P.

**B, 525-526**: 22 Feb 1790, John Leonard of Richmond County, Georgia, to Wm McDonald of Chester County, SC, for £100 lawful money of SC, 300 acres on waters of Fishing Creek in Chester County adj. Thomas Steel, Arthur Hickland, Benjamin Cook, granted to Robt Duke 23 June 1774, recorded in Book QQQ, page 526 and conveyed by said Duke to said John Leonard by deed 17 Jan 1779. John Leonard (LS), Wit: Fred Kimball Junr, Robt McKann (R), Robt Burnett. Proved in Chester County by the oath of Frederick Kimball Junr 23 Dec 1790 before Jas Knox, J.P.

**B, 526-527**: 25 Oct 1791, John Keterry of Chester County to Wm McDonald of same, for £95 s10, 191 acres on southwest side of Wateree River in Craven County adj. land granted to Saml Wagoner, land formerly laid out to John McKennie, which land was granted to his father Alexd Keterey by Gov. Montague 30 Oct 1776. John Ketterry (X) (LS),Wit: Moses McCoun, Mid'n McDonald. Elizabeth Stroud (formerly Ketery) renounced all claim to dower before James Knox, J.P. Proved in Chester County by the oath of Middleton McDonald 22 Jan 1791 before Jas Knox, J.P.

**B, 527-529 & 532:** Lease and release. 9 & 10 June 1774, John Wilson of Broad River, St. Marks Parish, planter, and wife Elizabeth, to Clayton Rogers of same, cordwainer, for £150 current money of SC, 150 acres granted 3 July 1772 to John Wilson, on a branch of Turky Creek, waters of Broad River adj. James Right. John Wilson (LS), Ellisabeth Wilson (X) (LS), Wit: Wm Kirkpatrick, Isaac Sadler, Francis Ray (X). Proved by the oath of Francis Ray 25 Jan 1792 before Jno Mills, J.P.

**B, 530:** John Renolds to John McCown d'r, Novem/r 1774. [inventory of goods]. Personally came John McCown and made oath that the acct of £1 s1 d6 sterling it being the ballance of £13 s18 sterling is just as stated against John Renolds, dated 9 April 1787 before Andrew Hemphil, J. P. Endorsed to Thomas Stroud 9 April 1787. Wit: Andrew Hemphil, John Morris (X).

**B, 530-531:** Benjamin Hagin of Camden District, SC, planter, bound to John Runolds of same, planter, in the penal sum of £500, 23 March 1782, that said Benjn Hagin shall make good title to 60 acres of land on Cold water Creek, part of 200 acres which said Benjm Hagin bought of John Brown adj. Hugh Wilson, Alexdr McCown, William Hagin, including the cleared land. Benjamin Hagin (X) (LS), Wit: James Mackey, Martin Reynolds. John Runalds assigned bond to the use of Thomas Dye 19 March 1785. Thomas Dye endorsed to Thomas Stroud 1 Jan 1788, wit: Henry Strange. Proved by the oath of Martin Runalds (mark) 22 Feb 1786 before Andrew Hemphil, J.P.

**B, 532:** [see above pages 527-529].

**B, 533-534:** 17 Sept 1791, James Knox, Esqr, of Chester County, Doctor, to Hugh McKelvy of same, planter, for 16 guineas, tract granted 1 Sept 1768 to James Knox, 100 acres on the bounty then in Craven now in Chester County, adj. Francis Hendrick, on waters of Rockey Creek, recorded in Book DDD, page 441. James Knox (LS)., Wit: Thomas McKelvey, James Niesbit.

**B, 535-536:** 10 Feb 1791, Richard Atkins of Chester County to James Walker of same, for £20 sterling, 150 acres on waters of Cataba River between said river and Fishing Creek, part of tract on which said Richard Atkins now lives, granted to Culp. Rich'd Atkins (LS), Wit: John McCrerey, Alexander Crawford, John Walker. Proved by the oath of Alexander Crawford 25 Jan 1792 before Phil Walker, J.P.

**B, 537-539:** 18 Jan 1792, John Studmant and wife Hannah of Fairfield County, SC, to Paul Guttery of Chester County, for £500, 190 acres, part of tract granted 11 Aug 1774 to John McKinney Senior, 300 acres, on Tinkers Creek fork of Fishing Creek adj. John McFadden, Wm. McKiney, Henry Culp, Augustus Culp & James Neely, and said John McKinney sold to Wm McKinny deceased 2 April 1777, recorded in the Auditors Office of said state 2 May 1787, and said Wm McKinney willed or bequeathed the one half or 150 acres of it to Hannah McKinney, his daughter, now wife of said John Studmant, will dated 20 Nov 1782, recorded in the Ordinaries office of said state, as likewise

50 acres by said will to said Studmant and wife being part of tract bought by said McKinney from Edward White. John Studmant (X) (LS), Hannah Studmant (X) (LS), Wit: Kennos Bell, David Bell, Wm Wiley. Proved by the oath of Thomas Bell 18 Jan 1792 before John Bell, J.P.

**B, 539-542**: 4 Dec 1786, Wm White & Jean his wife of Chester County, to James Kenedy of same, for £27 sterling, part of tract granted 30 May 1768 to John White deceased, 450 acres on north side of Broad River on Bullocks Creek Road adj. land surveyed for Joseph Cobb, land surveyed for Benjamin Ellis, and said Wm White being the lawful heir of said John White deceased, and said Wm White and Jane his wife conveyed part of said tract adj. Hugh Bonner, James Wilkies, 200 acres, and said James Kennedy is to let James Wilkie & his heirs while he lives on the planation where he is have the priviledge of a certain spring. William White (W) (LS), Jane White (mark) (LS), Wit: Wm Boyd, James Wilson, James Wilkings. Proved by the oath of James Wilkings 16 April 1791 before John Bell, J.P.

**B, 543**: John Gaston of Beaver Dam, waters of Rockey Creek, Chester county, bound in the penal sum of £150 sterling to be paid to James McGarrah, minister, 29 Oct 1791. John Gaston (LS), Wit: James Kell, Adam Edger. Said bond is to defend the said Mr. James McGarrah of a certain tract on the Beaver Dams containing 150 acres in Chester County, conveyed from James Carr to John Knox Jr. 14 Aug 1779, and now by said John Knox to said Mr. James McGarrah. Proved by the oath of James Kell 25 Jan 1792 before Philip Walker, J.P.

[page numbering is not consistent here]

**B, 541-542**: 11 Oct 1791, Drury Going of Chester County, planter, to Asa Tindall of same, planter, for love and affection said Drury Going has for his son in law Asa Tindall, tract of 100 acres granted to John Long 6 june 1785 and by said John Long conveyed to said Drury Going by deed 1 July 1788 in Chester County on a branch of Turkey Creek, waters of Broad River adj. land granted to James Kirkpatrick, Claton Rogers. Drury Going (mark) (LS), Wit: Bettreich Rogers, Sarah Rogers, Isaac Rogers. Proved by the oath of Isaac Rogers 24 Jan 1792 before Clayton Rogers, J.P.

**B, 542-543**: 13 Jan 1792, Drury Going of Chester County, to Robert Elliott of Union County, SC, for £1000 current money, two tracts in Chester County on Broad River, 250 acres including the plantation whereon the said Drewry Goings now lives, adj. Aaron Locqert's [Lockhert's], Aaron Lockert, Joseph Roberson, in all 350 acres, part of two tracts one granted to Benjamin Love 3 Feb 1754, the other granted to Mary McCullough 21 Jan 1775 [1752?], and by said Benjamin Love & Mary McCullough conveyed to Robert Elliott and said Robert Elliot conveyed to Drury Going. Drury Going (X) (LS), Wit: Job Going, John Hill, Isaac Going. Proved by the oath of Job Going 10 Feb 1792 before William Gaston, Judge Chester County Court.

**B, 544**: 23 Jan 1792, Agreement between Moses Seaberry of Chester County, SC, and John N. Bell of same, that said John Bell for £3 sterling shall received a gray roan horse thirteen hands high, eight years old, branded on the near thigh S. Moses Seaberry (X), Wit: John Robins.

24 Jan 1792, Agreement between Moses Seaberry of Chester County, SC, and Thomas Robins of same, that said Thomas Robins for £1 s15 d8 sterling shall received one sorrel mare a bout 15 years old, one pot & Skillet, one cotten wheel, and cards, one hog. Moses Seaberry (X), Wit: John Bell (X), Valentine Bell.

**B, 544-546**: 26 Sept 1791, John Humphres of Chester County to John Roden of same, for £50 sterling, 60 acres, part of 300 acres on east part of tract on a branch of Sandy River named by the name of Rockey branch, adj. lands of Charles Humphres, granted to John Humphres by SC 6 March 1786. John Humphres (J) (LS), Elizabeth Humphres (X), Wit: Aaron Allen Tharp (X), Joseph Watson (X). Proved by the oath of Aaron Allen Tharp 25 Jan 1792 before John Pratt, J.P.

**B, 546-548**: 20 Jan 1791, James Moffet of Wilks County, Georgia, planter, to Moses Cantzon of Lancaster County, SC, for £50 sterling, tract granted 22 Aug 1768 to James Moffit, 400 acres on waters of Sandy River the south branch thereof in Chester County, recorded in Book I No. 9, page 249. James Moffet (LS), Wit: Wm. Ferell, Jacob Jorden (X), Samuel Hunter. Proved in Lancaster County by the oath of Wm Ferrell 19 Jan 1792 before Robert Dunlap, J.P.

**B, 549-553**: Lease and release. 9 & 10 Nov 1778, Charles Spradling and Martha his wife of Camden District, SC, to John Bell of same, for £3200, tract granted 25 Dec 1754 by North Carolina to John Gordon, 640 acres on the head of the river on the north side of Broad River, the dividing ridge between it and Cataba, now she Ruth Gorden wife of John Gorden afterwards Anderson having obtained rights for the said land from said John Gorden's sons being heirs to the same, she conveyed to Charles Spradling. Charles Spradling (CS) (LS), Martha Spradling (X) (LS), Wit: Alexander Turner, Wm. Boyl, John Turner. Proved by the oath of Captain John Turner 17 May 1784 before Phil Pearson,J.P.

**B, 553-556**: 14 Jan 1792, Robert Elliott & Jean his wife of Union County, SC, to Drury Going of Chester County, SC, for £1000 lawful money of said state, two tracts on Broad River & waters thereon of Chester County, one tract of 250 acres including the plantation on which the said Drury Going now lives adj. Aaron Lockert, the other of 100 acres including part of Elliott's old fields, adj. Joseph Roberson; one granted to Benjamin Love 3 Feb 1754, the other granted to Mary McCullough 21 Jan 1772, and by said Benjamin Love & Mary McCullough conveyed to Robert Elliott. Robert Elliott (LS), Jean Elliott (X) (LS), Wit: Job Going, John Hill, Isaac Going. Proved by the oath of Job Going 23 Jan 1791 [*sic*] before Wm. Gaston, J. I. C.

**B, 556**: Charles Kitchen of Lawrence County, SC, planter, for £30 lawful money of SC, to Thomas Gather of Rockey Creek, Chester County, one negro woman named Philis, 1 Sept 1791. Test: John Kitchen. Proved by the oath of John Kitchen 24 Jan 1792 before Philip Walker, J.P.

**B, 557-558**: 7 May 1791, Patrick McGriff of Pinckney District, Chester County, to George Sadler of same, for £50 sterling, tract in Chester County whereon the said Sadler now lives, by a resurvey 129 acres, originally granted to Patrick McGriff for 200 acres 3 April 1786, but by an old survey of Mr. McNit Alexander, he takes out 71 acres. Patrick McGriff (LS), Wit: Edward Lacey, Miles.

**B, 558-560**: 9 July 1773, Edward White, cordwinder, of Craven County, SC, and wife Elizabeth, to William McKinny of same, for £100, tract granted 10 Jan 1771 to Edward White, 250 acres on Fishing Creek, craven County adj. John McFaden, James Ferguson, Andrew Martin. Edward White (LS), Elizabeth White (mark) (LS), Wit: Thomas Fulton, Andrew Locquert. Proved by the oath of Andrew Lockert 11 Jan 1774 before James Patton.

**B, 560-563**: 9 Sept 1771, James Ferguson and wife Agnes of Craven County, SC, planter, to Wm. McKinny of same, for £350, part of 300 acres granted 12 Dec 1768 to James Ferguson, on Fishing Creek adj. William McKay, Thomas Martin, 140 acres on north side of Fishing Creek, the creek being the dividing line betwixt James Ferguson's part and William McKinnys part. James Furguson (LS), Agnes Furguson (X) (LS), Wit: Edward White, William Wiley, Abraham Furguson. Proved by the oath of William Wiley before John Gaston 11 Sept 1771.

**B, 563-564**: 31 Jan 1791, Jeremiah Thomas and Mary his wife in Camden District, Chester County, to John Donald of same, for £50 lawful money of SC, 68 acres, part of 200 acres granted to Moses Bond 12 July 1766 on a branch of Sandy River. Jeremiah Thomas (LS), Mary Thomas (X) (LS), Wit: James Donald, John Boyd. Proved by the oath of James Donald 25 Jan 1792 before Elijah Nunn, J.P.

**B, 565-566**: 20 Jan 1792, William McGarity of Rockey Creek, Chester County, Camden District, SC, planter, to Francis Henderson of Rockey Creek, same county, planter, for £10 current money, 40 acres on waters of Rockey Creek surveyed for William McGarity adj.land surveyed for James Bigham, Frances Henderson. William McGarity (w) (LS), Wit: Wm Donaldson, Thomas McCulley. Proved by the oath of Thomas McCulley 25 Jan 1792 before Philip Walker, J.P.

**B, 566-567**: Jonathan Jones of Chester County for £65 to William Patton of York County, SC, a negro woman slave named Rose and her child named Judy, 5 Nov ___. Jonathan Jones (LS), Wit: Hugh Whiteside, Thomas Whiteside. Proved by the oath of Thomas Whiteside 21 Jan 1792 before Hugh Whiteside.

**B, 567**: Philip Walker, yeoman, of New Acquisition District,SC, bound to Samuel Weeir of state aforesaid, yeoman, in the sum of £1000, 14 Jan 1782, to make title to 100 acres of land on Rockey Creek adj. said Weeirs plantation, being the plantation the said Walker formerly lived on. Philip Walker (O) Wit: Philip Walker Esqr. Jan 3, 1787. Samuel Weiir assigned obligation to Saml Hambleton for his proper use, Samuel Weeir. Wit: James Knox.

**B, 567-568**: Thomas Gather of Camden District, Chester County, SC, for love, good [will], and affection to the heirs of Frances Kitchen wife of Charles Kitchen of Lawrence County, state aforesaid, four negroes two males & two females and their offspring, the males by name Ben & Harry, the females by name Esther & Dinah, now being in my possession, 23 Jan 1792. Thomas Gather (t), Wit: John Dye (X), Thos Morris. Proved by the oath of John Dye 24 Jan 1792 before Philip Walker, J.P.

**B, 568-569**: Nathan Sims of Chester County appoint my son Matthew Sims of same, my attorney to receive from the estate of William Hughs deceased, all my right, title, interest and portion that may be coming to me or my wife from the estate of said William Hughes, 5 Dec 1791. Nathan Sims (LS), Wit: Thomas Jenkins, Daniel Glenn, David Sims. Proved by the oath of David Sims 5 Dec 1791 before John Pratt, J.P.

**B, 569-570**: State of North Carolina, Cumberland County, Feb. 10th 1789. James Campbell and Alexander Campbell, being heirs at law of the estate of Reverend James Campbell, and that of our brother John Campbell deceased, to constitute and appoint our trusty and well beloved friend Robert Jamieson, to sell, make over and convey all the estate real or personal now belonging to the said James Campbell in the state of South Carolina for our use. James Campbell, Alexander Campbell. Test: John Clark. Proved in Chester County by the oath of John Clark 25 Jan 1792 before Philip Walker, J. P.

**B, 570**: South Carolina, Chester County. John Sealy for four shillings sterling to Peter Sealy, four negroes viz one woman named Sarah and one girl named Meriah, the youngest child of said Sarah's, also two boys the one named Jacob and the other Juness, sons of Hannah, 12 Sept 1791. John Sealy (LS), Wit: Saml Sealey (X), Jeremiah Terry. Proved by the oath of Saml Sealey (X) 21 Jan 1792 before John Pratt, J.P.

**B, 571-572**: 24 Jan 1792, Hugh Wilson of York County, SC, to Robert Wilson of York County, for ten shillings, tract on north side Broad River adj. Joseph Roberson, Francis Kilpatrick, Robert Black, Drury Going, 50 acres. Hugh Wilson (LS), Wit: James Jameson, Jean Keneday (X), Joseph Jameson.

**B, 572-573**: 1 Oct 1790, William Sharp of Chester County, planter, to John Bell, esquire, of same, for £200, tract on Sandy Creek, a branch of Broad River, as appears by plat surveyed by Isaac Perry, Deputy Surveyor, 16 Dec 1762, and granted to James Sharp, 6 April 1789, and conveyed from said

James Sharp to said William Sharp 2 De 1789. William Sharp (Seal), Wit: William McQuiston, Robert Murdock, Robert Andrew. Proved by the oath of Wm McQuestion 12 April 1792 before John Pratt, J.P.

**B, 574-576**: 8 Nov 1791, Adam Edgar of Rockey Creek, Chester County, Camden District, Taylor, to James McQuestion, Hugh Milling, and John Kell of same, planters, for £1 s17 d4 sterling, two acres and eighteen perches, part of tract granted 4 May 1775 to Benjamin Mitchell for 150 acres, recorded in Book XXX, page 345, and said Benjamin Mitchell having conveyed said tract to Adam Edgar, adj. James McAleansas, including the spring of water, and including the meeting house, to said James McQuestion, Hugh Milling & John Kell and the Congregation under the ministration of the Reformed Presbytery. Adam Edger (LS), Wit: Thos Donelly, William Edgar. Proved by the oath of Thos Donally 27 Jan 1792 before Elijah Nunn, J.P.

**B, 576-578**: 5 Jan 1790, Andrew Graham & Margaret his wife of Chester county, to Lard Burns of same, tract granted 7 March 1775 to said Andrew Graham, 100 acres on waters of Rockey Creek adj. James Knox, Francis Henderson, Benjamin Mitchell, Lard Burns. Andrew Graham (LS), Margaret Graham (mark) (LS), Wit: Samuel Henderson, Margaret McConnel (X).

**B, 578-580**: 9 May 1789, George Cherry & Jennett his wife of Rockey Creek, Chester County, Hatter, to John Johnstone, of Rockey Creek, taylor, for £12 sterling, 100 acres on Rockey Creek originally granted to said George Cherry 26 July 1774. George Cherry (LS), Jennet Cherry (O) (LS), Wit: James Young, William Kirkpatrick. Proved by the oath of Thomas McCauley (McCalla) 26 Jan 1792 before Andrew Hemphill, J.P.

**B, 580-582**: 15 Sept 1791, William iller & wife Margaret of Chester County, to Robert Morrison of same, for £30 sterling, 200 acres, part of tract granted 7 Jan 1788 to William Miller for 420 acres, on waters of north fork o Rocky Creek adj. Saml Weeir, Saml Hambleton, Robert Morrison, Robt Bradford, James Crawford, James Wiley, Thomas Blair. William Miller (Seal), Margaret Miller (Seal), Wit: Wm Weeir, Wm Boyd, Charles Orr.

**B, 583-584**: 15 Dec 1791, Philip Cohoon & wife Martha of Washington County, Georgia, to James Wood of Craven County, SC, for £80 sterling, 200 acres on south side of Catawba River joining waters of Fishing Creek, granted 1765 to George Hudson and by him conveyed to William Hudson and by said Hudson's heirs to said Philip Cohoon. Philip Cohoon (LS), Martha Cohoon (X) (LS), Wit: Solomon Wood J. P., James Cohoon, John McCreary. Proved in Chester County by the oath of John Cohoon 28 Dec 1791 before James Knox, J.C.C.

**B, 584-586**: 20 Oct 1787, Charles Orr, attorney in fact for Doctor Daniel Harper of Lancaster County, SC, yeoman, to William Orr & John Orr, sons of said Charles Orr, tract granted 6 Dec 1768, recorded in Auditors Office in Book I No 9, page 231, 28 Feb 1769, granted to Daniel Harper, 100 acres on so branch of Sandy River, the same tract of land being granted and invested in the said Charles Orr's hands by power of attorney. Charles Orr Atty as aforsd (LS), Wit: David Hunter, James Norton.

**B, 586-588**: 10 March 1792, Archebald Elliott Senior of Chester County, planter, to Archebald Elliott Junior of same place, planter, for £50 sterling, 250 acres in Chester county on the south fork of Fishing Creek adj. lines with land of the estate of Robert Gill deceased, Hugh Dodd, Joseph Walker, William Farriss. Archebald Elliott (AE) (LS), Wit: Hugh Whitesides, George Hill, Thomas Whitesides. Proved by the oath of George Hill 26 March 1792 before Hugh Whitesides, J.P.

**B, 588-590**: 6 Jan 1792, Robert Jameson of Rocky Creek, Chester County, Camden District, planter, to Gardner Miller of same, planter, for £40 sterling, 150 acres on Bullskin, a branch of Rocky Creek originally granted to Jasper Rogers by grant 10 July 2766, and conveyed 225 Dec 1770 to Reese Hughs who sold 10 & 11 Dec 1772 to Rev. James Campbell deceased, which tract of land devolved to his sons James Campbell & Alexander Campbell, heirs at law of said Rev. James Campbell deceased, who hath appointed said Robert Jameson to be their lawful attorney, 10 Feb 1789. Robert Jameson (Seal), Wit: Gardner Jameson, Archebald Boyd.

**B, 590-592**: 29 June 1792, John Chambers of York County, SC, yeoman, to John Latta of Chester County, Waggon maker, for £60, 200 acres, part of tract granted 21 Oct 1758 by North Carolina to William Neely, 400 acres then in Anson County but now in Chester County, on both sides Fishing Creek, west side Cataba River, conveyed to Saml Neely unto John Chambers 22 March 1789. John Chambers (LS), Wit: Hugh Whitesides Jr., Saml Neely, Hugh Whitesides. Proved by the oath of Saml Neely 23 June 1792 before Hugh Whiteside, J.P.

**B, 593-594**: 8 June 1792, Robert Morrison of Chester County, yeoman, to John McCullough of same place, planter, for £20, tract granted 23 June 1774 to Robert Morrison, 100 acres on a branch of Rocky Creek adj. Saml McCullough, James Crawford, Alexander Henry, William Furguson, Edward Henderson, Matthew Gaston, Alexander Roseborough, Bishop. Robert Morrison (LS), Wit: Ebenezer Elliott, Abraham Wright, Austin Culp.

**B, 595-596**: 9 Feb 1792, Samuel Neely of Chester County, yeoman, to Thomas Neely, Waggon maker, for £50 sterling, 150 acres, part of tract granted 27 March 1755 by North Carolina to Samuel Neely, 400 acres in Anson County, below the path next below the Saluda Waggon Road but now in South Carolina, Chester County, on both sides Fishing Creek. Samuel Neely (LS), Wit: John Mills, James Smith, Daniel Cook. Proved by the oath of John Mills, Esqr., before 17 May 1792 before Hugh Whiteside.

**B, 597-598**: 21 Dec 1791, James Dillard & Precilla his wife of Fairfield County, SC, to John Foote of Chester County, for £75 sterling, tract on south side

Sandy Creek commonly called River, 160 acres, less two acres excepted by said James Dillard & Prescilla his wife for a mill seat, part of larger tract of 200 acres granted to John Davis by SC in 1767. James Dillard (LS), Precilla Dillard (X) (LS), Wit: Nathan Jaggers, William Foote. Proved by the oath of William Foote 16 April 1792 before Rich'd Taliaferro, Clk Chester County Court.

**B, 598-599**: George Foote Senior of Chester County to his William Foote, one negro girl named Silva & one negro boy named Hanible, 2 March 1792. George Foote (LS), Wit: Benjamin Sherls, Saml Dawson, John Foote. Proved 16 April 1792 by the oath of Benjamin Sherls and John Foote before Rich'd Taliaferro, Clk Chester Cty.

**B, 599**: George Foote Senior of Chester County to his John Foote, one mulato girl named Rachel & one negro boy named Eli, 2 March 1792. George Foote (LS), Wit: Benjamin Sherls, Saml Dawson, Wm Foote. Proved 16 April 1792 by the oath of Benjamin Sherls and William Foote before Rich'd Taliaferro, Clk Chester County.

**B, 599-600**: Archebald Elliott of Chester County, planter, for £40 sterling, to Archebald Elliott Junr, a dark brown hose about 12 years old branded on the left shoulder A & on the buttock of the same side E, also one red cow about 7 years old marked with a crop of the right eat also one black heifer & two steers of two years old each, also two beds & their appurtenances, household furniture, two large iron potts, one Dutch over, two pewter dishes, one bason & six plates, 10 March 1792. Archebald Elliott (AE) (LS), Wit: Hugh Dodds, William Elliott. Proved by the oath of Hugh Dodds 26 June 1792 before Richd Taliaferro, Clk Chester County.

**B, 600-602**: 20 Jan 1787, James Arther & Agnes Turner, formerly the wife of Charles Arther, deceased, now the wife of John Turner of Fairfield County, to Thomas Farris of Chester County, for £20 sterling, part of tract granted 31 March 1753 by North Carolina to Mathew Patton, 320 acres on a creek named Ferrells Creek on west side Cataba River, conveyed from James Patton admr. of the estate of Matthew Patton to Michael Patton on which tract the said Michael Patton now lives, and said Michael Patton & Jean his wife sold 31 Dec 1778 to Charles Arthur deceased, 120 acres, part of said tract, recorded in Charleston in Book B No. 5, page 154, and said James Arthur heir to said Charles Arthur & Agnes Turner, formerly the wife of said Charles Arthur. James Arther (LS), Agnes Turner (mark) (LS), Wit: Wm Boyd, William Fearriss, John Turner. Proved 26 June 1792 by the oath of William Boyd before Rich'd Taliaferro, Clk Chester County. [The deed referred to can be found in *South Carolina Deed Abstracts 1776-1783*, by Brent H. Holcomb page 83].

**B, 602-603**: 15 Sept 1792, Edward Willson of Burk County, North Carolina, planter, to William Wood of Chester County, Pinckney District, SC, for £100 sterling, tract of 200 acres on north side Broad River on a small fork of Sandy

River called the Stony Fork adj. John Boser, Edward Wilson. Edward Wilson (X) (LS), Martha Wilson (X) (LS), Wit: Thomas B. Frankling, General Wilson. Proved by the oath of Thomas B. Franklin 1 Aug 1796 before John Pratt, J.P.

**B, 603-604**: 28 July 1792, William Hughs Senior of Ninety Six District, Union County, to Thomas Hughes Junior of Camden District, Chester County, for £50, tract on waters of Terrible Creek, a branch of Broad River adj. said Thomas Hughs, Thomas Crosbey, David Hays, 154 acres. William Hughs (LS), Wit: Wm. Embry, John Hughs, Isaac Hughs.

**B, 604-605**: 10 Dec 1789, Ephraim McCulley of Camden District, Chester County, to John Johnstone of same, for £12 sterling, 100 acres on Rockey Creek granted to Margaret McCulley 17 March 1775, which tract devolved unto the said Ephraim McCulley as heir at law of said Margaret McCulley deceased. Ephraim McCulley (LS), Wit: James Young, Thomas McCawley.
**B, 605-606**: 22 July 1774, John Harlowe of Craven County, SC, farmer, to John McKewn of same, tract granted 23 June 1774 to John Harlowe, for £100, 100 acres on waters of Rocky Creek adj. Ann Hanna, John Downey. John Harlowe (LS), Wit: James Harper (F), Robert Caldwell (RC). Proved by the oath of Robt Caldwell before John Gaston 9 Dec 1794.

**B, 607-608**: 7 Aug 1792, John McCool & Jane his wife of Chester County to Thomas McDaniel of Union County, tract granted 1753 by North Carolina, recorded in the Auditor's Office of South Carolina in Book I No. 9, page 20, 3 Aug 1768, granted to Adam McCool, 600 acres on east side Broad river and said Adam McCool did make over to John McCool by deed of gift, 235 acres on 10 Aug 1784, recorded in Book M No. 5, page 804 to 805 8 Dec 1784, adj. Joseph & John McCool. John McCool (Seal), Jean McCool (Seal), Wit: Thomas Brandon, Jas Love, Charles Sims, Adam McCool Junr, Margaret Gaston, John Gaston. Proved by the oath of Col. Thomas Brandon 7 Aug 1792 before Wm Gaston, J. C. C. Jane McCool relinquished dower 8 Aug 1792 before William Gaston, J. C. C.

**B, 609-611**: 15 Sept 1788, William Paul & James Paul, both of Chester County, to Abraham Furguson, for £7 s2 d-, 50 acres, part of tract granted to Henry McMurdy 3 April 1770 for 300 acres on Beaver Dam, north fork of Rocky Creek adj. James Furguson Turner, Sarah Knox, James Burnsly. William Paul, James Paul. Wit: William Lullington. Proved by the oath of William Gaston 8 Sept 1790 before James Knox, J.P.

**B, 611-612**: John McCool & Thomas Brandon of Union County bound to Thomas McDonald of same in the sum of £800 current money of SC, 7 March 1784, for John McCool to make title to Thomas McDanald to 200 acres which said John McCool had from his father Adam McCool. Wit: William Gaston, Charles Sims.

**B, 612-613**: 6 March 1792, Robert Wilson of York County, Sc, to Aaron Lockart of Chester County, for ten shillings, tract on north side Broad River adj. Joseph Robertson, Francis Ray, Robert Black, Drury Going, 50 acres, granted to Hugh Wilson 20 Nov 1771 by North Carolina. Robert Wilson (LS), Wit: John Lockart, Jno Johnsey (X). Proved by the oath of John Lockart 3 April 1792 before Philip Walker, J.P.

**B, 613-615**: 5 June 1770 [*sic*], William Stroud of Craven County, planter, and Sarah Stroud his wife, to Thomas Morton of same, planter, for £200, tract granted 17 May 1774 by SC, to William Stroud, 50 acres on waters of Rocky Creek, recorded in Book QQQ, page 352. William Stroud (W) (LS), Sarah Stroud (X) (LS), Wit: John Boyd, John Kell. Proved by the oath of John Kell 21 Dec 1779 before John Gaston, J.P.

**B, 613-615**: 9 Aug 1792, Christopher Strong and Elizabeth Strong and John Simonton & Mary Simonton his wife, all of state of SC, for £26 s5 sterling, to John Linn of Chester County, planter, tract granted 14 Oct 1774 to Elizabeth Strong, 100 acres, on north fork of Rocky Creek adj. John Gaston, recorded in Book GGG, page 213, said Christopher Strong and John Simonton with their wives being the sole heirs of said Elizabeth Strong now deceased. Christopher Strong (Seal), Elizabeth Strong (mark) (Seal), John Simonton (Seal), Margret Simonton (Seal), Wit: Thomas Morton, Robt Millin. Proved by the oath of Thomas Morton 15 Aug 1792 before John Mills, J.P.

[numbering not consistent here]

**B, 618-619**: 17 Feb 1792, Casper Sleger Senior of Chester County, to Casper Sleeger Junr of same, for £50 sterling, 150 acres on waters of Fishing Creek granted 24 Jan 1790 to said Casper Sleger Sr. Casper Sleger (Seal), Wit: Thos Walker, ----, John McCreary J.P. Receipt witnessed by Solomon Crook, John McCreary, J.P.

**B, 619-620**: 11 June 1789, Captain James Walkup & wife Margaret of Mecklenburg County, North Carolina, to James Boyd of Camden District, for £4000 SC money, 360 acres of land, part of tract formerly conveyed to William Pickens and Griffith Rutherford by King George II pattent, also by virtue of a deed from said Griffith Rutherford & Elizabeth his wife dated 16 J-- 1759 to said William Pickens, tract on west side Cataba River and on Rocky Creek. James Walkup (LS), Margaret Walkup (LS), Wit: Robert Davis, John Rogers, Jas Davis. Proved by the oath of Robert Davis 8 Nov 1792 before J. Donnom, J.P.

**B, 621 (or 623)**: South Carolina, Chester County. Robert Boyd in the County of Chester, whereas the said Robert Boyd is seized in fee by the death of his brother Samuel Boyd, late of Franklin County, State of Pennsylvania, of a tract of land in the county of franklin, being one six part of a tract of which the said Samuel Boyd, deceased was seized and possessed of, now said Robert Boyd appoints Rev. John Boyd, formerly of Franklin County, Pennsylvania, to sell, grant or convey the said land... dated 10 Dec 1792. Robert Boyd (Seal), Wit: Samuel Williamson, James Bratton. Proved by the oath of Saml Williamson 20 Dec 1792 before Jo Palmer, J.P.

**B, 622-623**: Lease. 6 Jan 1779, Robert Duke of Parish of St. Mark, SC, yeoman, to John Leonard of same, yeoman, for ten shillings, 300 acres in Craven County on waters of Fishing Creek between it & the Catawba River adj. land of Thomas Steel, Benjamin [Cook], Arthur Hicklin Junior, Robert Swan. Robert Duke (Seal), Wit: John Duke (X), Alexander McNiell. Proved in Camden District by the oath of Alexander McNiell 12 Jan 1779 before John Gaston, J.P. [see on page 82, B, 520-521 for release of this tract.]

**B, 623-624**: 27 July 1792, Edmund Lea & Nancy his wife of Craven County, SC, to Kasel Hardwick Junr of same, for £56 d1 d6 sterling, 100 acres granted 16 Jan 1772 to John Moberly, and transferred 1786 from said Moberly to Elizibeth Nunn, from Nunn to Edmund Lea. Edmund Lea (Seal), Nansey Lea (Seal), Wit: Ezekiel Sanders, Jas Hardwick. Proved by the oath of Jas Hardwick before Richd Taliaferro, Clk Chester County Court.

**B, 624-626**: 23 July 1789, Solomon Peters of State of SC to Willis Carrell of Chester County, for £60 sterling, 400 acres, half of 800 acres on NE side of Broad River near a branch of said River, granted to said Solomon Peters 17 May 1774. Solomon Peters (mark (Seal), Wit: Robert Collens, Jacob Crocker, Jessey Obroyand (mark). Proved 23 Dec 1790 by the oath of Jessey Obriant before John Bell, J.P.

**B, 626-627**: 5 Aug 1791, Hugh Thomas of Chester County, SC, for £100 sterling to William Arterberry of same, tract on waters of Sandy River, Wrights Mill Creek, 200 acres adj. Hollis Timms. Hugh Thomas (Seal), Wit: James Carr, Jane Thomas (X), Thomas Oneel. Proved 10 Aug 1792 by the oath of Thomas Oneal before Richd Taliaferro, Clk Chester County Court.

**B, 627**: 4 July 1790, William Roden of Chester County to Edman Mayfield of same, for £50 SC currency, 75 acres on the east side of Breshey fork of Sandy River adj. John Roden, James Attebary, Prisey Attebary, William Roden, Abraham Mayfield. William Roden (Seal), Mary Roden, Wit: Elisha Mayfield, Allen Mayfield. Proved by the oath of Elisha Mayfield before Elijah Nunn, J.P., 26 Jan 1792.

**B, 628**: 18 April 1792, John Walker, sadler, to William Morrow, Shoemaker, all of Chester County, for £180 s16 sterling, 100 acres on a small branch of Rocky Creek granted to Samuel Walker 18 May 1771, which tract afterwards upon the death of said Samuel Walker descended to said John Walker his eldest brother and heir by law. John Walker (Seal), Wit: Hu's McClure, William Walker.

**B, 628**: William Stroud of Chester County for £95 s10 to John Rattery, one negro fellow named London, 25 Oct 1791. William Stroud (X) (Seal), Wit: Jas Knox, Wm McDonald. By Saml Lacey, Depty Clk.

**B, 629**: 19 July 1784, William Thomas of Charlestown District, to Col. David Hopkins, Esqr., of Camden District, for £2000 sterling, tract in Ninety Six District on Twelve mile River & waters thereof, granted to William Thomas 16 July 1784, 640 acres adj. Col. Pu--. William Thomas (LS), Wit: Thomas Green Sr., Thomas Pitt. Proved 16 Dec 1784 by the oath of Thomas Green before Charles Sims, J.P.

**B, 629-630**: Jonathan Jones of Chester county to Joseph Jones of same, a small negro girl named Cate, two feather beds & furniture, four horses, including all the horse beasts I possess,also all the cattle I posses in number 15, also sheep, for £100, 16 Nov 1792. Jonathan Jones (LS), Wit: William Jones. Proved by the oath of William Jones 20 Nov 1792 before Rich'd Taliaferro.

**B, 630-631**: 5 Nov 1791, Elizebeth Miller of Chester County, to Thomas Miller of same, for £60, 100 acres, half of tract of 200 acres on a small branch of Rockey Creek adj. John Mills. Elizibeth Miller (mark), Wit: Charles Miller, James Miller, James Willson. Proved by the oath of James Wilson 3 Dec 1791 before John Bell, J.P.

**B, 631-632**: 3 Feb 1786, Thomas Roden of Camden District, to John Roden of same, for £40, 170 acres according to a platt & grant granted 21 Jan 1785 on waters of Sandy River adj. lands of Charles Umphres [Humphries]. Thomas Roden (Seal), Mary Roden (M) (Seal),Wit: Enoch Pearson, Daniel Head, William Head, Greenberry Roden, James Roden. Proved by the oath of Greenberry Roden before Rich'd Taliaferro, Clk Chester County.

**B, 632-633**: 14 June 1792, Michael Wornal, a poor boy, of Chester County, with the approbation of Joseph Timms, overseer of the poor, and John Terry of county aforesaid, wheel right, said Michael Wornal is bound as an apprentice until he shall come to the age of 21 or day of marriage. John Terry (Seal), Michael Wornal (X) (Seal), Wit: John Pratt, J.P. Michael Wornal's age is stated to be fifteen years and six months, dated 1 June 1792, Joseph Timms.

**B, 633-634**: South Carolina, Chester County. 25 April 1791, John Owen to Alexander McGaughey, for £40, tract where James McGaughey now lives, 200 acres, part of 532 acres in Chester County on waters of Sandy River granted to said John Owen 1 March 1790. John Owen (Seal), Wit: James McGaughey, Edw'd Griffin (mark), Robt Owen. Proved by the oath of Edward Griffin 25 Jan 1792 before Hugh Whiteside, J. P.

**B, 634-635**: 19 May 1790, William Roden of Chester County to Prissey Arthurberry of same, for £60 so currency, 75 acres on Smith Creek of Breshey fork of Sandy River adj. Thomas Morris, Robert Mayfield, William Roden.

William Roden (Seal), Mary Roden (Seal), Wit: Elisha Mayfield, Allen Mayfield. Proved by the oath of Elisha Mayfield 25 Jan 1792 before Elisha Nunn, J.P.

**B, 635-636**: South Carolina, Camden District. 12 June 1784, James Gore, planter, to Patrick McGriff, Col., both of district aforesaid, for £100, 100 acres, part of tract granted to Mr. Zachariah Isbell, 8 March 1763. James Gore (Seal), Wit: John Ashford Gore, Elisha Gore.

**B, 636-637**: 2 Jan 1790, James Nickle of Lancaster county ,SC, miller, to George Minnis of Chester county, weaver, for £30 sterling, 100 acres on a branch of Rocky & Fishing Creek,granted 28 July 1769 to Thos Patterson, and by him conveyed to said James Nickle.James Nickle (mark) (Seal), Wit: James Gaston, Thomas Gaston, Eli'r Alexander. Proved by the oath of Eliz'r Alexander 17 May 1790 before Joseph Lee, J.P.

**B, 638-640**: Lease and release. 27 & 28 Feb 1774, William Boyle of Craven County, SC, and wife Martha, to George Adams of same, for £130, 150 acres in Craven County on a branch of Rockey Creek called Bullskin branch, granted 13 May 1768 to Wm Boyle. William Boyles (Seal), Martha Boyles (X) (Seal), Wit: Alexander Turner, Jeremiah Meek (I). Proved in Camden District by the oath of Jeremiah Meek 14 March 1792 before Philip Walker, J.P.

**B, 641-642**: 14 June 1788, George Adams & Lydia his wife of Camden District, Chester County, planter, to James Douglass of same, planter, for £40 sterling, 150 acres on Bullskin branch, granted 13 May 1768 to William Boyles, surveyed 25 Jan 1768 for said William Boyle. George Adams (Seal), Lydia Adams (Seal), Wit: John Johnson, Thos McCalla. Proved by the oath of John Johnston 16 Feb 1792 before Philip Walker, J.P.

**B, 642-643**: 14 June 1788, George Adams & Lydia his wife of Camden District, Chester County, planter, to James Douglass of same, planter, for £25 sterling, 100 acres on Bullskin branch, granted 6 Nov 1786 to said George Adams and surveyed 6 May 1786. George Adams (Seal), Lydia Adams (Seal), Wit: John Johnson, Thos McCalla. Proved by the oath of John Johnston 16 Feb 1792 before Philip Walker, J.P.

**B, 644-645**: __ 1792, Hugh Thomas & Leah his wife of Chester County to Thomas Arterberry of same, for £25 sterling, 100 acres on waters of Sandy River adj. William Rainey, Wilson Henderson, John Thomas. Hugh Thomas (Seal), Leah Thomas (Seal), Wit: John Bennett, John Robinson, Presley Williams. Proved by the oath of Joseph Bennett 9 Aug 1792 before Richd Taliaferro, Clk Chester County Court.

**B, 645-647**: 22 July 1789, Solomon Peters of State of SC to Willis Carrell of Chester County, for ten shillings sterling, 400 acres, part of 800 acres on NE side Broad River near a branch of said River, granted to said Solomon Peters 17 May 1774 by SC. Solomon Peters (mark) (Seal), Wit: John Collins, Jacob

Crocker, Jesse Obroyand [O'Bryan] (X). Proved 23 Dec 1790 by the oath of Jesse Briant before John Bell, J. P. [See release for this tract on page 83, B, 624-626.]

**B, 647-648**: Alexander Wilson of Chester County for £4 s2 d6½ to Jeremiah Kingsley of same, mortgage of a likely young negroe wench named Patt, 5 Sept 1792. Alexander Wilson (X), Wit: Elijah Nunn, Stephen Clement. Proved in Chester County by the oath of Elijah Nunn Esqr 5 Dec 1792 before John Pratt, J.P.

### END OF DEED BOOK B

**C, 1**: Thomas Bragg of Chester County, yeoman, for £20 sterling to John Green of same, planter, one negro man named Cato, 19 Sept 1792. Thomas Bragg (LS), Wit: Philip Fox, Robert Hemphill. Proved by the oath of Philip Fox 15 April 1793 before Jno Mills, J.P.

**C, 2**: Austin Culp of Chester County, planter, for £40 sterling, one negro boy named Thom, also one bay mare of six years old, fifteen hands high, 8 Jan 1793. Austin Culp (Seal), Wit: William Whiteside, Henry Culp (X). Proved by the oath of William Whiteside 28 Jan 1793 before John Mills, J.P.

**C, 3-4**: 23 May 1791, Thomas Baker Franklin of Chester County, to James Stuart of same, for £12 s13 d4 sterling, 50 acres, part of 276 acres granted 3 Jan 1781 in Camden District on the south fork of Sandy River adj. land surveyed for Edward Wilson, James Stuart, Thomas Baker Franklin. Thos B. Franklin (Seal), Wit: Alexander Johnson, Hasel Hardwick, John Franklin. Proved by the oath of Hasel Hardwick 23 May 1791 before John Pratt, J.P.

**C, 4-5**: 14 June 1792, Francis Gore, a poor girl of Chester County, with the approbation of Joseph Timms overseer of the poor for the county aforesaid, and John Ashford Gore, planter, bound herself as apprentice to said John Ashford Gore until she comes to the age of 18 years. John Ashford Gore (Seal), Francis Gore (mark) (Seal), Wit: John Pratt, J.P.

**C, 5-7**: 17 Nov 1768, James Greer of St. Marks Parish, jober, to James Adams of same, planter, tract granted 13 May 1768 to said Greer, for £50, 100 acres on north side Broad River on Susa Boles branch, six feet wide, five inches deed, adj. land of Thos Rodin. James Greer (Seal), Wit: William Hadin, Abraham Adams (A), Hannah Oglethorp (mark). Proved 17 Nov 1768 by the oath of Wm. Hadin before John Oglethorp.

**C, 8-10**: 29 Aug 1792, Hugh White of York County, SC ,miller, to Samuel Neely & Thomas Neely of Chester County, yeomans, whereas said Hugh White is justly indebted to said Samuel & Thomas Neely, Robert Lusk & John Chambers in several sums of money, in the whole £200, partly on the security of a bond entered into by said Hugh White to John Walker 25 Aug 1794, and partly upon an account of money paid & laid out by the said Samuel & Thomas Neely for said Hugh White, mortgage of four plantations viz one granted to said Hugh White, 21 acres on Fishing Creek, two granted to Philip Walker containing 50 acres each on Fishing Creek including a Grist Mill, fulling mill & flax seed oil mill, the other granted to John Walker on Fishing Creek for 100 acres, and conveyed to said Hugh White by Philip & John Walker. Hugh White (Seal), Wit: David Neely, James Neely, Andrew Downing. Proved by the oath of David Neely 29 Aug 1792 before Hugh Whiteside.

**C, 10**: 4 Sept 1792, James Timms of Chester county to Hasel Hardwick Senr of same, for £6 sterling [record not completed].

[The numbers for pages 11 and 12 were apparently skipped and page 13 is blank.]

C, 14-16: 25 March 1793, Joel Anthony of Abeville County, SC, to John Owens of Chester County, for £20 sterling, 200 acres known by the name of Lewis's old place, granted to William Lewis 11 Aug 1774 and conveyed from him to John Anthony by deed adj. William Furguson, Josiah Kitchens, Daniel Moats, Thomas Haney on a branch of Sandy River. Joel Anthony, Wit: Hyram Traylor, William Griffin, Robert Owen.

C, 16-21: 10 June 1787, Agusteen Culp of State of North Carolina, to William Shadrick of Chester County, SC, tract granted 2 Jan 1786 to Augustin Culp, 95 acres on a small branch of Fishing Creek, waters of Cataba River. Augustine Culp (Seal), Wit: William McKinny, Thos Neely, Danl Cook. Proved by the oath of Thomas Neely 15 Apr 1794 before John McCreary ,J.P.

C, 21-23: 14 March 1793, William Shadrick for £50 sterling to Robert Fee, 30 acres on waters of Fishing Creek in Chester County adj. said Shadricks land, granted 4 Jan 1791 to Benjamin Rives and by him to said Shadrick. William Shadrick (X) (Seal), Wit: Thomas Neely, John McKanon, John Fleming. Proved by the oath of Thomas Neely 14 March 1793 before Hugh Whiteside.

C, 24-25: 15 Jan 1791, Benjamin Rieves, planter, of SC, to William Shadrick, planter, for £5, 30 acres, it being the west side of s'd Rives's land adj. Grear, part of 396 acres granted to said Rives adj. Swint. Benjamin Rives (Seal), Wit: Wm. Henderson, Jacob Cooper, Thomas Neely. Proved by the oath of Thomas Neely 15 Apr 1794 before John McCreary ,J.P.

C, 26-28: 15 March 1793, William Shadrick of Chester county, to Robert Fee, turner, for £50 sterling, 95 acres on waters of Fishing Creek adj. John McKanan, William Corath, Barnet, granted 2 Jan 1786 to Augstin Culp and by said Culp conveyed to Shadrick. William Shadrick (X) (Seal), Wit: Thos Neely, John McKanon, John Fleming. Proved by the oath of Thomas Neely 14 March 1793 before Hugh Whiteside.

C, 28-31: 18 March 1791, John McFadden of Chester County to Robert McFadden of same, tract granted 18 May 1770 to John McFadden, 331 acres on Fishing Creek adj. Matthews, Jacob Behley, Robert Martin, Andrew & Thomas Martin. John McFadden (Seal), Wit: William Willey, Joseph Booth, Richard Wyat. Proved by the oath of Wm Willey 7 Feb 1792 before John McCreary.

C, 32-35: 9 Nov 1792, Hugh Knox, Sheriff of Chester County, SC, to William Robertson of same, planter, whereas Owen Evans in the County Court of Chester did implead Joshua Repault by attachment on an action of Debt in June Court this present year 1792, did obtain final judgment, to be made of the lands & tenements of said Joshua Repault, judgement for £35 sterling with interest and £7 s2 cost, 200 acres on a branch of Sandy River called the Reedy fork, part of 600 acres granted to Richard Warring 23 Dec 1771, and said 200 acres conveyed by said Richard Warring to David Pruit and by David Pruit to Owen Evans and by Owen Evans to Joshua Repault, adj. Benjamin Carter, Edmund Russell, William Boyd, sold for £16 sterling to William Robertson. Hugh Knox (LS), Wit: William Morrow, Hugh Stewart, David Boyd.

C, 35-37: 23 Feb 1793, John Frankling and Mourning his wife of Chester County, to Jonathan Dungan of same, for £50 sterling, part of 200 acres on Flinthems Creek, granted to Thomas Frankling deceased, December 1772, which said John Frankling and Mourning his wife sell eighteen acres, on the north east of said tract adj. lines with William Trussell, Robert Kenedy, Thomas B. Frankling. John Frankling (Seal), Mourning Frankling (Seal), Wit: William Boyd, Jacob Dungan, James Kenedy. Proved by the oath of William Boyd 15 April 1793 before John Pratt, J.P.

C, 38-40: 23 Feb 1793, Thomas B. Frankling and wife Ann of Chester county to Jonathan Dungan of same, for £30 sterling, 77 acres on Flinthems Creek, the waters of Sandy River, part of two different tracts, one granted to Major Grissom 2 Oct 1786, 100 acres, granted to Thomas Baker Frankling; part of one granted 5 Feb 1787, 363 acres. Thos B. Frankling (LS), Ann Frankling (X) (LS), Wit: John Frankling, James Kenedy, Jacob Dungan. Proved by the oath of Jacob Dungan 15 April 1793 before John Pratt, J.P.

C, 40-43: 8 Nov 1792, Andrew Stevenson and Elizabeth his wife of Chester County to John Simonton of York County, SC, for £100 sterling, tracts of land containing by the patents 253 acres, the first granted to Andrew Stevenson 22 April 1790 for 103 acres; the second granted to John Carson 22 Nov 1784 for 50 acres and conveyed by lease and release 16 April 1788, recorded in Book A, page 435 and 535 to Andrew Stephens; the third granted to John Carson 13 May 1768, 100 acres and conveyed to Andrew Stephenson 7 Sept 1787, recorded in Book A, page 531 and 532, all said tracts on waters of Rockey Creek adj. Mary Harberson, Dougall Balentine, John Cooper, Benjamin Mitchell. Andrew Stephenson (LS), Elizabeth Stephenson (LS), Wit: William Boyd, Robert Harberson, William McCulloch. Proved 17 April 1793 by the oath of William McCullough before Richd Taliaferro, Clk Chester County Court.

C, 44-46: 13 March 1792, Thomas B. Frankling of Chester County, planter, to John Frankling of same, planter, for £40 sterling, 265 acres on Flinthems Creek, a branch of Sandy River granted to Minor Winn, Esqr., 6 March 1789 and transferred from him to said Frankling, and part of the said tract said Thomas B. Frankling sold to John Frankling, 45 acres on the south east side of said tract. Thos. B. Frankling (Seal), Wit: Allen DeGraffenreid, William Wood, Philip Knowling. Proved 26 June 1792 by the oath of Allen DeGraffenreidt before Richd Taliaferro, Clk Chester County Court.

C, 46-49: South Carolina, Pinckney District. 22 Jan 1793, Esam Frankling of county aforesaid, planter, to Thomas B. Frankling, of same, for £10 sterling,

CHESTER COUNTY SC DEED ABSTRACTS

128 acres surveyed for him 3 Jan 1792 on water sof Sandy River adj. Richard Taliaferro, Thomas Roden, granted to Esam Frankling in 1792, recorded in Book BBBB, page 55. Esam Frankling (+) (LS), Wit: Park McGriff, Wm Armour (X), Daniel Trussell (X). Proved 4 May 1793 by the oath of Col. Patt McGriff before Richd Taliaferro, Clk Chester County Court.

C, 49-51: 13 March 1792, Thomas Baker Frankling of Chester County, planter, to John Frankling of same, for £100, 202 acres on Flenthems Creek, a branch of Sandy River, part of four different tracts or grants of land; one tract of 50 acres granted to Thomas Frankling 24 Nov 1767, a part of 100 acres granted to Thomas B. Frankling 2 Oct 1786, part of 363 acres granted 5 Feb 1787, and a tract of 50 acres granted to Major Grissom 7 Aug 1786 and transferred from said Grissom to Thomas B. Frankling, all on waters of Sandy River. Thomas B. Frankling, Wit: Allen De Graffenreidt, William Wood, Philip Noland, James Stewart. Proved 26 June 1792 by the oath of Allen DeGraffenreidt before Richd Taliaferro, Clk Chester County Court.

C, 52-54: 20 Aug 1792, James Hughey & Sarah his wife of Chester County to John Frankling of same, for £100 sterling, 50 acres, part of 100 acres laid out unto Edward Flinthem 3 June 1766 on north side of Broad River on a small branch thereof called Flinthems Creek adj. John Hopkins, James Hughey, Thomas B. Frankling. James Hughey (LS), Sarah Hughey (LS), Wit: John Kenedy, Thos B. Frankling, John Weir. Sarah, wife of James Hughey relinquished dower 1792 before John Pratt, J.P.

C, 54-58: 25 March 1793, Hugh Knox, Sheriff of Chester County, to John Frankling of same, planter, whereas Samuel Culwell and Hugh Milling, exrs. of the estate of Alexander Miller deceased in the county court of Chester did implead Thomas B. Frankling and Notley Coates on an action of debt in June Court 1791 and did obtain judgment, and by writ of fieri facias to levy £42 sterling, sells tract of 297 acres on waters of Sandy River being part of several different tracts, to wit 45 acres part of 265 acres granted to Minor Winn 6 March 1786 and conveyed by Minor Winn to Thomas B. Frankling; 200 acres part of four different tracts, one of 50 acres granted to Thomas Frankling for 100 acres 24 Nov 1767, a part of 200 acres granted to Thomas B. Frankling 2 Oct 1786, a part of 363 acres granted 5 Feb 787, also a tract of 50 acres granted to Major Grissom 7 Aug 1786, and transferred from said Grissom to said Thomas B. Frankling, sold for £42 to John Frankling. Hugh Knox (LS), Wit: D. Sims, Saml Lacey. Proved by the oath of Samuel Lacey before Richd Taliaferro, Clk Chester County Court.

C, 58-60: 20 March 1790, James Hughey of Chester County to James Stewart of same, planter, for £50 sterling, 50 acres, part of 200 acres granted to Edward Wilson on a fork of Sandy River called the Stony Fork. James Hughey (LS), Wit: Thomas Jinkins, James Gore, James Hardwick. Proved by the oath of Thomas Jenkins 20 March 1790 before John Pratt, J.P.

C, 60-61: So Carolina, Kershaw County, Camden District. Robert Fullwood of Clarendon County sells to Thomas Gather, a negro fellow named Peter formerly the property of Moses Brown, 3 March 1792. Robert Fulwood (Seal), Wit: Thomas Dinkins. Proved in Chester county by the oath of Thomas Dinkins before Philip Walker, J.P., 29 April 1792.

C, 61-62: Charles Finchlea of Prince Fredericks Parish, Liber[ty] County, SC, planter, for £40 sterling, to James Head of said state, planter, one negro girl named Jemimah, 24 Dec 1792. Charles Finklea (X) (Seal), Wit: Thomas Finklea, George Head. Proved 16 April 1793 by the oath of George Head before Rich'd Taliaferro.

C, 62-63: South Carolina, Chester County. Archibald Elliott Junior of state and county aforesaid to David Davis, planter, for £14 sterling, tract on waters of Fishing Creek, 52 acres 2 roods, adj. Robert Gill. Archibald Elliott Junr (AE) (Seal), Wit: William Shaw, James Barron, Elijah Davis.

C, 63-65: 23 March 1791, William Stone & Elizabeth his wife of Chester County to Dennis Carell of same, for £100 sterling, part of 300 acres but by resurveying only 225 acres, granted to William Stone 17 June 1760, on a branch of Sandy Creek a branch of Broad River. William Stone (X) (Seal), Elizabeth Stone (X) (Seal), Wit: Robert Lemonds, James Head, Henry Head.

C, 65-67: Plat of 126 acres. 7 Jan 1793, John Gore & Mary his wife of Chester County to Nathan Coffee of same, for £100, 126 acres, part of tract granted to Zachariah Isbell 15 Oct 1762 adj. James Timms, Sampson Noland, David Boyd, on waters of Sandy River, tract from Zachariah Isbell to James Gore deceased, thence by said James Gore decd by his will to said John Gore. John Ashford Gore (Seal), Wit: William Boyd, Major Grissim (mark), Philip Noland. Proved by the oath of Philip Noland 25 April 1793 before Elijah Nunn, J.P.

C, 67-69: 17 April 1793, Thomas Fletchall of Chester County to Allen DeGraffinriedt of same, for £65 sterling, 85 acres on waters of Sandy River, part of tract granted to James Fletchall 5 Oct 1758 adj. Joseph Davis, Thomas Jinkins... Francis Rogers who is intitled by law to her dower of one third part during her life joined with said Thomas Fletchall. Thomas Fletchall (Seal), Fracis Rogers (X) (Seal), Wit: Hollis Timms, Thomas Saterwhite, Jeremiah Thomas. Proved by the oath of Hollis Timms 252 June 1793 before Elijah Nunn, J.P.

C, 70-71: 23 March 1791, Dennis Carrell & Sarah his wife of Chester County to William Stone of same, for £100 sterling, 300 acres by resurveying only 225 acres, part of said tract containing 77 acres on the north side of said tract, granted to William Stone 17 June 1760 on a branch of Sandy Creek a branch of road River adj. Daniel Price, this 77 acres transferred from John Stone, Moses Stone & Jacob Stone to said Dennis Carrel & William Stone 19 Oct

1783. Dennis Carrell (Seal), Sarah Carrell (X) (Seal), Wit: Robert Lemonds, James Head, Henry Head.

C, 72-75: 18 Feb 1785, John Morriss of Craven County, Camden District, St. Marks Parish, planter, and wife Mary, to James Bankhead of same, for £21 s8 d6 sterling, tract granted 23 June 1774 to John Morris, 200 acres on waters of Rocky Creek adj. John Cooper, Sarah Knox, Pattrick McGerity, recorded in Book QQQ, page 661. John Morriss (X) (Seal), Mary Morriss (X) (Seal), Wit: James McGarity, William McGarity (mark). Proved in Chester County by the oath of James McGarity 23 June 1793 before And'w Hemphill, J.P.

C, 75-77, 79-80: Lease and release. 11 & 12 March 1793, William Ford, eldest son & heir at law of Thomas Ford deceased, of Chester County, Pinckney District, SC, to James Clark of same, for £26 sterling, 50 acres, part of 100 acres granted to Thomas Ford 4 Oct 1768 on SW side of Cattawba River on a small branch of Rocky Creek known by the name of Hogues branch. William Ford (X) (Seal), Wit: Wm. Hawkins, Burrell Sandefer. Proved by the oath of William Hawkins 22 June 1793 before And'w Hemphill, J.P.

C, 78-79: 4 Sept 1792, Hasel Hardwick Senr of Chester County, to James Tims of same, for £6 sterling, 61 acres on waters of Sandy River, part of 500 acres granted to said Hardwick. Hasel Hardwick (Seal), Wit: Amos Timms, James Hardwick. Proved by the oath of Amos Timms 5 Sept 1792 before John Pratt, J.P.

C, 80-82: Mary Sims and William Sims of Chester County for consideration of a bond given by Nathan Sims deceased to David Hopkins for 16,000 pounds of merchantable tobacco, quit claim to Ferdinand Hopkins, all our part of parts of a certain tract of 160½ acres conveyed by David Hopkins to Nathan Sims late of Chester County, deceased, part of 321 acres granted to David Hopkins 5 Feb 1787. Mary Sims (Seal), William Sims (Seal), Wit: Robt Glenn, Richardson Mayo, Mary Vaughn (X).

C, 82-84: 27 July 1791, John Pugh of Chester County to Col. Edw'd Lacey of same, for £4 sterling that the said Lacey stands security for s'd Pugh unto Hambleton Brown payable on demand, also £14 s12 d6 which the said Pugh stands debtor to the said Lacey, as appears by his obligation of £12 bearing date 1 July 1790, also a settled account of £2 s12 d6, also said Pugh sells three cows, one young calf & a two year old & one year old heiffers, also one roand mare about seven or eight years old, branded IB, a bay coloured colt. John Pugh (Seal), Wit: Samuel Pugh, David Patterson. Proved by the oath of Saml Pugh before John Pratt, J.P.

C, 85-89: Lease and release. 31 July & 1 Aug 1788, John Steel of Chester County, planter, to Thomas Steel of same, for £60, 200 acres, half of tract granted 17 Nov 1771 to Catharine Steel for 400 acres on Fishing Creek, adj. land formerly belonging to Wm Gaston, land formerly belonging to John Gaston, land now surveyed for James Gaston, John White, land formerly belonging to John McFadden & Catharine Steel, John Leonard, and said Catherine Steel dying intestate, the said John Steel her son became heir of all her lands. John Steel (Seal), Margret Steel (Seal), Wit: John McCreary, Andrew Lockhart.

C, 90-91: 1 March 1793, John McCrary Esqr. of Chester County to John Bankhead of same, planter, for £25 sterling, 125 acres on the waters of Fishing Creek adj. said John Bankhead, James Gaston, John McDill, granted 5 March 1787 to said John McCreary. J. McCreary (Seal), Wit: Joseph Booth, James Eakin, Thomas Wood.

C, 92-93: 21 July 1787, Isham Strainge of Wilkes county, Georgia, to Andrew Kidd of county aforesaid, for £80, 200 acres on waters of Rocky Creek on a branch called Rocky Branch adj. John Winn, William McGomery [Montgomery], Randle Wright in the County of Fairfield. Isham Strange (Seal), Anne Wilson (Seal), Saml Wilson (Seal), Rachel Strange, Elizabeth Strange (mark), Sarah Lincecum (X), Wit: Isaac Ball, Jane Ball, James Robertson. Proved by the oath of James Robertson 26 Jan 1792 before Andrew Hemphill, J.P.

C, 93-94: Charles Wall of Chester County for natural love and affection to Jane Wallace, his niece, 100 acres granted to Bird Wall deceased on big Rocky Creek, south side Cataba River adj. Benjamin Street, William Nettles, Abraham Stover, William Will, by John Wall the right lawful heir of Bird Wall deceased, released to Charles Wall and William Wall by lease and release 29 Nov 1786, recorded in Chester County Book A, page 255, and said William Wall granted to said Charles Wall, 4 Aug 1790, also three cows, three breeding mares, two feather beds and furniture, a lott of pewter, two pots & one dutch Over, 18 April 1793. Charles Wall (Seal), Wit: Jon'n Hemphill, Hempton Stroud, William Wall. Proved by the oath of Hampton Stroud 21 May 1793 before Andrew Hemphill, J.P.

C, 95-96: 16 Aug 1791, Andrew Kidd of Chester county, planter, to Nathaniel Durham of same, planter, for £100 sterling, 200 acres on waters of Rocky Creek, granted to Michael Strange 2 April 1773. Andrew Kidd (Seal), Wit: John Polley, James Brown (X).

C, 96-98: 17 April 1788, Kemp T. Strother of Fairfield County, SC, to Ferdinand Hopkins of Chester County, for £1000 sterling, tract on Brushy Fork of Sandy River & the drains thereof, granted to David Hay 21 April 1775. K. T. Strother (Seal), Wit: M. Winn, Elisha Hunter. Proved in Fairfield County by the oath of Minor Winn Esqr., 12 Aug 1709 before J. Pearson, J.P.

C, 99-100: 18 June 1793, Robert Chapman of Union County to William Gaston of Chester County, for £3 s15, 200 acres on Wilsons branch, adj. estate Alexander Tomb deceased, granted to William Chapman brother to Robert Chapman and now deceased, 26 June 1787. Robert Chapman (Seal), Wit: Jo Brown, James Love Gaston, John Brown. Proved by the oath of Joseph Brown Esqr 25 June 1799 before John McCreary, J.P.

C, 100-102: 26 Nov 1792, Francis Greenwood and wife Elizabeth of Chester County to Robert Walker of same, for £50 sterling, 100 acres on branches of Sandy River granted to Ephraim Mitchell Esqr., 15 Oct 1784, recorded in Book ZZZ, page 372, adj. land of David Hudson, land claimed by Stephen Terry, conveyed by Ephraim Mitchell to David Hopkins 29 March 1785, then by David Hopkins to Francis Greenwood 26 Nov 1792. Frances Greenwood (Seal), Wit: John Pratt, Lydia Pratt (O), Jennet Pratt (mark). Proved by the oath of John Pratt Esqr., before Rich'd Taliaferro, Clk Chester County.

C, 102-104: 1 Nov 1792, David Hopkins and wife Mary of Chester county, for £100 sterling, 100 acres on branches of Sandy River granted to Ephraim Mitchell 15 Oct 1784, recorded in Book ZZZ, page 372, adj. land of David Hudson, land claimed by Stephen Terry, conveyed by Ephraim Mitchell to David Hopkins 29 March 1785. D'd Hopkins (Seal), Mary Hopkins (m) (seal), Wit: Samuel Harriss, Ferd'd Hopkins. Proved by the oath of Ferdinand Hopkins 26 Nov 1792 before John Pratt, J.P.

C, 104-105: James Gaston of Chester county for £32 sterling to Benjamin Morriss of same, one negro boy named Jeremiah, 21 May 1793. James Gaston, Wit: Mark Eaves, Samuel McCreary, J. McCreary. Proved by the oath of Samuel McCreary 22 June 1793 before John McCreary, J.P.

C, 105-107: Lease and release. 1 & 2 March 1793, Nathaniel Pace of Kershaw County, Camden District, to John Morriss of Pinckney District, Chester County, for £15 sterling, 55 acres on a ridge of Rocky Creek on the NW side Cataba River adj. Thomas Morris, Middleton, John Cooper. Nathl Pace (Seal), Wit: Elijah Banckston, Thomas Britton. Proved by the oath of Elijah Banckston 22 June 1793 before And'w Hemphill, J.P.

C, 108-110: __ May 1793, John Walker & Agnus his wife of Chester County to John Walker, son of Samuel Walker of same, for £60 sterling, tract on waters of Sandy River granted to said John Walker 2 Oct 1786, 130 acres adj. Jonathan Dungan. John Walker (Seal), Agnus Walker (X) (Seal)l Wit: Hugh Stuart, James Norton. Proved by the oath of Hugh Stuart 20 June 1793 before And'w Hemphill, J.P.

C, 110-111: 1 March 1784, James Burns of Camden District, planter, to Laird Burns, sadler of same, for £6 sterling, all the rights that the said Jas Burns has or can have to the estate of Laird Burns deceased of said district. James Burns (Seal), Wit: Robert Boyd, Hugh Wier (X). Proved by the oath of Hugh Wier 27 June 1793 before Philip Walker, J.P.

C, 112-114: 26 June 1793, William Boyd & Ann his wife of Chester county to James Sloan of same, for £26 s10 sterling, tract granted 14 Sept 1771 to William Housten, 100 acres on Bullskin run, adj. Micajah Pickett, and William Housten and wife Elinor conveyed said tract to William Boyd. William Boyd (Seal), Ann Boyd (Seal), Wit: John McDonald, James Nyle.

**C, 115-119**: 22 June 1793, James Bankhead of Chester County to Thomas McDill for £30 sterling, tract on a small branch of Rocky Creek adj. James Bankhead, Patrick Harbison, John McDill, Edward Lowance, 150 acres, part of tract granted to Samuel Frazor 16 June 1768, adj. Mary Bayely, and said Samuel Frazor and wife Elizabeth did convey 14 & 15 Dec 1768 to Richard Burkel, who conveyed 24 Feb 1774 to Joseph Milican who conveyed 12 & 13 April 1775 to Alexander Rogers, Doctor of Fisick, whose death it is devolved unto said John Gray and Rebecah as executors and heirs of said Alexander Rogers, who conveyed 3 & 4 Jan 1788 to James Bankhead. James Bankhead (LS), Wit: John McDill, Patrick Mcalla (mark), Samuel McDill.

**C, 119-120**: 26 June 1793, Josiah Hill of Chester County to Thomas Wallace of same, for £90 sterling, 339 acres on waters of Rocky Creek granted by patent to Josiah Hill 1786. Josiah Hill (Seal), Wit: John Pratt, D. Sims.

**C, 120-124**: 14 Jan 1788, John Gray & wife Rebecca of Fairfield County, to James Bankhead of Chester County, planter, for £23 sterling, 150 acres granted to Samuel Frazor 16 June 1768, on a branch of Rocky Creek, adj. Mary Bailey, and said Samuel Frazor & Elizabeth his wife did convey to Richard Burkloe who conveyed 23 & 25 Feb 1774 to Joseph Milligan, who conveyed 12 & 13 April 1775 to Alexander Rogers, Doctor of Phisic, by whose death it has devolved to said John Gray & Rebecca his wife as executors. John Gray (LS), Rebekah Gray (LS), Wit: Danl Cochran, James Hanna. Proved in Fairfield County 24 June 1793 by the oath of James Hanna before Arch'd McQueston, J.P.

**C, 124-126**: 4 Jan 1793, Samuel Atkins of Chester County to Henry Jordan of same, for £10, 225 acres on the Cataba River in Chester County originally granted to ____ Culp and by him conveyed to James Patton deceased & by Sheriffs titles conveyed to said Samuel Atkins adj. Rebecca Patton, Richard Atkins. Samuel Atkins (Seal), Wit: Thomas Baird, Thomas Wood, J. McCreary. Proved by the oath of John McCreary 25 Jan 1793 before Hugh Whiteside, J.P.

**C, 127-128**: 5 June 1793, Hugh Knox, Sheriff of Chester County, to Robert Walker of same, planter, whereas Richard Evans in the County Court of Chester did implead Thomas Baker Franklin, John Franklin & Sampson Noland in an action of Debt at July Term 1788, did obtain judgment for his debt, in the sum of £9 s3 sterling, sells 100 acres on waters of Sandy River adj. Richard Taliaferro, Jeremiah Davis, Thomas Roden, granted to Isham Franklin 2 July 1792, recorded in Book BBBB, page 57, and conveyed by said Isham Franklin to Thomas B. Franklin; sold to Robert Walker for £6 s15 sterling. Hugh Knox S. C. C. (Seal), Wit: John Mills Junr, Richard Evans, John Pratt.

**C, 129-130**: 25 June 1793, Wilson Henderson of Chester County, Pinckney District, to Robert Frost Senr of same, for £100 current money of SC, 276 acres on waters of Sealys Creek of Sandy River, granted 3 Dec 1787. Wilson

Henderson (Seal), Wit: Hollis Tims, William Estes, Joseph Tims. Proved by the oath of William Estes 25 June 1798 before John Pratt, J.P.

**C, 131-133**: South Carolina, Chester County. 17 May 1791, Thomas Baker Franklin of county aforesaid, planter, to Denniss Carrell of same, yeoman, for £20 sterling, 100 acres on waters of Flinthems Creek of Sandy River adj. Richard Head, James Hughey (plat included), part of 265 granted 6 March 1786 to Minor Winn, surveyed 25 Nov 1785, recorded in Book HHH, page 158, sold by Minor Winn to said Thomas Baker Franklin 22 May 1789. Thomas B. Franklin, Wit: James Huey, John Cockrell (X), Thomas Cockrell (X).

**C, 133-134**: 7 March 1793, John McCombs and wife Ann of Chester County to Parker Adkins of same, for £50 sterling, 50 acres granted to John McCombs 5 May 1786 for 640 acres on waters of Sandy River adj. Edward Lacey, Thomas Coburn, Parker Adkins. John McCombs. No wit.

**C, 135-138**: Edward Allen of Commonwealth of Massachusetts and Town of Salem for £157 s18 d3 sterling, to Ferdinand Hopkins of Chester County, all my right, title, and claim to five tracts of land: one tract of 322 acres granted to Littlebury Colville 1 Aug 1785 on Little River adj. Col. John Winn, Thomas Addison, David Hopkins, Hampton; tract of 640 acres granted to Daniel Colville 1 Aug 1785 on waters of Little River adj. Thomas Shannon; tract of 640 acres granted to Edward colville 5 Sept 1785 on waters of Broad River adj. David Hopkins, William Thomas, David Stephens; 640 acres granted to David Hopkins 15 Oct 1785 on waters of Little River of Broad River adj. Charles Coleman, David Richardson, John Richardson, David Hopkins, Nathaniel Harbin, William Tucker, Richard Crosby, David Lindsay; 350 acres granted to James Moore on Brushy fork & Sandy River including the fork of the said Brushey fork & Sandy River, known by the name of the place whereon James Moore formerly lived, also 50 acres adj. the same granted to John Steen[?], date 10 Feb 1793. Edw'rd Allen (seal), Wit: Robert Glenn, James Dillard.

**C, 138**: Levy Smith of Chester County for natural affection to my daughter Elizabeth Smith, a negro girl named Nelly about nine years old, 20 June 1793. Levy Smith (Seal), Wit: Joseph Bennett.

**C, 138-139**: Levy Smith of Chester County for natural affection to my daughter Salley Smith, a negro boy named Jack about six years old, 20 June 1793. Levy Smith (Seal), Wit: Joseph Bennett.

**C, 139-140**: 7 Feb 1792, John Colvin and wife Hannah of Chester county to Richard Head of same, for £150 sterling, 250 acres on waters of Stones Creek of Sandy River adj. John Cockrell, James Hughey, James Daugharty, John Colvin, granted 6 Feb 1786, recorded in Grant Book GGGG, page 511, granted to said John Colvin. John Colvin (Seal), Hannah Colvin (X) (Seal),

Wit: John Pratt, James Head, George Head (X). Proved by the oath of James Head & Geo Head before Richd Taliaferro, Clk of Chester County Court.

**C, 141-143**: 9 March 1771, Lucy Collins of Province of SC to Denniss Carrell of Craven County, said province, for £100, tract granted 17 Feb 1767 to said Lucy Collins, 100 acres on a branch of Broad River called Sandy Creek. Lucy Collins (X) (Seal), Wit: Anthony Duffield, William Stone (M), James Stone (O). Proved in Craven County by the oath of Anthony Duffield 16 March 1772 before Thomas Fletchall, J.P.

**C, 143-145**: 27 Feb 1792, Isaac Taylor of Chester County to Richard Head of same, for £50 sterling, 300 acres, part of 640 acres granted to said Richard Head 5 Feb 1787, adj. Moses Stone, John Stone, Isaac Taylor, on waters of Sandy River. Isaac Taylor (Seal), Jane Taylor (X) (Seal), Wit: James Head, Henry Head, Sarah Taylor. Proved by the oath of James Head 15 April 1793 before Richard Taliafferro, Clk Chester County Court.

**C, 145-147**: 7 Feb 1792, John Colvin of Chester County and wife Hannah to Richard Head of same, for £60 sterling, 100 acres on Sandy Creek, granted to Lucy Collins 17 Feb 1767 and transferred from said Lucy Collins to Dennis Carrell 9 March 1771 and from said Dennis Carrell to John Colvin 3 Feb 1784. John Colvin (Seal), Hannah Colvin (Seal), Wit: John Pratt, James Head, George Head (X). Proved by the oath of James Head & Geo Head before Richd Taliaferro, Clk of Chester County Court.

**C, 147-148**: Jacob Roberts to James Head, one negro man named Hall, but through disguise have been called Joseph about 36 years of age, for £30, 12 Dec 1792. Jacob Roberts (Seal), Wit: James Hughey, William Woodward, Richard Head. Proved by the oath of Richard Head 15 April 1793 before Richd Taliaferro, Clk Chester County.

**C, 148-150**: Charles Boyd of Chester County for natural love and affection to Ann, Jonathan, Nancy & William Dungan, children of Jacob Dungan, and Ann his wife; to Jonathan Dungan two sorrel horses; to Nancy & Ann, all the household furniture, sheep & cows; to William Dungan the drove of hogs, a loom, two saddles, all tools, 11 March 1793. Charles Boyd (Seal), Wit: William Boyd, Charles Boyd, John Cerd. Proved by the oath of William Boyd 15 April 1793 before John Pratt, J.P.

**C, 150-152**: South Carolina, Camden District. 3 Feb 1784, Denniss Carroll of district aforesaid, planter, to John Colvin, planter, for £500 south currency, tract on a branch of Broad River called Sandy Creek, 100 acres by grant dated 17 Feb 1767 by SC to Lucy Collins and conveyed by her to Dennis Carroll. Dennis Carrell (Seal), Wit: John Cockrell, John Pratt, William Armer (mark). Proved by the oath of John Cockrell before David Hopkins, J. P., 11 Nov 1784.

C, 152-157: 26 & 27 Aug 1790, Robert Rowand of Charleston, gentleman, to Miss Harriett Elliott Rowand & Charles Elliott Rowand, both of said city, for five shillings, five different tracts of land, viz one tract of 1500 acres surveyed for Jas Simmons 8 Sept 1772 and granted to Robert Rowand 28 Oct 1774 in Craven County on branches of the brushy fork, six miles below Loves Ford, adj. Clement Lempreer, Westly Wm Anderson; one other tract surveyed of Archibald Simpson & granted to said Robt Rowand for 1000 acres 28 Oct 1774 in Colleton County, the waters of Salt Catcher; three other tracts of land all granted to said Robert Rowand 28 Oct 1774 making together 1500 acres adj. each other in Orangeburg District, being part of what is called the three ponds. Robt Rowand (Seal), Wit: Mary Wells, Jas Rivers Maxwill, Alexdr Walker. Proved 13 Sept 1790 before Charles Linning, J. P., by the oath of Jas Rivers Maxwill.

C, 157-160: 4 Feb 1778, Benjamin Mitchell of Craven County, SC, District of Ninety Six, planter, & wife Susanna, to Adam Agers of same county, District of Camden, St. Marks Parish, Taylor, for £400, tract granted 4 May 1775 to Benjamin Mitchell, 150 acres on branches of Rocky Creek adj. said Benjamin Mitchell, recorded in Book XXX, page 345. Benjamin Mitchell (mark) (Seal), Susanna Mitchell (X) (Seal), Wit: John Sansom, Michael Blain. Proved in Camden district by the oath of Michael Blain 1 Sept 1778 before Philip Walker, J.P.

C, 160-162: James Winn of Fairfield County for £50 sterling, to Robert Gaston of Chester County, 90 acres on the north side of Fishing Creek. J. Winn, Wit: D'd Hamilton, Richard Gladney. Proved in Fairfield County by the oath of D'd Hamilton before J. W. Yongue, J.P.

C, 162-164: 13 May 1792, Thomas Morriss of Chester County to Peter Jones of same, for £18 sterling, 173 acres in Chester County on waters of Cataba River adj. Johnathan Hephill, Charles Wall, Donald McDonald, James Cloud, granted to said Thomas Morris 6 Feb 1792. Thomas Morriss (Sea,), Wit: Saml Lowrie, Robt Bradford.

C, 164-166: 18 Dec 1792, William Massey of Lancaster county to John Edwards of Chester County, for £100 sterling, 18883 acres in Chester County, part of two grants, 59 acres being on the north side of Fishing Creek adj. Laurence Galaher, John McCoun, Alexdr McCain; whereas by certain indentures from Alexdr McCoun to John McCoun and from John McCoun to Joshua Edwards and said Joshua Edwards having authorised William Robertson by power of attorney and sold to William Massey, 50 acres; also another tract of 122 acres granted to said William Massey recorded in Book YYYY, page 92. William Massey (Seal), Wit: Jas Shuffield, Joseph Massey, George Massey. Proved by the oath of James Shuffield 22 Jan 1793 before J. McCreary, J.P.

C, 166-167: South Carolina, Chester County. March 1st 1793. Sandy River. Alexander Willson of said county sells to Hasel Hardwick, planter, of same, a young negro wench named Patt, about ten years old. for six years. Alexander Wilson (mark), Wit: John Salse, William Estes. Proved by the oath of William Estes 5 June 1793 before Elijah Nunn, J.P.

C, 167-170: 23 Jan 1792, Walter Brown, planter, of chester county to Samuel McDill, Blacksmith, of same, for £30 sterling, tract granted 20 July 1772 to Walter Brown, 100 acres on a branch of Rocky Creek, on Rocky Creek. Walter Brown (mark) (Seal), Wit: John McDill, John Wilkens, Thos McDill. Proved by the oath of John Wilkins 28 Jan 1793 before Richd Taliaferro, Clerk of Chester County.

C, 170-173: 31 Aug 1791, James Cobb of Union County, SC, to William Boyd of Chester County, for £200 sterling, 100 acres, part of a tract granted 23 Dec 1771 to Richard Waring, 400 acres on a branch of Sandy River called the Cainey Fork adj. John Evans, Benjamin Carter, Edmond Russell, conveyed by said Waring to David Pruit 16 Oct 1775, recorded in Charleston 24 Aug 1778, in Book Y. No. 4, page 147 and 148, and from David Pruit to Nathaniel Cobb 16 Nov 1776. James Cobb (Seal), Wit: John Terry, Adam Williamson, Jones Taylor (X).

C, 173-176: 19 Feb 1793, John Culp, son of Peter Culp deceased, farmer, of Camden District, Chester County, to Philip Cline, planter of same, for £30 sterling, 75 acres on Fishing Creek, adj. said John Culp, said Philip Cline. John Culp (Seal), Wit: Hugh Whiteside, Austin Culp, Abraham Whitesides. Proved in Chester County by the oath of Austen Culp 19 Feb 1793 before Hugh Whiteside.

C, 176-178: South Carolina, District of Camden. 12 March 1785, John Hitchcock of District aforesaid, planter, to Hugh Stuart of same, blacksmith, for £1 sterling, 200 acres, part of 400 acres on a branch of Sandy Creek of Broad River, granted 27 Nov 1778 [sic]. John Hitchcock (Seal), Wit: James Gore, Richard Evans, John Pratt. Proved in Chester County by the oath of Rich'd Evans 28 Jan 1794 before Clayton Rogers, J.P.

C, 178-180: 2 March 1793, Hugh Knox, Sheriff of Chester County, to Thomas Neeley of same, waggon maker, whereas Philip Walker in the County Court of Chester did implied Daniel Cook on an action of Debt in June Court 1792, and obtained judgment and by a writ of fieri facias, to levy £24 s15 d20 sterling, sells tract of about 300 acres adj. Nathaniel Simple, John McKinney; and the other of 100 acres on waters of Fishing Creek; both tracts in the whole 350 acres, sold to Thomas Neeley for £25 s5 sterling. Hugh Knox Shff (Seal), Wit: Hu McCluer, Hugh Whiteside, William Whiteside. Proved by the oath of Hugh McClure 2 March 1793 before Hugh Whiteside.

C, 180-181: Thomas Morris for £10 sterling to Robert Walker of Chester County, one feather bed & other furniture in the house, four head of waggon horses which includes teem, 15 Jan 1793. Thomas Morriss (Seal), Wit: James H. Walker, Samuel Walker.

**C, 181-183**: 30 Nov 1792, Richard Nance & Mimah his wife of Chester county, Pinckney District, to Jas Timms of same, for £70 currency, tract on Sandy Creek, a branch of Broad River on north side of said Broad River, 112 acres, 50 acres of which land being part of 250 acres granted to Capt. Zachariah Isbell, which said 50 acres is on north side Sandy Creek adj. said Isbell; the other 50 acres granted to Thomas Roden 27 Sept 1769, adj.Zachariah Isbell, Jeremiah Pate, Thomas Roden, and the 12 acres is included between the two fifty acre tracts. Rich'd Nance (Seal), Gemima Nancy (Seal), Wit: Hollis Timms, Amos Timms, Danl Rogers (X).

**C, 183-186**: South Carolina, Chester County. 23 Aug 1792, John Hays & wife Mary of Chester County, blacksmith, to Christopher Strong, planter, of same, for £20 current money, 100 acres on south fork of Fishing Creek,adj. Christopher Strong, Robert Harper, William Wier, John Hays, Christopher Strong, part of it in a granted to Joseph Mitchell by North Carolina 26 Oct 1767 and conveyed down to James Jack and from said Jack to John Hays 26 Jan 1788, recorded in the Clerks Office of Chester County, the remainder of said tract of 100 acres is part of tract granted to Robert Harper 1 Sept 1785 and conveyed 31 March 1788. John Hays (Seal), Wit: Jno Mills, Robt Cooper. Proved by the oath of Robert Cooper 23 Aug 1792 before John Mills, J. P. Plat included showing land adj. Robert Harper, Christopher Strong, Robert Cooper, Wm Wier, Capt. Robert Cooper. Recorded by S. Lacey 1 Aug 1793.

**C, 186-189**: Lease and release. 27 & 28 June 1792, Abner Wilks & wife of Chester County, to James Blair of same, for £60 sterling, 150 acres on the south side of Hagues branch, part of tract laid out to John Rennolds for 300 acres on 15 Feb 1769, recorded in Book DDD, page 96, sold to Benjamin Street for £100 south currency 9 Sept 1769 and by said Benja Street & wife Mary to Abner Wilks for £22 sterling. Abner Wilks (Seal), Martha Wilks (X) (Seal), Wit: David Roddey, William Sprowl (O). Proved by the oath of William Sprowl 24 Jan 1793 before And'w Hemphill, J.P.

**C, 189-192**: 4 Jan 1793, Thomas Neely of Chester County to Henry Jordan of same, yeoman, for £10 sterling, tract granted 26 July 1774 to James Neeley, 320 acres on a branch of Fishing Creek adj. said Neeley, Wm. Kinney, a part of which tract being conveyed to Thomas Neeley, the deed recorded in Chester Court in January 1788 in Book A, page 337 and 338. Thomas Neeley (Seal), Wit: David Hyatt, Casper Sleeker, Britton Correl.

**C, 192-194**: 23 Oct 1792, Alexander Tenant of Chester County to Hugh Gaston of same, for £25 sterling, 147 acres on Wilsons Spring Branch of Bull Run, adj. said Hugh Gaston, adj. lands granted to Michael Dickson & John Walker of Bull Run, the said land granted to Alexander Tenant 1 Jan 1787. Alexander Tenant (mark) (Seal), Martha Tenant (mark) (Seal), Wit: Edward McDaniel, John Caldwell.

C, 194-197: 20 Dec 1784, Catherine Steel of Camden District, to William Reaves of said district, planter, for £500 sterling, tract granted 28 Nov 1771 to Catharine Steel, 200 acres on waters of Fishing Creek adj. John McFadden, John Leonard, said Catharine Steel. Catharine Steel (mark) (Seal), Wit: Wm Wiley, Wm. McDonald, Benjamin Reaves. Proved 31 Dec 1784 by the oaths of William McDonald and Benjamin Reaves before Jas Knox, J.P.

C, 197-198: 18 Nov 1782, Robert Morrison & Jennet his wife of Parish of St. Marks, SC, Taylor, to James Montgomery of same, for ten shillings, 100 acres on Culps Mill Branch. Robert Morrison (Seal), Janet Morrison (mark) (Seal), Wit: Jas Wylie, Alexdr Gaston.

C, 199-200: South Carolina, Chester County. 16 March 1793, William Cockrell of county aforesaid, planter, to Robert Nix of same, for 40 shillings, 90 acres surveyed for him 14 Nov 1792 in the District of Pinckney, Chester county, on waters of Sandy River adj. Archibald Roberts, Capt. Richard Taliaferro, Jeremiah Daviss, granted to William Cockrell 1792, recorded in Book BBBB, page 55. William Cockrell (X) (Seal), Wit: James Huey, Moses Cockrell (X). Proved by the oath of Moses Cockrell 16 July 1793 before John Pratt, J.P.

C, 201-202: 16 May 1793, Peter Jones, late Sheriff of Chester County, to Hugh Cooper, Blacksmith, whereas John Ferguson in the County Court of Chester did implied John Gillam on an act of Debt in the sum of £25 sterling in 1790 and obtained judgment, sells tract of 100 acres on Rocky Creek known by the name of Carrells old place, granted to Mary Biggam 1 Sept 1768. Peter Jones (Seal), Wit: John Ray (O), Jacob Breakfield, Robert Owen. Proved by the oath of John Ray 3 Aug 1793 before John Pratt, J.P.

C, 202-203: 21 Jan 1793, Jas Timms of Chester County to Daniel Rogers of same, for £20 sterling, 85 acres surveyed & granted to James Timms 15 March 1792 adj. Hasel Hardwick, John Donald, John Moultrie. Jas Timms (Seal), Wit: Rich'd Taliaferro, Judith N. Corbell.

C, 204-205: 24 June 1791, William Wilie & Isabella his wife of Chester County to John Hays of same, for £20 sterling, 100 acres, part of 898 acres granted to Wm Wilie 2 Nov 1789, adj. Wm Wilie, John McClure. William Wylie (Seal), Isabella Wylie (Seal), Wit: Samuel Knox, Robert Kelsey, Philip Walker. Proved by the oath of Philip Walker 26 Jan 1793 before John McCreary, J.P.

C, 205: Isaac Pritchard of Chester County indebted to Thomas Wallace of same, in the sum of £50 sterling, mortgage of one bay mare, two year old colts, four cows, three year old calves, two two year old heiffers, hogs, one waggon & Gears, my household furniture, 10 Feb 1790. Isaac Pritchard (Seal), Wit: Peter Sraine, Margaret Porter.

C, 205-207: 14 Nov 1791, David Patterson of Chester County to William Rainey of same, for £35 currency, tract whereon said Rainey now lives, 100 acres granted to David Patterson 4 Dec 1771. David Patterson (Seal), Wit: Josiah Hill, Arthur Travers.

C, 208-209: 25 Nov 1790, William Kirkland Junr of Fairfield County to William Good of Chester County, for £10, tract granted 16 March 1786 to William Kirkland, 150 acres on a branch of Turkey Creek. Be it remembered that a small corner cut off by an old survey we are to be answerable for. William Kirkland (Seal), Wit: Zec'h Kirkland, Edw'd Lacey.

C, 209-210: Robert Smith of York County, SC, appoints friend Philip Walker, Esq., of Chester County, lawful attorney, to receive all debts due, 8 Jan 1793. Robert Smith (Seal), Wit: Michl Hogan, Agnes Wenols, Wm. Galloway[?].

C, 210-211: 21 Oct 1792, Andrew Morrowson of Chester County, yeoman, to Matthew Morrowson & Anderson Morrowson Junior of same, sons of said Andrew Morrowson, for five shillings sterling, 150 acres on the main branch of Sandy River adj. Hardis, Ferguson. Andrew Morrowson (Seal), Wit: Phil. Walker, John Hemphill.

C, 211-214: 23 Jan 1793, James Smith of Camden District, planter, to James Hambleton of same, planter, for £40 sterling, tract granted 13 Oct 1772 to James Smith, 250 acres on north side Fishing Creek in Chester County. James Smith (Seal), Lilles Smith (Seal), Wit: Daniel Cooke, Robert Smith, John McCrorey. Proved by the oath of John McCrorey 23 Jan 1793 before Hugh Whiteside.

C, 214-217: 23 Jan 1793, James Smith of Camden district, planter, to James Hambleton of same, for £35 sterling, tract granted 25 April 1767, 83 acres on north side Fishing Creek. James Smith (Seal), Lilles Smith (Seal), Wit: Daniel Cooke, Robert Smith, John McCrorey. Proved by the oath of John McCrorey 23 Jan 1793 before Hugh Whiteside.

C, 217-220: 19 Nov 1782, Robert Morrison & Janet his wife of Parish of St. Mark, SC, Taylor, to James Montgomery of same, for £100, tract granted 8 March 1768, tract granted to Janet Campbell, 100 acres in Craven County on Jacob Culp's Mill Branch, Janet Campbell now Robert Morrison's wife. Robert Morrison (Seal), Janet Morrison (O) (Seal), Wit: James Wylie, Alexdr Gaston. Proved by the oath of James Wylie 1 March 1783 before Philip Walker, J.P.

C, 220-223: 28 July 1784, Augustine Culp & his wife Agnes of Camden District, SC, to Andrew Jeter of the State of Virginia, County of Greenville, for £60, tract granted 2 March 1768 to Elizabeth Craig 100 acres on the waters of Fishing Creek & on the great road that leads from Lyles's ford on Broad River to Land's ford on Catawba River adj. Tinker, Robert Brown, and said tract fell to George Craig by the death of the said Elizabeth Craig and by George Craig to Augustine Culp 4 June 1774. Augustine Culp (Seal), Agnus Culp (X) (Seal), Wit: Benjamin Reaves, John Tomlinson, James Massey.

C, 223-225: 28 July 1784, Augustine Culp & his wife Agnes of Camden District, SC, to Andrew Jeter of the State of Virginia, County of Greenville, for £60, tract granted 4 Oct 1768 to Robert Brown, part of 100 acres on the west side of Catawba River adj. Matthews, and said tract was conveyed by said Robert unto Henry Culp 6 Sept 1769 and said Henry Culp for £26 to Augustine Culp 6 March 1775, said tract being 26 acres adj. Wm McKinney, plat certified by Andrew McDowel. Augustine Culp (Seal), Agnus Culp (X) (Seal), Wit: Benjamin Reaves, John Tomlinson, James Massey.

C, 225-227: 28 Dec 1792, Andrew Jeter of State of Georgia, Columbia County, to Henry Jordan of Chester County, for £100, tract granted 2 March 1768 to Elizabeth Craig, 100 acres on the waters of Fishing Creek & on the great road that leads from Lyles's ford on Broad River to Land's ford on Catawba River adj. Tinker, Robert Brown, and said tract fell to George Craig by the death of the said Elizabeth Craig and by George Craig to Augustine Culp 4 June 1774. Andrew Jeter (Seal), Wit: Benjamin Reaves, Mary Reaves (X), William Reaves.

C, 228-229: 28 Dec 1792, Andrew Jeter of Columbia County, Georgia, to Henry Jordan of Chester County, for £10 sterling, tract granted 4 Oct 1768 to Robert Brown, part of 100 acres on the NW side of Catawba River adj. Matthews, and said tract was conveyed by said Robert unto Henry Culp 6 Sept 1769 and said Henry Culp for £26 to Augustine Culp 6 March 1775, said tract being 26 acres adj. William McKinney. Andrew Jeter (Seal), Wit: Benjamin Reaves, Mary Reaves (X), William Reaves.

C, 230-231: 23 Jan 1793, John Terry of Chester County to William Morriss of same, for £25 sterling, 54 3/4 acres, part of 200 acres granted to Stephen Terry 10 July 1766 on waters of Sandy River adj. Thos Humphries. John Terry (Seal), Wit: George Blissit, Reason Blissit, Stephen Blissit. Plat included.

C, 231-233: 6 Aug 1792, Hugh Knox, Sheriff of Chester County, to Alexander Robinson of Fairfield County, planter, whereas Alexander Robinson in the County Court of Chester did implied Robert McCleland on an action of Debt in June Court 1792 and obtained judgment, to levy £18 s19 d7 sterling, sells 350 acres on waters of Little River on a branch called Curless Creek, granted to John McCleland which devolved on Robert McCleland his son, now sold for £15 s10 sterling. Hugh Knox (Seal), Wit: Arch'd Boyd, Hance Hamilton.

C, 233-234: 22 Sept 1788, Robert Smith of Chester County for £70 sterling to John Wright of same, part of tract laid out for Ambrose Nixx adj. land of Thomas Roden, Robert Humphries, Ferguson, Mannon Gore, being 150 acres. Robert Smith (mark), Wit: John Fleetwood, Abraham Myers.

C, 234-235: 22 Sept 1788, Robert Smith of Chester County to John Wright of same, for £10 sterling, 23 acres, part of tract laid out for Mannon Gore & relapsed to Wm Young 21 Jan 1785. Robert Smith (mark), Wit: John Fleetwood, Abraham Myers.

**C, 235-239**: 24 Feb 1779, James Hanna of Parish of St. Mark, Craven County, to Samuel Caldwell of same, weaver, for £300, tract granted 8 Dec 1774, 10 acres in Craven County on the draughts of Fishing Creek adj. John Stevenson, Samuel Cross. James Hanna (mark) (Seal), Wit: Alexdr Gaston, Saml Wier, Matthew Johnson (X). Proved by the oath of Samuel Wier 23 Aug 1793 beore Phil Walker, J.P.

**C, 239-243**: 4 Aug 1792, James Gill & Mary his wife of York County, SC, planter, to Thomas Nesbett of Chester County, planter, for £20 sterling, 100 acres on waters of Fishing Creek in Chester County adj. Hugh Gaston, originally granted to Mary Gaston (now wife of Jas Gill) by granted dated 17 March 1775, recorded in Book NNN, page 292. James Gill (Seal), Mary Gill (Seal), Wit: Robert Steel, Henry Rea. Proved in Chester County by the oath of Robert Steel 17 Aug 1793 before J. McCreary, J,.P.

**C, 243-246**: 4 Feb 1782, John Ferguson of Camden District, Craven County, SC, planter, and wife Elizabeth to Robert Steel of same, for _____, tract granted 18 May 1773, 100 acres on a branch of Fishing Creek adj. Thos Peterson. John Ferguson (Seal), Elizabeth Ferguson (Seal), Wit: Edward McFadden, Samuel Ferguson. Proved in Chester County by the oath of Saml Ferguson 3 Jan 1789 before Andw Hemphill, J.P.

**C, 246-248**: 7 March 1788, Samuel Caldwell & wife of Fairfield County, planter, to Robert Steel of Chester County, planter, for £10 sterling, 100 acres on the draughts of Fishing Creek adj. John Stevenson, Samuel Cross. Saml Caldwell (Seal), Wit: Joseph Booth, James Peden. Proved by the oath of Joseph Booth 17 Aug 1793 before J. McCreary, J.P.

**C, 248-253**: Lease & release. 9 & 10 Sept 1787, Joseph Telford of Rocky Creek, Chester County, planter, to James McAlonan of same, for £60 sterling, tract granted 9 Sept 1774 to Benjamin Mitchell, 150 acres on a branch of Rocky Creek adj. Frances Henderson, and said Benjamin Mitchell sold to Robt McClelland 21 & 22 June 1776, recorded in Book B No. 5, page 149 and 150, 16 Aug 1779, and the heirs of Robt McClelland sold to Joseph Telford 16 & 17 Nov 1778. Joseph Telford (X) (Seal), Rachel Telford (mark) (Seal), Wit: Samuel Telford, Matthew Harbison. Proved by the oath of Matthew Harbison 15 June 1793 before Phil Walker, J.P.

**C, 254-260**: Lease & release. 16 & 17 Nov 1778, John McClelland of Craven County, Camden District, St. Marks Parish, SC, cooper, lawful heir of Robt McClelland now deceased, to Joseph Telford of same, planter, for £1010 old currency, 150 acres granted 9 Sept 1774 to Benjamin Mitchell, 150 acres on a branch of Rocky Creek adj. Frances Henderson, recorded in Book SSS, page 697, and said Benjamin Mitchell sold to Robt McCleland 21 & 22 June 1776. John McClelland (Seal), Wit: John Carson, Jas Harbison. N. B. Rebecca McClelland, formerly wife to Robert McClelland now deceased, for £336 s13 d4, for one third of this tract, confirm this instrument of writing. Rebecca McClelland (mark) (Seal). Proved in York County by the oath of Jas

Harbison. Proved by the oath of Matthew Harbison 30 April 1793 before Wm Love, J.P.

**C, 260-263**: 29 Jan 1791, Joseph Lyon of Chester County, yeoman, to Robert Harper of same, yeoman, for £100, 160 acres, part of tract granted 29 April 1768 by NC to Alex'dr Brown Senr, 290 acres in Macklenburgh County, NC, at the time of survey, but now in Chester County, on both sides So fork of Fishing Creek, adj. George Craig, Henry Culp, William Miller, John Boyd, David Lusk, including his plantation. Joseph Lyon (Seal), Wit: Wm Wilson, Wm Jack. Proved by the oath of William Wilson 27 Aug 1793 before John Mills, J.P.

**C, 263**: South Carolina, Chester County. Valentine Bell, planter, of county aforesaid, gives to daughter Mary Bell of same county, a likely negro girl about four years old named Edde, 22 June 1793. Valentine Bell (mark), Wit: William Bell.

**C, 263-264**: South Carolina, Chester County. Valentine Bell, planter, of county aforesaid, gives to daughter Sarah Bell of same county, a likely negro girl ten years old named Becca, 22 June 1793. Valentine Bell (mark), Wit: William Bell.

**C, 264-266**: 23 Feb 1792, James Houston of Chester County to Thomas Cabeen of same, for £10 current money, tract on waters of Sandy River granted to said James Houston 2 Oct 1786, 125 acres. James Houston (Seal), Wit: Edward Lacey, James Gordon. Proved by the oath of Col. Edward Lacey 16 Sept 1793 before John Pratt, J.P.

**C, 266-268**: 7 Feb 1793, Edward White Senr of Chester County, farmer, to Thomas White, for £5 sterling, tract granted 2 Jan 1792 to said Edward White on waters of Fishing Creek, part of plat of 160 acres on the north west side part of said tract. Edward White (Seal), Wit: Robert White, Robert Linn, John McCannon. Proved by the oath of Robert Linn 12 Feb 1793 before J. McCreary, J.P.

**C, 268-270**: 3 Aug 1793, Laird Burns & Jane his wife to Alexander English, for £105, 270 acres on Rockey Creek originally granted, one tract of 100 acres to Peter Culp by patent, and by him conveyed to Laird Burns 15 & 16 Sept 1762, recorded in Book P. No. 3, page 304, and by the will of said Laird Burns bequeath to his son Laird Burns; one tract of 100 acres granted to Andrew Graham 17 March 1775, entered in the Audr Gens office Bok M. No. 14, page 23, 3 Aug 1775, and part of a tract of 100 acres granted to Laird Burns 15 Oct 1784, recorded in grant book ZZZ, page 160, and lastly part of a tract of 148 acres granted to said Laird Burns 3 Sept 1792. Laird Burns (Seal), Jane Burns (X) (Seal), Wit: Philip Walker, George Morrow (mark). Proved by the oath of George Morrow 15 Aug 1793 before Philip Walker, J.P.

C, 271-272: 7 Jan 1793, Hugh Miller former sheriff of Camden District, Sc ,to John Mills of Chester County, for £67 s7 d5 sterling, whereas James Mitchell in the County of York did in the court of common pleas of Camden District implead William Jones & John Simpson, securities for James Landsbey on an action of debt in April Court 1786 and obtained judgment to levy £116 with interest from June 1784 sterling money, sells tract of 400 acres: 250 acres granted to granted to Henry Culp and 150 acres granted to Alexander Balentine. Hugh Milling late Sheriff C. D. (Seal), Wit: Saml. W. Yongue, D. Evans, Wm. Jones. Proved in Chester County by the oath of William Jones 20 July 1793 before Phil Walker, J.P.

C, 272-274: 20 Nov 1792, Thomas Holsey of Edgefield County, SC, to Richard Yarbrough of Chester County, for £20, 410 acres, part of 640 acres granted to said Thomas Holsey 5 Feb 1787, recorded in Grant Book RRRR, page 33, on waters of Sandy River & Little River, adj. William Murry, John Given, Wm. Paniel [Daniel?]. Thomas Halscel (Seal), Wit: Benjamin Halsell, Isaac Waggoner, Ephraim Padget (mark). Proved in Chester County by the oath of Benj Holsey 11 June 1793 before John Bell, J. P.

C, 274: 17 July 1784, Thomas Macklen for £1000 current money to David Hopkins of Camden District, 640 acres granted 16 July 1784 on the north side of the south fork of Saluda River, plat certified 8 June 1784. Thomas Macklen (Seal), Wit: John Terrey, Daniel Lehalf, Edwd McVeal[?].

C, 275: 17 Oct 1784, Samuel Thomson to David Hopkins of Camden District, for £1000 current money, 286 acres according to a plat and grant, granted 15 Oct 1784 on south fork of Saluda River adj. unknown, plat certified 8 June 1784. Saml Thomson (mark) (Seal), Wit: Edward S. Coleman, Wm. Wilcocks, Archibald Stubbs.

C, 276-277: 23 Oct 1784, William Susland, gentleman, to David Hopkins, Esq., of Camden District, for £1000 sterling, 640 acres on the District of 96 on great Rockey Creek, granted 16 Oct 1784. William Susland (X) (Seal), Wit: Joseph Hall, Edw'd S. Coleman.

C, 277-278: 17 Aug 1792, Thomas Holsey of Edgefield County to William Murrey of Chester County, for £10 sterling, 200 acres, part of 640 acres granted to Thomas holsey 5 Feb 1787 adj. Samuel Carter. Thomas Holsel (Seal), Mary Holsel (mark) (Seal), Wit: Rich'd Yarbrough, And'w Pannel (mark). Proved by the oath of Richard Yarborough 16 Sept 1793 before Richd Taliaferro, Clk Chester County Court.

C, 279-280: 1 July 1786, Solomon Peters of Orangeburgh District, SC, to Charles Coleman of Camden District, for £150 sterling, 400 acres granted to said Solomon Peters on a branch of Sandy River of Broad River on the northeast side of said Broad River, half of 800 acres granted to said Peters 1 May 1774. Solomon Peters (Seal), Wit: James Parks, John Coleman, George

Allcorn. Proved by the oath of Jas Parks & John Coleman 2 Aug 1787 before David Hopkins, J.P.

C, 280-281: 8 Nov 1793, James Adams of the State of Georgia, County of Greene, to William Bell of Chester County, SC, for £30, 100 acres on north side of Broad River on Susan Boles' branch, it being six feet wide and five inches deep, adj. Thomas Robins, granted to James Greer 13 May 1768. James Adams (Seal), Wit: Sarah Bell, Nancy Bell, Valentine Bell (X). Proved by the oath of Sarah Bell 16 Sept 1793 before Richd Taliaferro, Clk Chester County Court.

C, 282-283: 17 April 1793, James Timms & Patty his wife of Chester County, Pinckney District, to Thomas Fletchall of same, for £75 currency, tract on Sandy Creek of Broad River, 112 acres, 50 acres of which being part of 250 acres granted to Capt. Zachariah Isbell, and the other 50 acres granted to Thomas Roden 29 Sept 1769 adj. Zachariah Isbell, Jeremiah Pottes, Thomas Roden, and the 12 acres is included between the two fifty acre tracts. James Timms (Seal), Patty Timms (X) (Seal), Wit: Hollis Timms, Thos Saterwhite, Jeremiah Thomas. Proved by the oath of Hollis Timms 16 Sept 1793 before John Pratt, J.P.

C, 284: Claudius Charvin of Chester County sells to Edward Lacey of same, a certain blue roaned mare about 15 hands high, about 8 years old, paces, trots & Canters, for £25 sterling, 4 April 1789. Claud. Charvin ((Seal), Wit: John Miles, Richard Miles.

C, 284-287: Lease and release. 20 & 21 May 1789, Minor Winn of Mill Creek, Fairfield County, esquire, to Thomas Baker Franklin of Chester County, planter, for £ 64 s5, 265 acres on waters of Sandy River, adj. James Huey, granted to said Minor Winn 6 March 1786. M. Winn (LS), Wit: K. T. Strother, Wm. Evans. Acknowledged in open Court by Minor Winn 12 April 1794, D. Evans, Clerk of Fairfield County.

C, 288: John Mills Junr of Chester County for £80 sterling, to George Gill, silver smith, of same, a negro man slave named Guy, 13 June 1789. John Mills (LS), Wit: Arch'd Gill.

C, 288-290: 5 Jan 1792, Robert Jamieson to Gardiner Miller, for ten shillings, 150 acres on Bullskin, a branch of Rocky Creek in Chester County, originally granted to Jasper Rogers 10 July 1766, and conveyed from said Jasper Rogers 21 & 22 Dec 1770 to Reese Hughes, who granted by lease & release 10 & 11 1771 to Revd. Jas Campbell deceased, which said tract devolved to his sons Jas & Alexdr Campbell, who appointed said Robt Jamieson their attorney 10 Feb 1789 to sell said tract. Robert Jamieson (mark) (Seal), Gardiner Miller (LS), Wit: Gardiner Jamieson, Arch'd Boyd.

C, 290-291: 5 Nov 1791, Elizabeth Miller of Camden District, Chester County, to Thomas Miller of same, for ten shillings, 200 acres, being half of 400 acres in Craven County adj. land surveyed for John Mills (surveyed for Josiah Miller now deceased). Elizabeth Miller (mark), Wit: Charles Miller, James Miller, James Wilson. Proved by the oath of James Wilson 3 Dec 1791 before John Bell, J.P.

**C, 291-296**: 26 June 1786, Hugh Whiteside of Chester County, yeoman, to Samuel Leech of York County, yeoman, for £50 sterling, tract granted 7 Nov 1785 to Jane Walker, 200 acres on a branch of Fishing Creek, adj. James Robeson, and said Jane Walker hath impowered the above named Hugh Whiteside by letter of attorney to convey said tract. Hugh Whiteside (LS), Wit: Wm Whiteside, Thos Whiteside, Jas Patton.

Jane Walker of Chester County, SC, spinster, appoints Hugh Whiteside of same, her lawful attorney to sell 200 acres surveyed for her on north fork Fishing Creek, including improvement and Dwelling house that Samuel Galey now lives in, 27 Aug 1785. Jane Walker (X) (LS), Wit: Samuel Lusk, John Walker Junr.

**C, 296-299**: 14 Aug 1777, James Gill, late of Parish of St. Marks, SC, yeoman, to John Cooper of same, yeoman, for £200, tract granted 22 Sept 1769 by SC to James Gill, 200 acres on waters of the south fork of Fishing Creek in Craven County adj. John McNitt Alexander, George Glover deceased, John Davis, George Gill. James Gill (Seal), Wit: Christopher Streight, Jas Cooper, Geo Gill. Proved in Camden District by the oath of Christopher Streight 16 May 1785 before Jas Knox, J.P.

**C, 299-302**: South Carolina, Chester County. 4 Dec 1793, Thomas Roden of county aforesaid, planter, to Denniss Carrell of same, planter, for £90 sterling, 238 acres on waters of Sandy River on a creek called Welches fork, 200 acres granted 21 Jan 1785 to John Dougherty, surveyed 23 Aug 1784, recorded in Book AAAA, page 405, sold by said John Dougherty to said Thomas Roden 15 Feb 1787, also another 200 acres granted to John Dougherty 3 April 1786, recorded in Book KKKK, likewise a tract which Thomas Roden purchased to Martin Elam of 10 acres. Thomas Roden (Seal), Mary Roden (M) (Seal), Wit: Martin Elam, Moses Stone (X), George Elam. Proved by the oath of Martin Elam 15 Dec 1794 before John Pratt, J.P.

**C, 302-303**: South Carolina, Chester County. 31 Dec 1791, James Brown to Alexander Brown, both of state and county aforesaid, for £100, 116 acres on waters of Turkey Creek, part of tract laid out for & Granted to Catharine Brown 23 Jan 1773, and transferred by will of said Catharine Brown at her deceased to said Alexander Brown, and by him to James Brown. James Brown (Seal), Wit: Hambleton Brown, John Reed, George Conn (mark). Proved by the oath of Hambleton Brown 8 May 1792 before Jo. Brown, J. C. C.

**C, 304-308**: Lease and release. 7 & 9 June 1792, Hugh Boyles of Chester County to William Boyd of same, for £35 sterling, 100 acres on a branch of Rocky Creek adj. William Rottenberry, Solomon Holmes, granted 24 Aug

1770. Hugh Boyles (X) (Seal), Wit: Andrew Walker Junior, Andw Walker, Andw Crawford. Proved by the oath of Andrew Walker before John Bell, J.P.

C, 308-310: 19 Jan 1785, Agnes Hannah of Ninety Six District, SC, spinster, to Paul Ferguson of Camden District, for ten shillings, 200 acres on a branch of Rockey Creek adj. James McCluer, Elizabeth White. Agnes Hanna (X) (LS), Wit: William Starling, Thomas Hanna, James Hanna. Proved in Chester County by the oath of James Hanna 27 April 1794 before John Bell, J.P.

C, 310-314: Lease and release. 28 & 29 Feb 1774, George Adams of Craven County to Wm Boyles of same, for £100, tract granted 23 Aug 1770 to Geo Adams, 100 acres on a small branch of Rockey Creek adj. Wm. Rottenberry, Solomon Holmes. George Adams (Seal),wit: Samuel Craig, Andrew Walker, John Bell. Proved 1 Aug 1792 by the oath of Andrew Walker before John Bell, J.P.

C, 315: Elizabeth Miller of Rockey Creek, Chester County, for love and good will to my daughter Jane Knox of Fishing Creek, all my goods & chattles, household furniture, stock, etc., 2 Nov 1791. Elizabeth Miller (mark). Wit: Jas Miller, Charles Miller, Jas Wilson. Proved by the oath of James Wilson 3 Dec 1791 before John Bell, J.P.

C, 315-316: Sarah Golden of Chester County to my illegitimate daughter Salley Golden, a horse, saddle & bridle, 14 Nov 1792. Sarah Golden (mark (Seal), Wit: Richd Taliaferro, Clerk of Chester County.

C, 316-317: Alexander Wilson of Chester county for £19 s13 s2 to Hazel Hardwick of same, a negro girl named Patt or Patsey, 5 Oct 1793. Alexander Wilson (X) (Seal), Wit: John Pratt, Hugh Knox, Philip Noland. Proved by the oath of Philip Noland 5 Oct 1793 before Phil Walker, J.P.

C, 317-318: 27 Oct 1793, Thomas Cabeen of Chester County, Farmer, to Frances Neisbett, for £30, 125 acres on waters of Sandy River, granted to James Houston 2 Oct 1786, and to said Thos Cabeen by deed 23 Feb 1792. Thomas Cabeen (Seal), Wit: James McNeel, David Morrow. Proved by the oath of David Morrow 2 Nov 1793 before Phil Walker, J.P.

C, 318-320: 5 Oct 1793, John Gill Senior, farmer, and wife Sarah, of Chester County, for £50 sterling, 150 acres in Chester County, on Rocky Creek, including part of two different tracts, one granted to George Wier 18 May 1771 and afterwards conveyed by deed 20 Jan 1777 to said John Gill, and the other tract granted to John Gill by grant 20 Oct 1772 on Rocky Creek, at the mouth of a branch on the north side of Rocky Creek, adj. land granted to William Wilie. John Gill (Seal), Wit: William Whiteside, James Gill. Proved by the oath of Wm Whiteside 5 Oct 1793 before John Mills, J.P.

C, 320-323: 1 Sept 1789, John Belton and ___ his wife, of Camden District, surveyor, for £14 sterling to John Miles, tract on north side Broad River on

Mill Creek in Chester County, 100 acres, plat dated 11 Feb 1763. John Belton (Seal), Wit: Benjamin Perkins, J. Holzendorf. Proved in Lancaster County 4 Dec 1790 by the oath of Benjamin Perkins before Andrew Baskin.

C, 323-324: 10 Jan 1792, John Miles of County of Mercer in Kentucky in the state of Virginia, to Joseph Feemster of York County, SC, for £30 sterling, tract on Mill Creek, north side of Broad River, otherwise called Suseys Creek adj. land granted to Wm. Minter, Saml Givens, James Brown, Milles, known by the name of Mahafies land, in Chester County, granted to John Belton 14 Feb 1763, 100 acres. John Miles (Seal), Wit: Wm Miles, John Adair. Proved in Chester County by the oath of Wm Miles 13 Dec 1793 before Wm. Gaston, J. C. C.

C, 324-328: Lease and release. 31 Oct 1791, James Chesnut & Esther his wife of Chester County to Samuel Maphet, planter, of same, for ten shillings sterling, 150 acres on both sides of Little Rockey Creek, a branch of Cattawba River adj. George Cherrey, widow Carr, John Culp, granted 13 Aug 1756 to John Jacob Culp, conveyed from him to James Chesnut 4 & 5 Sept 1787. James Chesnut (Seal), Esther Chesnut (mark) (Seal), Wit: William Maffet, Hugh Park, William Chesnut. Proved by the oath of Hugh Park 2 Jan 1794 before John Bell, J.P.

C, 328-329: 18 Sept 1788, Rice Hughes Junr of Rockey Creek, Chester County, planter, to John Bankhead of Fishing Creek, said county, planter, for £65, tract granted 1 Feb 1768 to Robert Martin, 100 acres on Fishing Creek, recorded in Book BB, page 479. Rice Hughes (Seal), Wit: Joseph Booth, Richard Wyat. Proved by the oath of Richard Wyat 17 July 1793 before John McCreary, J.P.

C, 329-334: Lease and release. 4 & 5 Sept 1787, John Jacob Culp of Camden District, SC, to James Chesnut, planter, for £50 sterling, 150 acres on both sides Little Rocky Creek adj. Jas. Cherrey, Widow Carr, John Culp, granted 13 Aug 1756 to John Jacob Culp. John Jacob Culp (X) (Seal), Wit: Andrew Graham, Alexander Chesnut, John McDill.

C, 334-336: 2 Jan 1794, James Meek of Chester County, planter, to Hance Hambleton of same, for £36 sterling, 140 acres on a branch of Little River & Cobs Creek, part of tract granted to Thomas Kirkpatrick 16 June 1768, conveyed to said James Meek 17 & 18 Sept 1776. James Meek (Seal), Wit: William McQuiston, James Wylie, James Meek. Proved by the oath of William McQuiston 2 Jan 1794 before John Bell, J.P.

C, 336-337: 10 Aug 1793, Thomas Mitchell & Elisabeth his wife of Chester county to Elizabeth Moore of same, for £100 sterling, 190 acres, being a tract granted to Edward Atterberrey 7 Aug 1786 and transferred to said Thomas Mitchell. Thomas Mitchell (X) (Seal), Hepsabeth Mitchell (X) (Seal), Wit: Elias Mitchell, Isaiah Mitchell, David Mitchell. Proved by the oath of Isaiah Mitchell 14 Jan 1794 before John Pratt, J.P.

**C, 337-338**: Nicodemus Barnes of Chester ·County for £10 sterling, to Cornelius Dorely of same, mortgage of a certain gray mare branded RB & three head of cattle, and 25 head of hogs, two beds and furniture, 24 Jan 1794. Nicodemus Barns (Seal), Wit: Phil Walker, Caleb Barns (B). Proved by the oath of Calib Barns 25 Jan 1794 before Philip Walker, J.P.

**C, 338-339**: James Elliott of Lancaster County, SC, relinquish all my claim of a certain piece of land near Broad River in Chester County, for £50 sterling, formerly the property of Jas Elliott deceased, to Robert Elliott, 30 Sept 1793. James Elliott (Seal), Wit: Jo Duglass, Anthony Cox, John Elliott. Proved by the oath of Anthony Cox 31 Dec 1793 before W. Gaston, J. C. C.

**C, 339**: November 26th 1793. This day met at Mr. Valuntine Bell's, Thomas Hail & certain other neighbours on a Examination of a Slanderous report told on Miss Fieldor Bell which should have been told by said Thomas Hail which report the said Hail said he had from a certain woman under an infamious character which he the said Hail says he never believed & does confess his fault in telling after such another. In the presents of Thos Robins (X), William Bell, Thomas House, John Williams, George Conn, John Nielson, John Galliher. Proved by the oath of Wm Bell & John Wilson 25 Jan 1794 before Saml Lacey, D. Clk of Chester County Court.

October 30th 1793. Personally appeared before me Mary Seebree & Being duly sworn according to law deposeth & Saith that she had a report had prevailed by means of a certain Thomas Hail that a certain Fielder Bell had been found guilty of furnication with a certain negro man slave named George, the property of Voluntine Bell, now the said Mary on her oath doth say that she never knew nor heard of the said Fielder being guilty of any such crime, before J. Ker Alexander, J.P.

**C, 340-341**: Plat of 97 acres showing adj. land owners Thomas Humphreys, James Timms.

1 March 1793, Peter Nance & Ursilla his wife of Fairfield County to Sampson Noland of Chester County, for £100 sterling, 97 acres, part of tract of land granted to Thomas Roden 17 Feb 1767, adj. Thomas Humphreys, Jas Timms. Peter Nance (Seal), Wit: William Boyd, Thomas Wilkes (T), Edmond Tilley (X). Proved by the oath of Wm. Boyd in Chester County 23 Dec 1793 before John Pratt, J.P.

**C, 342-343**: 4 Feb 1794, Sampson Noland of Chester County, to Nathan Coffee of same, for £35 sterling, 50 acres on waters of Sandy River, granted to Thomas Roden 17 Feb 1767, and said Thomas Roden conveyed to Peter Nance deceased, and from said Peter Nance deceased to his son Richard Nancy by his will, and from said Richard Nance to his brother Peter, and from said Peter to Sampson Noland. Sampson Noland (Seal), Wit: Nicholas Colvin, William Price. Plat included. Proved by the oath of Nicholas Colvin 4 Feb 1794 before John Pratt, J.P.

C, 344-346: 21 Jan 1794, George Morriss & wife Agnes of Chester County for £50 sterling, to Benjamin Morriss of same, two tracts of land joining together by two separate grants, one granted to said George, 166 acres 6 Oct 1788, recorded in Book XXXX, page 387; the other of 34 acres, a part of grant to Hugh Montgomery and by him conveyed to Moses Reeves and by said Reeves to Christopher Morgan and by said Morgan and Martha his wife to George Morriss 5 Feb 1788. George Morriss (LS), Agnes Morriss (LS), Wit: Josiah Allen, William Sibley, Andrew Hemphill. Proved by the oath of William Sibley 27 Jan 1794 before And'w Hemphill, J.P.

C, 346-349: 24 Nov 1789, Alexander McCown of Chester County to Thomas Stroud of same, for £300, tracts granted 18 May 1773 and 19 Aug 1774 to Alexr McCown, 150 each, on a branch of Rockey [Creek], adj. Wm. Nettles, Barber, Alexr McCown, Wilson, Wiegen, Higins. Alexander McCown (LS), Wit: James McCown, Martin Runnolds. Proved by the oath of James McCown 4 Dec 1793 before John McCreary, J.P.

C, 349-350: Richard Smith of Chester County for £65 sterling to Jonathan McKey of same, one negro girl named Bett about 14 years of age. Richard Smith (Seal), Wit: Thomas Morriss, Burrell Sandifur (X), George Morriss. Proved by the oath of Burrell Sandifur 26 Dec 1793 before Andw Hemphill, J.P.

C, 350: South Carolina, Chester County. Personally appeared James Walker of county aforesaid and made oath that a certain grey or white horse about 14 hands three inches high about nine or ten years old branded on the mounting shoulder 3E which said James Walker tolled before me, that the said horse is dead & that not through any neglect of his but by worms, 23 Nov 1793. Jas Walker, John McCreary, J.P. Deposition of John Walker 23 Nov 1793 also.

C, 351-352: 26 Jan 1794, Jonathan Jones & Bethsheba his wife of Chester County to John Thompson of same, for £20 sterling, 55 acres, part of tract granted to Jonathan Jones 2 Oct 1786 for 114 acres. Jonathan Jones (LS), Bethsheba Jones (mark) (LS), Wit: Wm Boyd, Joseph Timms, John Walker. Proved by the oath of John Walker 1 March 1794 before John Mills, J.P.

C, 352-354: Frances Henderson of £25 sterling to Abraham Ferguson of same, one grey geldin about 13½ hands high, one sorrel horse 13½ hands high, one black horse cold, also nine head of cattle marked with a crop off each ear & A split[?] in each ear, and twelve head of hogs with the mark aforesaid, and household and kitchen furniture, 8 Jan 1794. Frances Henderson (mark) (LS), Wit: Philip Walker, Saml Jack (I). Proved by the oath of Samuel Jack 8 Jan 1794 before Phil Walker, J.P.

C, 354-355: 18 Oct 1793, John Hagans and wife Elizabeth of Chester County to Alexander Crafford of same, for £5 sterling, tract of 14 acres on the bank of Cattawba River beginning per a certificate of John Gaston dated 19 Nov

1772, part of tract granted to John McClenahan. John Hagans (Seal), Elizabeth Hagans (Seal), Wit: Hugh Hagans, Robt King, Wm Hageains.

C, 355-357: So Carolina, Chester County. 13 Nov 1793, Dennis Carrell of county aforesaid, planter, to John Colvin of same, for £50 sterling, 100 acres on waters of Flinthems Creek of Sandy River adj. Dennis Carrell, Richard Head, James Huey, part of 265 acres granted to Minor Winn 6 March 1786, surveyed 25 Nov 1785, recorded in Book HHHH, page 158, conveyed by Minor Winn to Thomas Baker Franklin 22 May 1789, and then to Dennis Carrell 17 May 1791. Dennis Carrell (LS), Sarah Carrell (LS), Wit: Nicholas Colvin, Joseph Rice, Jesse Simpson. Plat included. Proved by the oath of Nicholas Colvin 23 Jan 1794 before John Pratt, J.P.

C, 357-358: 17 Jan 1789, Owen Evans of Chester County to Mary Evans of same, for £50 sterling, 100 acres on waters of Sandy River, south fork, surveyed for Owen Evans 1 Jan 1771, recorded in Book JJJJ, page 456. Owens Evans (Seal), Wit: Richard Evans, Adam Williamson. Proved by the oath of Richard Evans 24 Jan 1794 before Richd Taliaferro, Clk Chester County.

C, 358-360: 29 July 1793, Abraham Myers of Chester County to Nathaniel Norward of same, for £100, 50 acres, part of 640 acres granted to James Atterberry 4 Sept 1786 on Smiths Creek, a branch of Brushy Fork, adj. Nathal Norward, Wm Norward. Abraham Myers (Seal), Sarah Myers (X) (Seal), Wit: Elijah Nunn, Josiah Cook, Allen Mayfield. Proved by the oath of Allen Mayfield 19 Dec 1793 before Elijah Nunn, J.P.

C, 360-361: 29 July 1793, Abraham Myers of Chester County to William Norward of same, for £100, 50 acres, part of 640 acres granted to James Atterberry 4 Sept 1786 on Smiths Creek, a branch of Brushy Fork, adj. Nathal Norward, Wm Norward. Abraham Myers (Seal), Sarah Myers (X) (Seal), Wit: Elijah Nunn, Josiah Cook, Allen Mayfield. Proved by the oath of ALlen Mayfield 19 Dec 1793 before Elijah Nunn, J.P.

C, 362: John Edward of Chester County for £80 sterling to Arthur Shufield of same, a negro boy named Jacob about 17 years old, 16 Nov 1792. John Edward (Seal), Wit: Alexdr Crafford, James Patton. Proved by the oath of Alexander Crafford 28 Jan 1794 before John McCreary, J.P.

C, 362-364: South Carolina, Pinckney District. 7 Aug 1793, Thomas Stevenson and Mary his wife to James Egger, both of Chester County, said district, for £30 sterling, 100 acres, part of lands granted to James Adair by patent 5 Feb 1787 adj. Thos Hail, Jas Adair, Wm Minter, including the improvements. Thomas Stevenson (Seal), Mary Stevenson (Seal), Wit: William Egger, John James Norton, Sarah Stevenson. 20 Jan 1794 proved by the oath of Wm Egger before Richd Taliaferro, Clk Chester County Court.

C, 364-366: 18 May 1793, David Hopkins of Chester County to Elias Mitchell of same, for £100 sterling, tract on north side Broad River, part of tract granted to David Hopkins 16 July 1784, on the upper side of the mouth of little Turkey Creek on the bank of Broad River. Dd. Hopkins (Seal), Wit: Mary Hopkins (Seal), Wit: Thomas Mitchell (X), Ferd'd Hopkins, H. Anderson. Proved by the oath of Thomas Mitchell 16 Nov 1793 before Elijah Nunn, J.P.

C, 366-368: 16 May 1793, Ferdinand Hopkins of Chester County to Thomas Mitchell of same, for £100 sterling, part of tract granted to James Oneal 26 Aug 1774 and since conveyed by said Oneal to Ferdinand Hopkins on north side Broad River on the bank of Broad River, below Wilcoxes branch adj. Thomas Hughey, 202 acres. Ferd'd Hopkins (Seal), Wit: Elias Mitchell, Isaiah Mitchell. Proved by the oath of Isaiah Mitchell 16 Nov 1794 before Elijah Nunn, J.P.

C, 368-369: 26 Oct 1793, James Timms, Admr. of George Carter deceased, of Chester county, for £5 to Samuel Carter, a tract on waters of Sandy River, 32 acres. James Timms (Seal), Wit: Joseph Bennett, Thomas Oneel. Proved by the oath of J. Bennett and Thomas Oneel 26 Oct 1793 before Richd Taliaferro, Clk Chester County Court.

C, 369-370: John McGlamery of Chester County, yeoman, for £50 sterling, to James English of same, cloathier, a negro boy named Sank about 19 years of age, 11 May 1792. John McGlamery (Seal), Wit: John Mills, Mary Mills. Proved by the oath of John Mills before Richd Taliaferro, Clk Chester County.

C, 370-371: 26 Oct 1793, James Timms, Admr. of George Carter deceased, of Chester county, for £10 to Thomas ONeel, a tract of 89 acres. James Timms (Seal), Wit: Joseph Bennett, Saml Carter. Proved by the oath of Joseph Bennett and Saml Carter 26 Oct 1793 before Richd Taliaferro, Clk Chester County Court.

C, 371-372: 30 Sept 1793, John Carter and wife Elizabeth of Chester county to Henry Cotterell of same, for £100 sterling, tract on waters of Sandy River, 400 acres, recorded in Grant Book SSS, page 168. John Carter (Seal), Elizabeth Carter (X) (Seal), Wit: William Atteberry. Proved 2 Oct 1793 by the oath of William Atterberry before Richd Taliaferro, Clk Chester County Court.

C, 373-374: 29 March 1793, Thomas Eakins & wife Elizabeth of Chester County to Robert Eakin of same, for £24, tract on waters of Mill Creek including the plantation on which the said Robert Eakin now lives, 150 acres, granted to said Thomas Eakin 8 July 1774. Thomas Eakins (Seal), Elizabeth Eakin (Seal), Wit: Robert Davis, Thomas Eakin Junr, Alexander Eakin. Proved by the oath of Thomas Eakin Junr 24 Jan 1794 before Richd Taliaferro, Clk Chester County Court.

**C, 374-376:** 25 March 1793, Hugh McCown of Chester County to James McCown of same, for £20 sterling, 100 acres on a branch of Little River, part of a tract granted to Edward Nixon in 1772, and conveyed from sd Nixon to Robert McCown by lease and release and from him to Hugh McCown. Hugh McKeown (Seal), Wit: Wm. McQuiston, Isaac Bean, Samuel McCown. Proved by the oath of Samuel McKeown 28 Aug 1793 before John Bell, J.P.

**C, 376-377:** 8 Oct 1793, John Hagans of Chester County to Alexander Crafford of same, for £5 sterling, tract of 263 acres granted to John Lance, on north west side of Catawba River. John Hagans (Seal), Elizabeth Hagans (Seal), Wit: Hugh Hagans, Robert King, William Hageains.

**C, 377-378:** 12 Jan 1791, William Worthy of Chester County, to Thomas Cowsart of same, for £1 lawful money, 100 acres, part of 2331 acres, granted to David Hopkins 15 July 1784. William Worthy (mark) (Seal), Wit: James McCall, Frances Rea (X), John Cousart. Proved by the oath of John Cowsart and Francis Ray 25 Jan 1794. Recorded 16 March 1794.

END OF DEED BOOK C

**D, 1-3**: 19 Oct 1793, Christopher Strong of Chester County, planter, to William Blackstokes of same, for £150 sterling, 350 acres on waters of Fishing Creek in the forks of said creek, originally granted to sundry persons & at sundry times; to Charles Strong 200 acres 4 May 1775, and 100 of which was granted to Joseph Mitchell and the remaining part to Robert Harper, in a deed of conveyance by John Hays to said Christopher Strong 23 Aug 1792, recorded in Chester County Deed Book C, page 283, and remaining 50 acres granted to said Christopher Strong 1 Feb 1790. Christopher Strong (Seal), Wit: John Mills, George Hill, Edward Blackstock. Proved by the oath of George Hill 20 Oct 1793 before John Mills, J.P.

**D, 3-4**: Joseph Hurst of Northumberland County, Virginia, for loving affection to my daughter Judith Nutt Corbell, one negro girl Sarah with all her future increase instead of a negro girl Hannah being sold for a good purpose and was made over in a deed by Peter Corbell to me to me the said Joseph Hurst as a trustee for the said Judith N. Corbell in a former deed dated 13 Dec 1784, dated 21 March 1789. Joseph Hurst (Seal), Wit: Rogers Sinclair, Joseph Hurst Junr. Proved at a court held for Northumberland County on Monday the 19th October 1789 by the oath of Joseph Hurst Junr. Certified by Thomas Pollard, deputy Clerk of said county.

**D, 4-5**: Peter Corbell of Northumberland County, Virginia, for love and affection to my wife Judith Nutt Corbell, to Joseph Hurst, trustee, four negroes Winney, Hannah, Billy and Alse and their future increase, with one good feather bed & furniture, 13 Dec 1784. Peter Corbell (Seal), Wit: Elisha Harcum, Zacariah Barr. Acknowledged in open court Northumberland County 13 Dec 1784. Catesby Jones, Clk. Certified by Thomas Pollard, deputy Clerk of said county.

**D, 5-6**: 30 Dec 1793, William Bell & Mary his wife of Chester County to John Nichols Bell of same, for £30 sterling, tract on Susey Bowls branch adj. Thomas Robins, John Nichols Bell, granted 13 May 1768 to Jas Green by SC. William Bell (Seal), Mary Bell (X) (Seal), Wit: James Robison, Joseph Robison, Amie McBey (X). Proved by the oath of James Robison 31 Dec 1793 before Wm Gaston, J. C. C.

**D, 7-9**: 2 Oct 1780 [sic for 1784?], John Walker and Ann his wife of Camden District, SC, to John Hagans of same, for £14 sterling, tract granted to Robert McClanchan 5 Feb 1754, a tract on west side Cattawba River, then in Anson County, North Carolina, which tract said McClenehan conveyed to Thomas Land, 193 acres, and the said Thomas Land conveyed to George Sleager Senior of Northampton County, Pensylvania, and by said Sleager to said Geo Sleager Junr, further Isaac Taylor obtained the Kings Patent 8 July 1774 (since running the boundary line between North & South Carolina), for 350 acres on west side of the Cattawba River in South Carolina, 14 acres whereof said Taylor conveyed to the said Geo Sleager Junr 21 Feb 1775, and is part of the same land which was conveyed to said George Sleager Junr, and the same 14 acres conveyed to said John Walker 23 Aug 1778. John Walker (Seal), Ann

Walker (Seal), Wit: John Burnet, Margaret Burnet, Jane Patton (mark). Proved by the oath of Jane Patton in Chester County 14 Sept 1792.

**D, 9-11**: 2 Oct 1784, John Walker and Ann his wife of Camden District, SC, to John Hagans of same, for £178 s11 d5 sterling, tract granted to Casper Culp 5 Feb 1754, 200 acres on west side Cattawba River, then in Anson County, North Carolina, which tract said Casper Culp conveyed to John Lance, and the said John Lance to John Walker, adj. Gasper Sleager, age 1000 acres belonging to said Casper Culp 25 Sept 1753, 52 acres and nine perches of which tract conveyed to John Lance 23 Aug 1778. John Walker (Seal), Ann Walker (Seal), Wit: John Burnet, Margaret Burnet, Jane Patton (mark). Proved by the oath of Jane Patton in Chester County 14 Sept 1792.

**D, 12-13**: 21 Dec 1793, George Roden of Chester County and wife Darkes to Abner Wilkes of same, for £65 sterling, tract on waters of Sandy River, part of tract granted to James Stepp 26 July 1774 and conveyed by Stepp to John McColpin and by him to James Wilkison and by Wilkeson to Abraham Myers & Sarah his wife, adj. Wilkes line, Joseph Watson, Ferguson, to Starns Creek, Bonds' line. George Roden (X) (Seal), Darkis Roden (X), Wit: Elijah Nunn, Jesse Meadows. Proved by the oath of Jesse Meadows 21 Dec 1793 before Elijah Nunn, J.P.

**D, 13-15**: 16 July 1792, John Reynolds of Fairfield County, to Thomas Stroud of Chester County, for £50, 270 acres in Chester County on waters of Rockey Creek, adj. Robt Williams, Wm Wilson, John Smith, Hugh Wilson, John Brown, granted 1 Aug 1791 to said John Reynolds. John Reynolds (I) (Seal), Wit: Thomas Neely, Isbell Weer (X), John McCreary. Proved by the oath of Thomas Neely 10 Nov 1792 before John McCreary, J.P.

**D, 15-16**: 1 Aug 1793, Edward Atterberry of Chester County, SC, to Levi Myers of same, for £100 sterling, 20 acres, part of tract granted to Edward Atterbury on the south west side of Brushey Fork Creek, including the dwelling house and mills now in possession of Abraham Myers. Edward Atterberry (X) (Seal), Wit: Elijah Nunn, Obediah Mayfield, Abraham Myers. Proved 25 Jan 1794 by the oath of Abraham Myers before Richd Taliaferro, Clk Chester County.

**D, 17-18**: 10 Dec 1793, Col. David Hopkins and wife Mary of Chester county to Matthew McCalla of same, for £40 sterling, 250 acres on waters of Broad River on little Turkey Creek granted to David Hopkins 16 July 1784, part of tract of 2331 acres. David Hopkins (Seal), Mary Hopkins (Seal), Wit: James McCalla, John Anderson, James McCalla. Proved by the oath of James McCalla 20 Jan 1794 before Elijah Nunn, J.P.

**D, 18-20**: 25 Jan 1794, James Hughey of Chester County, SC, to John Franklin of same, for £20 sterling, 34 acres, part of tract granted to William Cockrell (Bounty) and made over toe said James Hughey, 100 acres granted to William Cockrell 2 July 1792, on waters of Sandy River, adj. Thomas Baker, Major

Minor Winn (Plat included). James Huey (Seal), Wit: Richard Evans, Wm. Stuart. Proved by the oath of Richard Evans 25 Jan 1794 before John Pratt, J.P.

D, 20-23: Lease and release. 15 & 16 Feb 1788, William Ford Senior of Chester County to William Storman of same, for £10 sterling, tract on Heages branch of Rockey Creek adj. Wm Ford Senior, Samuel Erwin, David Carrell, granted to Wm Ford Senior 6 April 1786, 25 acres. William Ford (Seal), Wit: James Clark, John Yarborough, William Ford. Proved by the oath of John Yarborough 21 March 1788 before And'w Hemphill, J.P.

D, 23-26: Lease and release. 15 & 16 Feb 1788, William Ford Senior of Chester County to William Storman of same, for £20 sterling, 50 acres on Heages branch of Rockey Creek adj. William Sandifur, part of tract granted to William Sandifur and sold to William Ford. William Ford (Seal), Wit: James Clark, John Yarborough, William Ford. Proved by the oath of John Yarborough 21 March 1788 before And'w Hemphill, J.P. Receipt witnessed 13 Dec 1793 by And'w Dun, John Ford Junr (X).

D, 26-28: Lease and release. 15 & 16 Feb 1788, William Ford Senior of Chester County to William Storman of same, for £10 sterling, tract granted to Isham Dansby 5 Jan 1773, 27 acres, part of tract formerly belonging to John Land & conveyed to Henry Hales and then to William Ford, adj. William Sandefur Senior, John Lott, Wm. Ford. William Ford (Seal), Wit: James Clark, John Yarborough, William Ford. Proved by the oath of John Yarborough 21 March 1788 before And'w Hemphill, J.P.

D, 29-32: Lease and release. 15 Nov 1792, Isaac Garrick & Elizabeth Garrick to Richard Gather, for £60, 289 acres on waters of Rockey Creek adj. John Winn Junior, John Ellis, granted to Jacob Brown 22 Jan 1787. Isaac Garrick (Seal), Elizabeth Garrick (X) (Seal), Wit: John Winn, John Gunthrop, Andrew Hemphill. Proved by the oath of John Winn 15 Nov 1792 before Andrew Hemphill, J.P.

D, 32-34: 7 Sept 1791, Abraham Myers and Sarah is wife of Chester County to George Roden of Union County, for £70, tract on waters of Sandy River, part of tract granted to James Stepp 26 July 1774, and conveyed by Stepp to John McColpin, and by John McColpin to James Wilkeson and by Wilkeson to Abraham Myers, adj. Wilkeson's line, on Starns Creek, Bond's line. Abraham Myers (Seal), Sarah Myers (X) (Seal), Wit: Joseph Watson, Abner Wilkes, Jeremiah Roden (mark). Proved by the oath of Abner Wilkes 21 Dec 1793 before Elijah Nunn, J.P.

D, 34-36: 12 Nov 1793, James Bigham of Rockey Creek in Chester County, and wife Jane planter, to James Martin of same, planter, for £20, tract granted 31 Aug 1774 to Jas Bigham, on waters of Rockey Creek, 450 acres adj. John Walker, Wm McKennies, recorded in Book SSS, page 397. James Bigham (Seal), Jane Bigham (X) (Seal), Wit: Saml Bigham, George Wier. Proved by the oath of Geo Weir 38 Jan 1794 before Rich'd Taliaferro, Clk Chester County.

**D, 37**: Thomas Baker Franklin of Chester County, planter, for £60 sterling, to Notly Coats of same, one negro wench named Hannah about 25 years of age, 20 Dec 1793. Thomas B. Franklin (Seal), Wit: Charles Coats, Jas Coats (X).

**D, 37-39**: 21 Jan 1794, William Wood & wife Sarah of Chester County to John Allen of same, for £25 sterling, 75 acres, part of tract granted to Edward Wilson, 250 acres on north side of Broad River on a small fork of Sandy River called Stoney fork, adj. John Baker, Edward Wilson, and said Edward Wilson did make over to Wm Wood by deed 15 April 1792, and recorded in Chester count 17 Sept 1792 in Book B, page 364, 25 acres adj. Stephen Siddle's line (plat included). William Wood (Seal), Sarah Wood (X) (Seal), Wit: Thomas Jinkins, William Boyd, William Mobley. Proved by the oath of William Boyd 27 Jan 1794 before John Pratt, J.P. Sarah Wood, wife of Wm. Wood, relinquished dower 27 Jan 1795 before John Pratt, J.P.

**D, 40-42**: 10 Dec 1793, David Eakins & Margaret his wife of Chester County to John Quenton of same, for £30 sterling, 125 acres on waters of Turkey Creek, part of 300 acres granted to David Eakins 23 May 1787. David Eakins (wax), Margaret Eakins (mark) (wax), Wit: James Young, James Quenton, James Hendrick. Proved by the oath of Jas Quenton 28 Jan 1794 before Elijah Nunn, J.P.

**D, 42-45**: Lease and release. 1 & 2 Dec 1793, James McKown & Wife Hannah of Pinckney District, Chester County, to John Prentice of same, for £20, 133 acres on Fishing Creek adj. Jas McKown, John Leonard, Nicholas Thompson, recorded in Grant Book BBBB No. 2, page 49, granted 6 Feb 1792, and conveyed to James McCown 7 Dec 1792. James McCown (wax), Hannah McCown (X) (wax), Wit: John McKown, Alexander McKown, James Ratch (mark). Proved by the oath of Capt. John McCown 23 Jan 1794 before John McCreary, J.P.

**D, 45-48**: 7 Dec 1792, Voluntine Weathers & wife Sarah of Camden District, Fairfield County, to James McCown of Chester County, for £-- sterling, 133 acres on Fishing Creek, Chester County, adj. James McCown, John Leonard, Nicholas Thompson, William Nettles, recorded in Grant Book BBBB No. 2, page 49, and another tract of 62 acres adj. James Cloud, on Fishing Creek, recorded in Grant Book BBBB No. 2, page 51, the 133 acres granted 6 Feb 1792 and the 62 acres granted 7 May 1792. Voluntine Weathers (mark (Seal), Wit: John McCown, Wm Morris ()X. Proved by the oath of Capt. John McCown 22 Jan 1794 before John McCreary, J.P.

**D, 48-50**: 13 Aug 1793, John Bigham (the oldest brother of Jane Bigham deceased) of Mecklenburg County, North Carolina, planter, to Samuel Telford of Chester County, SC, for £25 sterling, 100 acres in Chester County on waters of the north fork of Rockey Creek, known by the name of the Bever Dam, adj. John Bell, Jacob Sutton, John Gaston, Rev. Mr. McGarra's, granted 9 Nov 1774 to Jane Bigham. John Bigham (Seal), Wit: Joseph Gaston, George Graham, James Graham. Proved in Chester County by the oath of Joseph Gaston 27 Jan 1794 before John McCreary, J.P.

**D, 50-52**: 18 July 1786, John Dick & Margaret his wife of Chester County to Joseph Montgomery of same, for £185 SC money, 100 acres on waters of Rockey Creek adj. Robert Weathers, John McCown. John Dick (Seal), Margaret Dick (X) (Seal), Wit: James Montgomery, John McClurkin. Proved by the oath of James Montgomery 28 Jan 1794 before Hugh Whiteside.

**D, 52-54**: 22 Aug 1774, Robert Kirkpatrick & wife Agnes of Craven County, SC, to William Wylie of same, for £100 SC money, 100 acres on west side Cattawba River adj. Archibald Powel. Robert Kirkpatrick (Seal), Agnes Kirkpatrick (Seal), Wit: James Grier, James Dunn, Wm. Rottenberry (M). Proved in Chester County by the oath of James Dunn 28 Jan 1794 before Hugh Whiteside.

**D, 55-57**: 10 May 1786, James Grier & wife Martha of Maclinburgh County, North Carolina, to James Dunn of Chester County, SC, for £800 old South Carolina currency, 200 acres on waters of Cattawba River between said river and Fishing Creek adj. John Fleming, Jane Campbell, George Sleeker, John Walker. James Grier (Seal), Martha Grier (Seal), Wit: James Mountgomery, Samuel Atkins. Proved in Chester County by the oath James Montgomery 28 Jan 1794 before Hugh Whiteside.

**D, 57-59**: 6 Aug 1774, John Fleming and wife Martha of Craven County, SC, to James Greer of same, for £100 SC currency, 200 acres on waters of the Cattawba River between said river and fishing Creek adj. John Flemming, Jane Campbell, George Sleeker, John Walker. John Fleming (Seal), Martha Fleming (X) (Seal), Wit: John Davis, John Burnett, Wm. Wylie. Proved by the oath of William Wylie 28 Jan 1794 before Hugh Whiteside.

**D, 59-63**: 25 March 1793, John McCown of Chester County to James McCown of same, for £5 sterling, 37 acres on a branch of Little River, granted to John McCown 4 June 1787, recorded in Book VVVV, page 92. John McCown (Seal), Wit: William McQueston, Bean Isaac, Samuel McKown. Proved by the oath of Samuel McCown 28 Aug 1793 before John Bell, J.P.

**D, 63-69**: Lease and release. 31 July & 1 Aug 1792, Alexander Johnston, deputy Surveyor, of Chester County, Pinckney District, to Samuel McCown, son of Hugh McCown, of same, for £20 sterling, 100 acres, part of 1410 acres granted to said Alexdr Johnson 1 Jan 1787. Alexandr Johnston (Seal), Wit: John Currey, James McKeown. Proved by the oath of James McKown 11 March 1793 before John Bell, J.P.

**D, 69-70**: Charles Coats of Chester County, planter, for £50 sterling, to Notley Coats, a negro boy named Harry about 18 years of age. Charles Coats (C) (wax), Wit: Alexander Johnston, Samuel Craige. Proved 28 Jan 1794 by the oath of Samuel Craige before Richd Taliaferro, Clk of Chester County.

**D, 70-71**: Charles Coats of Chester County, planter, for £40 sterling, to Notley Coats, a negro wench named Clare about 22 years of age. Charles Coats (C) (wax), Wit: Alexander Johnston, Samuel Craige. Proved 28 Jan 1794 by the oath of Samuel Craige before Richd Taliaferro, Clk of Chester County.

**D, 71-72**: Charles Coats of Chester County, planter, for £15 sterling, to Notley Coats, a negro girl named Esther about 3 years of age. Charles Coats (C) (wax), Wit: Alexander Johnston, Samuel Craige. Proved 28 Jan 1794 by the oath of Samuel Craige before Richd Taliaferro, Clk of Chester County.

**D, 72-75**: James Smith of Craven County on Fishing Creek and wife Matty to James McCammon on Fishing Creek, same county, weaver, for £200, 200 acres on the west side of the Cattawba River & north side of Main Fishing Creek on Smith's branch commonly called the Still house branch, ad. Mary Smith, tract granted to John Smith by North Carolina in 1768, and said John Smith by his will did give to Jas Smith, 10 July 1782. James Smith (Seal), Martha Smith (mark) (Seal), Wit: David Hunter, William McCammon (X). Proved by the oath of William McCammon 21 Feb 1784 before Hugh Whiteside.

**D, 75-78**: 3 Sept 1771, Abraham Dye & wife Sarah of Craven County, SC, for £100, to William Leard of same, 150 acres, part of tract granted 7 April 1770 to Abraham Dye for 300 acres on a branch of Rockey Creek. Abram Dye (wax) (Seal), Sarah Dye (wax), Wit: Rees Hughes, Thos Garrott (T), Elisha Garrott (E). Proved 3 April 1771 by the oath of Thomas Garrott before Peter Grant.

**D, 78-80**: _____ 1776, Susanna Wade, Spinster, to William Herbison, Weaver, both of Province of SC, for £200, 200 acres on waters of Saludy on the north side of said river adj. Robt Spin[?], John Williamson, William Steward, John Glenn, Wm Cox, said 100 acres granted to said Susanna Wade 8 July 1774. Susanna Wade (X), Wit: Conrod Fethner, Sarah Tinesly (X). Proved by the oath of Conrod Fethner 27 -- 1779 before William Arther, J.P.

**D, 81**: John Rainey of Chester County, planter, for love, good will and affection to my son Samuel Rainey of same county, planter, at my death, 75 acres, part of tract of land I now live on, the north side of the tract with the old plantation on it, 1 Jan 1790. John Rainey (X) (Seal), Wit: Frances Greenwood, James Pratt (P). Proved by the oath of James Pratt 20 March 1794 before John Pratt, J.P.

**D, 82-83**: South Carolina, Pinckney District. 18 Dec 1793, John Ferguson of County of Pendleton, SC, planter, to John Ray of same, planter, for £90 sterling, 256 acres granted to said John Ferguson 7 May 1787 on waters of Sandy River adj. Widow Ferguson, Jas Douglass, Jas Bigham, James Pagan, Peter Coonrod. John Ferguson (Seal), Wit: Robert Owen, Samuel Lacey Senr,

John Ramsey. Proved by the oath of John Ramsey 28 Dec 1794 before John Mills, J.P.

**D, 83-85:** 11 Nov 1793, John Fleeming the elder of the Town of Columbia, to John Fleeming the younger, son & heir apparent of the said John Fleeming the elder, of same place, for natural love and affection, all the lands & *personal property hereinafter mentioned, to wit, one tract of 327 acres on Mill Creek west side of Cattawba River granted to James Land & by him conveyed to Jacob Hanas Culp to the said John Fleeming the elder; three negroes Bob, Nan & Doll, my new waggon, geers & five horses, also the house & lot now in possession of said John Fleeming the elder, with household furniture. Jno Fleeming Senr (wax), Wit: John Clark, Joseph Fleming, Ann Work Fleming. Proved in Camden District, Richland County by the oath of John Clark 13 Nov 1794 before John Calvert, J.P. Recorded in Richland County Deed Book A, folio 549 and 500, 14 Nov 1793. Examined by Martyn Atkins, D. C. C.

**D, 85-86:** 25 July 1789, Francis Watson of Camden District, Chester County, to Robert Watson of same, for £25 sterling, 50 acres, part of tract of 100 acres laid out to said Francis Watson on waters of Sandy River on north side of the River, on the old Saludy Road adj. Thomas Jenkins, Allen Burton. Francis Watson (mark) (Seal), Wit: Thomas Hughs, John Watson. Proved by the oath of Thomas Hughs Junr 15 March 1794 before Elijah Nunn, J.P.

**D, 87-88:** 15 Sept 1792, John Peoples of Macklinburgh County, North Carolina, to William Merrian of Fairfield County, SC, for £20 sterling, tract in Chester County on waters of Rockey Creek, 300 acres granted to Margaret Peoples in September 1768. John Peoples (Seal), Hannah Peoples (mark) (Seal), Wit: Thomas McCulley, John Long.

**D, 88-91:** Grant. For £9 6/8 sterling paid by Francis Bremar & Peter Freneau, into the Treasury, as tenants in common & not as joint tenants, 400 acres (surveyed for Richard Allen 30 Sept 1784) in the District of Camden on waters of Sandy River adj. John Ozburns, John Sealy, Peter Sealy, John Wood, 500 acres, 3 April 1786. Plat included, certified 1 March 1786, recorded 7 Dec 1786 by D. Mazyck, Register. Assigned by Francis Bremar & Peter Freneau of Charleston for five shillings to Richard Allen of Sandy River, 7 Dec 1786. Wit: Peter Neufville, Robert Forster. Recorded in Book V No. 5, page 519, 7 Dec 1786. Proved in Charleston District by the oath of Robert Forster 7 Dec 1786 before John Vanderhorst, J.P. [This deed is also found in South Carolina Deed Abstracts 1783-1788, page 324, by Brent H. Holcomb.]

**D, 91-92:** An Inventory of the goods & Chattles of Elizabeth Miller of Rockey, Chester county, as delivered by deed of gift unto Jeannet Knox, Fishing Creek, County aforesaid, dated 2 Nov 1791, 7 horses, 12 cows, 7 sheep, 15 hogs, 1 waggon with her appurtenances, household furniture consisting of beds & bedding &c., 2 Nov 1791. Elizabeth Miller (mark). Wit: Saml Wright, James

Miller, Charles Miller, James Willson. Proved by the oath of James Willson 2 Dec 1791 before John Bell, J.P.

**D, 92-97**: Lease and release. 18 & 19 Nov 1775, William Bond & his wife of Craven County, SC, to Edwards Henderson of same, for £300, 100 acres adj. John Bond, near Sealys Creek of Sandy River. William Bond (Seal), Alce Bond (B) (Seal), Wit: William Gaston, John McCluer, Martha McCluer. Proved in Camden District by the oath of William Gaston before Willm Brown, J.P. [The release shows the wife of William Bond as signing by mark "Marth Bond."]

**D, 98-102**: Lease and release. 14 & 16 April 1770, Moses Bond of Craven County, SC, to William Bond of same, for £100, 100 acres adj. John Bond on Sealys Creek a branch of Sandy River. Moses Bond (X) (Seal), Usly Bond (X) (Seal), Wit: Richard Jenkins, John Davis, Awbrey Noland. Proved in Craven County by the oath of Richard Jenkins 16 April 1770 before Thos Fletchall.

**D, 103-104**: 1 Oct 1793, Stephen Ferguson of Chester County to Nathaniel Henderson of same, for £100 sterling, 100 acres on waters of Turkey Creek. Stephen Ferguson (Seal), Wit: Richard Wright. Proved 1 Oct 1798 by the oath of Richard Wright before Rich'd Taliaferro, Clk Chester County.

**D, 105-108**: 16 Sept 1793, William Rainey and wife Elinor of Chester County to William Robinson of same, for £50 sterling, 100 acres granted to said Rainey, recorded in Book WWW, page 458. William Rainey Senr (mark) (Seal), Elinor Rainey (mark) (Seal), Wit: Charles M. Boyd, David Boyd, William Rainey. Proved by the oath of Charles Boyd 1 March 1794 before John Bell, J.P.

**D, 108-110**: 13 Nov 1793, Jeremiah Thomas & Mary his wife of Chester County to Mary Sims of same, for £85 sterling, parcel of land whereon they now live except 68 acres conveyed to several persons &* now in the possession of John Carter, said tract containing 200 acres before the division, now 132 acres. Jeremiah Thomas (Seal), Mary Thomas (X) (Seal), Wit: Lewis Sanders (X), William Sims, D. Sims. Proved 2 Nov 1793 by the oath of William Sims who swore that Jeremiah Thomas Mary his wife conveyed to Mary Sims, widow of Nathan Sims, before Rich'd Taliaferro, Clk C. C. C.

**D, 110-112**: 8 Nov 1793, William Watson of Chester County and wife Bethiah to John Watson of same, for £10 sterling, 100 acres granted 9 Sept 1774 to Leonard Pratt and conveyed to said William Watson, on Martins branch of Sandy River. William Watson (X) (Seal), Bethiah Watson (X) (Seal), Wit: Richard Yarborough, John Hedgpeth (X), Absolum Littlefield (X). Proved by the oath of Absolum Littlefield 13 Nov 1793 before John Pratt, J.P.

**D, 112-116**: South Carolina, Chester County. William Watson & Bethiah his wife for £50 to John Hedgpeth of Fairfield County, 78½ acres on NE side Broad River on Martins branch of the south fork of Sandy River, it being the east part of 939 acres granted to William Head Senr 5 March 1787 but transferred from said Wm Head to Wm Watson, 9 Nov 1793. William Watson (X) (Seal), Bethiah Watson (B) (Seal), Wit: John Watson, Wm Grubs, Enoch Grubs (O). Proved by the oath of Enoch Grubs 29 March 1794 before John Pratt, J.P.

**D, 116-119**: South Carolina, Chester County. John Watson & Bethiah his wife for £60 to Enoch Grubs of Fairfield County, 100 acres on Martins branch of Sandy River, granted to Leonard Pratt 9 Sept 1774, memorial entered in Book M No. 13, page 406 conveyed from Leonard Pratt to William Watson 28 Oct 1787, recorded in Chester County Book B, page 60, also transferred from said William Watson to John Watson 8 Nov 1793. William Watson (Seal), Bethiah Watson (X) (Seal), Wit: Eli Cornwell, John Hedgpeth (X), William Grubs. Proved by the oath of John Hedgpeth 29 March 1794 before John Pratt, J.P.

**D, 120-123**: 2 -- 1779, William McKinney of the Parish of St. Marks, SC, yeoman, to William Manson of same, yeoman, for £2000, 150 acres, part of grant 8 Aug 1774 to John McKinney Senr, 300 acres in Craven County on Tinkers Creek, fork of Fishing Creek adj. John McFadden, said William McKinney, William Taylor, Henry Culp, Augustin Culp, James Neely, conveyed to William McKinney 1777. William McKinney (X) (Seal), Wit; Wm Willey, John McKinney. Proved in Camden District by the oath of William Willey 7 April 1785 before Jas Knox, J.P.

**D, 123-127**: 20 Dec 1785, William Manson of State of North Carolina, yeoman, to Thomas Farrel of Camden District, SC, tract granted 11 Aug 1775 to John McKinney, 140 acres, part of 300 acres on Tinkers Creek fork of Fishing Creek adj. John McFadden, Wm McKinney, Wm. Taylor, Henry Culp, Augusteen Culp, James Neely, conveyed 2 April 1777 to Wm McKinney and then sold to Wm Manson 150 acres of said tract, 2 Nov 1779. William Manson (Seal), Wit: Wm Wiley, Wilson Henderson, Wm McKinney. Proved in Chester County by the oath of Wm Wiley 12 Feb 1794 before John McCreary, J.P.

**D, 127-130**: 26 March 1794, Thomas Farrel of Chester County and wife Martha to Henry Jordan of same, for £100 sterling, tract granted 11 Aug 1774 to John McKinney Senr, 300 acres on Tinkers Creek adj. John McFadden, William McKinney, Wm. Taylor, Henry Cup, Augustine Culp, James Neely, conveyed to Wm McKinney 2 April 1777, and said William McKinney sold to Wm Manson, 150 acres of said tract 2 Nov 1779, and said Manson conveyed to Thomas Farrell, 140 acres of said tract. Thomas Farrel (seal), Martha Farrel (X) (Seal), Wit: Williamson Harper (X), William Rives, David Barr. Proved by the oath of Wm Rives 19 April 1794 before John McCreary, J.P.

**D, 131-133**: Plat of 150 acres. 1 Jan 1794, Thomas Baker Franklin & Ann his wife of Chester County to Stephen Liddle of same, 150 acres, part of tract granted to Edward Wilson containing 150 acres on north side Broad River on a small fork of Sandy River called Stony Fork, adj. John Bosher, Edward Wilson, and said Edward Wilson conveyed to William Woodley by deed 15

April 1792, recorded in Chester County 17 Sept 792 in Book B, page 384, and Wm Wood conveyed to Thomas B. Franklin. Thomas B. Franklin (Seal), Ann Franklin (X) (Seal), Wit: Allen DeGraffinreidt, Eli Cornwell, John Allen. Acknowledged by Thomas Baker Franklin in open court 21 April 1794. Jas Knox, one of the Judges. Saml Lacey, Clk. Ann, wife of Thomas B. Franklin, relinquished dower 21 April 1794 before John Pratt, J.P.

**D, 133-137**: 9 Aug 1792, John McCollough of Chester County to George Augustus Hill of same, store keeper, for £10 sterling, 50 acres, part of tract granted 23 June 1774 to Robert Morrison, 100 acres on a branch of Rocky Creek adj. Samuel McCullough, James Crafford, Alexander Henery, William Ferguson, Edward Anderson, Matthew Gaston, Alexander Rosborough, Bishop, conveyed by Robert Morrison 9 June 1792. John McCollough (Seal), Wit: William Knox, Thomas Wright. Proved by the oath of William Knox 21 April 1794 before Elijah Nunn, J.P.

**D, 137-139**: 1 March 1794, William Paul of Chester County to Abraham Ferguson of same, for £35, 200 acres on the waters of Bever Dams or north fork of Rockey Creek adj. Robert Fullerton, James Turner, Sarah Knox, John Ferguson, Abrm Ferguson, James Bunsly. William Paul (Seal), Wit: Adam Ferguson, John Ferguson (X), Alexdr Morton. Proved by the oath of Adam Ferguson 19 April 1794 before John McCreary, J.P.

**D, 139-142**: South Carolina, Chester County. Jacob Barker & wife Catherine of state aforesaid for £40 sterling, to Archibald Roberts of county aforesaid, 59 acres, the SW part of 200 acres granted to William Carter deceased, and was transferred from John Carter, who is son & heir of said William Carter deceased, to Jacob Barker Senr, 30 Jan 1794, on a branch of Sandy River. Jacob Barker (Seal), Catherine Barker (X) (Seal), Wit: John Jinnings, Thos Franklin, John Robards. Proved by the oath of John Jinnings 1 May 1794 before John Pratt, J.P.

**D, 143-144**: 21 Oct 1793, Charles Nix of Winton County, SC, to Archibald (Archilis) Roberts of Chester County, for £30, 50 acres, part of 450 acres granted to Edward Nix 13 Aug 1763, now adj. John McCorpin, Sandy River. Charles Nix (wax), Anne Nix (X) (wax), Wit: Robert Nix (X), Samuel Still (X), John Thomas. Proved in Chester County by the oath of Robert Nix 18 Feb 1794 before John Pratt, J.P.

**D, 145-147**: 21 Oct 1793, William Blackstokes to Christopher Strong, for five shillings, 350 acres in the fork of Fishing Creek, and the same parcel of land which Christopher Strong conveyed to the Rev. William Blackstocks, mortgage for 5 years, in the sum of £160 sterling, to be paid in four different installments commencing 3 Nov 1794. William Blackstock (seal), Wit: John Mills, George Hill, Edward Blackstock.

**D, 147**: Articles of agreement 28 Sept 1793, between Alexander English and Stephen Fitshaw, that said Stephen is to dig a mill race in the space of five weeks from the date hereof to the liking of the mill right and according to his directions. Stephen Fitshaw, Alexdr English, Wit: Alexr Downing, James Hamilton.

**D, 148-150**: 24 Jan 1793, Peter Jones of Chester County, yeoman, to George Gill, yeoman, whereas Peter Jones standeth indebted to said George Gill in the sum of £35 sterling, partly by a debt due unto the state of John Gill deceased, and partly by sums of money paid & laid out by said George Gill for said Peter Jones, mortgage of two tracts: 173 acres on waters of Cattawba River, granted to Thomas Morris, one of 50 acres on south side of the south fork of Fishing Creek, part of tract granted to Jonathan Jones. Peter Jones (wax), Wit: William Weir, John Mills, John Mullen. Proved by the oath of William Weer 24 Jan 1793 before John Mills, J.P.

**D, 150-152**: 27 July 1792, Ezekiel Saunders of Chester County, to Hasel Hardwick Junior of same, for £3 s13 d6 sterling, 7 acres, part of tract granted to said Sanders 21 Jan 1785 adj. said Ezekiel Sanders, on waters of Sandy River. Ezekiel Sanders (Seal), Wit: James Hardwick. Proved by the oath of James Hardwick before Rich'd Taliaferro, Clk C. C. C.

**D, 152-153**: George Cherrey of Chester County for £50 sterling to Daniel Green of same, one negro boy named Toney. George Cherrey (Seal), Wit: James McCown, Joshua Smith, Andrew Hemphill.

**D, 153-154**: Recd from son Laird Burns full satisfaction for my dowry both real & personal left me by the wil of my deceased husband, 27 Feb 1796. Jennet Burns (X), Test: Philip Walker, George Morrow (mark). Proved by the oath of George Morrow 29 Jan 1794 before Elijah Nunn, J.P.

**D, 154-155**: 22 May 1804. Edward Atterberry of Chester County and wife Keziah to Abraham Myers of same, for £50 sterling, 100 acres, part of tract granted to said Edward Atterberry, 5 March 1787. Edward Atterberry (X) (Seal), Keziah Atterberry (mark) (Seal), Wit: James Wilkinson, David Davidson Mitchell. Proved by the oath of David D. Mitchell 13 June 1795 before Saml Lacey, Clk C. C. C.

**D, 155-157**: 18 Nov 1793, Richard Atterberry of Chester County to Charles Morris of Newberry County for £50, 142 acres in Chester county on waters of the Brushey Fork. Richard Atterberry (X) (Seal),Wit: Elijah Nunn, Myhill Smith, William Norwood. Proved by the oath of William Norwood 18 Nov 1793 before Elijah Nunn, J.PO.

**D, 157-161**: Lease and release. 16 & 17 June 1792, Daniel Brown, Executor of Jacob Brown deceased, to John Polley of same, for £500, 122 acres on waters of Rockey Creek granted to John Winn Junr adj. Hugh Montgomery, John Ellis, granted to said Jacob Brown 5 March 1787. Daniel Brown executor of will of Jacob Brown deceased (Seal), Wit: S. W. Yongue, John Woodward,

R. F. Winn. Proved by the oath of S. W. Yongue 3 June 1794 before D. Evans, C. F. C. [Clerk, Fairfield County]

[page after 160, document incomplete]: Jennet Walker of Chester County for natural affection to my two grandsons John Walker (son of Saml Walker), two cows & Calves, to Thomas Walker (son of said Samuel Walker), one year old heifer, one gray horse, six pewter plates, one feather bed & furniture, 14 head of hogs, all my household furniture & stuff [see D, 257-258, page 133.]

D, 162-165: Lease and release. 3 & 4 May 1794, John Polley to Samuel Farriss for £5, 122 acres on the waters of Rockey Creek adj. land granted to John Winn Junr, Hugh Montgomery, John Elliss, granted to Jacob Brown 4 March 1787. John Polley (Seal), Wit: Andrew Dunn, Littleton Isbell, John Wright. Proved -- June 1794 by the oath of Andw Dunn before Andw Hemphill, J.P.

D, 166: South Carolina, Chester County. Thomas Bragg of Chester County, planter, for £38 sterling, one negro woman named Rose, 27 Dec 1793. Thos Bragg (Seal), Wit: Robert Hemphill, Mary Mills.

D, 166-169: Lease and release. 9 & 10 June 1794, Nathaniel Durham of Chester County to William Collans of same, blacksmith, for £14, 100 acres waters of Rockey Creek, part of grant of 200 acres granted to Mitchell Strange, on the north side of said grant. Nathaniel Durham (LS), Wit: William Stone, George Egnew (mark). Proved by the oath of William Stone 10 June 1794 before Andw Hemphill, J.P.

D, 169-171: 25 Jan 1794, John Franklin & Mourning his wife of Chester County to Peter Corbell Junr of same, for £100 sterling, 200 acres in Chester County on Flintons Creek of Sandy River, part of four different grants, one granted to Thomas Franklin 24 Nov 1767, 100 acres, part of one granted 24 Dec 1772 to said Thomas Franklin, 200 acres, part of one grant to Major Gresham in October 1786, 100 acres, and one granted to Thomas Baker Franklin 5 Feb 1787, all on waters of Sandy River (plat included). John Franklin (Seal), Mourning Franklin (X) (Seal), Wit: John Weir, Jacob Dungan, William Brittain. Proved by the oath of John Weir and William Brittain 25 Jan 1794 before Elijah Nunn, J.P.

D, 172-174: 13 Dec 1793, Elijah Nunn, Esqr. & wife Frances of Chester County to Thomas Roden of same, for £45 sterling, 124 acres on waters of Brushey Fork, waters of Sandy River, granted to John Roden 15 Oct 1784, recorded in Book QQQ, page 279, transferred from said John Roden to Elijah Nunn 24 Dec 1790. Elijah Nunn (Seal), Frances Nunn (X) (Seal), Wit: Thomas Wilks (X), William Wilks, William Bond. Proved by the oath of Thomas Wilks 13 June 1794 before John Pratt, J.P.

D, 174-176: William Mansinger, late of Macklinburgh County, but since the division of the county, now in the County of Cabarrus in North Carolina, to Nicholas Ridenour of same county of Cabarrus, bound to Philip Hafely of

Camden District, SC, in the sum of £200 NC money, 29 Jan 1794; whereas the said William Mansinger in consideration of £100 bought and obtained a piece of land on the west side of Cattawba River in Camden County SC, adj. Jas Drafton, 200 acres, by indenture 19 Nov 178 conveyed by James Drafton to William Mansinger, for £45 NC money, and whereas the said Philip Hafely to presume the legalities of the right & titles of said William Mansinger to the said land might be defective, and therefore brought some uneasiness. William Mansinger (wax), Nicholas Ridenouer (wax), Wit: William Slyker (M), J. Linnback. Proved in Chester County by the oath of William Slyker 13 June 1794 before Hugh Whiteside.

**D, 177-180**: 25 March 1794, James Crawford & wife Mary of Chester County to John McGuire of same, sadler, for five shillings, tract granted 8 March 1768 to Mary Campbell, wife of James Crawford, 100 acres on waters of Rockey Creek in Chester county (then Craven), adj. Danl Kelsey. James Crawford (Seal), Mary Crawford (mark) (Seal), Wit: Jno McCulley, Jno Johnston, John Armour. Proved by the oath of Jno McCulley 13 June 1794 before Andw Hemphill, J.P.

**D, 180-186**: Lease and release. 11 May 1794, Richard Wooley Senior of Chester County, planter, and wife Elizabeth to Francis Lee of same, for £70 sterling, 200 acres on a branch formerly called Bowers Mill Creek but now a branch on the waters of Little River, part of 400 acres granted to Jacob Bowers 3 Aug 1768, and conveyed by him to Richard Wooley Senior 9 Aug 1768. Richard Woolley Senr (Seal), Eliz'th Woolley (Seal), Wit: Alexdr Gordon, James Turner. Proved by the oath of James Turner 13 June 1794 before Elijah Nunn, J.P.

**D, 186-188**: 10 Dec 1793, William Archer of Chester County to Thomas Bell of same, for £60 sterling, 190 acres on waters of Rockey Creek. William Archer (mark), Isebala Archer (X) (Seal), Wit: John Speer, Thomas Morton. Proved by the oath of John Speer 4 June 1794 before John McCreary, J.P.

**D, 188-191**: 7 Feb 1792, Thomas Fariss of Chester County, yeoman, to Samuel Lusk of same, yeoman, for £10, part of tract granted 6 Sept 1790 to Thomas Fariss, 640 acres on waters of Cattawba River adj. Michael Patton, James Dunn, James Crawford, John McNitt Alexander, Joseph McKinney, Samuel Lusk, Jas Robison. Thomas Fearis (wax seal), Wit: Samuel Lusk, Robert Robinson, William Patton. Proved by the oath of Samuel Lusk Junior 28 Nov 1792 before Hugh Whiteside. Plat of 233 acres, part of 640 acres included.

**D, 191-192**: Jesse Miller of York County, SC, yeoman, for £50 sterling, to Samuel Lusk of Chester County, yeoman, a negro woman slave named Eder, 9 July 1793. Jesse Miller (wax seal), Wit: Nathaniel Barker (X).

**D, 192-193**: 9 June 1794, Ferdinand Hopkins of Chester County to Josiah Cook of same, for £1000 SC money, 100 acres, part of a survey on north side of Old Saluda Road, leading from the old Cattawba Nation, granted 15 Oct

1784, on waters of Sandy River adj. James Fletchall, certified 9 Oct 1784. Ferd'd Hopkins (seal), Wit: Robert Glenn, Is. Dansby. Proved by the oath of Robert Glenn 24 June 1794 before Saml Lacey, Clk of Chester County Court.

**D, 193-194**: 13 April 1794, Rebeckah Patton of Chester County to James Harbison of same, 80 acres, part of tract granted to Rebeckah Patton on west side of the Cattawba River, Chester County near Land's ford, adj. James Harbison, John Fleming, William Oneal. Rebecca Patton (Seal), Wit: James Walker, Ezekiah Ingram, John Walker. Proved 24 June 1794 by the oath of James Walker before Saml Lacey, Clk.

**D, 194-195**: 12 May 1794, William Shaw and wife Ann of Chester County, to Edmund Lee of same, for £50 sterling, tract on waters of Sandy River, 100 acres, part of tract of land the said William Shaw now dwells on adj. William Shaw, James Timms. William Shaw (Seal), Ann Shaw (LS), Wit: William Boyd, John Wright.

**D, 196-197**: 19 Oct 1793, Edmund Lee & wife Nancy of Chester County to Jeremiah Thomas of same, for £100 sterling, 126 acres. Edmund Lee (Seal), Wit: Joseph Bennett, William Atteberry.

**D, 197-199**: 15 May 1793, Minor Winn, Esquire, of Fairfield County, for £50, to Henry Jordan of Chester County, 29 acres in Chester County on west side Cattawba River adj. Shff Fennell's land, William Shadrack, John McCannon, Elisha Craig, granted 5 March 1787 surveyed for Benjamin Rives, recorded in Book TTTT, page 26. M. Winn (Seal),Wit: Mark Eaves, Obed Kirkland, R. F. Winn. Proved by the oath of Mark Eaves 17 June 1794 before Jas Knox, J.C.C.

**D, 199**: Elijah Nunn of Chester County for £80 sterling to Asa Darby of same, one negro woman Esther and two children Anaka & Moses, 1 Sept 1793. Elijah Nunn (seal), Test: Michael Gore.

**D, 199-202**: 12 August 1785, Arthur Hicklin of Camden District, SC, to David Bell of same, tract granted 28 Aug 1767 to John Pike, 200 acres on the straight fork of Rockey Creek, and said Arthur Hicklin Senior sold to David Bell for £750 old current money of SC. Arthur Hicklin (X) (Seal), Wit: Andw Hemphill, John McCown, George Hicklin. Proved by the oath of Andrew Hemphill 27 June 1792 before John Pratt, J.P.

**D, 202-205**: 19 Feb 1794, David Wear, Stiller, of Chester county, to David Bell of same, for £30 sterling, part of tract granted 26 Sept 1789 to Thomas Baker Franklin, 103 acres on a small fork of Rockey Creek adj. David McDill, John Mebon, David Bell, Archibald Coulter, David Wear, and said Thomas Baker Franklin did sell to David Wear, and said David Wear sells to David Bell, 50 acres of said tract. David Wear (Seal), Wit: James Chesnut, Alexander Chesnut, John McDill. Proved by the oath of Alexander Chesnut 20 Feb 1794 before John Mills, J.P.

**D, 205-207**: South Carolina, Chester county. 23 Nov 1793, William Mobley of county aforesaid to Thomas Estes of same, for £100, 100 acres on Sandy Creek granted 6 June 1766. William Mobley (wax seal), Wit: Thomas Jinkins, Dewitt Allen. Proved 24 June 1794 by the oath of Thomas Jinkins before Saml Lacey, Clk. C. C. C.

**D, 207-208**: 9 May 1794, William Manson, yeoman of State of SC to Henry Jordan, planter, for £5, 10 acres, the east end of a tract of Mason's land adj. James Neeley, Augustine Culp, on west side of Cattawba River. William Manson (Seal), Wit: John Staret, John Cooper, Benja Rives. Proved by the oath of Benjamin Rives 12 May 1794 before John McCreary, J.P.

**D, 208-209**: 24 April 1790, Benjamin Rives, yeoman, of SC, to William Henderson, planter, for £5, 100 acres, it being the south of said Rives land adj. Matthew Pattern's land. Benjamin Rives (Seal), Wit: William Henderson, Wilson Henderson, Sarah Rives (mark).

**D, 209-211**: 13 Feb 1787, Archibald Roberts of Camden District, SC, to Thomas Franklin of same, for £10 sterling, 100 acres, part of tract granted to said Archibald Roberts 18 Oct 1784. Archibald Roberds (Seal), Unis Roberds (X), Wit: John Franklin, Lewis Franklin (X), Ann Franklin (X). Proved by the oath of John Franklin 26 Feb 1789 before John Pratt, J.P.

**D, 211-213**: 7 July 1794, Benjamin Morriss, planter, of Chester count, to Burrell Morris & Jackson Morris, nephews to said Benjamin Morris & sons to George Morriss, for natural love and affection, and five shillings, 200 acres of land where George Morriss now lives to be equally divided between them then come to age, the said land being a part of two tracts adj. together, one granted to George Morris and other to Hugh Montgomery, and by said George Morris granted to Benjamin Morris, 21 Jan 1794 on SW side Cattawba River, recorded in Book C, page 344, Chester County. Benjamin Morriss (LS), Wit: Jonathan Mackey (X), John Steel. Proved by the oath of John Steel 8 July 1794 before Andrew Hemphill, J.P.

**D, 213-215**: 19 March 1787, Robert Martain & wife Sarah of Chester County to William Massey of Lancaster County, SC, two grants dated 13 Feb 1768 and 19 Aug 1774, to Andrew Martin, 100 acres and another to Robert Martin, 50 acres, on west side Fishing Creek. Robert Martin (LS), Sarah Martin (mark) (LS), Wit: William McDonald, Williamson Harper (W). Proved by the oath of Wm McDonald 10 July 1793 before James Knox, J. C. C.

**D, 216-217**: 31 May 1794, Josiah Hill of Chester County to Samuel Given of same, for £10 sterling, 110 acres, part of 12,700 acres adj. Voluntine Bell, Hezekiah Alexander, James Adair and said Josiah Hill. Josiah Hill (wax LS), Wit: Thos Wallace, Jas McCown. Acknowledged in open Court June 1794 by Josiah Hill. Plat included, certified 12 Dec 1789 by W. Gaston, D. Surv.

**D, 218-220**: 7 March 1794, William Paul of Chester County, planter, & Isbel Paul his wife, to George Wier of same, for £29, tract granted 1 Sept 1768 to James Paul, on waters of Rockey Creek, 200 acres adj. John Weir, Burnsides, plat recorded in Book DDD, page 435, reserving that part already laid off by a prior grant for a grave yard or place of interment. William Paul (Seal), Isabel Paul (X) (Seal), Wit: Samuel Bigham, Thomas Bell, John Speer. Proved by the oath of Samuel Bigham 27 June 1794 before Saml Lacey, Clk C. C. C.

**D, 221-223**: 5 Nov 1793, James Bigham of Rockey Creek in Chester County, planter, to Samuel Bigham of same county, planter, for £30, tract granted 1 Oct 1787, to James Bigham, 300 acres on both sides of Beaver Dam branch, waters of Rockey Creek adj. widow Katerees, Thomas Morris, William Stroud, Margaret McCreary, recorded in Grant book UUUU, page 481. James Bigham (Seal), Jane Bigham (X) (Seal), Wit: Jas Martin, George Wier. Proved by the oath of George Weir 27 June 1794 before Saml Lacey, Clk C. C. C.

**D, 223-227**: 30 Dec 1779, John Love, yeoman, and wife Martha, & James Love, yeoman & wife Jennet of Camden District, SC, to William Gaston, yeoman of same, for £100, part of tract granted 3 Sept 1753 to William Love, 800 acres on Turkey Creek on north side Broad River, Craven County, but at the time of granting thought to be in Anson County, North Carolina, and the creek now called Turkey Creek was then called Loves Creek, and the above named William Love dying intestate, the above named John Love being the next oldest brother of said William Love deceased and by being heir according to law to all the lands which the said William Love was possessed of at his death, and by a grant 5 Oct 1763 by SC to James Love, 300 acres within the aforementioned 800 acres granted to William Love deceased, now conveys 90 acres of said tract on which the said William Gaston doth now dwell. John Love (Seal), Martha Love (Seal), James Love (wax seal), Jennet Love (mark) (wax seal), Wit: Jno Countryman, Jonathan Poston, Jane Love. Proved in Camden District by the oath of Jno Countryman 1 Jan 1780 before John Gaston, J.P.

**D, 227-228**: Elizabeth Weir & Joseph Weir of Chester County, bound to James Meeck of same, in the sum of £50 sterling, 26 March 1792; that the above bound Elizabeth Weir & Joseph Wier do keep the said James Meeck clear of trouble or molestation from a certain Thomas Chambers. Elizabeth Weir (mark) (Seal), Joseph Weir (Seal), Wit: Andrew Graham, Hance Hambleton, James Chesnut.

**D, 228-232**: Lease and release. 20 & 21 Aug 1782, John Caskey & Esther his wife of Camden District to James Meek of same, planter, for £275, 200 acres on a branch of Rockey Creek adj. Andrew Miller, Jasper Rogers, granted 8 Def 1775 to John Caskey. John Caskey (wax), Esther Caskey (mark) (wax), Wit: John Turner, John Bell, William Dunn. Proved by the oath of William Dunn 9 March 1793 before John Bell, J.P.

131

**D, 233**: South Carolina, Chester County. William Love of county aforesaid for £78 to Robert Elliott of same, one gray mare about six years old, about five foot two inches high, one riding carriage with harniss, 22 July 1794. W. Love (Seal), Wit: Anthony Cox, James Love. Proved by the oath of Anthony Cox 14 Aug 1794 before W. Gaston, J. C. C.

**D, 233-235**: 25 March 1794, James Atteberry & Darcus his wife of Chester County to David Davidson Mitchell of same, for £100, 150 acres, part of tract granted to James Atteberry 4 Sept 1786. James Atteberry (Seal), Darcas Atteberry (mark) (Seal), Wit: William Norwood, James Wilkinson. Proved by the oath of Wm Norwood 30 May 1794 before Elijah Nunn, J.P.

**D, 235-237**: 7 July 1794, John White & wife Sarah of Chester County to David Davidson Mitchell of same, for £100 sterling, 103 acres on both sides of the Brushey fork granted to said John White 4 Jan 1790. John White (wax), Sarah White (X) (wax), Wit: William Norwood, Isaiah Mitchell. Proved by the oath of Isaiah Mitchell 11 July 1794 before Elijah Nunn, J.P.

**D, 237-241**: Lease and release. 7 & 8 July 1786, David Mitchell of Chester County, turner, to David Davidson Mitchell of same, for twenty shillings, tract on east side of the Brushey fork of Sandy River, part of 150 acres granted to said David Mitchell 21 Jan 1785. David Mitchell, Mary Mitchell (X), Wit: John White, Isaiah Mitchell. Proved by the oath of John White and Isaiah Mitchell 23 Feb 1789 before Dd. Hopkins, J.P.

**D, 241-244**: 15 Sept 1793, Thomas Blair Senr & his wife Margaret of Chester County to Thomas Blair Junr of same, for £100 sterling, tract granted 4 June 1787 to James Blair, 163 acres on waters of Rockey Creek, also a tract granted to Thomas Blair Senr, 200 acres, adj. Thomas Blair Senr, Philip Walker Esqr. Thos Blair Senr (wax), Margaret Blair (X) (wax), Wit: William Neisbet, Phil Walker. Plat included. Proved by the oath of William Niesbet 15 Dec 1793 before Phil Walker, J.P.

**D, 244-246**: 3 March 1792, James Blair of Rockey Creek in Chester County, to Thomas Blair of same, tract granted 4 June 1787 to James Blair, 160 acres adj. James Wylie, Robert Walker, Philip Walker, Thomas Blair, recorded in Book TTT, page 219. James Blair (Seal), Wit: John Robinson, James Magors. Proved by the oath of James Magors 14 Jan 1794 before Philip Walker, J.P.

**D, 247-248**: 13 Aug 1784, Hugh McCluer & wife Jane of Camden District, to Benjamin Love of same, for £50 sterling, 300 acres granted to Benjamin Elliss and conveyed to James McCluer 5 Aug 1769 and left by will to Hugh McCluer dated 1769. Hugh McCluer (wax), Jane McCluer (X) (wax), Wit: Alexander Gaston, John Woods, Wm Gaston. Proved by the oath of Alexdr Gaston 13 Aug 1784 before Jax Knox, J.P.

**D, 248-249**: 2 March 1789, William Gaston of Chester County to Benjamin Love of same, for £1, tract being part of grant to William Gaston 3 Sept 1787,

50 acres adj. Benjamin Love's old corner. Wm Gaston (wax), Wit: Stewart Brown, John Cubit, Janet Cubit (mark). Proved by the oath of Stewart Brown 1 Aug 1794 before Wm Gaston, J. C. C.

**D, 250-251**: 18 Nov 1791, Drewry Goen & Sarah his wife of Chester county to William Love Senr of same, for £200, tract granted to William Gaston 3 Sept 1787 and by him conveyed to said Drewry Goen adj. James Wright. Drewry Goyen (mark) (Seal), Sarah Goyen (Seal), Wit: William Hughes, Benjamin Love (B), William Gaston. Proved by the oath of Benjamin Love 3 Dec 1791 before W. Gaston, J.C.C.

**D, 251-252**: 2 March 1789, William Gaston of Chester County to Stewart Brown of same, for £1, tract on Mill Creek, part of tract granted to William Gaston 3 Sept 1787, 50 acres. William Gaston (wax), Wit: John Cubit (mark), Janet Cubit (mark), Benjamin Love (B). Proved by the oath of Benjamin Love 21 Aug 1794 before William Gaston, J.C.C.

**D, 253-254**: 27 Dec 1793, Levy Smith of Chester County to Thomas Franklin of same, for £10 sterling, 200 acres, part of tract granted to Thomas Jinkins 17 May 1792 on waters of Sandy River adj. Thomas Jinkins. Levy Smith (Seal), Ann Smith, Wit: Zechariah Wade, William Sims, Wm McGregor (X). Proved by the oath of Zachariah Wade 18 Feb 1794 before John Pratt, J.P.

**D, 255-256**: Reece Hughs of Chester County, planter, for love, good will & affection to my loving son James Hughs of same, planter, tract of land whereon I now live, 493 acres on Rockey Creek, 24 Feb 1794, reserving to Reece Hughs during his life time 150 acres bought from Thomas Garrett. Reece Hughs (Seal), Wit: Alexander Morton, Eliz'a Lard (X). Proved by the oath of Alexdr Morton 22 Aug 1794 before John McCreary, J.P.

**D, 256-257**: 12 March 1793, Frances Barrott of Chester County to Joseph Loving, brother of said Frances Barrott, for natural love and affection and £1 sterling, one black walnut desk, one mare of brown color, one bed & bedstead and furniture, chairs, and all other property. Frances Barrott (X) (Seal), Wit: Elijah Nunn, James Loving (I), Mary Loving (X). Proved by the oath of Mary Loving 13 Aug 1793 before Elijah Nunn, J.P.

**D, 257-258**: Janet Walker of Chester County for natural affection to my two grandsons John Walker (son of Saml Walker) two cows & calves, to Thomas Walker (son of said Samuel Walker), one year old heifer, one gray horse, six pewter plates, one feather bed & furniture, 14 head of hogs, all my household furniture & stuff...25 Aug 1794. Jennet Walker (mark) (LS), Wit: Joseph Liles, Jas Kannedy.

**D, 258-259**: South Carolina, Chester County. 8 June 1793, Josiah Hill of county aforesaid, planter, to Herman Kolb of York County, SC, sadler, for £15 sterling, 103 acres on waters of Sandy River, the south corner of a tract surveyed & granted by patent 6 Nov 1786 to James Adair. Josiah Hill (wax seal), Wit: Samuel Lacey, Samuel Pugh. Proved by the oath of Samuel Lacey 25 Sept 1794 before Saml Lacey, Clk, C. C. C. Plat included shows adj. Hardens corner, dated 23 May 1793 by James Fowler.

**D, 260-261**: 13 Aug 1794, John Rainey of Chester County to Thomas Rainey of same, for £100 sterling, 54 acres, part of a tract of 100 acres conveyed from Major Grisham to said John Rainey 26 July 1789. John Rainey (X) (Seal), Wit: John Trussell, Clayborn Wright, Daniel Trussell. Plat included showing adj. land owners John Hopkins James Trussell, Major Grisham, by Will Boyd. Proved by the oath of John Trussell 15 Sept 1794 before John Pratt, J.P.

**D, 261-263**: 2 Dec 1791, Richard Land, the eldest son & heir of James Land, deceased, of Fairfield County, Camden District, SC, to Andrew Hemphill of Chester County, Pinckney District, for £40 sterling, 240 acres on both sides Little Rockey Creek, granted to John Matthews and by him conveyed to James Land 6 Feb 1778, recorded in Book Y No. 4, page 276. Richard Land (X) (Seal), Wit: Moses Hollis, Moses Hollis Junr. Proved in Fairfield County by the oath of Moses Hollis 23 Jan 1794 before John Turner, J.P. [The deed referred to can be found in *South Carolina Deed Abstracts 1776-1783*, page 19, by Brent H. Holcomb.]

**D, 263**: Plat: Pursuant to precept from George Hunter Esqr., dated 5 June 1753, I have admeasured unto Thomas Land, 400 acres on Rockey Creek, the South side of Catawba River above 40 miles from the Catawba Town, 23 March 1754. Saml Wyly Depy Survr. Copy take from Surveyor General's Office, Town of Columbia, Jan 18th 1794.

**D, 264-265**: 28 June 1793, William Sandefur Senior of Chester County to Samuel Ferguson of same, for £45 sterling, 50 acres, part of tract granted to said William Sandefur for 200 acres, the said 50 acres on the south side of Hagues branch, and branch of Rockey Creek adj. James Stinson, William Stormont, Burrell Sandifur, & late in the occupancy of said Burrell Sandifur, and known by the manders of said Hagues Creek as a dividing line. William Sandefur (X) (Seal), Wit: Andrew Hemphill, Samuel Sandifur (X). Proved by the oath of Samuel Sandifur 29 June 1794 before Andw Hemphill, J.P.

**D, 265-267**: 3 Aug 1790, Littleton R. Isbell, the right lawful heir of Henry Isbell deceased, and Ann Isbell his wife, & Elizabeth Stewart, the former wife of the said deceased, to Samuel Ferguson for £70 sterling, 100 acres granted to James McCluer on Rockey Creek, and said James McCluer granted to Thomas Dye & James Hemphill Senr, and by said Thomas Dye & James Hemphill Senr to Henry Isbell for £600 old currency 6 Nov 1773. L. R. Isbell (wax), Ann Isbell (X) (wax), Elizabeth Stewart (E) (wax), Wit: Andrew Hemphill, William Steenson. Proved by the oath of Andrew Hemphill 5 Oct 1790 before James Knox, J.P.

**D, 267-269**: 3 Aug 1790, Littleton R. Isbell, the right lawful heir of Henry Isbell deceased, and Ann Isbell his wife, & Elizabeth Stewart, being formerly the wife of the said deceased, to Samuel Ferguson for £70 sterling, 100 acres in the fork of Rockey Creek, adj. John McFadden, William Wilson, James McCluer, granted to Andrew Hemphill and conveyed by said him to Henry Isbell 20 July 1775. L. R. Isbell (wax), Ann Isbell (X) (wax), Elizabeth Stewart (E) (wax), Wit: Andrew Hemphill, William Steenson. Proved by the oath of Andrew Hemphill 5 Oct 1790 before James Knox, J.P.

**D, 269-271**: 2 Aug 1790, Littleton R. Isbell & Ann his wife to Richard Featherstone, all of Chester county, for £40 sterling, 50 acres on south side of Big Rockey Creek, south side of Little Rockey Creek adj. James McCluer, John Yarbrough, part of 250 acres granted to John Land, 16 July 1765, recorded in Book ZZ, page 161, and conveyed to John Yarbrough and by him to Littleton R. Isbell. L. R. Isbell (wax), Ann Isbell (mark) (wax), Richd Featherston, Wit: Andrew Hemphill, William Steenson. Proved by the oath of Andrew Hemphill 5 Oct 1790 before James Knox, J.P.

**D, 271-273**: 25 Sept 1792, Abner Wilkes of Chester County to Samuel Ferguson of same, for £10 sterling, 20 acres on north side of Hagues branch, part of tract granted to John Rennolds and known by the manders of said branch. Abner Wilkes (Seal), Wit: And'w Hemphill, Benjamin Strange. Proved by the oath of Benjamin Strange 5 Jan 1793 before And'w Hemphill, J.P.

**D, 273-274**: 3 March 1794, John Fleming of Camden District to William Richardson Davie of Hallifax Town, North Carolina, for £8 s16 SC money, all my half of tract in Chester County, Pinckney District, granted to said William Richardson Davie & John Fleming 5 Dec 1791. John Fleming (Seal), Wit: John Fleming (Seal), Wit: Robert Karr, David Patton, Tristram Patton. Proved in York County by the oath of Robert Karr 20 Sept 1794 before Alexr Moore, J.P.

**D, 274-276**: 17 Aug 1793, Alexander Patton, Tristram Patton & Rebecca Patton to William Richardson Davie for £167 s10 SC money, land sold by Casper Culp to Matthew Patton in Chester County on west side Cattawba River, part of tract of 97 acres formerly the property of said Culp, 225 acres. Alex'dr Patton (wax), Tristram Patton (wax), Rebecca Patton (wax), Wit: Joseph Davie, William Barnett, Robert Karr. Proved in York County by the oath of Robert Karr 20 Sept 1794 before Alexander Moore, J.P.

**D, 276-278**: 27 May 1794, Alexander Walker Senr, planter, of Chester County, to Samuel Walker, Alexander Walker Junr, William Guy Walker, Robert Walker, & James Walker, for natural love & affection to his beloved grandsons, sons of Philip Walker deceased, and for five shillings, one negro boy named Jack to Alexander Junr, one negro boy named Ceasar to William Guy Walker, one negro girl named Sall to Robert Walker, one negro woman named Phoebe to James Walker, 100 acres of land on which I now live on the north fork of Rockey [Creek], adj. land of Peter Nance, Thomas Blair, Francis Ray, Philip Walker. Alexander Walker (X) (Wax), Wit: Andw Hemphill, Caleb

Barns (B). Proved by the oath of Andrew Hemphill 15 Sept 1794 before John McCreary, J.P.

**D, 278-281**: Lease and release. 27 & 28 Sept 1792, James Pagan, Taylor, of Chester County, to John Ramsey, planter, for £55, 216 acres on head waters of Sandy River, waters of Broad River, granted to said James Pagan 5 June 1786, recorded in Grant Book LLLL, page 338. James Pagan (wax), Wit: Hugh Whiteside, Thos Neeley, Robert Walker. Proved by the oath of Thomas Neeley 28 Sept 1792 before John Mills, J.P.

**D, 282-284**: 20 Dec 1793, Dennis Carrell & wife Sarah of Chester County to Allen De Graffenreidt of same, for £200 sterling, part of tract of 300 acres, 108 acres granted to William Stone, 17 June 1760 on a branch of Sandy Creek, conveyed from John Stone, Moses Stone & Jacob Stone to Dennis Carrell & William Stone 19 Oct 1783, and from William Stone to Dennis Carrell 23 March 1791. Dennis Carrell (LS), Sarah Carrell (X) (LS), Wit: John Pratt, Wm Hobson, Mabry Thomas. Proved by the oath of William Hobson 25 Oct 1794 before Saml Lacey, Clk C. C. C.

**D, 284-285**: 29 Oct 1794, Edward Lacey & Jane his wife of Pinckney District, to Peter Coonrod of same, for £60, 100 acres on waters of Susey Bowls branch, granted to Edward Lacey 29 April 1788, recorded in Book No 13, also Book M No 12, page 142. Edw'd Lacey (wax), Jane Lacey (wax) (wax), Wit: Arthur Travers, Thomas B. Franklin, Hugh Cooper. Proved by the oath of Arthur Travers 29 Oct 1794 before Saml Lacey, Clk C. C. C.

**D, 286-287**: 25 March 1794, William Rainey of Chester County to Richard Atteberry of same, for £10, tract on which the said Atteberry now lives, 100 acres granted to said William Rainey 4 Dec 1771. William Rainey (X) (Seal), Wit: Richard Wright, Richard Woolley Senr. Proved by the oath of Richard Woolley Senr 11 Nov 1794 before Saml Lacey, Clk.

**D, 287-289**: 3 Dec 1791, William Barrow of York County to James Morrow, now of same, for £40 sterling, tract on waters of Sandy River adj. lands of George Sadler, Josiah Hill, Mr. Parker, on the south side of Loves road leading from Fishing Creek to Broad River. William Barrow (Seal), Wit: Philip Sandifur, Eliz'a Sandifur, D. Gordon. Proved in York County by the oath of David Gordon 16 April 1793 for Jo Palmer, J.P.

**D, 289-290**: Ann McCurdy of Chester County, spinster, appoint Robert Sanderson of said county, my true and lawful attorney to receive of Rhoda McCurdy & William McCurdy of the County of Pendleton, SC, all sums of money due me, 14 Nov 1794. Ann McCurdy (Seal), Wit: Gardiner Miller. Proved in Chester County by the oath of Gardiner Miller 15 Nov 1794 before Elijah Nunn, J.P.

**D, 291**: Philip Walker impowers William Walker to act and do everything concerning a tract of land in the State of Georgia, originally ranted to John

Bell and by him conveyed to my brother John Walker, sadler, of Chester County, 23 Sept 1794. Philip Walker (Seal), Wit: Josiah Porter, William Bohannan. Proved in Chester County by the oath of William Bohannan 6 Dec 1794 before John Mills, J.P.C.C.

**D, 291-294**: 17 May 1794, George Augustus Hill & Jane his wife of Chester County, planter, to John McGuire of same, for £10 sterling, tract granted 23 June 1774 to Robert Morrison, 50 acres on a branch of Rockey Creek adj. Samuel McCullough, James Crawford, Alexander Henry, William Ferguson, Matthew Gaston, Alexander Rosborough, Bishop, conveyed to said George Augustus Hill by John McCulloch by a deed 9 Aug 1792. George Augustus Hill (Seal), Jane Hill (X) (wax), Wit: George Johnston, John Lackey. Proved by the oath of George Johnston 11 Sept 1    794 before Andw Hemphill, J.P.

**D, 294-296**: 25 Oct 1790, William Patton of Union County, SC, and wife Jane to Robert Patton of York County, SC, for £20 sterling, 100 acres, part of tract granted 31 March 1753 to William Patton, 386 acres, now in the state of South Carolina in Chester County, near the Trading path on the south side of the Cattawba River. William Patton (Seal), Jane Patton (mark) (Seal), Wit: Alexander Eakin, Robert Patton, William Patton. Proved in Chester County by the oath of Alexander Akins 7 Dec 1790 before Francis Adams, J.P.

**D, 296-297**: 24 July 1794, Robert Patton of Richland County, SC, to Isaac McFadden of Chester County, for £20 sterling, 100 acres, part of 186 acres on south side Cattaba River, granted to William Patton. Robert Patton (wax), Wit: Thomas Johnston, William Wilson, John Patton. Proved by the oath of Thomas Johnston 17 Dec 1794 before Hugh Whiteside.

**D, 297-299**: 22 Jan 1795, John Porter & Jane his wife of Chester County, to Thomas Porter of same, for £20 SC money, 150 acres on waters of Fishing Creek including the improvements where he now lives, part of a tract of 400 acres granted to sd. John Porter 4 May 1775 by William Bull, Gov. of SC... John Porter (Seal), Jane Porter (O) (Seal), Wit: Jas Ferguson, Hugh McCluer, John Ferguson. Proved by the oath of Hugh McCluer 22 Jan 1795. "The Bill of sale recorded in Book A, page 138."

**D, 299-301**: 5 Aug 1794, John Mills of Chester County, Esqr., to William Wilson of same, planter, for £50, tract granted 10 May 1768 to Robert Glover, 250 acres on James McCluer's spring branch, south fork of Fishing Creek, conveyed to Henry Culp 21 Sept 1768, and by said Culp to Jonathan Jones 6 June 1772 and by Jonathan Jones to James Langshy 19 Jan 1786 and by Hugh Milling, Sheriff of Camden District, to John Mills. John Mills (wax seal), Wit: George gill, William Jones, John Mills (X). Proved by the oath of John Mills Senior 1 Jan 1795 before Hugh Whiteside.

**D, 301-303**: 23 Oct 1794, John Culp of Chester county, planter, to William Wilson of same, yeoman, for £60, mortgage of a negro woman slave named Margaret formerly belonging to the estate of Peter Culp deceased, and tract of 75 acres adj. Philip Cline, John Latta, Thomas Latta, including the house & improvements where the said John Culp now lives, also a negro woman named Patt, payment due 30 March 1797. John Culp (wax), Wit: Hugh Whiteside, Robert Harper, Proved by the oath of Hugh Whiteside 28 Oct 1794 before John Mills, J.P.

**D, 303**: John Culp of Chester County for £50 sterling to William Wilson, negro woman slave named Margaret, 20 Oct 1794. William Elliott, Charles Orr. Proved by the oath of Charles Orr 1 Jan 1795 before Hugh Whiteside.

**D, 304-305**: South Carolina, Fairfield County. William McQuiston of Fairfield County, planter, for £50 sterling, to James McQuiston of Chester county, 200 acres in Chester County on waters of Rockey Creek adj. James Stuart, Michael Dickson, granted to me, said William McQuiston, 4 June 1787. William McQuiston (wax), Wit: Arch'd McQuiston, Wm. McQuiston. Proved 16 July 1794 by the oath of Arch'd McQuiston before Hugh Milling, J.P.

**D, 305-307**: 6 April 1794, William Whiteside of Chester County to Thomas Whiteside of York County, for £30 sterling, 100 acres, part of tract granted 29 April 1768, 200 acres at the time of survey supposed to be in North Carolina, Macklenburgh County, but now in South Carolina, on west side Cattawba River, on the north side of Main Fishing Creek, both sides of the Cainey run, on both sides of the waggon road, near William Neely's line, conveyed to Samuel McKinney by James Smith & Lillies his wife 21 June 1774 and by Saml McKinney to George Kelsey 29 Jan 1780 and to William Whiteside by George Kelsey 24 March 1789. Wm Whiteside (wax), Wit: Hugh Whiteside, James Turner, Jas Turner (X). Proved by the oath of Hugh Whiteside 12 Nov 1794 before Hugh Whiteside.

**D, 308-310**: 6 Jan 1795, Edward Lacey, Sheriff of Pinckney District, SC, to Col. John Pearson of Fairfield County, whereas Col. John Pearson in the court of common pleas holden at Camden for the district of Camden did implead John McWilliams in an action in case upon attachment in November Term 1792, to levy the sum of £119 sterling, also £19 s3 d11, sells tract on waters of Sandy River adj. Mr. Bowers and vacant land, granted to John Miller 177-, sells to John Pearson for £30 sterling. Edw'd Lacey Shff P. D. (wax), Wit: Wm Hobson, Jo Pearson Jr., Hugh Stuart. Proved in Chester County by the oath of John Pearson Junior 6 Jan 1795 before Saml Lacey, Clk, C. C. C. G.

Plat: South Carolina, Craven County. Pursuant to a precept to me directed by John Bremar, Esqr., Dpty Surv Genl dated 6 April 1773, I have admeasured and laid out to John Miller 300 acres on the dreans of Sandy River adj. Mr. Bowers, certified 20 April 1773. David Hopkins, D. S. Copy from Surv Genls Office, Columbia, Nov. 4th 1792.

**D, 310**: South Carolina, Chester County. James Bigham personally appeared and made oath that a certain large black horse with a blaze in his face, all his feet white, trots & paces, branded on the mounting shoulder AS, had on when taken up a large bell, which horse this deponent tolled agreeable to law 30 October last, 25 Dec 1794. James Bigham before John McCreary.

**D, 311-312**: 1 Dec 1794, William Cloud of Fairfield County, sadler, to Joseph Cloud of same, sadler, for £100 sterling, tract of 200 acres on a branch of Rockey Creek in Chester County, granted 1 June 1770 to said William Cloud. William Cloud (wax), Wit: James Cloud, Anna Cloud. Proved by the oath of James Cloud 25 Jan 1795 before John McCreary, J.P.

**D, 312-314**: 20 Dec 1794, William Cloud of Camden District, sadler to James Cloud of Chester County, Pinckney District, sadler, for £54 sterling, 150 acres on waters of Fishing Creek in Craven County, now Chester County, granted 3 June 1765 to said William Cloud, also tract of 100 acres on south side of Cattawba River adj. Mr. Cloud, Aaron Alexander, granted 21 Feb 1772 to said William Cloud. William Cloud (wax), Wit: Anna Cloud, Joseph Cloud. Proved by the oath of Joseph Cloud 21 Jan 1795 before John McCreary, J.P.

**D, 314**: John McCool of Chester County for £50 sterling to John Cherrey, a negro man named Sam, 2 Oct 1795. John McCool (Seal), Wit: James Anderson. Proved by the oath of James Anderson 28 Jan 1795 before John McCreary, J.P.

**D, 314-315**: South Carolina, Chester County. 22 Nov 1794, Thomas Roden to Jeremiah Roden, both of county aforesaid, planters, for £16, tract on waters of Sandy River, part of tract surveyed & granted to William Kirkland, 26 Nov 1785, 77 acres adj. Stuart Brown. Thomas Roden (X) (wax), Wit: James Fowler, William Roden (W), Leonard Roden. Proved by the oath of William Roden 25 Nov 1794 before Elijah Nunn, J.P.

**D, 315-316**: 1 Sept 1794, Daniel Cook of Chester County to Samuel Lowrie of same, for £20 sterling, 50 acres on waters of Fishing Creek on east side of said creek, part of 300 acres granted to Patrick Hambleton in 1768. Daniel Cook (wax), Wit: John McGlammery (X), John Lockheart, James Lockheart (mark). Acknowledged by Daniel Cook 27 Jan 1795 in open court.

**D, 317-318**: 9 Sept 1794, Michael Patton and Jane his wife of York County, SC, to James White, son of Hugh White, Esqr., of Lancaster County, SC, 200 acres whereon the said Michael Patton now lives, and part of 320 acres conveyed by James Patton to said Michael Patton by deed 25 July 1763, on waters of Ferrels Creek, 120 acres of which has since been conveyed to James Currey, and whereas Hugh White, father of said James White, hath become bound to said Michael Patton & wife Jane in his bond for £100, to provide & furnish said Michael Patton & wife Jane with what provision & cloathing may be necessary for them. Michael Patton (mark) (wax), Jane Patton (mark) (wax), Wit: John Simpson, David Patton, Sarah Simpson. Proved by the oath of John Simpson 23 Jan 1795 before Hugh White, J. L. C. C.

**D, 318-319**: 9 Dec 1794, Robert Brodie & wife Mary to Elizabeth Simpson, for twenty shillings, 391¼ acres on west side Cattawba River adj. William Catton, James Patton, James Simpson. Robert Brodie (mark) (wax), Mary Brodie (X) (wax), Wit: Thomas Johnston, Elender Johnston, Martyn Alken. Proved by the oath of Martyn Alken 11 Dec 1795 before W. Falconer, J.P.

**D, 319**: George Long of Chester County to Samuel Clement of Granville County, North Carolina, one negro girl named Jude, 9 Feb 1792. George Long (X) (Seal), Wit: Jon'thn Knight, William Estis. This bill of sale shall be discharged by paying 66 silver dollars with lawful interest on or before 15 Oct next, 9 Feb 1792. Samuel Clement (Seal), Wit: Jon'thn Knight.

**D, 320**: 21 Dec 1786, David Hopkins in Chester County to Josiah Cook of same, for £150 sterling, 155 acres on the waters of Brushey fork adj. David Hopkins, Michael Arterberry. D'd Hopkins (wax), Wit: Jeremiah Kingsley, Michael Arterberry. Proved 26 Jan 1795 by the oath of Jeremiah Kingsley before Saml Lacey, Clk.

**D, 321-322**: 7 Oct 1791, Willis Carrell of Chester County to Charles Atterberry of same, for £25 sterling, 50 acres, part of 800 acres on NE side Broad River near a branch of said River, granted to Solomon Peters 17 May 1774, conveyed by Solomon Peters to said Willis Carrell 23 July 1789. Willis Carrell (seal), Wit: Wm Graham, Philip Noland. Proved by the oath of William Graham 14 Feb 1792 before Elijah Nunn, J. P.

**D, 322-323**: 29 July 1793, Nathan Atterberry of Chester County to William Rainey of same, for £145, 176 acres, part of tract granted to Nathan Atterberry 7 Nov 1789, recorded in Book B. No. 5, page 19, on Welches branch. Nathan Atteberry (X) (LS), Wit: Elijah Nunn, John Wilkinson. Proved by the oath of Elijah Nunn 27 Jan 1795 before Reuben Lacey.

**D, 323-325**: 18 April 1789, William Archer of Rocky Creek, Chester County, planter, & Isbel Archer his wife, to John Galaspie of same, planter, for £16 s6 d3 sterling, 100 acres, part of tract granted 2 March 1768 to William Archer, 350 acres on waters of Rockey Creek, recorded in Book CCC, page 291. William Archer (mark) (wax), Isbel Archer (X) (wax), Wit: Robert Archer, Hugh Parker, Thomas Galaspie. Proved by the oath of Thomas Galaspie 22 Jan 1795 before And'w Hemphill, J.P.

**D, 326**: Levy Smith of Chester county bound to Josiah Cook of same, in the penal sum of £500 sterling, 8 March 1795, to make title to said Josiah Cook of tract of 100 acres whereon the said L. Smith now lives, and 100 acres joining the said land, surveyed for Fletchall & land surveyed for Calligan. Levy Smith (LS), Wit: Elijah Nunn. Proved by the oath of Elijah Nunn 24 Jan 1795 before Saml Lacey, Clk.

**D, 326-327**: 28 Dec 1793, Robert Williams, Blacksmith, of Chester County, to James Wier planter, of same, for £10 sterling, 50 acres on waters of Big

Rockey Creek, part of 400 acres granted to said Robert Williams 6 July 1784. Robert Williams (X) (Seal), Wit: George Eggnew (L), William Telford (mark). Proved by the oath of George Eggnew 29 Dec 1793 before And'w Hemphill, J.P.

**D, 328-329**: 16 Sept 1795, John Hagins of Chester County and wife Elizabeth to Benjamin Rives of same, for £95 sterling, 193 acres, it being the lower part of a tract granted to Casper Culp. John Hagins (Seal), Elizabeth Hagins (Seal), Wit: Williamson Harper (mark), James Patton, James Dunn. Proved by the oath of James Dunn and Williamson Harper 2 Jan 1795 before John McCreary, J.P.

**D, 329-330**: Plat of 106 acres adj. John McWilliams, Robert Coulter, John McDill. 5 Feb 1794, John McCrorey Senr of Chester County to Robert Torbet of same, for £40 sterling, 106 acres, part of tract granted to said John McCrory Senr 1 Oct 1787, 120 acres adj. John McWilliams, John McDill, Robert Coulter. John McCrorey (Seal), Wit: John McCullouch (O), David Kilpatrick, Jane McCrorey.

**D, 330-332**: 4 Oct 1794, William Gaston & Anne his wife of Chester County to James L. Gaston of same, for £150 sterling, tract on Kirkpatrick's branch, waters of Turkey Creek, in the counties of Chester & York, 231 acres, part of 150 acres granted to Robert Tindall 15 May 1771 and 204 acres being part of 750 acres granted to William Gaston 7 July 1788, and 83 acres being part of tract granted to Robert Kirkpatrick 7 June 1788, adj. John R. Love, James Love, Robert Tindall, William Gaston. James Kirkpatrick. Wm. Gaston (wax seal), Anne Gaston (mark) (wax seal),Wit: James Adair, John Brown, William P. Gaston. Proved by the oath of John Brown 26 Jan 1795 before Jo Brown, J. P.

**D, 332-334**: 5 Dec 1791, John McKinney of Chester County to Ralph McFadden of same, for £500, 95 acres, part of tract granted 18 Aug 1763 to Wm McKinney Senr deceased, 200 acres on both sides of Fishing Creek. John McKinney (wax seal), Wit: William Wyley, William McKinney. Proved by the oath of William Wyley 26 Jan 1795 before Jno Mills, J.P.

**D, 334-336**: 13 Nov 1791, William McKinney Junr of Chester County to Ralph McFadden of same, for £50, tract granted 13 Oct 1778 [*sic*] to William McKinney, 100 acres on Fishing Creek. William McKinney (wax seal), Wit: William Wylie, John McKinney. Proved by the oath of William Wylie 26 Jan 1795 before Jno Mills, J.P.

**D, 336-338**: 1 Nov 1794, Isaac McFadden, John Ferguson Senr, Pleasant Wm Ferguson, all of Chester County to Thomas Adams of same, for £50, tract granted 6 Nov 1784 to Isaac McFadden, John Ferguson, Pl William Ferguson, 112 acres on the wt branches of Fishing Creek. Isaac McFadden (Seal), mark of John Ferguson (X) (Seal), Pl W. Ferguson (Seal), Wit: Wm Wylie, Jas

McClenahan, John Wylie. Proved by the oath of William Wylie 26 Jan 1795 before Jno Mills, J.P.

**D, 338-339**: 2 Jan 1795, John Reed & Isabella his wife of Chester County to James Love Gaston of same, for £52 SC money, 100 acres granted to John McNit Alexander 10 Oct 1765 on both sides of Susey Bowls branch. John Reed (Seal), Isabella Reed (X) (Seal), Wit: Aaron Lockheart Junr, John Gaston, John Williams. Proved by the oath of John Gaston 21 Jan 1795 before Joseph Brown, J. C. C. G.

**D, 339-341**: 16 Dec 1791, Edward Strange of Camden District, Chester county, planter, to Samuel Ferguson of same, planter, for £30 sterling, part of tract granted 25 Feb 1769 to John Reynolds, 300 acres on both sides of Hagues branch adj. James Montgomery, 100 acres. Edmund Strange, Wit: Samuel Boyd, Thomas Nickles. Proved by the oath of Thomas Nickels 24 Nov 1794 before Andw Hemphill, J.P.

**D, 342-343**: 30 Jan 1794, Andrew Morrison Senr of Chester County to Samuel Lowrie, attorney at law of York County ,SC, for £15 sterling, 100 acres in Chester County on SE side Sandy River, 242 acres granted to said Andrew Morrison 4 Dec 1786. Andrew Morrison (Seal), Wit: Wm. Smith. Proved 21 Jan 1795 by the oath of Wm Smith Esquire in Chester County before Jo. Brown, J. C. C.

**D, 343-344**: 16 July 1794, Robert Kirkpatrick of York County, SC, to William Gaston of Chester County, for £5 s5, 240 acres on waters of Turkey Creek granted to Robert Kirkpatrick 7 July 1788. Robert Kirkpatrick (Seal), Wit: James L. Gaston, Mary Brown, Charlotte Land. Proved by the oath of Charlotte Land 21 Jan 1795 before Jo Brown, J.P.

**D, 344-345**: 4 Feb 1795, Alexander Crafford & wife Elizabeth of Chester County to William Richardson Davie of Hallifax County, North Carolina, for £23 sterling, 14 acres on the bank of Cattawba River, by certificate of John Gaston 19 Nov 1772, part of tract granted to Robert McClenahan. Alexander Crafford (Seal), Elisabeth Crafford (Seal), Wit: Joseph Davie, James Crafford, Joseph Gray. Proved in York County by the oath of Joseph Davie 6 Feb 1795 before Jo Palmer, J.P.

**D, 346-347**: 4 Feb 1795, Alexander Crafford & wife Elizabeth of Chester County to William Richardson Davie of Hallifax County, North Carolina, for £65, 163 acres, part of tract granted to John Lanse. Alexander Crafford (Seal), Elisabeth Crafford (Seal), Wit: Joseph Davie, James Crafford, Joseph Gray. Proved in York County by the oath of Joseph Davie 6 Feb 1795 before Jo Palmer, J.P.

**D, 347-348**: 12 Nov 1794, William Tidwell of Elbert County, Georgia, to Stephen Mayfield of Chester County, SC, for £100 sterling, 100 acres, part of tract granted to Richard Atterberry 1 Aug 1785 and transferred by said

Atterberry to William Tidwell, on the Brushy fork, waters of Sandy River. William Tidwell (W) (wax seal), Wit: James McBee, Absillum Tidwell. Proved 12 Nov 1794 by the oath of William HigginBotham, one of the Justices for Elbert.

**D, 349-350**: 27 Oct 1794, Patrick Harbison of Chester County to Rev. Robert McCullough of same, for £10 sterling, 22 acres on a branch of little Rockey Creek adj. said Patrick Harbison, James Bankhead, Samuel Frazier, Thomas McDill, said land granted to Patrick Harbison 3 April 1786. Patrick Harbison (P) (wax seal), Wit: James Peden, James Harbison, John Belley. Proved by the oath of James Harbison 26 Jan 1795 before Jno Mills, J.P.

**D, 350-352**: 27 Oct 1794, Patrick Harbison of Chester County to Rev. Robert McCullough of same, for £80 sterling, 200 acres on a small branch of Rockey Creek adj. John Adams, land granted to Patrick Harbison 13 May 1788. Patrick Harbison (P) (wax seal), Wit: James Peden, James Harbison, John Belley. Proved by the oath of James Harbison 26 Jan 1795 before Jno Mills, J.P.

**D, 352-354**: 27 Jan 1794, Thomas Baker Franklin of Chester County to William Shaw of same, for £100 sterling, 113 acres granted to said Thomas B. Franklin 5 Nov 1792 adj. Alexander Johnston, Agnes Lyles, Thomas Franklin, Notley Coats. Thomas B. Franklin (Seal), Wit: W. Hughes, P. Corbell, Thomas Kennedy. Proved by the oath of Thomas Kennedy 31 March 1795 before Saml Lacey, Clk. C. C. C.

**D, 354-357**: 7 June 1792, Peter Jones (late) sheriff of Chester County, to John Walker, planter, whereas Edward Lacey, Colonel, in the County Court of Chester, did implead William Nance on an action of debt in April Court 1790 and did obtain judgment, to levy the sum of £11 s6 d6 sterling, by writ of fieri facias, said Peter Jones sells 400 acres on Rockey Creek adj. Steel, Walker, Henry, William Ballentine, David Hunter, John Adams, Richd Carrell, said tract granted to Peter Nance & he died intestate and said lands became the property of William Nance his oldest son & heir. Peter Jones Shff (wax seal), Wit: John Wylie, Christopher Streight. Proved by the oath of Christopher Streight 28 July 1792 before John Mils, J.P. Plat included: Pursuant to a precept directed by Egerton Leigh, Surveyor General, 1 Nov 1768, I have surv'd and laid out unto Peter Nance 400 acres on Rockey Creek in Craven County adj. Steen, Walker, William Ballentine, William Hunt, John Adams. Certified 21 April 1769 John Winn, D. S.

**D, 357-360**: Lease and release. 12 & 13 Feb 1795, Robert McCullough of Chester County to Mary Nouse of said district, for £13, 63 acres part of a grant to said Robert McCullough for 200 acres on west side of Cuttawba River on waters of Little Rockey Creek and known by the name of James Black's old plantation adj. Samuel Sloan, Robert McCullough, William Stormont, granted 1 June 1787. Robert McCullough (Seal), Wit: John Graham, Alex'dr

McKown. Proved by the oath of John Graham 15 Feb 1795 before And'w Hemphill, J.P.

**D, 360-362**: 23 March 1795, Michael Dickson and wife Sarah of Pendleton County, SC, to Hugh Darrough of Chester County, for £10 sterling, 299¼ acres adj. Dickson's corner, Carter's line, part of tract granted to Michael Dickson 5 Sept 1785. Michael Dickson (Seal), Sarah Dickson (O) (Seal), Wit: David Shelton, Nicholas Bishop, Hugh Dickson. Proved by the oath of Hugh Dickson 7 April 1795 before Saml Lacey, Clk. C. C. C. G.

**D, 362-363**: 14 March 1795, Hugh Knox, Sheriff of Chester County, to Samuel Guy of York County, SC, planter, whereas James Hemphill in the County Court of Chester did implead Philip Walker Esqr in an action of debt in January Court 1793 and obtained judgment, by writ of fieri facias to levy £201 s17 d6, sells negro boy Titus about 6 years old for £27 s10 sterling. Hugh Knox S. C. C. (seal), Wit: John McCulley, Francis Henderson. Acknowledged by Hugh Knox Esqr 20 April 1795 before Saml Lacey, Clk C. C. C. G.

**D, 363-364**: 14 March 1795, Hugh Knox, Sheriff of Chester County, to Samuel Guy of York County, SC, planter, whereas James Hemphill in the County Court of Chester did implead Philip Walker Esqr in an action of debt in January Court 1793 and obtained judgment, by writ of fieri facias to levy £201 s17 d6, sells negro girl Hannah about 3 years old for £19 s10 sterling. Hugh Knox S. C. C. (seal), Wit: John McCulley, Francis Henderson. Acknowledged by Hugh Knox Esqr 20 April 1795 before Saml Lacey, Clk C. C. C. G.

**D, 365-366**: 14 March 1795, Hugh Knox, Sheriff of Chester County, to Samuel Guy of York County, SC, planter, whereas James Hemphill in the County Court of Chester did implead Philip Walker Esqr in an action of debt in January Court 1793 and obtained judgment, by writ of fieri facias to levy £201 s17 d6, sells negro woman Phillis about 30 years old for £28 sterling. Hugh Knox S. C. C. (seal), Wit: John McCulley, Francis Henderson. Acknowledged by Hugh Knox Esqr 20 April 1795 before Saml Lacey, Clk C. C. C. G.

**D, 366-367**: William Armor of Chester County appoint Thomas Jinkins of same lawful attorney to recover all such estate real & personal which shall appear to be my right either by deed of gift, will or fell to me by heirship in the state of North Carolina. William Armor (A) (wax), Wit: William Miller, Edward Halsell (E). Proved by the oath of Edward Halsell 24 April 1795 before John Pratt, J.P.

**D, 368**: Daniel Thomas Senr of Craven County, SC, for £300 current money of SC to Daniel Thomas Junr of same, a negro woman slave named Joan & child named Beck, 11 Sept 1772. Daniel Thomas (wax seal), Wit: David Hopkins, Anderson Thomas. Proved in Pinckney District by the oath of David Hopkins 22 April 1795 before Chris'r Johnson, J.P.

**D, 369**: Thomas Jinkins of Chester County for £25 sterling to William Lacey of same, a negro boy named Jacob about seven years of age, of a black complexion, stout & well made, 20 April 1795. Thomas Jinkins (seal), Wit: Samuel Lacey, John Wilson. Acknowledged by Thomas Jinkins 20 April 1795 in open court.

**D, 370**: 21 March 1795, Samuel Lowrie, Attorney at law, To John Russel of Sandy River in Chester County, for 12½ guineas, tract on waters of Sandy [River] originally granted to Saml Lowrie 1 Dec 1788, 104 acres, dated 21 March 1795. Saml Lowrie (Seal),Wit: Daniel Trussell (mark), George Rochford. Proved by the oath of Daniel Trussell 20 April 1795 before Saml Lacey, Clk. C. C. C.

**D, 371**: Elijah McCurdy son of Ann McCurdy (a Transient woman), by order of Chester County Court & Consent of one of the Overseers of the Poor, placed & Bound an apprentice in the planting or farming business to James & Rosa McCalla of Chester County, until 17 Jan 1815 at which time the said Elijah McCurry will arrive at the full age of 21 years, 21 Feb 1795. Elijah McCurdy (wax seal), James McCalla (wax seal), Rosa McCalla (mark) (wax seal), Wit: Elijah Nunn, Joseph Timms.

**D, 371-376**: Lease and release. 24 & 25 Nov 1788, Elenor White of Chester County to John Williams of same, for £20, 100 acres on the dividing ridge between Sandy River & Rockey Creek in Craven County adj. Benjamin Allis, granted to Elinor White 12 Aug 1768. Elinor White (mark) (wax seal), Wit: James Kennedy (X), William White. Proved by the oath of James Kennedy before John Bell, J.P., 16 April 1791.

**D, 376-378**: 4 Oct 1794, Peter Coonrod of Pinckney District, Chester County to Solomon Owen of Camden District, Kershaw County, for £50 sterling, 150 acres, part of 380 acres on waters of Sandy River adj. one Douglass, John Ferguson, Lewis, granted to James Nickleson 3 April 1786 and conveyed from said Nickleson to David McCalla and from David McCalla to Peter Coonrod. Peter Coonrod (was seal), Wit: Hugh Mellone, Bartholomew Peek, Charles Raley Junr. Proved by the oath of Charles Raley 20 April 1795 before Elijah Nunn, J.P.

**D, 378-379**: 11 March 1795, Richard Head and wife Sarah of Chester County, planter, to Allen DeGraffinreidt of same, merchant, for £15 sterling, 70 acres, part of 196 acres granted to said Richard Head 6 Feb 1792 on south side of the south fork of Sandy River on a branch called Cockrells branch adj. land surveyed for Wm. Stone. Richard Head (seal), Sarah Head (seal), Wit: Thomas Gore, John Price, James Oneal (mark). Proved by the oath of Thomas Gore 11 March 1795 before John Pratt, J.P.

**D, 380-381**: 11 March 1795, Richard Head and wife Sarah of Chester County, planter, to Allen DeGraffinreidt of same, merchant, for £10 sterling, 32 acres, part of 196 acres granted to said Richard Head 6 Feb 1792 on north side of the south fork of Sandy River on a branch called Cockrells branch adj. land surveyed for Wm. Stone. Richard Head (seal), Sarah Head (seal), Wit: Thomas Gore, John Price, James Oneal (mark). Proved by the oath of Thomas Gore 11 March 1795 before John Pratt, J.P.

**D, 381-383:** 11 May 1795, Paul Ferguson Senr and wife Anne of Chester county, planter, to Paul Ferguson Junr, for £100 sterling, 100 acres on the waters of Sandy River on the north side of Chester County Court House, granted to said Paul Ferguson Senior 7 Aug 1786, recorded in Book MMMM, page 178, adj. said Paul Ferguson Senior, Curtis Caldwell, Benjamin Reedar. Paul Ferguson (wax seal), Anne Ferguson (X) (wax seal), Wit: James Quinton, Mary Graham (mark), William Jones. Proved by the oath of Mary Graham 15 May 1795 before Saml Lacey, Clk Chester County Court.

**D, 384-388:** Lease and release. 14 & 15 March 1783, Samuel Sloan of Camden District and wife Agness to John Mebin of same, for £100, 100 acres in Craven County on So fork of Rockey Creek adj. Jonathan Dungamens, James Car, granted 17 March 1775. Samuel Sloan (wax), Agness Sloan (mark) (seal), Wit: Stafford Currey, John Stormand, Samuel Erwin. Proved in Chester county by the oath of John Stormand 16 March 1796 before And'w Hemphill, J.P.

**D, 388-392:** Lease and release. 2 & 3 June 1794, John Gwinn of Fairfield County, Camden District, planter, to Nezereus Whitted of same, planter, for £50 sterling, 100 acres on Little River in Chester County, granted 20 Aug 1767, recorded in Book BBB, page 163. John Gwinn (LS), Wit: Francis Lee, John Wagers (X), Thomas Shannon. Proved by the oath of Francis Lee 6 June 1795 before Saml Lacey, Clk of Chester County Court.

**D, 392-393:** 24 Feb 1793, William Hermon of Chester County to John Hermon of same, for £10, 100 acres on the south side of the north fork of Bull Skin, part of a tract laid out for & granted to William Collin, 200 acres, 20 July 1772, conveyed to said William Hermon 23 Feb 1793. William Hermin (LS), Wit: Gar'dr Jamieson, Robt Jamieson. Acknowledged in open court by William Hermon.

**D, 393-395:** 25 Dec 1790, Abel Johnston and wife Sarah of Chester County to William Kenney of same, planter, for £25 sterling, 138 acres on waters of Rockey Creek granted to said Abel Johnston 5 April 1790. Abel Johnston (X) (Seal), Sarah Johnston (X) (Seal), Wit: James Kenney, James Magors, James Walker. Proved by the oath of James Kenney 24 June 1795 before Saml Lacey, Clk of the court.

**D, 396-397:** Plat of 150 acres included. 1 Jan 1794, William Wood & wife Sarah of Chester County to Thomas B. Franklin of same, for £100 sterling, 150 acres, part of tract granted to Edward Wilson in Craven County now Chester County, 250 acres on the north side of Broad River on a small branch of Sandy River called Stoney fork, adj. John Bosher, Edward Wilson, conveyed to said William Wood by deed 15 April 1792, recorded 17 Sept 179- in Book

**B, page 384.** William Wood (Seal), Sarah Wood (X) (Seal), Wit: Martin Elam, Letishe Stone (mark). Proved by the oath of Martin Elam 24 June 1795 before John Pratt, J.,P.

**D, 398-399:** 13 March 1794, William Watson of Chester County to James Oneal of same, for £30 sterling, 146 acres on waters of Sandy River near a creek called Martins branch. William Watson (W) (Seal), Wit: Samuel Stone, Joshua Wade. Proved by the oath of Joshua Wade 26 April 1794 before John Pratt, J.P.

**D, 399-403:** Lease and release. 19 & 20 Sept 1792, John McClurkin & wife Margaret of Fairfield County to Andrew Walker of Chester County for £100 sterling, part of 518 acres granted 1 Oct 1787 to said John McClurkin, on waters of Rockey Creek adj. Elizabeth Chambers, Wilson, William Boils, William Boyd, John Burns, 259 acres. John McClurkin (Seal), Margaret McClurkin (mark) (Seal), Wit: George Kennedy, John Boyls. Proved 18 April 1795 by the oath of John Boyls before William McQuiston, J. P.

**D, 404:** Robert Dunlap of Chester County bound to Thomas Baker Franklin of same, in the penal sum of £100 sterling, 27 Apr 1789, to make title to 100 acres of land that he bought of said Franklin. Robert Dunlap (R) (Seal), Wit: John Burns, John Franklin. Proved by the oath of John Franklin 13 June 1795 before John Pratt, J.P.

**D, 404-405, 408-410:** Lease and release. 8 & 9 Dec 1794, Thomas Stroud of Chester County to Ebenezer Elliott of same, for £56 sterling, 160 acres on the east side of Beaverdam Creek adj. Hugh Wilson, Daniel Green, William Nettles, Thomas Stroud. Thomas Stroud (X) (wax seal), Wit: John McCown, James McCown, Edward Steudman. Proved by the oath of James McCown 13 Feb 1795 before John McCreary, J.P.

**D, 406-408:** 1 April 1777, Casper Sleeker & wife Elizabeth of Craven County, SC, planter, to John Featherston of same, planter, for £150 current money, tract granted 23 Jan 1773 to Casper Sleeker, 150 acres, half of 300 acres on draughts of Fishing Creek adj. David Lomand, Hickland, John White, John McFadden. Casper Sleger (Seal), Elizabeth Sleger (X) (Seal), Wit: Marshil Jones, William Crook, Beckey King Collson (X). Proved in Camden District 26 Nov 1777 by the oath of Beckey King Colson before James Simpson.

**D, 408-410:** [see above with 404-405]

**D, 410-412:** 22 Aug 1794, John Featherston and wife Willey of Richland County, SC, to William Giles of Chester County, for £100 sterling, tract on waters of Fishing Creek on the north side, 150 acres, being one half of 300 acres granted to Casper Sleeker 23 Jan 1773, conveyed by said Slicker to said Featherston 1 April 1777. John Featherston (wax seal), Willey Featherston (wax seal), Wit: Richard Featherson, Samuel Bell, Lucey Featherson (X).

Proved in Chester County by the oath of Richard Featherston 18 April 1795 before John McCreary, J.P.

**D, 412-413**: Plat of 10 acres adj. Edward Self, Robert Underwood, James Leigh. South Carolina, Pinckney District, Chester County. 12 Dec 1794, Robert Lemonds, planter, of county aforesaid, to James Leigh of same, for £2 s6 d8, 10 acres on a branch of Sandy River called Stones fork or creek, part of 155 acres granted to said Robert Lemmonds 2 Oct 1786, recorded in Book OOOO, page 130. Robert Lemonds (wax seal), Wit: Jane Johnston (X), William Dushel, Richard Johnson. Proved by the oath of Richard Johnston 25 June 1795 before E. Nunn, J.P.

**D, 413-415**: 23 Jan 1795, William Goad & wife Mary of Chester County to Hugh Reid of same, for £60, tract granted 6 March 1786 to William Kirkland, 150 acres on a branch of Turkey Creek. N. B. Be it remembers that a small corner cut off by an old survey we are not to be answerable for. William Goad (wax seal), Mary Goad (mark) (wax seal), Wit: E. Nunn, James McCalla. Proved by the oath of Elijah Nunn 25 June 1795 before Saml Lacey, Clk of the Court.

**D, 415**: John Davis, sons of John Davis decd, by order of Chester County Court & Consent of Gen Edward Lacey, Gardian of said John Davis, is bound an apprentice to the sadler's trade to Robert Tindall Junr of Chester County, until 25 June 1800 at which time the said John Davis will be discharged from this indenture, 25 June 1795. Edward Lacey (seal), Robert Tindall (Seal), Wit: E. Nunn, J.P.

**D, 415-416**: James Graham of Chester County of Pinckney District sold to James McCaw a negro boy named Sampson for £30 sterling, 5 Dec 1793. James Graham. Wit: James Chesnut, Andrew Graham. Proved by the oath of Andrew Graham 19 March 1795 before John Pratt, J.P.

**D, 416-419**: Lease and release. 22 & 23 June 1795, Robert Kelsey of Chester County to John McNinch of same, for £50 sterling, 100 acres in Craven County now Chester on a branch of Rockey Creek adj. Henry Smith, granted to Thomas Kelsey 6 Feb 1773, recorded in Book TTT, page 242, the said Thomas Kelsey deceased intestate & Hugh Kelsey the eldest brother being the heir to said tract did convey to Robert Kelsey conveyed to Robert Kelsey 2 Jan 1788. Robert Kelsey (Seal), Wit: Andrew Graham, James Robinson, Arch'd Kell. Acknowleged in open court 25 June 1795 by Robert Kelsey.

**D, 419-420**: 20 Jan 1795, Hez. Alexander of Macklenburgh County, North Carolina, to Thomas Stevenson of Chester County, SC, for £50 north currency, tract granted to him 27 Sept 1766 on waters of South fork of Susa Bowl's Branch of Turkey Creek on both sides of Floyds waggon road near Moses McCarter, 200 acres. Hez. Alexander (seal), Wit: James Eager, Hugh Stevenson, Joel Alexander. Proved in Chester County 13 June 1795 by the oath of James Eager.

**D, 421-423**: 11 Dec 1794, Denniss Carrell & wife Sarah of Chester County to Samuel Moberley of Fairfield County, planter, for £90 sterling, 128 acres on the waters of Sandy River on a creek thereof called Welches fork in Chester county, granted to John Dougherty 23 Aug 1784, memorial entered in Book AAAA, page 405, transferred from said John Dougherty to Thomas Roden 5 Feb 1787, also another tract of 100 acres granted to said John Dougherty 3 April 1786, recorded in Book KKKK, and transferred from said John Dougherty to Thomas Roden, adj. Isaac Taylor, James Dougherty, part of the same survey which was granted to Thomas Roden, also another parcel of land purchased by said Thomas Roden of Martin Elam, 10 acres, transferred from said Thomas Roden to Denniss Carrell 4 Dec 1793, recorded in Book C, page 299 11 Dec 1793. Denniss Carrell (wax seal), Sarah Carrell (X) (was seal), Wit: Edward Mobley, Charles Arterbery (mark), Elizabeth Carrell (X). Proved by the oath of Edward Mobley 25 June 1795 before Thomas Jinkins, J.P.

**D, 423-424**: 9 June 1795, David Kilpatrick of Chester County to John Hermon, for £8 33½ acres on both sides north fork of Bullskin, part of tract granted to David Kilpatrick 4 Nov 1798. David Killpatrick (seal), Wit: William Hermon, Robert Torbit. Proved by the oath of William Hermon 25 June 1795 before Hugh Knox, J.P.

**D, 424-426**: South Carolina, Chester County. Archibald McQuiston of Fairfield County, planter, for £25 sterling to James Cooper of county aforesaid, doctor, 100 acres on a branch of Rockey Creek called Bull Run, granted to John Henderson and by him conveyed to Archibald McQuiston 16 Aug 1785, dated 3 Jan 1793. Archibald McQuiston (wax seal), Wit: Andrew McQuiston, Hugh McQuiston, James McQuiston. Proved 15 June 1795 by the oath of Andrew McQuiston before William McQuiston, J.P.

**D, 427-428**: 8 March 1794, James Young of Chester County to William Gaston for £10 sterling, tract on Jack Love's branch of Turkey Creek, adj. land granted to James McCawley, David Aekins, David Hopkins, Margaret Bowden, 200 acres, part of a tract of 295 acres granted to the said Young 7 Feb 1791, adj. James McCawley, John Anderson, James Johnston, William Gaston, Hopkins. James Young (wax seal), Wit: John Anderson, John Young, Sarah Young (mark). Proved by the oath of John Anderson 2 April 1795 before John McCreary, J.P.

**D, 428-429**: 29 Jan 1795, Jonathan Hemphill and wife Esther of Chester County to Henry Dye of same, for £30 sterling, 100 acres on waters of Rockey Creek adj. Alexander's old place, land surveyed for Reece Hughs, Jonathan Hemphill. Jon. Hemphill (Seal), Esther Hemphill (X) (Seal), Wit: William Stone, John Dye (X), Charles Kitchen. Proved by the oath of William Stone 23 June 1795 before Andw Hemphill, J.P.

**D, 429-430**: John McMullin of York, fuller, for £100 sterling to Josiah Leak, the following property which is now discharged of the attachment which Hugh & Thomas White has levied on it, being my property, one black mare & colt, one cow red, one bay mare, one large pot and oven, one tub and paid, flat iron, one saddle & two bridles, 25 bushels of corn, 2 suits of Clothes, one jacket & breeches, five yards jeans, one pair cotten stockings, a quantity of cotton and flax thread, 23 yrds linsey cloth, one pair boots, one pair of shoe brushes, one house bell, one fur hat, one shirt, 2 neck cloths, blue vat & butels, 15 pieces of cloth finished and pressed, 21 pieces dyed and ready for finishing. John McMullen (LS), Wit: James Galt. Proved in Chester County by the oath of James Galt Esqr 29 June 1795 before E. Nunn, J.P.

**D, 430-431:** 27 Feb 1793, William Hermon & John Hermon, both of the County of Chester, SC, to Robert Jamieson of same, for £3 sterling, 100 acres, on the SW side of a tract of land laid out and granted to William Collins 20 July 1772, by deed of conveyance to the said William Hermon who did convey one half of land to John Hermon & now each jointly and separately do convey a part of their land to Robert Jamieson supposed to contain 100 acres. William Hermon (Seal), John Herman (Seal), Wit: Gard'r Jamieson, Forsith McLonem. Proved by the oath of Garner Jamieson in Chester County 27 June 1795 before Hugh Knox, J.P.

**D, 432:** 23 Feb 1793, William Collins of Chester county to William Hermon of same, for £16, tract on Bull Skin, a branch of Rockey Creek in Chester county, being a tract laid out for & granted to said William Collins 20 July 1772. William Collins (Seal), Wit: Gar'dr Jamieson, Daniel Cook. Proved by the oath of Garner Jamieson 27 June 1795 before Hugh Knox, J.P.

**D, 433-434:** 16 Nov 1791, William McCaw Senr of Chester County to Samuel McCaw of same, for £5 sterling, 100 acres on the Bull run branch of Rockey Creek, adj. Thomas McFie, Samuel Wier. William McCaw (wax seal), Wit: Edward McDaniel, Hervy McCary. Proved by the oath of both wit 27 June 1796 before Hugh Knox, J.P.

**D, 434:** South Carolina, Chester County. Personally appeared Rhoda Russell who being sworn deposeth that she had a title bond form John Humphries to this Deponant 7 two of her children for 50 acres of land & she thinks the land was to bound on Sealeys Creek & include the place whereon this deponant now lives, which bond was taken out of her possession on the evening of the 23rd of this instant or either lost or mislaid so that she cannot find it, that the above mentioned bond was wrote by William Embrie & signed in his presence, 27 June 1795. Rhoda Russel (X), E. Nunn, J.P.

**D, 434-435:** 22 Oct 1784, Alexander Miller of Camden District, SC, to James Owens of same, for £101 s5 sterling, 100 acres on a branch of little Rocky Creek. Alexander Miller (Seal), Wit: Abram Miller, Thomas Steel (T). Proved by the oath of Thomas Steel 21 June 1795 before Andrew Hemphill, J.P.

**D, 436:** South Carolina, Chester County. Thomas Roden Senr being duly sworn deposeth that William Roden Junr is the lawful heir of William Roden Senr who was nephew to & lawful heir of John Winman decd who formerly lived in Cuthbert County in Maryland which said John Winman died without any lawful issue & further this deponent saith that after the death of said John Winman that he was informed that John Gray sent word to the said William Roden Senr to come & Take possession of a tract of land which as the property of said John Winman decd & Further this deponant saith that the reason why the s'd William Roden did not immediately go & Take possession of said John Winman's estate was his living in Virginia, 28 July 1795. Thomas Roden Senr. E. Nunn, J.P.

**D, 437-438**: 3 Oct 1786, James Owens of Chester County to Robert Harper of same, for £100 sterling, 100 acres on a branch of Little Rockey Creek. James Owens (X) (Seal), Wit: Samuel Ferguson, Thomas Steel (T). Proved by the oath of Thomas Steel 21 June 1795 before And'w Hemphill, J.P

**D, 438-440**: 17 Nov 1774, Daniel Coutney of Camden District, SC, to James Harper of same, for £200 tract granted 2 April 1773, 100 acres on Rockey Creek adj. James Hemple, recorded in Book OOO, page 287. Daniel Cottney (wax seal), Wit: Charles Hemphill, Robert Harper (mark). Proved by the oath of Robert Harper 1 June 1784 before James Knox, J.P.

**D, 441-442**: 18 Sept 1790, Catharine McKain of Camden District, Fairfield County, to Robert Harper of Chester County, said district, for £30 sterling, 200 acres on a branch of Little Rockey Creek adj. Isaac Taylor, James Strong. Catharine McKain (mark) (Seal), Wit: Robert McCullough, Abram Miller. Proved by the oath of Robert McCollough 21 June 1795 before And'w Hemphill, J.P.

**D, 442-444**: 17 Oct 1782, Hugh Boyd & Rachel Harper of Rockey Creek & John Richman of Wateree Creek, all in Camden District, SC, to Robert Harper of same, for £200, tract granted 2 April 1773 to Daniel Cotney, 100 acres on Rockey Creek adj. James Hemphill, and conveyed by Daniel Cottney to Robert Harper deceased, and the said Harper willed said tract to the above named persons. Hugh Boyd (X) (Seal), John Richman (I) (Seal), Rachel Harper (mark) (Seal), Wit: Samuel Erwin, Samuel Sloan, Wm. Lowry. Proved by the oath of Samuel Erwin in Camden District 18 June 1784 before Samuel Knox, J.P.

**D, 445-446**: 16 Aug 1779, John McDonald of State of Virginia, Augusta County, to Alexander Miller of Camden District on Rockey Creek, for £300 lawfull current money of South Carolina, tract on a branch of Rockey Creek, vacant on all sides, 100 acres. John McDonald (Seal), Wit: Hugh McDonald, Patrick Lowry, William Lowry. Proved in Chester County by the oath of William Lowry 21 June 1795 before Andw Hemphill, J.P.

**D, 446-450**: Lease and release. 13 Aug 1787, Thomas Baker Franklin of Chester County, planter, to David Weir Senr of same, for £30 sterling, 103 acres on a small fork of Rockey Creek adj. David Bell, David McDill, John Mebin, Archibald Coulter, David Wier. Thomas Baker Franklin (Seal), Wit:

John Bell, Thomas McClurkin. Proved by the oath of Thomas McClurkin 11 March 1793 before John Bell, J.P.

**D, 451-453**: 24 Nov 1777, John McLilly and wife Elizabeth of Camden District, Mecklinburgh and State of North Carolina, weaver, to William Martin and Mary his wife of Camden District, Craven County, tract granted 16 Dec 1766 by SC to John Black, 150 acres between Cattawba & Broad River adj. John Russel, land surveyed for said John Black. John McLilley (Seal), Wit: Hugh Stuart, William Martin. Proved by the oath of Hugh Stuart 17 Oct 1795 before Hugh Knox, J.P.

**D, 453-455**: 5 Sept 1795, Archibald Martin of Chester county to James Martin of same, for £40 sterling, 50 acres, part of 150 acres granted to John Black by grant 16 Dec 1766 adj. John Russel, and said John Black did sell to John McLilley recorded in Book N, number 445-7, and said John McLilley did sell to William Martin 24 Nov 1777, and William Martin did give and bequeath said 50 acres to Archibald Martin. Archibald Martin (wax seal), Sarah Martin (mark) (wax seal), Wit: George Williamson, Robert Caldwell. Proved by the oath of Robert Caldwell 11 Oct 1795 before Hugh Knox, J.P.

**D, 455-457**: Daniel McElduff of Lancaster County, SC, for £1000 sterling, to Walthal Burton of North Carolina, one negro man slave named Will with a negro woman named Phoebe his wife and their children, also a negro man named Charles & Cate his wife & their children, 20 Feb 1796. Daniel McElduff (LS), Wit: John Pratt, J.P., Thomas Jinkins, J.P.

Before John Pratt and Thomas Jinkins appeared Daniel McElduff and made oath that whilst he lived in the Elinoise on the Mississippi that he the deponant were feloniously rob'd of a number of negroes, viz named William & Phoebe his wife & her children, Charles & Cate his wife and her children, taken by a certain Jack Clam Morgan & that his deponant declares on oath that he never bargain sold nor impowered any other person to make rights to the above negroes, as he has now conveyed them to Mr. Walthal Burton, 20 Feb 1796.

22nd Feb 1796. I do hereby signed over all my right, title & Claim to within Bill of sale unto William Jinkins for valued received. Walthal Burton, Wit: Martin Elam. Proved by the oath of Martin Elam 25 July 1796 before Thomas Jinkins, J.P. Proved by the oath of John Pratt, Esqr., 26 July 1796 before El. Nunn, J.P. Recorded 27 July 1796.

**D, 457-458**: Francis Robinson of Edgefield County appoint John Tims of Chester County, SC, my lawful attorney to ask, demand, sue for, recover & receive of James Conner of the State of North Carolina, Mecklenburgh County, a certain negro woman named Beck or Rebecca & a child named Nelly & others the increase of said negro Beck or Rebecca, which negro is claimed by me Francis Robinson as my property, 11 Aug 1796. Francis

Robinson (Seal), Wit: Amos Tims, Richard Robinson. Proved by the oath of Amos Tims 10 Aug 1796 before John Pratt, J.P.

**D, 458**: South Carolina, Chester County. Sarah Stroud (X), wife of Thomas Stroud, relinquished dower to Ebenezer Elliott, 8 Feb 1797 before W. Gaston, J. C. C.

### END OF DEED BOOK D

E, 1A: James L. Gaston of Chester county for $215 to Jehu Hoskins of the City of Charleston, 100 acres granted to John McNit Alexander 13 Oct 1765 on Susy Bowles branch, waters of Broad River, dated 23 April 1798. Jas L. Gaston. N. B. The above premises to be delivered to Jehu Hoskins or his agent the first day of January 1799.) Wit: John Gaston William Johnsey, John Windsor (X). Proved by the oath of William Johnsey 24 April 1798 before Wm. Gaston, J.C.C. Jane Gaston, wife of James L. Gaston, relinquished dower 24 April 1798 before Wm. Gaston, J.C.C.

E, 1-2: 25 Feb 1793, James & Richard Johnston of Chester County to William McQuiston, of same, for £12 sterling, 100 acres on a branch of Little River beginning where Mr. Alexander Johnston's and William McQuiston's lines intersect, part of a plat granted to Alexander Johnson 1 Jan 1787, recorded in Book PPPP, page 497. James Johnston (Seal), Richard Johnston (Seal), Wit: Andrew Graham, James Chesnut, Robert Andrew. Proved in Chester County by the oath of Robert Andrew 29 March 1798 before John Bell, J. P.

E, 3: At a court held continued and held by adjournment for Chester County 29 June 1795, Present Edward Lacey, one of the Judges of Chester County. Ordered that a Dedimus Potestatem issue to any two magistrates in the County of Bedford, State of Virginia, to take the acknowledgements of John Walker of county & state aforesaid of two deeds of conveyance of two several tracts of land in the County of Chester, made to James Galt upon the death of two witnesses present at the execution of said deeds of conveyance. Dedimus dated 31 July 1795. Saml Lacey, Clk of Chester County Court.

E, 4-5: 23 April 1795, John Walker of State of Virginia, County of Bedford, to James Galt of South Carolina, District of Pinckney for £50 sterling, 116 acres on Susey Boles branch, a branch of Turkey Creek, part of tract of 350 acres granted to Catharine Brown 23 Jan 1773, and said 116 acres conveyed from said Catharine Brown to William Brown by deed 10 Dec 1783, and from said William Brown to John Walker 9 April 1788. John Walker (Seal), Wit: John Crumpacker, Elizabeth Crumpacker (X). Pursuant to a Commission from the County Court of Chester, we have caused John Crumpacker and Elizabeth Crumpacker to come before us and they made oath that they saw the within mentioned John Walker signed the deed, 12 Aug 1795. James Callaway (wax seal), Thos Holt (wax seal).

E, 5-7: 23 April 1795, John Walker of State of Virginia, County of Bedford, to James Galt of South Carolina, District of Pinckney for £50 sterling, two surveys, 590 acres on Susey Boles branch, a branch of Turkey Creek, one of which surveys was granted to Aaron Lockheart and by legal deed is now vested in said John Walker, and other said to contain 190 acres granted to said John Walker. John Walker (Seal), Wit: John Crumpacker, Elizabeth Crumpacker (X), Peter Crumpacker (X). John Walker of Bedford County, Virginia, but formerly of Chester County, South Carolina, miller, do acknowledge the receiving of £50 sterling, 23 April 1795. Pursuant to a Commission from the County Court of Chester, we have caused John

154

Crumpacker and Elizabeth Crumpacker to come before us and they made oath that they saw the within mentioned John Walker signed the deed, 12 Aug 1795. James Callaway, Thos Holt.

E, 7-9: 4 March 1795, Robert Lemond of Chester County to Robert Andrews of same, for £40 sterling, 105 acres granted to Robert Lemonds 2 Oct 1786, excepting 40 acres sold by said Lemond to Jeremiah Grisham on the east side of said tract, and also 10 acres sold by said Lemond to James Lea, on the north side of said tract, recorded in Book OOOO, page 160. Robert Lemond (wax seal), Wit: Robert Murdock, Edward Blackstock, William Omelveney. Proved by the oath of Robert Murdock before William McQuiston, J. Q., 4 March 1795.

E, 9-10: 23 June 1795, John McWaters of Chester County to Robert Archer & William Peden (executors of the estate of William Archer deceased) of county aforesaid, for £10 s20 d10, tract of land on which I now live, 100 acres granted to John Baylie on waters of Rockey Creek. John McWaters (LS), Wit: Anthony Savage, James Pedan.

E, 10-11: 18 July 1795, Peter Nance of the State of North Carolina, County of Surrey, planter, to William Bradford of Chester County, SC, for £50 sterling, 108 acres, part of tract granted to Thomas Roden and conveyed to said Peter Nance. Peter Nance (wax seal), Wit: Jacob McCraw, James Graham, Samuel Freeman. Proved by the oath of James Graham 21 Sept 1795 before Saml Lacey, Clk Chester county Court.

E, 11-13: 28 July 1795, Robert Tindall (shoe-maker) of Chester county to Robert Tindall (sadler) of same, for £10 sterling, 100 acres, part of 400 acres granted to Philip Grisham 17 May 1774, on the south branch of Mill Creek of Turkey Creek, north side of Broad River, which 400 acres was conveyed to said Robert Tindall by John Grisham, elder son to the said Philip Grisham, 5 Feb 1785. Robert Tindall (Seal), Wit: Stephen Ferguson, Samuel Gelliher, Samuel Lowery. Proved by the oath of Stephen Ferguson 28 Sept 1795 before Reubin Lacey, J.P.

E, 13-14: 7 July 1787, William Taylor of Lancaster County, planter, to William Peden of Chester County, planter, for £400, tract granted 17 Dec 1772 to Jacob Taylor, 200 acres on both sides of Rockey Creek adj. Hugh McDonald. William Taylor (Seal), Wit: Anthony Savage, James Peden. Proved by the oath of James Peden Esqr., 21 Sept 1795 before Wm McQuiston, J.P.

E, 13-17: Lease and release. 23 & 26 Aug 1787, Thomas McClurkin of Chester County, planter, to David Weir of same, planter, for £40 sterling, 100 acres on waters of Rockey Creek, granted 16 June 1768. Thomas McClurkin (Seal),Wit: John Bell, Matthew McClurkin. Proved by the oath of Matthew McClurkin 11 March/May 1793 before John Bell, J.P.

**E, 18-19**: Plat showing adj. land owners Richd Warring & Wm Boyd, Richd Evans, John Evans, Owen Evans. 21 July 1795, William Boyd & wife Ann of Chester County to David Boyd of same, for £40 sterling, part of two plantations, one granted to Richard Waring & the other to William Boyd 4 Jan 1790 on waters of Sandy River, adj. John Evans, Richard Evans, Richard Evans, Richard Warring & William Boyd, Owens Evans deceased. Wm Boyd (Seal), Wit: Ann Boyd (Seal), Wit: Wm Rainey, Jas Woodburn, Wm Boyd. Acknowledged in open court by William Boyd 21 Sept 1795, Saml Lacey, Clk, C. C. C.

**E, 19-20**: 26 Aug 1792, Thomas McElhany of Chester County, planter, to Stephen Titshaw, planter, of same, for five shillings, tract granted 7 May 1792 to Thomas McElhaney, 296 acres surveyed to him by William Boyd by virtue of a warrant dated 9 Nov 1791 on waters of Rockey Creek adj. William Miller, James Knox, Robert Gaston, Robert Walker, Robert Miller. Thomas McElhaney (wax seal), Wit: Samuel Wright, Isaac Shillhouse (X). Proved by the oath of Isaac Shillhouse 27 Aug 1792 before John Mills,J.P.

**E, 20-21**: 4 May 1795, John Allen of Chester County to Samuel Allen of same, for £100 sterling, tract on south side of the Lick Branch, 175 acres, part of two tracts of land as I john Allen purchased of George Standford & Zacariah Kitchen, adj. Marrains, Boyd. John Allen (Seal), Wit: William Hudson, James Glenn (X). Proved by the oath of James Glenn 16 Oct 1795 before J. McCreary, J.P.

**E, 21-23**: 14 Oct 1795, Stephen Siddle & Mary his wife of Chester County to Cornelius Dorsey of same, for £100 sterling, 150 acres, part of tract granted to Edward Wilson, in Craven County, now Chester County, 250 acres on north side Broad River on a small fork of Sandy River called Stoney fork adj. John Baker, Edward Wilson, conveyed by Edward Wilson to William Wood 15 April 1792, recorded 17 Sept 1792 in Chester County in Book B, page 384, and said William Wood did convey to Thomas Baker Franklin and said Franklin to Stephen Siddle. Stephen Siddle (S) (wax seal), Mary Siddle (wax seal), Wit: William Bradford, John Allen. Proved by the oath of William Bradford 31 Oct 1795 before Saml Lacey Clk of Chester County Court.

**E, 23-24**: 30 April 1794, John Bigham of Maclenburgh County, NC, planter, to John Bell of Chester County, SC, for £10 sterling, 100 acres on Rockey Creek adj. John Burns, Michael Dickson, John Burns, John Walker, granted to John Bigham 9 Nov 1774. John Bigham (wax seal), Wit: Thomas McCullough, Matthew Knox. Proved by the oath of Thomas McCullough 31 Oct 1795 before Saml Lacey, Clk Chester County Court.

**E, 24-25**: 4 Aug 1795, George Lewis of Chester county to Robert Ferguson & Abraham Ferguson of same, for £1 s8, 2 acres on west side of Fishing Creek, part of tract granted to William McFadden, 24 Jan 1770, 200 acres transferred by said McFadden to George Lewis, said two acres by plat of William Gaston 7 March 1795, adj. William Wylie, to said Robert & Abraham Ferguson as members of the Baptist Church for the publick benefit of the Baptist constituted in 1795 by advise & directions of the Bethel Association of the Baptist Church and known by the term of Hopewell Church. George Lewis (wax seal), Wit: James Fowler, Samuel Bradley, Walter Lock (mark). Proved by the oath of Walter Lock 15 Aug 1795 before John McCreary, J.P.

**E, 26-27**: 25 Oct 1788, Robert Ferguson & wife Elizabeth of Chester county to Abraham Ferguson of same, for £100, part of tract granted 10 May 1768 to James Ferguson Senr, 200 acres on SW side Catawba River between Fishing Creek & Rockey [Creek], and said James Ferguson released one half of said tract to said Robert Ferguson 11 June 1787. Robert Ferguson (wax seal), Elisabeth Ferguson (X) (wax seal), Wit: Wm Gaston, John Collins. Proved by the oath of William Gaston 9 Sept 1790 before Jas Knox, J.P.

**E, 28**: 2 May 1795, James Adair & wife Mary of Chester County to Aaron Lockert of same, for £40 sterling, 250 acres on waters of Mill Creek, part of tract of 12,700 acres granted to Josiah Hill 7 July 1786 adj. Jane Young. James Adare (wax seal), Mary Adare (wax seal), Wit: James Tyner, John Estes, Marget Adare. Proved by the oath of John Estes 11 July 1795 before E. Nunn, J.P.

**E, 29**: 2 May 1795, James Adair & wife Mary of Chester County to Aaron Lockert of same, for £40 sterling, 100 acres on waters of Mill Creek, tract granted to Jane Young 1 Sept 1768 adj. Jane Young. James Adare (wax seal), Mary Adare (wax seal), Wit: James Tyner, John Estes, Margret Adare. Proved by the oath of John Estes 11 July 1795 before E. Nunn, J.P.

**E, 30-31**: 29 Jan 1791, Abraham Markley of City of Charleston, SC, to Thomas McCulley of Chester County, for £35 sterling, 200 acres as laid down in the original plat & grant to Thomas Lehre of 200 acres, recorded in Book RRRR, page 324. Abr'm Markley (wax seal), Wit: John Bleair, Abr'm Tyson. Proved 15 Feb 1793 by the oath of John Blair before Philip Walker, Esq. Proved by the oath of John Bleair 14 Nov 1795 before Hugh Knox, J.P.

**E, 31-32**: James Adair of Pinckney District, Chester county, to James L. Gaston of same, a negro girl named Harriett, 5 Nov 1795. James Adare, Wit: Robert Owen, Amos Timms. Proved by the oath of Robert Owen 21 Nov 1795 before Edward Lacey.

**E, 32-34**: Lease and release. 25 & 26 Oct 1795, James Phillips & Philip Pearson of Fairfield County, planters, to Henry Mabin of Chester County, for £37 sterling, 150 acres on Little Rockey Creek in Chester county adj. Peter Sandifur, William Ford, William McCluer, Widow Erwin, granted 3 Jan 1769 to Mary Dunsheth. James Philips (seal), Phil: Pearson (Seal), Wit: Robert Bryson, John Dodds. Proved by the oath of Robert Bryson 27 Nov 1795 before Andw Hemphill, J.P.

E, 35-36: 15 June 1790, William Miller & Margaret his wife of Chester County to Cornelius Dorsey of same, for £40, 80 acres, part of tract granted 7 Jan 1780 [sic] to William Miller for 420 acres on waters of North fork of Rockey Creek adj. Samuel Weir, Rea's land, Samuel Hamelton, Robert Morrow, Robert Bradford, James Crawford, James Wylie, Thomas Blair. William Miller (wax seal), Margert Miller (mark) (wax seal), Wit: Hu McCluer, Phil: Walker. Proved by the oath of Hugh McCluer, Esqr., 23 Dec 1795 before Hugh Knox, J.P.

E, 36-37: John McWatters of Chester County for £10 s12 to John McCreary of same, one negro woman named Violet county born about 30 years of age, also three feather beds, covering & steds, 16 Jan 1795. John McWatters (wax seal), Wit: James Norton, Samuel Telford. Proved by the oath of James Norton 26 Jan 1795 before E. Nunn, J.P.

E, 37-38: 24 July 1795, Jonathan Jones & Bethsaba his wife of Chester county to John Miller of same, for £15 sterling, tract granted to Jonathan Jones 2 Oct 1786, 114 acres on south fork of waters of Fishing Creek adj. John Thompson, Peter Eaves[?], Edward Martin, William Jones, Jonathan Jones. Jonathan Jones (wax seal), Bathshaba Jones (mark), (seal), Wit: Robert Harper, James Cook (mark). Proved by the oath of Robert Harper 31 Dec 1795 before Hugh McCluer, J.P.

E, 38-39: 13 Oct 1795, John McGuire of Chester County to Guy McFadden of same, planter, for £10 sterling, tract granted 23 June 1774 to Robert Morrison, 50 acres on a branch of Rockey Creek adj. Samuel McCullough, James Crawford, Alexander Henry, William Ferguson, Edward Anderson, Matthew Gaston, Alexander Roseborough, Bishop, conveyed to George Agustes Hill by John McCullough and from Hill to John McGuire, recorded in Chester County Book D, page 291. John McGuire (Seal), Jane McGuire (Seal), Wit: Alexander Martin, William Blair, James Bigham. Proved by the oath of Wm. Blair 17 Dec 1795 before Hugh McCluer, J.P.

E, 40-41: 18 May 17--, John McGuire of Chester County, to Guy McFadden of same, planter, for £40 sterling, tract granted 8 March 1768 to Mary Campbell now wife of James Crawford, 100 acres on waters of Rockey Creek adj. Daniel Kelley, conveyed by James Crawford and Mary his wife to John McGuire 25 March 1794, recorded in Chester County Book D, page 177. John McGuire (Seal), Jane McGuire (Seal), Wit: Alexander Martin, Wm Blair, James Bigham. Proved by the oath of Wm. Blair 17 Dec 1795 before Hugh McCluer, J.P.

E, 41-43: 30 June 1795, James Harbison of Turkey Creek, York County, planter, to James Kell of Rockey Creek, Chester county, planter, for £30, tract granted 15 Oct 1784 to James Harbison, 150 acres on waters of Rockey Creek adj. Philip Walker, Henry Stone, Dugal Ballantine, surveyed in a warrant for said James Harbison 6 Jan 1793 on 26 March 1793, grant recorded in Book AAAA, page 168. James Harbison (wax seal), Margaret Harbison (mark) (wax seal), Wit: John Harbison, Patrick Spence, John Harbison. Proved by the oath of John Harbison 27 Nov 1795 before Hugh Knox, J.P.

**E, 43-44:** 15 July 1795, Francis Kirkpatrick of Chester County to Andrew Letzinger of same, for £30 sterling, 247 acres on the waters of Fishing Creek adj. Nightingale, Samuel Hambleton, Peter Robison, Thomas White, Granted 54 Aug 1793 to Francis Kirkpatrick. Francis Kirkpatrick (wax seal), Wit: John McCreary, Abraham Walker, Samuel Telford. Proved by the oath of John McCreary 1 Jan 1796 before Saml Lacey, Clk C. C. C.

**E, 44-46:** 17 Feb 1795, James Cooper & Margaret Cooper, of Chester County to John Ferguson of same, for £20 sterling, tract granted 14 Oct 1774 to James Cooper, 100 acres on waters of the Beaver Dam fork of Rockey Creek adj. Sarah Knox. James Cooper (Seal), Margaret Cooper (X) (Seal), Wit: John Collins, John Cooper. Proved by the oath of John Collins 10 July 1795 before Joseph Gaston, J.P. Recorded 11 Feb 1796.

**E, 46-48:** 25 Jan 1796, John Dick, planter, and wife Margaret, of Chester County to Agnus Ray, otherwise Miller, otherwise Allen, of same, for £38 sterling, tract on a small branch of Rockey Creek adj. John Watson, John Sudmon, Charles Spradling, granted to said John Dick Dec 1774, recorded in Book TTT, page 553. John Dick (Seal), Margret Dick (mark) (Seal), Wit: Staff'd Currey, Samuel Moffet, Hugh Brown. January Term 1796 acknowledged in open court by John Dick and wife Margaret. Recorded 11 Feb 1796.

**E, 48:** James Adare of Chester county to James L. Gaston, a mulatto boy named Phil for $120, 5 Jan 1796. James Adare (seal), Wit: John Brown, Alex'dr Brown. 28 Jan 1796, Acknowledged in open court by James Adare. Recorded 11 Feb 1796.

**E, 48-49:** James Adare of Chester County to James L. Gaston of same, a negro boy George for $150, 5 Jan 1796. James Adare (LS),Wit: John Brown, Alex'dr Brown. 28 Jan 1796, acknowledged in open court by James Adare. Recorded 11 Feb 1796.

**E, 49-50:** 24 Oct 1795, Samuel Lowrie, Esqr., Attorney at Law, to John Graham, son of William Graham, shoe maker, the former an inhabitant of York County, the latter of Chester, for £20, tract on waters of Sandy River, 100 acres adj. John Carson, John Pugh, across the waggon Road. Saml Lowrie (LS), Wit: William Graham. 25 Jan 1796 acknowledged in open court by Samuel Lowrie. Recorded 11 Feb 1796.

**E, 50-52:** 3 Jan 1793, William Taylor and wife Elizabeth of Lancaster County, District Eastward of the Wateree, SC, to James Taylor of Chester county, Pinckney District, for £100, part of tract granted 8 July 1774 to Isaac Taylor, 350 acres on west side Cattawa River, and by said Isaac Taylor, a part of said land was conveyed to George Sliger 21 Feb 1775, 235 acres, and said Isaac Taylor did convey to Jacob Taylor a part of said tract, 100 acres, and the said

William Taylor who is the eldest son of Jacob Taylor who died intestate. William Taylor, Elizabeth Taylor (X), Wit: John Barr, George Vickery (X). Proved by the oath of John Barr 25 Jan 1796 before Jas Crafford, J.P. Recorded 12 Feb 1796.

**E, 52-54**: 10 March 1794, John Winn Junr, Sheriff of Fairfield County, Esquire, to Richard Gaither of Chester County, whereas James Rainey and John Winn of said county, planters, being justly indebted until Charles Picket & William Lewis, and said Picket & Lewis did for the recovery of such debt commence an action in the County Court of Fairfield against the said James Rainey & John Winn, and in June Term 1791 at Winnsborough, they did recover judgment for £64 s18 d2 and £1 s1 d4 damages, now by a writ of fieri facias dated 10 July 1791, sheriff sells 107 acres, part of 300 acres on waters of Rockey Creek adj. Mitchel Stranger, granted to Jesse Minton and after sundry conveyances conveyed by James Read to John Winn, now sold to said Richard Gaither for £3 s10. John Winn Junr, Sheriff of Fairfield County (wax seal), Wit: D. R. Evans, George Lott (X). Proved in Chester County by the oath of George Lott 22 Jan 1796. Recorded 12 Feb 1796. Plat of 107 acres certified 3 Jan 7194 by And'w McDowell showing adj. land owner Aaron Roberts, Nathaniel Dorems[?].

**E, 54-55**: South Carolina, Chester County. Jeremiah Davis & wife Frances of county aforesaid for £50 sterling, to James Jinnings of same, 100 acres on Martins Branch of Sandy River adj. Barker, Solomon Peters, part of 300 acres granted in 1784, recorded in Book GGGG, page 138, to said Davis, 20 Dec 1794. Jeremiah Davis (Seal), Frances Davis (X) (Seal), Wit: Rich'd Yarbrough, John Jennings. Proved by the oath of John Jennings 19 Sept 1795 before Thomas Jenkins, J.P.

**E, 55-56**: 18 Nov 1795, Charles Humphries Senior of Chester County to Amos Timms Senior of same, for £100 sterling, tract on waters of Sandy River, 100 acres granted to Lazarus Moore 24 Nov 1767 and conveyed to William Roden and from Wm Roden to Charles Humphries Senior. Charles Humphries (mar) (Seal), Wit: Thomas Humphries, John Timms, Alse Humphries. Proved by the oath of John Timms 26 Jan 1796 before John Pratt, J.P. Recorded 15 Feb 1796.

**E, 56-57**: William Colvin of Chester County for £60 sterling to Hasel Hardwick Junior of same, a negro man named Limbrick of a black complexion, well made & about eighteen or twenty years of age, 8 May 1795. William Colvin (X) (wax seal), Wit: E. Nunn, John Pratt. Proved by the oath of John Pratt 26 Jan 1796 before E. Nunn, J.P. Recorded 15 Feb 1796.

**E, 57-58**: State of Georgia. 22 Feb 1790, John Leonard of Richmond County, state aforesaid, planter, to William McDonald of Chester County, for £100 lawful current money of SC, tract on waters of Fishing Creek betwixt that & The Cattawba River in Chester County, bounded when surveyed on Rateree, Thomas Hances, Thomas Addison, 200 acres granted to John Henderson 2?

June 1744 and recorded in Book QQQ, page 267, conveyed by said Henderson to said John Leonard by deed 7 Jan 1779. John Leonard (wax seal), Wit: Robert McKann (R), Fredk Kimball Junr, Benjamin Burnett. Proved by the oath of Fredk Kimball Junr 28 Dec 1790 before Jas Knox, J. P. Recorded 15 Feb 1796.

**E, 58-59**: 22 Aug 1795, William Nance of Chester County to Elizabeth Nance of same, for £50 sterling, 400 acres on Rockey Creek, granted to Peter Nance Feb 1772. Wm. Nance (Seal), Wit: Thomas Saterwhite Evans, Robert Smith (R), Richard Nance. Proved by the oath of Thomas Saterwhite Evans 22 Aug 1795 before Joseph Brown, J. C. C., 22 Aug 1795. Recorded 15 Feb 1796.

**E, 60**: 30 Nov 1793, Charles Humphries of Chester County to Absolum Humphries of same, 100 acres on the drafts of Sandy River adj. James Ferguson, granted 11 Feb 1773. Charles Humphries (C) (Seal), Wit: Thomas Stokes, Thomas Humphries. Proved by the oath of Thomas Humphries 26 Jan 1796 before John Pratt, J.P. Recorded 15 Feb 1796.

**E, 60-61**: 10 Oct 1795, Abner Wilkes of Chester County, to Jesse Wall of same, for £80, 250 acres on the draughts of Sandy River adj. Adam Ferguson. Abner Wilkes (Seal), Martha Wilkes (X) (Seal), Wit: Absolum Humphries, Richard Humphries. Proved by the oath of Absalum Humphries 10 oct 1795 before E. Nunn, J.P. Recorded 17 Feb 1796.

**E, 61-62**: Plat of 90 acres. South Carolina, Pinckney District, Chester County. 29 June 1795, Nathan Arthurberry of said county to Moses Grisham of same, for £60, 90 acres on Welches branch of Sandy River, part of tract of 200 acres granted to said Nathan Arthurberry 7 Dec 1789. Nathan Arthurberrey (X) (wax seal), Wit: Thomas Oneel, Noah Bennett, William Murray (X). Proved by the oath of William Murray 26 Jan 1796 before John Pratt, J.P. Recorded 17 Feb 1796.

**E, 62-63**: Plat of 100 acres. 17 Nov 1795, Hugh Ross of Chester County to William Ross of same, for £100 sterling, 100 acres on waters of Rockey Creek adj. Hugh Boner, William White, Hugh Ross, part of 400 acres granted to Hugh Ross Senr 21 April 1774, and said Hugh Ross Senr dying intestate, and said Hugh Ross Junr being eldest son and heir to Hugh Ross deceased. Hugh Ross (Seal), Wit: James Brown, George Kennedy, William White. Proved by the oath of James Brown 26 Jan 1796 before E. Nunn, J.P. Recorded 17 Feb 1796.

**E, 63-65**: 14 Dec 1795, Hugh Ross of Chester County to Abraham Ross of same, for £50 sterling, 200 acres on head waters of Rockey Creek, part of 400 acres granted to Hugh Ross Senr 21 April 1774, and said Hugh Ross Senr dying intestate, and said Hugh Ross Junr being eldest son and heir to Hugh Ross deceased. Hugh Ross (Seal), Wit: James Brown, George Kennedy, William White. Proved by the oath of James Brown 26 Jan 1796 before E.

Nunn, J.P. Recorded 17 Feb 1796. Plat included showing adj. land owners Joseph Cobb, Hugh Ross.

**E, 65-66**: 9 Jan 1796, Hugh Ross of Chester County to Francis Ross of same, for £25 sterling, 100 acres on head waters of Rockey Creek, part of 400 acres granted to Hugh Ross Senr 21 April 1774, and said Hugh Ross Senr dying intestate, and said Hugh Ross Junr being eldest son and heir to Hugh Ross deceased. Hugh Ross (Seal), Wit: James Brown, George Kennedy, William Ross. Proved by the oath of James Brown 26 Jan 1796 before E. Nunn, J.P. Recorded 17 Feb 1796. Plat included showing adj. land owners Joseph Cobb, Hugh Ross, William White.

**E, 66-67**: South Carolina, Fairfield County. David McQuiston of county aforesaid for £25 sterling, to Samuel McAlilley of Chester county, 100 acres on a small branch of Rockey Creek called Bullrun, part of 400 acres granted to said David Mcquiston, 8 July 1774, adj. Benjamin Love, William Martin, dated 24 Sept 1795. David McQuiston (wax seal), Wit: Hance Hambleton, Hugh McQuiston, John Williams. Proved in Chester county by the oath of William McQuiston 24 Sept 1795 before Hance Hambleton. Recorded 18 Feb 1796.

**E, 67-69**: 24 Jan 1795, Daniel Cook of Chester county, taylor, to John McCroary of same place, carpenter, for £50 sterling, tract granted 1 Sept 1768 to Patrick Hambleton, 300 acres on waters of Fishing Creek adj. Samuel Hambleton, and conveyed by said Patrick Hambleton to Daniel Cook 6 Aug 1788 (except 50 acres on the west side adj. lands belonging to William McCammon). Daniel Cook (wax seal), Wit: John Barr, James Lockhart (mark), William Lyle. Proved by the oath of James Lockhart 25 Jan 1796 before Hugh Whiteside. Recorded 18 Feb 1796.

**E, 69-70**: 18 Jan 1796, James Mitchell and wife Nancy of Chester County to David Stephens of same, for £10 sterling, tract on the bank of Wilsons Creek, 60 acres. James Mitchell (X) (wax seal), Nancy Mitchell (X) (Seal), Wit: Abner Stephens, Mary Stephens. Proved by the oath of both wit. 22 Jan 1796 before E. Nunn, J.P. Recorded 19 Feb 1796.

**E, 70-71**: 29 Oct 1795, William Fariss of Fairfield County to Thomas Arterberrey of Chester County, for £25, 100 acres on waters of Sandy River. William Fearys (Seal), Mary Fearys (mark) (Seal), Wit: Edward Self, Nathaniel Henderson. "A Deed of conveyance from William Fariss to Thomas Arterberrey for 100 acres originally granted to Fariss by His Excellency Lord Montague 1771." Proved by the oath of Nathaniel Henderson 3 Nov 1795 before Reuben Lacey, J.P. Recorded 19 Feb 1796.

**E, 71-72**: James Timms of Chester County for 128 dollars to Robert Walker of same, a part of two tracts on Sandy River, adj. Adam Walker, John Donald, Henry Harden, two tracts granted to James Timms, 1 June 1795 and 7 Sept 1795. Plat included. Dated __ Jan 1796. James Timms (Seal), Wit: Will Boyd,

Thomas Flechall, Joseph Bennett (X). Acknowledged in open court January Term 1796 by James Timms. Recorded 19 Feb 1796.

**E, 72-73**: James Timms of Chester County for $51.24 to Adam Walker of same, a part of tract on Sandy River, adj. Adam Walker, Henry Harden, tract granted to James Timms 7 Sept 1795. Plat included. Dated 28 Jan 1796. James Timms (Seal), Wit: Thomas McGriff, Ralph Harden, Will Boyd. Acknowledged in open court January Term 1796 by James Timms. Recorded 19 Feb 1796.

**E, 73-75**: 11 Jan 1796, David Hopkins of Chester County to James Mitchell of same, for £30 sterling, tract on Wilsons Creek of Broad River, 117 acres. D'd Hopkins (Seal), Mary Hopkins (Seal), Wit: Fer'd Hpkins, William Davenport. Proved by the oath of William Davenport 19 Jan 1796 before E. Nunn. Recorded 22 Feb 1796.

**E, 75**: Robert Harper of Green County, Georgia, for £150 sterling, to Patrick McGriff of Chester county ,one negro woman slave named Silvey, about 23 years of age, and three negro children named Peter, Harry & Dawkins, 25 Nov 1791. Robt Harper (wax seal), Wit: James Harper, Samuel Lacey, Robert Patterson. Proved by the oath of Samuel Lacey 28 Jan 1796. Recorded 22 Feb 1796.

**E, 75-77**: 8 July 1795, James McKown of Chester county to John McKown, for £100 sterling, 122 acres on Fishing Creek on the south side thereof, part of two tracts, one of 300 acres granted to Alexander McKown 21 April 1774 and the other 100 acres granted to Laurence Gallaher 3 Nov 1770. Jas McCown (wax seal), Wit: Wm Morriss (X), Sampson McKown, Elijah Rutledge (X). Proved by the oath of William Morris 20 Jan 1795 before John McCreary, J.P. Plat included at the joint request of Alexander McKown Senr and Capt. John McKown, adj. Laurence Gallaher, 10 Feb 1794. Jas Bredin, D. S.

**E, 77-78**: Mathew Sims of York County for £50 sterling quit claim to Ferdinand Hopkins, to all my part of a tract of 160½ acres conveyed by David Hopkins to Nathan Sims late of Chester County, deceased, part of 321 acres granted to David Hopkins 5 Feb 1787 on Little Sandy River and known by the place whereon Nathan Sims formerly lived, 26 Jan 1796. Matthew Sims (Seal), Wit: Wm. Hobson, Chas Sims. Proved by the oath of Charles Sims 26 Jan 1796 before Thomas Jinkins, J.P. Recorded 22 Feb 1796.

**E, 78-80**: 17 Feb 1792, Isaac McFadden of Chester County, planter, to Pleasant William Ferguson of same, planter, for £100, 100 acres, part of tract granted 15 Aug 1772 to Robert McFadden decd, 150 acres adj. Henry Culp, Thomas Fulton, John Smith, William Taylor. Isaac McFadden (wax seal), Wit: Wm Wylie, James Ferguson. Proved by the oath of James Ferguson 17 Feb 1792 before Jno Mills, J.P. Recorded 24 Feb 1796.

**E, 80**: Elizabeth Morris, mother to John Morris, of Chester County,k for £5 sterling, to John Morris, eight head of cattle, one feather bed & furniture & Chest, 7 July 1795. Elizabeth Morriss Senr (mark) (LS), Wit: James Rateree (J), Andw Hemphill. Proved by the oath of James Rateree 7 July 1795 before And'w Hemphill, J.P. Recorded 24 Feb 1796.

**E, 81-82**: 13 Jan 1796, John Miller of Chester County to John Allen of same, for £50 sterling, 200 acres on Fishing Creek surveyed for Arthur Duff by John Wade, dept surv, 4 May 1757 certified for Robert Swann by order of council dated 6 June 1758 and recorded in Book 6, page 346. John Miller (wax seal), Wit: George Perrey, Samuel Thomson. Proved by the oath of Samuel Thomson 25 Jan 1796 before And'w Hemphill, J.P.

**E, 82-83**: John McWaters of Chester County for £11 s4 d8 sterling to John Allen of same, one negro woman named Violet aged about 30 years or upwards, 25 Jan 1796. John McWaters (Seal),Wit: Samuel Thomson, George Perrey. Proved by the oath of Samuel Thomson 25 Jan 1796 before And'w Hemphill, J.P. Recorded 2 March 1796.

**E, 83-84**: 14 Nov 1795, John Dick of Chester County to William White for £100 sterling, 100 acres on waters of Sandy River originally granted to said John Dick 6 Feb 1786, recorded in Book FFFF, page 442. John Dick (Seal), Margaret Dick (mark) (Seal), Wit: George Kennedy, James Brown, James Kennedy (X). Proved by the oath of James Kennedy 2 Dec 1796 before Hugh Knox. Recorded 2 March 1796.

**E, 84-86**: 7 May 1795, James McCammon of Chester county, weaver, to Hugh Lockhart of same, taylor, for £40 sterling, tract granted 1768 by North Carolina to John Smith, 200 acres on the north side of Fishing Creek on Smiths branch commonly called the Still-house branch adj. Mary Smith, James Smith, son & heir of said John Smith, did convey 10 July 1782 to said James McCammon. James McCammon (wax seal), Wit: Hugh Whitesides, Andrew Lockhart, John Lockhart. Proved by the oath of Andrew Lockhart 7 May 1795 before Hugh Whiteside. Recorded 3 March 1795.

**E, 86-88**: 10 Jan 1795, Matthew Gaston & wife Anne of Rowan County, North Carolina, to David Porter of same, for £37 s10 proc. money of NC, tract in the County of Craven, SC, on waters of Rockey Creek adj. Edward Henderson, David Hunter, 100 acres. Matthew Gaston (Seal), Anne Gaston (Seal), Wit: John Porter, John Adams. Proved in Chester County by the oath of John Porter 9 July 1794 before Wm. Gaston, J. C. C. Recorded 3 March 1796.

**E, 88-90**: 31 Oct 1795, James Martin & Alexander Martin of Chester County to John Douglass of same, for £120 sterling, 150 acres between Cataba and Broad Rivers, adj. John Russell, granted to John Black 16 Dec 1766 by SC, recorded in Book H No. 8, page 144, conveyed by John Black to John McAlilley recorded in Book N No. 4, page 457, and said John McAlilley conveyed to William Martin, recorded in Chester County Book D, page 451, and said William Martin did by his will give to James Martin and Alexander Martin & Archibald Martin, and said Archibald Martin conveyed his 50 acres to said James Martin 5 Sept 1795, recorded in Book D, page 453. James Martin (I) (Seal), Elisabeth Martin (V) (Seal), Alexander Martin (Seal), Wit: George Kennedy, Hugh Ross, William Ross. Proved by the oath of Hugh Ross 3 Dec 1795 before Hugh Knox, J.P. Recorded 3 May 1796.

**E, 90-92:** 13 Jan 1788, Joseph Walker and wife Ann of Chester County to John Walker of same, young man, for £50 sterling, 100 acres granted to John Walker Senr, father to said John Walker, by patent 21 Nov 1766 by SC, transferred from Joseph Walker to John Walker, on the dry fork of Sandy Creek. Joseph Walker (wax seal), Wit: William Boyd, James McNeal, Thomas Walker (X). Proved by the oath of William Boyd 20 Feb 1796 before Saml Lacey, Clk of Chester County Court.

**E, 92-93:** Whereas James Greer of York County, SC, did enter as my security into a bond given to James Hanna Senr for the payment of £30 sterling,in consequence of which & his present desire of being secured for so doing, I sell to him the tract of land whereon I now live in Chester county, 200 acres, with a brown mare & Colt 8 or 9 years old, a brown ____ about 7 or 8 years old, another brown mare & colt about 5 years old, a brown mare about 4 years old, 4 cows & Calves, about 20 head of hogs, with my present crop and household & kitchen furniture, to hold intrust till said Robert Brown pay his demands, 17 Aug 1794. Robert Brown (mark) (LS), Wit: John Murphey, Robert Murphey. Proved in York County by the oath of Robert Murphey before ____. Recorded in York County in Book C, pages 374, 9 Sept 1794. Recorded in Chester County 3 March 1796.

**E, 93-94:** 2 March 1779, James Wilson & Elinor Wilson his wife of Rockey Creek, Camden District, planter, to John Burns of same, for £800, tract granted 3 April 1772 to James Wilson, 200 acres on the branch of Rockey Creek adj. James Wyley. James Wilson (LS), Elinor Wilson (mark) (LS), Wit: James Meek, John McCaw. Proved in Chester County by the oath of James Meek 7 March 1796 before William McQuiston, J.P. Recorded 15 March 1796.

**E, 95-97:** 19 Oct 1791, John Culp of Chester County to Samuel Maphet of same, for £10 sterling, tract granted 17 Jan 1788, 65 acres on the south fork of Rocky Creek, to John Culp adj. George Cherry, Jacob Culp, David Fairy, James Chesnutt. John Culp (O) (Seal), Wit: James McMillan, Wm Kirkpatrick, James Weir (mark). Proved 19 Oct 1791 by the oath of William Kirkpatrick 18 March 1796 before James Paden, J.P. Recorded 19 March 1796.

**E, 97-98:** 2 Jan 1796, Robert Frost of Chester County to Philip Noland of same, for £100 SC money, 276 acres adj. Robert Frost, on waters of Sealeys Creek of Sandy River. Robert Frost (Seal), Wit: Samuel Sealey (X), Joshua Gore, Sampson Noland. Proved by the oath of Samuel Sealy 9 March 1796 before Robert Owen, J.P. Recorded 21 March 1796.

**E, 98-99**: 2 Jan 1796, Robert Frost of Lincoln County, North Carolina, to Philip Noland of same, for £100 SC money, 100 acres, part of a larger tract adj. John Bond deceased, near Sealeys Creek a branch of Sandy River, adj. John Bond. Robert Frost (Seal), Wit: Samuel Sealey (X), Joshua Gore, Sampson Noland. Proved by the oath of Samuel Sealy 9 March 1796 before Robert Owen, J.P. Recorded 21 March 1796.

**E, 100**: John Burns of Chester County, Pinckney District, for £45 sterling to Alexander Boyd of Chester County, Pinckney District, 100 acres taken off or from a plantation of 200 acres surveyed and granted to James Wilson 1772 in Craven County now Chester on a branch of Rocky Creek adj. James Wiley, and said James Wilson conveyed the said plantation of 200 acres to John Burns in 1779, and said plantation now granted to Alexr Boyd by John Burns is bounded by James Douglas, 3 March 1796. John Burns (Seal), Wit: Samuel Omelveny, Andrew Crawford, George Kennedy. Proved by the oath of George Kennedy 5 March 1792 before Samuel Lacey, Clk. Recorded 23 March 1796.

**E, 101-102**: William Robinson of Chester County for £95 sterling to Samuel McKay of same, 100 acres on waters of Sandy River adj. Chester Court House, granted to William Rainey 17 March 1775 and conveyed from William Rainey & wife Elenor to William Robertson 16 Sept 1793, dated 7 March 1796. William Robinson (Seal), Wit: William Crawford, Robert Owen. Maryan Robinson, wife of William Robinson, relinquished dower 17 March 1796 before Edward Lacey, J.C.C. Proved by the oath of William Crawford 17 March 1796 before Edward Lacey, J.C.C.

**E, 102-103**: South Carolina, Chester County. 25 Dec 1794, Peter Sealey of county aforesaid for £10 to John Allen of same, 50 acres on s'd Sealy's corner on Jinkins Path, Jinkins' line, said Allen's corner, Richard Allen. Peter Seely (wax seal), Wit: Thomas Eastes, Dewit Allen, Isaach Allen (X). Proved by the oath of Isaac Allen 29 March 1796 before Samuel Lacey, Clk of Chester County Court. Recorded 1 April 1796.

**E, 103-104**: 15 Dec 1795, Stephen Titshaw of Chester County to James McCluer of same for £10 s17 sterling, part 32½ acres, part of two tracts, the one granted to Robert Gaston 4 Nov 1772 and conveyed to Stephen Titshaw on waters of Rocky Creek, the other granted to Thomas McElhany 7 May 1792 and conveyed to Stephen Titshaw 14 Nov 1795, adj. Robert Walker, Robert Miller. Stephen Titshaw (wax seal), Wit: James Elliott, John Knox. Proved by the oath of John Knox before Hugh McCluer, J.P. [no date]. Recorded 2 April 1796.

**E, 105-106**: 9 Jan 1796, John Titshaw & wife Nancy of Chester County to Jane Porter (alias Johnston alias Gaston) widow, for £20 sterling, 167 acres on the drafts of Rockey Creek, being part of two tracts, one granted to Robert Gaston for 100 acres 4 Nov 1772 and conveyed by Robert Gaston and wife Jennet to said Stephen Titshaw 14 Nov 1794; the other granted to Thomas McElhaney by grant 7 May 1792, 196 acres and conveyed by Thomas

McElhany to Stephen Titshaw, adj. James Knox (Plat included). Stephen Ditshaw (Seal), Nancy Ditshaw (O) (Seal), Wit: Samuel Lowry, William Morton, Thomas Porter. Proved by the oath of William Morton 9 Jan 1796 before Hugh McCluer, J.P. Recorded 4 April 1796.

**E, 106-108**: 14 Nov 1795, Robert Gaston and wife Jennet of Chester County to Stephen Titshaw for £70 sterling, 200 acres on draughts of Rockey Creek adj. James Knox, John McKewn, granted to said Robert Gaston 4 Nov 1772. Robert Gaston (wax seal), Jannet Gaston (O) (wax seal), Wit: James McCluer, Joseph Gaston. Proved by the oath of James McCluer 17 Nov 1795 before Hugh McCluer, J.P. Recorded 4 April 1796.

**E, 108-109**: 23 Sept 1797, Thomas Neal of Chester County to William Murry of same, for £50 sterling, 89 acres granted to James Timms as administrator of George Carter, in pursuance of an act of General Assembly passed 28 March 1778 and an ordinance of the state passed 26 March 1784 for the purpose of granting lands to the soldiers as therein set forth from the 28 Sept 1792, land adj. Thomas Stokes, do make over all my interest of 89 acres of land to said William Murry. Thomas ONeale (LS), Wit: Joseph Bennett, Jane Lacey, Edw'd Lacey. Proved by the oath of Joseph Bennett 15 March 1796 before Edward Lacey. Recorded 5 April 1796.

**E, 109-110**: 4 Nov 1795, John McCombs of Chester County, planter, to William Murrey of same, for £250 sterling, 600 acres on waters of Sandy River. John McCombs (LS), Wit: Joseph Bennett, Sylvanus Eastes, James Grant (mark). Proved by the oath of Joseph Bennett 15 March 1796 before Edward Lacey. Recorded 5 April 1796.

**E, 110-111**: Sampson Noland of Chester County, planter, for £130 sterling to Phillip Noland, sundries to the amount of £68 s9, 18 Jan 1796. Sampson Noland (wax seal), Wit: Pat McGriff, Joseph Timms. (Inventory of goods including one slave, not named). Proved by the oath of Patrick McGriff 9 March 1796 before Robert Owen, J.P. Recorded 6 April 1796.

**E, 112**: William Reedy of Chester County bound to Samuel Omblevaney of same, planter, in the sum of £150 sterling in gold or silver specie at the rate of four shillings & Eight pence to the dollar or one pound one shilling & nine pence to the guinea, 5 Oct 1795, to make sufficient title to 150 acres adj. David Weir, John McKee, Thomas McKee, known as McCollister's old place, against 10 March 1796. William Reedy (LS), Wit: David Weir, James Chesnutt. Proved by the oath of James Chesnut 5 April 1796 before William McQuistion, J.P. Recorded 12 April 1796.

**E, 113**: Michael Henderson of Chester County, SC, for £7 s10 sterling to William Graham of same, one certain sorrel horse three years old this spring about 13½ hands high, a star in his forehead, the off hind foot white, trots naturally (late the property of Josiah Hill), 30 March 1796. Michael Henderson (LS), Wit: Samuel Lacey, Thos Cabeen. Proved by the oath of Thomas Cabean 30 March 1796 before Samuel Lacey, Clk. C. C. Ct.

**E, 113-114**: Plat of 100 acres pursuant to the desires of Gen. Edward Lacey & John Johnsey, 21 March 1796 by John Minter. Adj. land owners Aaron Lockhart, Gen Edwd Lacey, Jane Young.

Josiah Hill of Chester County, yeoman for $100, to Joseph Johnsey, 100 acres on Mill Creek, a branch of Turkey Creek, 9 April 1796. Josiah Hill (wax seal), Wit: Arthur Travers, Samuel Lacey. Proved by the oath of Arthur Travers 9 April 1796 before Samuel Lacey, Clk. C. C. C. Recorded 13 April 1796

**E, 114-115**: Josiah Hill of Chester County, yeoman, for £100 sterling, to Robert Ash of York county, SC, planter, 300 acres in Chester County on waters of Sandy River, part of 12,700 acres granted to said Josiah Hill, 8 April 1796. Josiah Hill (wax seal), Wit: James Morrow, Thomas Cabeen, James Vance (O). Plat included showing adj. land owners Joseph Wilson, Robert Ash. Proved by the oath of Thomas Cabeen 9 April 1796 before Samuel Lacey, Clk. C. C. C. Recorded 9 April 1796.

**E, 116**: William Stuart and wife Jane of Chester County for $50 to Margaret Steel of same, 59 acres, part of tract of 736 acres granted to James Stuart 1 Dec 1788, conveyed to William Stuart 22 Sept 1795 by deed, 18 April 1796. William Stuart (Seal), Jane Stuart (Seal), Wit: Hugh Knox, John Knox. Acknowledged by William Stuart in open court April Term 1796. Recorded 16 May 1796. Plat included showing adj. land owners Samuel Walker, James Stuart, Charles Miller.

**E, 116-117**: Samuel Carter of Chester County, bound to Edward Blackstock of same, in the sum of £500 currency, 20 Nov 1794, to make title to tract whereon I now live, 350 acres. Samuel Carter (Seal), Wit: Peter Corbell, Richard Head. Proved by the oath of Peter Corbell 18 April 1796 before Hugh Knox, J.P. Recorded 16 May 1796.

**E, 117-119**: 30 Dec 1795, Mary Evans of Chester County to Matthew McClintock of same, for £80 sterling, 100 acres in Chester county on waters of Sandy River on a branch thereof called the south fork, granted to Owen Evans 1 May 1786, surveyed for said Owen Evans 1 Jan 1771, recorded in Grant Book IIII, page 456, and said Owen Evans did convey to Mary Evans by deed 17 Jan 1789, recorded in Chester County Book C, page 357. Mary Evans (Seal), Wit: Owen Evans, James Kennedy, John Willson. Proved by the oath of John Willson 18 April 1796 before John Pratt, J.P. Recorded 17 May 1796.

**E, 119-120**: Plat of 82 acres showing adj. land owners Peter Holsey, John Colman, Jean Coleman, on Welches branch, by Richard Johnson.

Willis Carrell of Fairfield County for £25 sterling to Ephraim Lyles of Chester county, tract on Welches branch of Sandy River, per plat, whereon the said Lyles now lives, 9 March 1796. Willis Carrell (wax seal), Wit: Richard Johnston, Joseph Huey (O), Charles Arthurbery (8). Proved by the oath of Joseph Huey 9 April 1796 before John Pratt, J.P.

E, 120-121: 1 Dec 1795, John Trussel of Chester County to John Weir of same, for £20 sterling, tract on waters of Sandy River, 104 acres granted to Samuel Lowrie 4 Nov 1788 adj. Grisham, Jos Trussel, Thomas B. Franklin, David Morrow, William Nunn, David Prewit, conveyed by Samuel Lowrie to John Trussel. John Trussel (Seal), Wit: D. Boyd, Pat McGriff. Proved by the oath of Col. Patrick McGriff 18 April 1796 before E. Nunn, J.P. Recorded 18 May 1796.

E, 121-122: __ Jan 1796, Sampson Noland of Chester County to Job Henson of same, for £30 sterling, 50 acres on waters of Sandy River, granted to Thomas Roden 27 Feb 1767 by SC, conveyed to Peter Nance and by Peter Nance to Sampson Noland, part of tract of 100 acres, adj. Elijah Nunn, Thomas Fletchall. Sampson Noland (wax seal), Wit: Philip Noland, Thomas B. Franklin. Proved by the oath of Thomas B. Franklin 18 April 1796 before Saml Lacey, Clk,. C.C.C. Recorded 18 May 1796.

E, 123-125: Lease and release. 15 & 16 Sept 1791, Christopher Strong, weaver, of Chester county to Samuel Ervin, weaver, for £30 sterling, 300 acres on waters of Rockey Creek adj. Henry Isbell, Widow Dunnseeth, grant recorded in Book XXX, page 155, memorial entered in the Auditor Generals Office in Book M no. 14, page 121, 26 Sept 1775, granted to said Christopher Strong, 4 April 1775. Christopher Strong (C) (LS), Wit: Andw Hemphill, Samuel Ferguson. Proved by the oath of Samuel Ferguson 13 Nov 1792 before Andw Hemphill, J.P. Recorded 18 May 1796.

E, 125-126: South Carolina, Chester County. James Timms for $10 to Job Henson, 17½ acres granted to James Timms 6 Oct 1794 adj. Roden, Jeremiah Kingsley, 24 March 1796. James Tims (Seal), Wit: Richard Hanson, Richard Nance. Proved by the oath of Richard Hanson 18 April 1796 before Saml Lacey, Clk C. C. C. Recorded 18 May 1796.

E, 126-129: 5 Aug 1794, John Mills of Chester County, Esqr., to Samuel Knox of same place, planter, tract granted 10 May 1768 to Robert Glover, part of 250 acres on James McCluer's spring branch, waters of south fork of Fishing Creek, conveyed to Henry Culp by Glover 21 Sept 1768 and conveyed by Culp to Jonathan Jones 6 June 1772 and by Jones to James Langsbey 19 Jan 1785, and by Langsbey to William Jones, then taken by execution at the suit of James Mitchell as William Jones's property and as security for said Langsbey by Hugh Milling, Esqr., Sheriff of Camden District, and conveyed to John Mills, 100 acres of said tract adj. William Jones, Peter Jones, Stone. John Mills (wax seal), Wit: William Jones, Peter Jones, Jonathan Jones. Proved by the oath of Jonathan Jones 18 April 1796 before Hugh Whiteside. Recorded 19 May 1796. Plat included.

**E, 129-131**: 18 April 1796, Samuel Knox, Planter, and wife Catharine of Chester County to Robert Hemphill of same, schoolmaster, part of tract granted 10 May 1768 to Robert Glover, 250 acres on waters of the south fork of Fishing Creek, on Jas McCluer's spring branch, conveyed to Henry Culp by said Glover 211 Sept 1768, to Jonathan Jones June 1772 and by Jonathan Jones to James Langsby 19 Jan 1785, by said Langsbey to William Jones, and taken by execution at the suit of James Mitchell as William Jones's property, conveyed by John Mills to said Samuel Knox 5 Aug 1794, 100 acres adj. William Jones, William Wilson, John Mills. Samuel Knox (S) (wax seal), Catharine Knox (mark) (wax seal), Wit: William Wilson, Christopher Streight. Acknowledged in open court 19 April 1796. Recorded 19 May 1796.

**E, 131-133**: 11 March 1794, Hugh Knox, Sheriff of Chester County, to William Moore of same, planter, whereas the state of SC did by Samuel Lowrie, Esqr., attorney in the county Court of Chester, implead John Humphreys on an action for bastardy, in 1793 and did obtained judgment in the same court for the fine & cost of suit to be levied on the goods & chattles lands and tenements of said John Humphreys, on fieri facias issued to the Sheriff, to be made £7 s7 d6 sterling, sells 100 acres (being part of 300 acres granted to Thomas Morris deceased 2 May 1785) on Sterns branch of Brushey fork of Sandy River, adj .Jacob Morris, Richard Morris, which 100 acres was bequeathed to said James Morris by the will of Thomas Morris decd, and conveyed by said James Morris to John Humphreys 1 Nov 1791, sold for £5 s6 sterling. Hugh Knox S. C. C. (wax seal), Wit: William Graham, John Knox. Proved by the oath of William Graham 25 April 1796 before Saml Lacey, Clk C. C. C. Recorded 19 May 1796.

**E, 133-135**: 8 Oct 1795, Jeremiah Roden and wife Mary of Chester County to Joseph Bennett Junr of same, for £16 sterling, 100 acres, part of tract granted to Thomas Morris deceased 2 May 1785 on Sterns branch, waters of Sandy River adj. Jacob Morris, Richard Morris, said 100 acres was bequeathed to James Morris by the will of Thomas Morris deceased and conveyed to John Humphreys by deed 1 Nov 1791, and sold by the sheriff to William Moore 11 March 1794. Jeremiah Roden (I) (LS), Mary Roden (X) (LS), Wit: Thomas Atteberry (X), James Bennett (mark), Richard Anderson (X). Proved by the oath of James Bennett before E. Nunn, 9 Oct 17905. Recorded 19 May 1796.

**E, 135**: John Donald of Chester County for £50 sterling, to John Carter of same, 68 acres, 20 Jan 1796. John Donald (Seal), Wit: Elisha Lyon, Benjamin Carter. Proved by the oath of Benjamin Carter 18 April 1796 before Saml Lacey, Clk C. C. C. Recorded 20 May 1796.

**E, 135-137**: South Carolina, Pinckney District, Chester County. 19 Jan 1795, Hugh Cooper, Blacksmith, to John Owen, both of county aforesaid, for £30, 100 acres on Rockey Creek, granted to Mary Biggam 1 Sept 1768 and conveyed from John Carryl (husband of said Mary Biggam) to John Gillam & then taken by execution, at the suit of John Ferguson against John Gilliam by Peter Jones (then sheriff) sold to Hugh Cooper. Hugh Cooper (wax seal), Wit: Edward Lacey, James Owen, Robert Owen. Proved by the oath of Edward Lacey 27 Jan 1795 before E. Nunn, J.P. Recorded 29 May 1795.

**E, 137-138**: South Carolina, Pinckney District, Chester County. 14 June 1794, Thomas McGriff Senr to John Owen, both of said county, for £38 sterling, 100 acres granted to Robert Kirkpatrick by patent 1 Sept 1768 and conveyed from said Robert Kirkpatrick to Josiah Kitchen and by Josiah Kitchen to Patrick McGriff and by said Patrick McGriff to Thomas McGriff Senr, on a branch of Sandy River. Thomas McGriff (T) (wax seal), Wit: Samuel Lacey, Peter Coonrod, Robert Owen. Proved by the oath of Samuel Lacey 27 Jan 1795 before E. Nunn, J.P. Recorded 20 May 1795.

**E, 138-139**: South Carolina, Chester County. 29 Oct 1790, John Gill to John Owen, both of county aforesaid, for £55 sterling, 143 acres including John Anthoney's old mill on Sandy River (being the south end of a tract of 200 acres granted to John Anthoney 25 April 1774) adj.John Lands, Josiah Kitchens. John Gill (wax seal), Wit: Robert Owen, Josiah Porter, James Pagan. Proved by the oath of Josiah Porter 27 Jan 1795 before E. Nunn, J.PO. Recorded 20 May 1796.

**E, 139-143**: Lease and release. 23 Sept 1794, Captain James Porter of Macklenburgh County, North Carolina, to William Knox of Chester County, SC, yeoman, for £200 sterling, 200 acres granted to Edward Henderson 15 May 1772 and since conveyed to Hugh Morton and by said Hugh Morton to said James Porter, on a small branch of Rockey Creek called Hunters branch. James Porter (wax seal), Wit: Thomas Porter, Mary Porter (mark), James Montgomery. Proved in Chester County by the oath of Thomas Porter 7 May 1796 before Hugh McCluer, J.P. Recorded 23 May 1796.

**E, 143-145**: 30 Aug 1792, John McCullough of Chester County, planter, to Abraham wright of same, part of tract granted 23 June 1744 [*sic*] to Robert Morrison, 100 acres on a branch of Rockey Creek adj. Samuel McCullough, James Crafford, Alexdr Henry, William Ferguson, Edward Henderson, Matthew Gaston, Alexander Roseborough, 62 acres. John McCollough (wax seal), Wit: Thomas Wright, William Knox. Proved by the oath of William Knox 7 May 1796 before Hugh Knox, J.P. Recorded 23 May 1796.

**E, 145-148**: 7 Jan 1796, David Porter & wife Flora of Chester County to Abraham Wright of Macklenburgh County, North Carolina, for ten shillings sterling, tract on waters of Rockey Creek adj. Edward Henderson, David Hunter. David Porter (Seal), Flora Porter (Seal), Wit: James Douglass, William Knox, Joseph Kennedy. Proved by the oath of William Knox 7 May 1796 before Hugh Knox, J.P.

**E, 148-149**: 6 May 1796, Solomon Owen of Chester County to John Owen Junr of same, for £24 sterling, 50 acres adj. Henry Smith, John Owen Senr, it being the south end of a tract granted to James Nicholson 3 April 1786 and conveyed to David McCalla and from him to Peter Coonrod and then to Solomon Owen. Solomon Owen (X) (wax seal), Wit: William Smith, Charles Raley, Cornelius Mellone. Proved by the oath of Charles Raley 6 May 1696 before R. Owen, J.P. Recorded 27 May 1796.

**E, 149-150**: John Owen of Chester County for £25 sterling to Edward Griffin, 100 acres, part of two tracts, one granted to William Killen and the other to John Owen, 3 May 1796. John Owen (Seal), Wit: Hugh Cooper, John Cooper, Thomas McCulloch. Proved by the oath of Thomas McCulloch 3 May 1796 before R. Owen, J.P. Recorded 27 May 1796.

**E, 151-152**: 4 Feb 1795, William Moore of Chester County to Jeremiah Roden of same, for £50 sterling, 100 acres, part of a tract granted to Thomas Morris deceased 2 May 1785 on Starns branch, waters of Brushy fork of Sandy River, the middle part of the said tract, adj. Jacob Morris, Rich Morris, bequeathed to James Morris by the will of Thomas Morris and conveyed to John Humphries by deed 1 Nov 1791 and sold by Hugh Knox, Sheriff, under execution to said William Moore. William Moore (Seal), Wit: Major Edge (M), R. Nunn, Stephen Mayfield (X). Proved by the oath of Major Edge 4 Feb 1795 before E. Nunn, J.P. Recorded 27 May 1796.

**E, 152-153**: Plat of 200 acres adj. Thomas Cabean, Wm Miles. Josiah Hill, yeoman of Chester County for $100 to James Vants of same, 200 acres on head waters of Sandy River adj. William Miles, Thomas Cabean, and said Josiah Hill, dated 20 May 1796. Josiah Hill (wax seal), Wit: Robert Lacey, Edward Lacey. Proved by the oath of Gen. Edward Lacey 20 May 1796 before Saml Lacey, Clk of Chester County Court. Recorded 27 May 1796.

**E, 153-157**: Lease and release. 28 & 29 Dec 1769, Robert Archer of Craven County, SC, to William Gladden of same, for £300, 100 acres on the north fork of Rockey Creek, granted 8 March 1768 to Robert Archer. Robert Archer (X) (wax seal), Wit: William Archer (X), Charles Waters (M). Proved in Craven County by the oath of William Archer and Charles Waters 29 Dec 1769 before Peter Grant. Recorded 28 May 1796.

**E, 157-160**: Lease and release. 17 & 18 Sept 1775, Hugh Wilson of Craven County, SC, to William Moore of the province of North Carolina, for £150 paid by William Gladden, 100 acres on Beaverdam Creek, being the north fork of Rockey Creek, granted 18 March 1768 to Robert Archer. Hugh Wilson (H) (wax seal), Wit: Andrew Hemphill, Wm Nisbet, James Barber, James Moore. Proved by the oath of William Niesbet 24 Aug 1782 before Andrew Baskin, J.P. for Camden District. Recorded 20 May 1796.

**E, 160-162**: 18 Sept 1775, Hugh Wilson of Craven County, SC, to William Moore of Macklinburgh County, North Carolina, for £500, 183 acres on

Beaverdam branch of Rockey Creek, granted by North Carolina in 1755 to Townsend Robinson and afterwards conveyed to said Hugh Wilson by Thomas Hallmark 15 Sept 1766 Hugh Wilson (mark) (wax seal), Wit: William Nisbet, John Greer. Proved by the oath of William Niesbet 24 Aug 1782 before Andrew Baskin, J.P. for Camden District. Recorded 20 May 1796.

**E, 162-163**: 31 July 1793, Rebeccah Moore, John Stuart & Hugh Coffee, lawful heirs to the estate of William Moore deceased, them being of the county of Macklinburg, North Carolina, to Archibald Walker of same, that the said premises was willed to Elinor Moore now wife of said Archibald Walker, & the said Rebekkah Moore, John Stuart & Hugh Coffee, and they agree to convey to said Archibald Walker all these pieces or parcels of land in Chester county on the north fork of Rockey Creek, with another tract on Beaverdam branch of Rockey Creek, 183 acres, in the whole 283 acres. Rebecka Moore (P) (Seal), John Stewart (Seal), Hugh Coffey (Seal), Wit: William Quirey, John Lemond. Proved in Lancaster County by the oath of William Quirey 9 Feb 1795 before Robert Montgomery, J.P. Recorded 30 May 1796.

**E, 163-165**: Archibald Walker, Fuller, of Mecklenburg County, NC, to John Stephenson of same, blacksmith, for £100 proc. money, 100 acres in Chester county on the north fork of Rockey Creek, tract granted to Robert Archer 8 March 1768, sold to William Gladden, then to Hugh Wilson, then to William Moore 17 Sept 1775, and said William Moore by his will bequeathed to Elinor Moore the wife of Archibald Walker, 18 Nov 1794. Archibald Walker (Seal), Wit: Israel Davis, John Gillon. Proved 5 Jan 1795 by the oath of Israel Davis before John Craig, J.P. for Lancaster county. Recorded 30 May 1796.

**E, 166-168**: Archibald Walker, Fuller, of Mecklenburg County, NC, to John Stephenson of same, blacksmith, for £183 proc. money, 183 acres in Chester county on the beaverdam branch of Rockey Creek, tract granted to Townsend Robinson by North Carolina, afterwards by a south patent to Hugh Wilson, 20 July 1775, and said Hugh Wilson conveyed to William Moore of North Carolina, 18 Sept 1775, and said William Moore by his will bequeathed to Elinor Moore the wife of Archibald Walker, 18 Nov 1794. Archibald Walker (Seal), Wit: Israel Davis, John Gillon. Proved 5 Jan 1795 by the oath of Israel Davis before John Craig, J.P. for Lancaster county. Recorded 30 May 1796.

**E, 168-170**: 27 Oct 1779, Samuel Fulton and wife Frances of Camden District, SC. to Robert McCullough of same, for £500, tract granted 9 Sept 1774 to Samuel Fulton, 150 acres adj. William Wood, Samuel Fulton, Archibald Cater, John Lee. Samuel Fulton (wax seal), Frances Fulton (E) (wax seal), Wit: Andrew Graham, Thomas McClurkin, Jesper Rodgers. Proved by the oath of Andrew Graham 28 May 1796 before Hugh Knox, J.P.

**E, 170-173**: 2 July 1790, Robert McCullough & wife Jane of Chester County, planter, to William Reedy of Chester County, Blacksmith, for £100 sterling, tract granted 9 Sept 1744 [*sic*], to Samuel Fulton, adj. William Woods, Samuel Fulton, Archibald Coulter, John Lee, and conveyed to Robert McCullough 27

Oct 1779. Robert McCullough (wax seal), Jane McCullough (mark) (wax seal), Wit: John Stormand, Andrew Graham. Proved by the oath of Andrew Graham 28 May 1796 before Hugh Knox, J.P. Recorded 1 June 1796.

**E, 173-174**: William Jones, Portugee (as he says), & Agnes Jones wife (apparently), alias Agness Dolliherd, as natural Guardian of John Jones, hath jointly and amicably this day put & bound as a servant their said son John about four years of age unto Andrew Morrison, planter( all parties of Chester county), and after the manner of a servant to serve him the said Andrew Morrison until the full end term of his minority or until he arrives at the age of 21 years next ensuing, 7 June 1796. William Jones (X) (LS), Agness Jones (X) (LS), And'w Morrison (D) (LS), Wit: Saml Lacey, Matthew Morrison, Thomas Walker (X). Recorded 8 June 1796.

**E, 174-175**: Joseph Hinckle of Chester County for $150 to William Lacey of same, one strawberry roan coloured horse about 14 hands high, seven years old, branded on the off buttock, M, paces natural, also one yellow bay mare about 13½ hands high, about 13 or 14 years old, branded on the near shoulder thus IA, trots natural, & her sorrel year old mare colt, neither docked nor branded, also five cows & calves, six yearlings of different marks & colours, being taken by execution as the property of Thomas Cabean for his arrears of General Tax, 17 June 1796. Joseph Hinkle (Seal), Wit: Saml Lacey, Robt Lacey. Proved by the oath of Robert Lacey 17 June 1796 before Saml Lacey, Clk. Recorded 20 June 1796.

**E, 175-177**: Haunce Hamilton of Chester County mortgage for $171 to Hugh Gaston of same, 140 acres in Chester County on branches of Little River & Cobbs Creek adj. Wilson, said sum to be paid with lawful interest 21 May 1798, dated 23 May 1796. Haunce Hamilton (wax seal), Wit: Hugh Knox, Jiney Knox (mark). Proved by the oath of Hugh Knox, Esquire, 24 June 1796 before Edward Lacey, J.C.C. Recorded 11 July 1796.

**E, 177**: 16 Feb 1796, James Bole & wife Isabella of Chester County to David Pendergress of same, for £50 sterling, 200 acres granted to James Bole 4 Sept 1786 on Broad River. James Bole (Seal), Isabella Bole (mark) (Seal),wit: Thomas Whitehead, Thomas McCraght. Proved by the oath of Thomas Whitehead 27 July 1796 before E. Nunn, J.P. Recorded 5 Aug 1796.

**E, 177-178**: 22 Jan 1796, James Martin of Rocky Creek in Chester County to John McWire of same, for £30 sterling, tract granted 21 Aug 1774 to James Biggam, recorded in Book SSS, page 397, 100 acres (which contained 450 acres) conveyed by James Biggam and wife Jane to said James Martin, recorded in Chester County Book D, page 34, land adj. William McGarrity. James Martin (wax seal), Mary Martin (X) (wax seal), Wit: John Linn, John Kell Senr. Proved by the oath of John Linn 20 July 1796 before Joseph Gaston, J.P. Recorded 5 Aug 1796.

**E, 178-179**: Plat of 200 acres adj. John Humphry, John Roden, Charles Humphreys, John Seely, Wm Esthers.

John Humphreys & wife Elizabeth of Chester county for $213 to Peter Petree of same, 110 acres on waters of Sealeys Creek, a branch of Sandy River adj. John Roden, John Humphrys, John Sealey, William Esther, Charles Humphrys, ___ June 1796. John Humphries (LS), Elisabeth Humphries (X) (LS), Wit: Hasel Hardwick, Thomas Stokes. Proved by the oath of Hasel Hardwick 27 July 1796 before E. Nunn, J.P. Recorded 5 Aug 1796.

**E, 180**: James Gordon of Chester County, blacksmith, for $20 to Rueben Lacey, Esqr., of same, one pair of smiths bellows, one anvil, one vise, one pickhorn, four hammers, three pair of Tongs, one sledge hammer, one pair of bell sheers, Butteredge, one pair of Pinchers & some small punches, 1 April 1796. James Gordon (wax seal), Wit: Robert Tindall, John Veale. Proved by the oath of Robert Tindall Jr., 27 July 1796 before E. Nunn, J.P. Recorded 5 Aug 1796.

**E, 180-182**: 8 Feb 1796, Samuel Neeley of Chester County, yeoman, to William Neeley of same, blacksmith, for £10 tract granted 2 March 1796 to Samuel Neeley, 41 acres (surveyed for him 12 Feb 1796) on waters of Cattawba River by lines running south east by the Cattaba Indians land, George Kelso's, Samuel Neeley. Samuel Neely (wax seal), Wit: Hugh Whiteside, Thomas Latta, James Neely. Proved by the oath of Thomas Latta 18 Feb 1796 before Hugh Whiteside, J.P. Recorded 5 Aug 1796.

**E, 183-185**: 6 Feb 1796, Samuel Neeley of Chester County, yeoman, to William Neeley of same, blacksmith, for £30 tract granted 4 May 1767 to Philip Walker, 100 acres in the Parish of St. Marks, adj. Lusk on Fishing Creek, conveyed by Philip Walker to said Samuel Neeley 22 Nov 1768, memorial entered in Book L No 11, page 31. Samuel Neely (wax seal), Wit: Hugh Whiteside, Thomas Latta, James Neely. Proved by the oath of Thomas Latta 18 Feb 1796 before Hugh Whiteside, J.P. Recorded 8 Aug 1796.

**E, 185-186**: Thomas Stanford & wife Martha of Chester County for £40 sterling, 160 acres on the north fork of Rockey Creek called Beaverdam, granted to Samuel Ervin 5 Nov 1787 adj. James Ballentine, the widow, and John Ratteree, 7 June 1796. Thomas Stanford (wax seal), Martha Stanford (mark) (wax seal), Wit: Robert Bailey, Hardy Stroud. Proved by the oath of Hardy Stroud 7 June 1796 before James Peden, J.P. Recorded 8 Aug 1796.

**E, 187-188**: 9 Feb 1791, James Bankhead of Chester county, planter, to Robert Fullerton Junr of same, planter, for £20 s5 d8 tract granted 23 Feb 1768 to James Blankhead [sic] on the Bounty, 100 acres in Craven County on a small branch of Rockey Creek, recorded in Book DDD, page 273. James Bankhead (I) (Seal), Mary Bankhead (mark) (Seal), Wit: George Wier, Samuel Bigham. Proved by the oath of George Wier 25 July 1796 before Saml Lacey, Clk. C. C. C. Recorded 11 Aug 1796.

**E, 188-190**: 6 Aug 1795, John Bell Esqr of Fairfield County to Alexander Boyd of Chester County, for £30 sterling, 200 acres in Chester County on the head waters of Rocky Creek, part of plat granted to John Bell Esqr 27 May 1787, recorded in Book TTTT, page 247. John Bell (Seal), Wit: William McQuiston, John Bell. Proved by the oath of John Bell 6 Aug 1795 before William McQuiston, J.P. Recorded 12 Aug 1796.

**E, 190-191**: 14 April 1796, Ferdinand Hopkins of Chester County to Peter Thomas of Union County, for £20 sterling, tract on north side of Sandy River in Chester County adj. lands of Wade Hampton, George Foote Senr, & the Crausbys. Ferd'd Hopkins (Seal), Wit: Charles Sims, John White. Proved by the oath of Charles Sims Esqr & John White 14 April 1796 before E. Nunn, J.,P. Recorded 12 Aug 1796.

**E, 191-193**: 13 Sept 1795, William hogan and wife Ann of Union County to Peter Thomas of same, for £100, tract in Chester County on north side Sandy River, 80 acres, part of tract granted to John Davis Senr, but when the 80 acres which this deed now specifies is deducted, the remainder is in possession of Mr. George Foot. William Hogans (wax seal), Ann Hogans (X) (wax seal), Wit: Jere'h Hamilton, Thomas Ward, James Thomas. Proved in Union County by the oath of Thomas Ward 26 June 1795 before W. Hogans, J.P. Recorded 12 Aug 1796.

**E, 193**: Daniel Thomas Senr of Craven County, SC, for £300 to James Thomas of same, one negro wench named Juda, a negro girl named Let and one named Jude a child, 11 Sept 1772. Daniel Thomas (wax seal), Wit: Daniel Thomas Junr, Robert Alcorn. Proved in Pinckney District by the oath of Col. David Hopkins who sore to the hand writing of Daniel Thomas Senr, Daniel Thomas Junr and Robert Alcorn, 14 April 1796 before Charles Sims, J.P., and E. Nunn, J.P. Recorded 17 Aug 1796.

**E, 193-194**: South Carolina, Chester County. James Gordon of county aforesaid for $200 to Anna Brown of same, a negro boy named Stephen about 18 years of age, 11 March 1796. James Gordon (wax seal), Wit: John Wallace (mark). Proved by the oath of John Wallace 12 March 1796 before E. Nunn, J.P. Recorded 17 Aug 1796.

**E, 194-195**: Josiah Hill of Chester County, yeoman, for $200 to Hugh Gordon of same, 190 acres on Mill Creek, a branch of Turkey Creek, adj. Voluntine Bell, Thomas Stevenson, and land granted to Daniel Travers, part of tract granted to said Josiah Hill for 12,700 acres, dated 18 July 1796. Josiah Hill (seal), Wit: Edward Lacey Junr, Saml Lacey. Proved by the oath of Edward Lacey 18 July 1796 before Saml Lacey, Clk. Recorded 22 Aug 1796.

**E, 195-197**: 4 Feb 1795, Thomas Neely of Chester County, Waggon maker, to William Lyle of York County, planter, for £50, tracts granted 21 March 1768 to Samuel Hambleton, 250 acres on waters of Fishing Creek adj. Nathaniel Semple, John McKinney, the other granted 1785, conveyed by Samuel

Hambleton to Daniel Cook 4 Nov 1789 and was taken in execution as the property of said Daniel Cook at the suit of Philip Walker and sold by the Sheriff to Thomas Neely, 2 March 1793. Thomas Neely (wax seal), Wit: John Barr, Hugh Whiteside, John McGlammery (X). Proved by the oath of John Barr 6 Feb 1795 before Hugh Whiteside. Recorded 22 Aug 1796.

**E, 197-199**: Lease and release. 14 & 15 Jan 1788, William Storment of Chester County to William Ford Senr of same, for £50 sterling, 200 acres, part of 300 acres on NW side Cattawba River on a branch of little Rockey Creek adj. Peter Sandifur, Matthew McClurkin, Widow Dunn. William Storment (Seal), Wit: Wm Ford, Jas Clark, John Yarbrough. Proved by the oath of William Ford Junr 22 March 1788 before Andrew Hemphill, J.P. Recorded 23 Aug 1796.

**E, 199**: South Carolina, Union County. William Jackson of district aforesaid to Col. Thomas Brandon, one negro woman about 35 years of age called Rachel and 2 children called Aff a girl and Abram a boy, for 80 guineas, 13 Sept 1785. William Jackson (X) (Seal), Wit: Joseph Songs, George Story Junr, William McJunkin. Proved in open court by the oath of George Story and recorded 28 Dec 1785 by John Haile, C. C., in Book A, page 2.

Thomas Brandon assigned his right to negro woman Rachel & her increase Aff & Abram except being already sold & conveyed away to John Thomas McCool, William Love McCool & to their only use, 7 Nov 1794. Thomas Brandon (Seal), Wit: Christopher Brandon. Proved in Union County by the oath of Christopher Brandon 25 Aug 1796 before Thomas Brandon, J. C. C. Recorded 30 Aug 1796.

**E, 199-201**: Lease and release. 14 & 15 March 1788, William Ford Senr of Chester County to William Ford Junior of same, for £10 sterling, 200 acres, part of 300 acres on a branch of Little Rockey Creek adj. Peter Sandifur, Matthew McClurkin, Widow Dunshee. William Ford Senr (Seal), Wit: John Ford, George Hood. Proved by the oath of John Ford 22 March 1788 before Andw Hemphill, J.P. Recorded 7 Sept 1796.

**E, 201-203**: 8 Feb 1796, Margret Beasley, George Beasley & Mary his wife, Adam Beasley, all of Fairfield County to William Rives of Chester County, for £100, 200 acres on waters of Fishing Creek adj. John McFadden, granted 15 July 1768, also 150 acres adj. Jacob Beasley, James Neely, John Swint, Robert Martin, granted to Jacob Beasley 15 June 1770, both tracts granted to Jacob Beasley and at his death invested in the above mentioned Margret Beasley, George Beasley and Adam Beasley. George Beasley (B) (wax seal), Mary Beasley (X) (wax seal), Margret Beasley (mark) (wax seal), Wit: Robt Gibson, Benjamin Booth, John Cameron. Proved by the oath of Benjamin Boothe 12 July 1796 before Joseph Gaston, J.P. Recorded 7 April 1796.

**E, 203-204**: 19 March 1796, David Hopkins of Chester County to David Mitchell, son of Mary Mitchell, for £20 sterling, part of larger tract on the dreans of Wilsons Creek including the plantation whereon the said David Mitchell & his mother now lives, 125 acres. D'd Hopkins (Seal), Wit: Mashack Willis, William Clark (X). Proved by the oath of William Clark 19 March 1796 before Elijah Nunn, J,P. Recorded 7 Sept 1796.

**E, 204-205**: 8 Sept 1789, George Stanford of Chester County to John Allen of same, for £22 s10 d5 sterling, tract on a branch of Rockey Creek, 68 acres. George Stanford (wax seal), Wit: George Ingram, William Martin. Proved by the oath of George Ingram 23 June 1790 before Andw Hemphill, J.P. Recorded 7 Sept 1796.

**E, 205-207**: 31 Aug 1789, William Bishop of Cumberland [no state indicated], planter, to David Porter of Chester County, SC, for £25, tract granted 3 April 1786 to William Bishop, 100 acres on waters of Fishing Creek. William Bishop (Seal), Wit: Joseph Gaston, Nicholas Bishop, David Hunter. Proved by the oath of Joseph Gaston before Hugh McCluer [no date indicated]. Recorded 8 Sept 1796.

**E, 207**: Jacob Dansby of Chester County, SC, for $500 to John Cowsart of same, two horses viz one dark bay mare, one dark bay horse, also four head of cow kind, two feather beds & furniture, one barshear plow, one shovel plow, one pot, one oven, one skillet, one dish, six pewter plates, one man's saddle, one woman's saddle, one loom & tacklings, one linnen wheel, six tin cups, 16 July 1796. J. Dansby (Seal), Wit: James Wilkinson, James Atteberry. Proved by the oath of James Atterberry 25 July 1796 before E. Nunn, J.P. Recorded 8 Sept 1796.

**E, 207-208**: Reese Hughs of Chester County for £50 sterling to John Lackey, 113 acres on waters of Rocky Creek, adj. Mr. Alexander, William Cloud, Jonathan Hemphill, 10 Feb 1796. Rece Hughes (Seal), Wit: Isaac Hughes, Reuben Taylor. Proved by the oath of Isaac Hughes 11 Feb 1796 before Joseph Collins, J.P. Recorded 8 Sept 1796.

**E, 208-209**: 11 May 1796, John McDonald of Chester County to Neuman McCollum of same, for £16 sterling, 10¼ acres, part of tract granted to John McDonald by the state dated 6 May 1793 in Pinckney District, waters of Brushey Fork, a branch of Sandy River adj. Newman McCollum, William Wilkes. John McDonald (Seal), Elisabeth McDonald (E), Wit: Jo Watson, Richard Wilkes, Thomas House. Proved by the oath of Richard Wilks 27 July 1796 before E. Nunn, J.P. Recorded 10 Sept 1796.

**E, 209-210**: 8 Feb 1796, Samuel Neely of Chester County, yeoman, to Hugh Whiteside of same place, Esqr., for £4, tract granted 2 March 1795 to Samuel Neely, 59 acres surveyed for him 11 Feb 1795 on the north side of Fishing Creek adj. Hugh Whiteside, Esqr., Samuel Neely, Andrew McCance, Samuel McCance. Samuel Neely (wax seal), Wit: Thomas Latta, William Neely, James Neely. Proved by the oath of Thomas Latta 23 July 1796 before Hugh McClure, J.P. Recorded 10 Sept 1796.

**E, 210-212**: 26 Dec 1793, Thomas Wilks of Chester County, planter, to Richard Wilks of same, for natural love and affection to his son Richard wilks, and for five shillings, tract of land whereon Thomas Wilks now lives, 117 acres adj. Abraham Mayfield, Wilks. Thomas Wilks (wax seal), Wit: Elijah Nunn, Francis Wilks. Proved by the oath of Francis Wilks 27 July 1796 before E. Nunn, J.P. Recorded 10 Sept 1796.

**E, 212-213**: 4 March 1795, John Humphries of Chester County and wife Elizabeth to William Estes of same, for £150 sterling, 109½ acres. John Humphries (J) (LS), Elisabeth Humphries (X) (LS), Wit: Stephen Clement, J. Waler. Proved by the oath of Stephen Clement 14 July 1796 before E. Nunn, J.P. Recorded 10 Sept 1796.

**E, 213-214**: South Carolina, Chester County. 22 June 1795, Richard Allen of county aforesaid to Cornelious Dorsey of same, for £30, 100 acres, part of tract that Richard Allen now lives on. Richard Allen (X) (LS), Mary Allen (X) (LS), Wit: Peter Seely, Stephen Blissit. Proved by the oath of Stephen Blissit 2 Aug 1796 before Saml Lacey Clk. Recorded 10 Sept 1796.

**E, 214-215**: 22 July 1796, Lewis Morriss to William Johnson, both of Chester County, for five shillings sterling, on the road to Hughes, in an pond on the Columbia Road. Lewis Morriss (Seal), Wit: John White, John Dyel (X). Acknowledged in open court July Term 1796. Recorded 12 Sept 1796.

**E, 215-217**: 5 Aug 1794, John Mills of Chester County, Esqr., to William Jones of same, blacksmith, for £68, tract granted 30 Oct 1767 to William McKinney, 150 acres on James McCluer's spring run, waters of said run falls into Fishing Creek, adj. George Glover, said tract conveyed to James Balentine, and taken under execution at the suit of James Michel on the estate of William Jones & security for James Langsbey by Hugh Milling, Sheriff, sold to John Mills, Esqr. Jno Mills (wax seal), Wit: Geo Gill, Wm Wilson, Jno Mills (X). Proved by the oath of William Wilson 22 Jan 1796 before Hugh Whiteside. Recorded 12 Sept 1796.

**E, 217-218**: Plat of 54 3/4 acres. 24 Oct 1794, William Morris of Chester county to Thomas Stones Senr of Fairfield County for £4 sterling, 54 3/4 acres, part of tract granted to Stephen Terry 10 July 1766 for 200 acres on cainey fork of Sandy River, adj. Thomas Humphries. William Morriss (Seal), Wit: John Terry, Jeremiah Terry, Michael Wornal.

**E, 218-219**: 15 Feb 1794, Peter Seely to John Jaggers, both of Chester County, part of tract granted 1791 recorded in Grant Book D No. 5, page 262, adj. Thomas Jenkins. Peter Seely (wax seal), Wit: Henry Bacor (X), Sarah Bacor (B). Acknowledged in open court July Term 1796 by Peter Seely. Recorded 12 Sept 1796.

**E, 219-221**: 22 July 1796, Pleasant William Ferguson & Mary Ferguson his mother, both of Chester County, to Abraham Ferguson Junr, for £10 sterling, tract granted 6 April 1768 to Saml Knox deceased, 100 acres on Fishing Creek, adj. William McKinney, Thomas Martin, conveyed to William Lard 21 Jan 1769 and by William Lard 23 Aug 1771 to James Ferguson. Pleasant Wm. Ferguson (wax seal), Mary Ferguson (X) (wax seal), Wit: Wm Wylie, James Ferguson, John Ferguson. Proved by the oath of James Ferguson 25 July 1796 before Hugh McCluer, J.P. Recorded 12 Sept 1796.

**E, 221-222**: 23 July 1796, Pleasant William Ferguson & Mary Ferguson his mother, both of Chester County, to James Ferguson, for £50 sterling, part of tract granted 23 Dec 1768 to James Ferguson Senr deceased, 300 acres on Fishing Creek, 140 acres being sold to William McKinney, likewise 20 acres of said remaining part of 300 acres is to be laid off to the survey joining above it from the mouth of the spring branch at the creek or deep ford up the creek to joining the line that the said Mary Ferguson lives on, the remainder being 140 acres. Pleasant Wm. Ferguson (wax seal), Mary Ferguson (X) (wax seal), Wit: Wm Wylie, John Ferguson, David Adams. Proved by the oath of John Ferguson 25 July 1796 before Hugh McCluer, J.P. Recorded 12 Sept 1796.

**E, 223-224**: 22 July 1796, Pleasant William Ferguson & Mary Ferguson his mother, both of Chester County, to John Ferguson Junr, for £50 sterling, part of tract granted 23 Oct 1774 to John Graves of 100 acres adj. William McKinney, James Ferguson, conveyed by John Graves to James Ferguson Senr decd 28 Aug 1776. Pleasant Wm. Ferguson (wax seal), Mary Ferguson (X) (wax seal), Wit: Wm Wylie, Jas Ferguson, David Adams. Proved by the oath of James Ferguson 25 July 1796 before Hugh McCluer, J.P. Recorded 12 Sept 1796.

**E, 224-225**: 17 March 1796, John Allen of Chester county to Thomas Leonard of same, for £100 sterling, 93 acres, part of three separate grants on the north side of Lick branch, a branch of Rockey Creek, to wit 50 acres granted to said John Allen 1 Sept 1787, also part of said tract on the north side of said Lick branch and now in the possession of said John Allen & indentured by Zachariah Kitchens to said John Allen 13 Nov 1783, recorded in Book A No. 6, page 397 18 Dec 1788 in Charleston District, also part of tract granted to George Stantford and by said George Stanford granted to John Allen 8 Sept 1789. John Allen (Seal), Wit: James McCown, Thomas Findley. Proved by the oath of James McCown 30 Aug 1796 before Joseph Gaston, J.P. Anna Allen (O), wife of John Allen, relinquished dower 12 Aug 1796 before Edward Lacey, J. C. C.

**E, 226**: Alexander Blair of Chester County for £16 sterling to John Cowsert of same, one gray mare, one cow & yearling, one loom & tacklings, 22 May 1796. Alexander Blair (O) (Seal), Wit: J. Dansby, James Cowsert. Proved by the oath of Jacob Dansby 27 July 1796 before E. Nunn, J.P. Recorded 14 Sept 1796.

**E, 226-227**: 6 Aug 1796, Edward Lacey former Sheriff of Chester County to Andrew Crawford of same, that John Turner did in the court implead John

Holeman on an action of debt in 1787 and did obtain judgment, by writ of fieri facias, sheriff sells 28 April 1788, two tracts in the whole 150 acres, one tract of 50 acres granted to John Lea 18 June 1764 and conveyed from said Lea to John Turner and from John Turner to said John Holeman, the other tract of 100 acres granted to James Cobb, 19 Feb 1767 and from said Cobb to John Turner, and said Edward Lacey then Sheriff did sell to James Graham of said county, for £6 s6 sterling. Edwd Lacey (LS), Wit: Peter Corbell, William Omelveny. Proved by the oath of Peter Corbell 6 Aug 1796 before Saml Lacey, Clk. Recorded 25 Sept 1796.

**E, 228**: William Gaston & wife Ann of Chester County to Samuel McCreary of same for £20 sterling, 100 acres granted to William Gaston 30 Oct 1767 on waters of Fishing Creek, 11 March 1796. Wm Gaston (wax seal), Ann Gaston (B) (wax seal), Wit: James L. Gaston, Aaron Lockheart, John Williams. Proved by the oath of Aaron Lockhart 11 March 1796 before Wm. Gaston, J. C. C. Recorded 14 Sept 1796.

**E, 228-229**: South Carolina, Chester County. James Kilpatrick of county aforesaid for $1000 to Reuben Lacey, one negro boy slave about fourteen years of age named Bob, also one negro girl named Moriah about 15 years of age, has no thumb ont he left hand and has one crooked finger on the same hand, also one small bay horse about 13 years old, about 13 hands high, branded on the mounting buttock I, trots natural, also one bay mare about 13 years old, about 14 hands high, branded on the near jaw C, trots natural, also two feather beds & furniture, 17 Sept 1796. James Kilpatrick (LS), Wit: Samuel Given, Edward Given. Proved by the oath of Samuel Given &Y Edward Given 19 Sept 1796 before E. Nunn, J.P. Recorded 27 Sept 1796.'

**E, 229-230**: Plat. Pursuant to a precept dated 7 July 1767, I have admeasured and laid out unto Aaron Lockhart, 100 acres on Turkey Creek, a branch of Broad River, certified 10 Sept 1767. William Glascock, Depy Surv. Certified to be a true copy 6 Sept 1796 at Columbia by Peter Bremar, Pro Surv. Genl.

Aaron Lockhart of Chester county, planter, for £50 to James Adair of same, 100 acres granted to me 2 Aug 1768 on Bowls branch called Mill Creek, 20 Sept 1796. Aaron Lockert (wax seal), Wit: James Love, Aaron Lockert Junr. Proved by the oath of Aaron Lockert Junr 12 Sept 1796 before Jo. Brown, J. C. C.

**E, 230-231**: South Carolina, Chester County. 1 Nov 1785, William Killen to John Owen, both of county aforesaid, for £12 sterling, 350 acres on a branch of Sandy River plat certified 30 Aug 1784. William Killen (wax seal), Wit: Hugh Miller, John Williams, John Carson. Proved by the oath of John Carson 21 Oct 1786 before John Carson. Recorded 22 Oct 1796.

**E, 231-232**: John Owen of Chester County for $200 to Robert Owen of same, 200 acres granted to John Anthony 25 April 1774 on a creek of Sandy River adj. John Land, Josiah Kitchens, dated 24 Oct 1796. John Owen (wax seal),

Wit: John Ray (O), Cornelious Mellone, John Brown. Proved by the oath of John Brown 25 Oct 1796 before Edwd Lacey, J. C. C. Recorded 28 Oct 1796.

**E, 232-233**: John Owen of Chester County for $200 to David Owen of same, two tracts of land, one of 100 acres granted to Robert Kirkpatrick 1 Sept 1768 on a creek of Sandy River; also one tract of 97 acres granted to me 1 Dec 1788 on a creek of Sandy River adj. Robert Kirkpatrick, Nicholson, William Killen, dated 24 Oct 1796. John Owen (wax seal), Wit: John Ray (O), Cornelious Mellone, John Brown. Proved by the oath of John Brown 25 Oct 1796 before Edwd Lacey, J. C. C. Recorded 28 Oct 1796.

**E, 233-235**: John Owen of Chester County for $2408 to John Brown of same, all the negroes, horses, cows, hogs, goods household & stuff & implements of household in the schedule hereunto annexed, dated 24 Oct 1796. John Owen (wax seal), Wit: John Ray (O), Cornelious Mellone. Proved by the oath of Cornelious Mellone 24 Oct 1796 before R. Owen, J.P. Recorded 31 Oct 1796. Schedule includes negro man named Ned about 28 years old, negro man named Guy about 21 years old, negro woman named Nan about 20 years old & child named Peter, one negro girl called Silveh about 15 years old.

**E, 235-236**: John Brown of Chester county for $2408 to Robert Owen of same, all the negroes, horses, cows, hogs, goods household & stuff & implements of household in the schedule hereunto annexed, dated 25 Oct 1796. John Brown (wax seal), Wit: George Brakefield, Charles Railey. Proved by the oath of Cornelious Mellone 24 Oct 1796 before R. Owen, J.P. Recorded 31 Oct 1796. Schedule includes negro man named Ned about 28 years old, negro man named Guy about 21 years old, negro woman named Nan about 20 years old & child named Peter, one negro girl called Silveh about 15 years old. Proved by the oath of George Brakefield 28 Oct 1796 before Edwd Lacey, J. C. C. Recorded 31 Oct 1796.

**E, 236-238**: John Owen of Chester County to Robert Owen of same, for $1000, several tracts of land, a part of a tract of 350 acres granted to William Killen 5 Dec 1785 & conveyed to me from said William Killen on a branch of Sandy River, 250 acres adj. John Sadler, Edward Griffin; part of a tract of 300 acres granted to John Sadler in 1769 and conveyed from said John Sadler to me 22 Sept 1788, 100 acres on the said branch of Sandy River adj. John Pugh; part of tract of 532 acres granted 1 March 1790 adj. Alexander McGaughey; also part of 200 acres granted to William Lewis 11 Aug 1774 and conveyed from William Lewis to John Anthony & from Joel Anthony heir apparent of said John Anthony to me 25 March 1794, 130 acres adj. land surveyed for Robert Kirkpatrick adj. John Anthony, and land some to William Malone adj. Henry Smith, dated 31 Oct 1796. John Owen (wax seal), Wit: Daniel Adkins (mark), Bart'w Griffin, Solomon Griffen. Proved by the oath of Solomon Griffin 31 Oct 1796 before Saml Lacey, Clk. Recorded 10 Nov 1796.

**E, 238-239**: 18 May 1796, William Pannell of Fairfield County to John Whitted of Chester County for £30 sterling, 154 acres granted to William Pannell 5

June 1786, recorded in Grant Book LLLL, page 242, adj. George Thomas, Israel Legmour, John Lee. William Pannell (Seal), Wit: Nar's Whitted, Richard Yarbrough, Gideon Whitted. Proved by the oath of Gideon Whitted 11 Oct 1796 before Robert Owen, J.P. Recorded 10 Nov 1796.

E, 239: 7 July 1796, Francis Lee of Chester County to John Whitted of same, for £100 sterling, tract on waters of Little River, 200 acres adj. land surveyed for John Guinn. Francis Lee (seal), Wit: Gideon Whitted, Alex'dr Gordon. Proved by the oath of Gideon Whitted 11 Oct 1796 before Robert Owen, J.P. Recorded 10 Nov 1796.

E, 240: Plat showing adj. land owner Stephen Terry. Jeremiah Kingsley of Chester County for £100 sterling to Thomas Stokes Senr & Junr, both of same, 154 acres on waters of Sandy River, 27 Sept 1796. Jeremiah Kingsley (LS), Wit: John Humphries (J), Thomas Humphries. Proved by the oath of John Humphries 11 Oct 1796 before Saml Lacey, Clk. Recorded 10 Nov 1796.

E, 240-241: South Carolina, Chester County. Nat'n Greg Campbell of county aforesaid in consideration of the part payment of a note to Edward Blackstock, one horse, saddle & Bridle at £10 also one field of corn at £13, also 22 pieces of cloth £177, one chest of books at £11, also notes & settled accts at £50, one silver watch at £7, dated 20 Sept 1796. Natn Greg Campbell (Seal), Wit: Archibald Wilson, John Lay. Proved by the oath of John Lay 26 Sept 1796 before William McQuiston, J.P. Recorded 10 Nov 1796.

E, 241-242: James Timms for $100 to John Scarbrough, tract of 23 3/4 acres, and another tract of 8 acres, both tracts granted to James Timms by Gov. William Moultrie, dated 31 Oct 1796. James Timms (Seal), Wit: Jeremiah Sadler, Peter Nance, Walter Timms (X). Proved by the oath of Jeremiah Sadler 2 Nov 1796 before E. Nunn, J.P. Recorded 11 Nov 1796.

E, 242: South Carolina, Chester County. Sandy River, December 31st 1794. James Head of county aforesaid, planter, sells to John Roden, planter, one negro woman named Hall about 37 years old. James Head (Seal), Wit: Greenberry Roden, John Stermatt Head, James Roden. Proved by the oath of James Roden 11 Oct 1796 before Saml Lacey, Clk. Recorded 11 Nov 1796.

E, 242-244: 23 Feb 1795, Richard Johnston of Chester County, surveyor, to John McKeown of same, planter, for £20 sterling, 150 acres on branches of Little River & Sandy River, part of plat granted to Alexander Johnson 1 Jan 1787, recorded in Book PPPP, page 497. Richaid Johnson (wax seal), Wit: Thomas Polley, James McKeown. Plat included showing road to Charleston, adj. land owners Samuel McKeown, Robert Murdock, Alexander Johnston. Proved by the oath of James McKeown 28 July 1796 before William McQuiston, J. P. Recorded 11 Nov 1796.

E, 244-245: 14 April 1796, John McEwen Senr of Fairfield County, SC, to Isaac Hudson of Chester County, for £50 sterling, three tracts of 100 acres each, the one being a part of 300 acres granted to David Hunter 5 Oct 1764, and there hath been 200 acres laid off to Alexander Rosborough in a square parallel to the SW line of the original tract, the other tract of 100 acres granted to William Ballentine 13 May 1768 on waters of Rockey Creek on Hunters branch, granted to David Hunter, the third tract 100 acres dated 8 De 1774 granted to Agness Hannah adj. William Ballentine, David Hunter, Ralph Baker, the first mentioned tract conveyed from David Hunter, the second tract conveyed from William Ballentine & Uxor, the third from William Hays & Uxor, the whole leased to John McEwen. John McEwen Senr (O) (wax seal), Wit: Allen Hudson, Alexander McKewn. Proved by the oath of Allen Hudson 13 Sept 1796 before Hugh Knox, J.P. Recorded 11 Nov 1796.

**E, 245-247**: Thomas Addison of Lancaster County, SC, for £100 current money, to William McDonald of Chester County, 195 acres in Chester county on west side of the Cattawba River adj. Thomas Leonard, Wm McDonald, 16 Aug 1796. Thomas Addison (wax seal), Wit: Francis Mothershead, Chris'r Mothershead. Esther Addison (X), widow, relinquished dower 16 Aug 1796 in Lancaster County before Danl Wade, J. L. C. Proved in Lancaster County by the oath of Francis Mothershead 16 Aug 1796 before Danl Wade, J.L. C. Plat included showing road from John Strets to McDonald's ford, spring drain of Fishing Creek, dated 9 Dec 1791. Jas Bredin, D. S.

State of South Carolina, Lancaster District. Personally appeared Glass Caston and John Caston Senr who depose that a certain tract on the west side of Cattawba River adj. lands surveyed for Daniel McDonald and John Leonard as we understand was called the property of Thomas Adersons since the year 1760, 10 Aug 1796. Glass Caston, John Caster, before Jas Ingram, J.P. Recorded 12 Nov 1796.

**E, 247-248**: South Carolina, Chester County. 9 Aug 1796, Cornelious Dorsey of county aforesaid to John Allen of same, for £15 sterling, 25 acres, part of a tract that said Cornelious Dorsey purchased of Stephen Siddle adj. James Stuart. Cornelious Dorsey (wax seal), Martha Dorsey (X)) (wax seal), Wit: Thomas Estes, Hezekiah West, Philip Ozburn (X). Proved by the oath of Philip Osburn 12 Nov 1796 before Saml Lacey, Clk.

**E, 248-249**: 8 Aug 1794, Archibald Brown of Camden District, Craven County, SC, weaver, to John Bell of same, for £13 sterling, planter, tract granted 4 May 1775 to Archibald Brown, 97 acres on waters of Bull skin a branch of Rockey Creek adj. Patrick Harbison, John Nixon, Walter Brown, Andrew Miller, the widow Rogers, John Adams. Archibald Brown (wax seal), Wit: George Ingram, Joseph Booth. Proved by the oath of Joseph Booth 8 Nov 1796 before Joseph Gaston, J.P. Recorded 14 Nov 1796.

**E, 249-251**: 24 Aug 1787, John Bell of Beaver Dam, Chester County, Camden District, St. Marks Parish, to John McCroary of same, planter, for £12 sterling, tract granted 4 May 1775 to Archibald Brown, 97 acres [see preceding deed]. John Bell (wax seal), Wit: Joseph Booth, John Kell. Proved by the oath of

Joseph Booth 18 Nov 1796 before Joseph Gaston, J. P. Recorded 14 Nov 1796.

**E, 251-252**: William Knox & Patience his wife of Chester County to John Cherrey of same, 200 acres in Chester County, being a tract granted to Edward Henderson and conveyed by said Henderson to Hugh Morton and by Morton to James Porter and by Porter to said William Knox, 11 Nov 1796. William Knox (LS), Patience Knox (O) (LS), Wit: Thomas Davis, David Morrow. Proved by the oath of Thomas Davis & David Morrow 11 Nov 1796 before E. Nunn, J.P. Recorded 18 Nov 1796.

**E, 252-253**: 11 Nov 1794, Thomas Stevenson & wife Mary of Chester County to Thomas Hail of same, for £50, tract on waters of Mill Creek of Turkey Creek, part of 350 acres granted to James Adair 5 Feb 1787. Thomas Stevenson (Seal), Mary Stevenson (Seal), Wit: James Morrow, David Stevenson, Hugh Stevenson. Proved by the oath of James Morrow 21 Nov 1796 before Saml Lacey, Clk. Recorded 21 Nov 1796.

**E, 253-254**: John Owen of Chester County for £40 to John Peoples of same, 100 acres on waters of Rockey Creek, granted to Mary Biggam 1 Sept 1768, recorded in Book DDD, page 523. John Owen (LS), Wit: Saml Lacey Junr, Cornelius Mellone. Rachel Owen (X), wife of John Owen, relinquished dower 26 July 1796 before Edw'd Lacey, Judge C. C. C., 26 July 1796. Proved by the oath of Cornelius Mellone 8 Sept 1796 before John Pratt, J.P. Recorded 4 Jan 1797.

**E, 254-255**: 2 March 1792, Hugh Henry of Abbeville County to James Elliott of Chester county, for £17 sterling, 100 acres on Rockey Creek adj. land surveyed for Hugh McDonald, the original in the surveyor general's office 12 Sept 1792 and granted to Alexander Henry 21 March 1768, and by virtue of the will of his deceased brother, 2 March 1793. Hugh Henry (Seal), Elizabeth Henry (O), Wit: James Douglass, "the other name torn out." Proved by the oath of James Douglass before John Bell, J.P., and the other witness was John Crafford, 1 Jan 1794. Recorded 4 Jan 1797.

**E, 255-256**: Ferdinand Hopkins of Chester County for £15 to David Stephens of same, tract on Wilsons Creek, part of a larger tract adj. land formerly laid out for William Clark, 50 acres, dated 6 Dec 1796. Fred: Hopkins (Seal), Wit: Abner Stephens (mark), David Mitchell. Acknowledged in open court 24 Jan 1797. Recorded 2 Feb 1797.

**E, 256-257**: 4 Feb 1796, Paul Guthrie of Chester County, carpenter, to William King of same, minister of the Gospel, tract granted on the Bounty to Margret Campbell now Margret Wright, wife of said Abraham Wright, 2 March 1768, and said Abraham Wright and wife Margret did convey to John Bell, and said Paul Guthrie being executor of said John Bell's will does not sell to William King for ten shillings. Paul Guthry (wax seal), Wit: John Cooper, James McLonan, William Edgar.

**E, 257-258**: 4 Feb 1796, Paul Guthrie of Chester County, carpenter, to William King of same, minister of the Gospel, for £50 sterling, tract granted 4 May 1775 to Alexander Porter, 100 acres on the north fork of Rockey Creek adj. William Stroud, Margaret Campbell, James Bigham. Paul Guthry (wax seal), Wit: John Cooper, James McLonan, William Edgar. Acknowledged in open court 24 Jan 1797. Recorded 2 Feb 1797.

**E, 258-259**: William Massey of Lancaster County, SC, for £100 sterling to Thomas Dugan of Chester County, 50 acres on the west side of Fishing Creek adj. land granted to John McFadden adj. William McFadden, originally granted to Robert Martin 19 Aug 1774 and purchased by said William Massey 19 March 1787, recorded in Chester County 6 June 1794, dated 27 Feb 1796. William Massey (Seal), Wit: William Taylor, Jacob Jarvis (X), George Lewis. Proved in Chester County by the oath of George Lewis 23 Jan 1797 before Joseph Gaston, J.P. Recorded 2 Feb 1797.

**E, 259**: William Massey of Lancaster County, SC, for £100 sterling to George Lewis of Chester County, 100 acres near Fishing Creek on the great road between John Lee's & Land's ford on the Cataba River originally granted to Andrew Martin 18 Feb 1768, willed by Andrew Martin to Robert Martin & sold by him to William Massey 19 March 1787, recorded in Chester County 6 June 1794, dated 11 March 1796. William Massay (Seal), Wit: Thomas Dugan, William Taylor, Jacob Jearvis (X). Proved in Chester County by the oath of Thomas Dugan 24 Jan 1797 before Hugh Knox, J.P. Recorded 6 Feb 1797.

**E, 260**: 19 Jan 1795, Williss Carrell of Chester County to John Liles son of William Liles of same, for £20 sterling, 150 acres adj. Isaiah Coleman's corner, part of tract of 800 acres granted to Solomon Peters 17 May 1774, and transferred from Solomon Peters to Williss Carrell. Williss Carrell (Seal), Wit: Joseph Whitney, Martin Elom. Proved by the oath of Martin Elom 21 Jan 1797 before Thomas Jinkins, J.P. Recorded 7 Feb 1797.

**E, 260-261**: 19 April 1796, James Galt of Union County to James Harbison of Chester County, for 25 Spanish milled dollars, whereas Moses Thompson in the county court of Chester did implead John Flemming formerly of said county on an action of debt & obtained judgment for his debt, and in consequence of which judgment did issue to the sheriff and delivered to Hugh Knox, Esquire, then Sheriff, to sell lands & tenements of said John Fleming for £12 s1 d11½ levied, and Hugh Knox did on 7 Dec 1791 to James Galt sell 483 acres on NW side Cattawa River granted to John Fleming. James Galt (Seal), Wit: Andrew Crosset, Alexander Harbison, William Crosset. Proved by the oath of William Crosset 24 Jan 1797 before Jos Gaston, J.P. Recorded 13 Feb 1797.

**E, 262**: 21 Dec 1786, David Hopkins of Chester County to Richard Jones of same, for £100 sterling, 100 acres adj. William Worthy and David Hopkins, Mark Robertson, part of tract granted to David Hopkins for 2331 acres 15

July 1784. D'd Hopkins (wax seal), Wit: Jeremiah Kingsley, Meshack Williss. Proved by the oath of Meshack Williss 24 Jan 1797 before E. Nunn, J.P.

**E, 263-264**: 3 July 1790, Andrew Graham of Chester County, Camden District, Blacksmith, and wife Margaret, to Hugh McMillian of same, planter, for £10 sterling, tract granted 6 Feb 1773 to Margret Coulter, 100 acres on waters of Rockey Creek adj. Mary Coulter, Joseph Carlye, recorded in Book FFF, page 249. Andrew Graham (wax seal), Margret Graham (X) (wax seal), Wit: Archibald Coulter, James Strong. Acknowledged in open court 13 Feb 1797. Recorded 13 Feb 1797.

**E, 264-265**: Elisabeth Nance of Chester County for $70 to James McClure of Chester County, 60 acres adj. David Hunter, William Ballentine, part of tract granted to Peter Nance 20 April 1769, dated 26 Oct 1796. Elisabeth Nance (wax seal), Wit: William Boyd, Richard Nance, Samuel Lowrie. Plat included. Proved by the oath of William Boyd 26 Jan 1797 before Hugh McCluer, J.P. Proved by the oath of Samuel Lowrie 26 Jan 1797 before Hugh McCluer, J.P. Recorded 13 Feb 1797.

**E, 265-266**: Thomas Blair of Chester County for £58 s10, to James Taylor, a negro wench named Sarah, 4 March 1795. Thomas Blair, Jane Blair (wax seal), Wit: John Blair, William Blair, James Blair. Proved by the oath of John Blair 25 Jan 1797 before Hugh Whiteside. Recorded 13 Feb 1797.

**E, 266-267**: David Grisham of Chester County for £50 sterling, to Jeremiah Grisham of same, tract on a branch of Stones fork of Sandy River adj. Notley Coats, Alexander Johnston, Jeremiah Grisham, 18 Aug 1796. David Grisham (D) (wax seal), Wit: Alexander Gordon, William Dufhel, Richard Johnston. Proved by the oath of William Duffle (Duphel) 25 Jan 1797 before John Pratt, J.P. Recorded 13 Feb 1797.

**E, 267**: Austin Culp of Chester County, planter, for £50 sterling, to John Culp of same, one negro boy named Tom, eight years old, 2 Nov 1796. Austin Culp (Seal), Wit: Robert Millen, Elijah Davis. Proved by the oath of Robert Millen 26 Jan 1797 before Hugh Whiteside, J.P. Recorded 13 Feb 1797.

**E, 267-268**: 14 Feb 1797, William Kenney, planter, to Samuel Walker, planter, all of Chester County, for £45 s10 sterling, 138 acres on a branch of the south fork of Rockey Creek adj Francis Henderson, James Harbison, Philip Walker, Peter Nancy, Daniel Oaks, Doctor James Knox, granted to Abel Johnston 4 April 1790 and conveyed to said William Kenney. Wm. Kenney (Seal), Wit: William Blair, Jennet Blar (mark), Elizabeth Blair (C). Proved by the oath of William Blair & Jennet Blair 14 Feb 1797 before John McCreary, J.P. Recorded 16 Feb 1797.

**E, 268-269**: 6 Aug 1793, Hampton Stroud of Chester County to John Jaggers of same, for £25 sterling, part of tract whereon the said Hampton Stroud now lives on the west side of a branch known by the name of the long branch, a draft of big Rockey Creek, part of tract granted to Hampton Stroud 15 Sept 1791, recorded in Book D No 5, page 61 adj. John Jaggers, Jonathan Hemphill, Robert Robertson. Hampton Stroud (mark) (wax seal), Wit: Joseph Strange, Jeremiah Jaggers. Acknowledged in open court 26 Jan 1797. Recorded 16 Feb 1797.

**E, 269-270**: Thomas Leonard of Chester County for £450 sterling, to Henry Harrison of same, 450 acres on west side of the Cattawba River at McDonald's ford, 21 July 1796. Thomas Leonard (wax seal), Wit: John Edwards, John Rataree (mark), Elisabeth Rataree (X). Proved by the oath of John Edwards 7 Sept 1796 before Joseph Gaston, J.P. Recorded 16 Feb 1797.

**E, 270-271**: Francis Erwin of Chester County for £70 sterling, to Charles McCrea of same, tract adj. lands of William Crook, Joseph Edwards, Solomon Crook, 200 acres, tract taken up and secured by Archibald Clark in 1770, dated 11 Jan 1797. Francis Erwin (wax seal), Wit: Charlotte Harrison (X), John Edwards, H. Harrison. Proved by the oath of Henry Harrison 18 Jan 1797 before Joseph Gaston, J.P. Recorded 16 Feb 1797.

**E, 271-274**: Lease and release. 26 & 27 Sept 1783, John Stormount of Camden District, and wife Elizabeth to James Duglas of same, for ten shillings, 100 acres on west side of Fishing Creek adj. James Henry, John Downey, granted 12 Aug 1768 to James Crafford and conveyed by James Crafford to John Stormount 1 Sept 1778. John Stormond (wax seal), Elizabeth Stormond (R) (wax seal), Wit: William Boyd, Robert Bailey (R), David Stormount. Proved by the oath of William Boyd 25 Jan 1797 before Hugh McCluer, J.P. Recorded 16 Feb 1797.

**E, 274-275**: 23 Jan 1797, William Rives & wife Mary of Chester County to David Hyatt of same, for £80 sterling, 240 acres on both sides of Fishing Creek, granted to Jacob Beasley & at his decease invested by heirship in Margret Beasley, George Beasley and Adam Beasley and by them conveyed to William Rives. William Rives. William Rives (wax seal), Mary Rives (X) (wax seal), Wit: Thomas Neely, Willey Crook, Jemima Crook (mark). Proved by the oath of Thomas Neely 24 Jan 1797 before James Crafford, J.P. Recorded 17 Feb 1797.

**E, 275**: 12 Nov 1796, Elijah Nunn of Chester county to John Service of same, for £20 sterling, 100 acres, part of a tract granted to Jacob Dansbey 1 Sept 1794 adj. John Morton. E. Nunn (seal), Wit: William Boyd, G. Williamson, John Service. Acknowledged in open court 25 Jan 1797. Recorded 17 Feb 1797.

**E, 276**: South Carolina, Chester County. Elijah Davies of county aforesaid, chair maker, to Austin Culp, planter, for £43 d15 sterling, 160 acres on the head of a small branch Samuel Wharrey's corner, granted to George Smith 9 Jan 1767 and conveyed to said Davis 25 & 26 Aug 1774. Elijah Davis (wax seal), Wit: Joseph Gaston, William Whiteside, Henry McKinney. Proved by the oath of William Whiteside 8 Nov 1796 before Hugh McCluer, J.P. Recorded 17 Feb 1797.

**E, 277**: John Mills of Chester County, planter, for $100 to John Millen, 108 acres granted to Daniel Elliott and by him conveyed to said John Mills, on south side Fishing Creek adj. Archibald Elliott, James McCullough, Joseph Gaston, George Craige, 26 Nov 1796. John Mills Senior (X) (wax seal), Wit: Robert Millen, Robert Hemphill, William Milling. Proved by the oath of Robert Millen 9 Jan 1797 before Hugh Whiteside. Recorded 17 Feb 1797.

**E, 277-278**: Joseph Boyd of Chester County for £70 sterling, to Robert Kelly, a negro boy named Ephraim, 5 Jan 1797. Joseph Boyd (wax seal), Wit: William Wilson, Geo Gill. Proved by the oath of Wm Wilson 5 Jan 1797 before Hugh Whiteside. Recorded 17 Feb 1797.

**E, 278**: Hugh Thomas of Union County for £50 sterling to Thomas Oneal of Chester County, 111 acres in Chester County adj. Faris, Thomas Atterberrey, 27 Aug 1796. Hugh Thomas (Seal), Wit: Joseph Wilson, Thomas Hollingsworth, Joseph Bennett. Proved by the oath of Joseph Bennett 25 Jan 1797 before E. Nunn, J.P.

**E, 279**: Thomas B. Franklin of Chester County to James Green Timms of same, a sorrell mare about 13½ hands high, 9 years old with a small blaze in her face brand with R on her near shoulder, trots naturally, for £4 s6 sterling, 23 Nov 1796. Thomas B. Franklin (Seal), Wit: William Boyd, James Gilchrist (X). Proved by the oath of William Boyd 25 Jan 1797 before E. Nunn, J.,P. Recorded 18 Feb 1797.

**E, 279-280**: 24 July 1790, John McColpin of Chester County to James Wilkinson of same, for £100, tract on waters of Sandy River, part of tract granted to James Steep 26 July 1774, and by Steep conveyed to John McColpin adj. Bond, Ferguson, 200 acres. John McColpin, Wit: Joseph Watson, Abraham Myers. Proved by the oath of Abraham Myers 13 Sept 1791 before Elijah Nunn, J.P. Recorded 18 Feb 1797.

**E, 280-281**: Plat of 70 acres on Fishing Creek adj. William McKinney, John Graves, Peter Wylie, William Taylor.

Hugh Knox of Chester County for $60 to John Simpson of same, 70 acres in Chester County, part of 100 acres granted to me 4 July 1785, 12 March 1796. Hugh Knox (wax seal), Wit: John Cowen, Thomas Wright. Jane Knox (mark), wife of Hugh Knox, relinquished dower 27 July 1796 before Edward Lacey, J. C. C. Recorded 20 Feb 1797.

**E, 281**: John Allen & William McDonald of County of Chester County, to Charles Kitchen of same, in the sum of £200 sterling, 21 March 1796, whereas the said John Allen & Charles Kitchen hath two suits at Law now depending in Pinckney District Court wherein the said Allen is Plaintiff  said Kitchen

Defendant, and said parties hath agreed to refer the same to the judgment of Mr. Henry Harrison & James Crafford, Esqr., with leave to choose an umpire. John Allen (Seal), William McDonald (Seal), Wit: Samuel Telford, John McCreary. Recorded 18 March 1797.

**E, 282**: David Sims of Chester County appoints Charles H. Sims of same, lawful attorney to receive from Mr. James Adair or whoever may be considered the lawful manager of the estate of Nathan Sims, deceased, my legacy or part of the said estate, 26 Dec 1796. David Sims (Seal), Wit: Daniel Colvin, James Huey. Proved by the oath of James Huey 18 Sept 1797 before Hugh Knox, J.P.

The Ear mark of Mr. Hugh Gaston's cattle as directed by him to be recorded is a crop off the left ear and a slit in the right ear.

The Ear mark of Joseph Ferguson's stock & he returns to me is a swallow fork in the left ear & a half crop in the right ear off the upper side.

END OF DEED BOOK E

F, 1: Plat. Pursuant to the desires of Messes General Edward Lacey & Aaron Johnsey, I have admeasured 69 acres from General Lacey to Aaron Johnsey, Nov 1796. John Minter.

Josiah Hill of Chester County, yeoman for $43 to Aaron Johnsey, 59 acres on Mill Creek, part of 12,700 acres granted to said Josiah Hill, dated 7 Nov 1796. Josiah Hill (Seal), Wit: Saml Lacey Junr, Samuel Lacey. Proved 7 Nov 1796 by the oath of Samuel Lacey before Saml Lacey, Clk.

F, 1-2: 27 March 1795, Charles Creighton, planter, and wife Margaret of Chester County for £38 s16 sterling, to Joseph Montgomery of same, 179 acres, part of tract granted to Samuel McCance on waters of Fishing Creek adj. Andrew McCance, Samuel Neely. Charles Creighton (X) (Seal), Margret Creighton (mark) (Seal), Wit: Daniel Oneal, William Armstrong, James Montgomery. Proved by the oath of James Montgomery 12 July 1795 before Jno McCrearey, J.P. Recorded 22 Feb 1797.

F, 2-3: South Carolina, Pinckney District. 6 March 1794, Solomon Peters, planter, of district aforesaid to Willis Carrell of same, for £20 sterling, part of tract on Welches Fork of Sandy River, 800 acres granted to Solomon Peters 17 May 1774, recorded in Book QQQ, page 341. Solomon Peters (mark) (wax seal), Wit: Saml Levers, John Lay, William Dushel. Proved by the oath of John Leigh 21 Jan 1797 before Thomas Jinkins, J.P.

F, 3-4: South Carolina. James Timms of Chester County for $30 to James Loving in the state aforesaid, tract of land granted to Ephraim Mitchell 16 Oct 1784 and conveyed to said James Timms, adj. Moses Bond, 100 acres on the waters of Sandy River, 23 Jan 1797. James Timms (Seal), wit: William Boyd, Wilson Henderson, Jeremiah Thomas. Proved by the oath of William Boyd 24 Jan 1797 before Saml Lacey, Clk. Recorded 23 Feb 1797.

F, 4-5: Plat of 13 acres, "Mr. Carter's land." James Donald of Chester County for $60 to John Carter, 13 acres granted to John Donald on waters of Sandy River, 8 Nov 1796. James Donald (Seal), Wit: Will Boyd, James Timms. Recorded 28 Feb 1797.

F, 5: James Timms of Chester County for $15 to John Carter, 9 acres, part of tract granted to James Timms adj. Moses Bond on waters of Sandy River, 8 Nov 1796. James Timms (Seal), Wit: Will Boyd, James Donald. Proved by the oath of William Boyd 24 Jan 1797 before Saml Lacey, Clk.

F, 6: South Carolina, Chester County. Robert and Elisabeth Fullerton of county aforesaid for £30 sterling to Thomas Moore of same, 100 acres, a tract granted to James Blankhead, recorded in Book DDD, page 273, and conveyed by said Blankhead to said Robert Fullerton, recorded in Book E, page 186-188, dated 24 Aug 1796. Robert Fullerton Junr (wax seal), Elisabeth Fullerton (wax seal), Wit: William Telford, Alex'dr Morton, William Blair. Proved by the oath of William Telford 8 Sept 1796 before Hugh McCluer, J.P. Recorded 24 Jan 1797.

**F, 7**: 11 May 1796, William Nettles of Camden District, Kershaw County to William Steenson of Pinckney District, Chester County, for £70 sterling, 200 acres on waters of Fishing & Turkey Creek adj. Alexander McCown, Joseph Kershaw, McCown, recorded in book LLLL, page 466 to said William Nettles, 3 July 1786. William Nettles (Seal), Wit: Eli Gather, Andrew Hemphill. Recorded 16 March 1797.

**F, 8**: Paul Ferguson Senior of Chester County for £100 sterling to Rueben Lacey, Esquire, 200 acres on a branch of Sandy River on the great road above Chester County Court House adj. Samuel Woodside, granted to said Paul Ferguson Senior, recorded in the Auditor's Office Book M No. 12, page 69, dated 28 Jan 1797. Paul Ferguson (wax seal), Wit: Notley Coats, William Sims. Proved by the oath of William Sims 28 Jan 1797 before E. Nunn, J.P. Recorded 17 March 1797.

**F, 9**: James Timms of Chester County for $60 to William Boyd of same, 180 acres on waters of Buffellow Creek in York County adj. Peter Buzeley, granted to said Timms 6 Oct 1794, deed dated 26 Jan 1797. James Timms (Seal), Wit: Edw'd Lacey, Elisabeth Tims (E). Proved by the oath of Genl. Edward Lacey 28 Jan 1797 before Robert Owen, J.P. Recorded 20 March 1797.

**F, 9-10**: James Timms of Chester County for $60 to William Boyd, 200 acres on waters of Buffelow Creek adj. Reason Jenkins, Samuel Morgan, Thomas Bridges, granted to said Timms 6 Oct 1794, deed dated 26 Jan 1797. James Timms (Seal), Wit: Edw'd Lacey, Elisabeth Tims (E). Proved by the oath of Genl. Edward Lacey 28 Jan 1797 before Robert Owen, J.P. Recorded 20 March 1797.

**F, 10-11**: South Carolina, Chester County. John Glover of Edgefield County, SC, to William Estes of Chester County, for £100, tract on Jewels fork, waters of Sandy River, 270 acres, part of tract granted to said Glover for 200 acres 21 Jan 1785, recorded in Book CCCC, page 180, adj. William Brittain, 14 Jan 1797. John Glover (Seal), Wit: Stephen Clement, Silvanus Estes. Proved 8 March 1797 in Chester County by the oath of Silvanus Estes before E. Nunn, J.P. Recorded 20 March 1797.

**F, 11-13**: 20 Jan 1785, Agness Hannah of Ninety Six District, spinster, to Paul Ferguson of Camden District, weaver, for £100 tract granted 8 Dec 1775 to Agness Hannah, 200 acres in Craven County on a branch of Rockey Creek adj. James McCluer, Elisabeth White. Agnes Hannah (X) (wax seal), Wit: William Sterling, Thomas Hannah, James Hanna. Proved by the oath of James Hannah 27 April 1793 before John Bell, J.P. Recorded 20 March 1797.

**F, 13-14**: South Carolina, Chester County. John Glover of Edgefield County for £100 sterling to William Estes of Chester County, 100 acres on a branch of Sandy River, waters of Broad River, granted to Hollis Timms, 14 Jan 1797. John Glover (Seal), Wit: Stephen Clement, Silvanus Estes. Proved 8 March 1797 in Chester County by the oath of Silvanus Estes before E. Nunn, J.P. Recorded 23 March 1797.

**F, 14-15**: James Timms for $33 to John Bennett, 33 acres granted to James Timms in Chester county on waters of Sandy River, 25 Jan 1797. James Timms (Seal), Wit: John Gaston, James Fletchall, Daniel Rogers (X). Proved by the oath of Thomas [*sic*] Fletchall, 26 Jan 1797, signed James Fletchall, before John Pratt, J.P. Recorded 23 March 1797.

**F, 15**: James Timms of Chester County for $40 to William Boyd of same, 20 acres on waters of Buffelow Creek in York County adj. John Morgan, Peter Quinn, 25 Jan 1797. James Timms (Seal), Wit: Daniel Rogers (X), James Timms (X). Proved by the oath of Daniel Rogers 27 Jan 1797, before John Pratt, J.P. Recorded 23 March 1797.

**F, 15-16**: 16 Feb 1797, William Morton of Chester County to John Orr of same, for ten shillings, 30 acres on waters of Rockey Creek adj. John McWaters, A. Burnsides, John Bailey, John Coulter, James Park. William Morton (Seal), Wit: William Archer, Elijah Hagood, James Standford (mark). Proved by the oath of William Archer 18 Feb 1797 before James Peden, J.P. Recorded 23 March 1797.

**F, 16-17**: 9 March 1797, Robert Williams of Chester County to John Egnew of same, yeoman, for $199, 150 acres in Chester county on waters of Rockey Creek adj. George Egnew, Hardy Stroud, John Morris, also intersected by 50 acres by the aforesaid Williams to James Weir & bound by lands belonging to the said Weir. Robert Williams (mark) (Wax seal), Elisabeth Williams (mark) (wax seal), Wit: John Barber (mark), Mary Barber (X). Proved by the oath of John Barber 9 March 1797 before John McCreary, J.P. Recorded 23 March 1797.

**F, 18-19**: John Bailey of Chester County for £30 sterling to James Galaspie of same, tract on waters of Rockey Creek granted to said John Bailey adj. George Weir, Thomas Bradshaw, James Galaspie, James Parks, Alexander Burnsides, whereon John McWaters now lives, 28 Feb 1797. John Bailey (LS), Wit: Joseph Gaston, Thomas Gillespie, John McCreary. Proved by the oath of Joseph Gaston 28 Feb 1797 before John McCreary, J.P. Susannah Bailey (X), wife of John Bailey, relinquished dower in Fairfield County 7 March 1797 before John Turner, J. F. C. Recorded 23 March 1797.

**F, 19**: Alexander Walker of Chester County for natural love and affection to my grandson William Walker of same (son of Philip Walker, esqr., deceased), a negro girl named Hannah about fifteen years of age now int he possession of Martha Walker in the state of Georgia, 20 Feb 1797. Alexander Walker (X)

(Seal), Wit: James Walker, Elisabeth Walker. Proved in Chester County by the oath of James Walker 6 March 1797 before Hugh Knox, J.P.

**F, 20**: John Leonard of Washington County, Georgia, for £75 sterling to Thomas Findley of Chester County, SC, 100 acres on waters of Fishing Creek, granted to said John Leonard 30 May 1763, dated 16 Nov 1796. John Leonard (Seal), Agness Leonard (Seal), Wit: Middleton McDonald, John Weaver (X), William Dunnavant. Proved by the oath of William Dunnavant 23 Jan 1797 before Joseph Gaston, J.P. Recorded 31 March 1797.

**F, 20-21**: Camden District, October 24th 1795. Robert Thompson of Richland County, SC, planter, to John Harmon of Chester County, planter, for £30 sterling, 150 acres on waters of Little River adj. Gordon, Young, McKown, McQuiston. Robert Thompson (wax seal), Margaret Thompson (mark), Wit: Samuel Penny, James Young, Elisabeth Patterson. Proved in Richland County by the oath of Samuel Penny before Andrew Patterson, J.P. Recorded 31 March 1797.

**F, 21-22**: John Hermon of Chester County, planter, to James Young of same, for £30 sterling, 150 acres on waters of Little River adj. Gordon, Young, McKown, McQuiston, 13 Nov 1795. John Hermon (mark) (Seal), Elisabeth Harmon (mark) (Seal), Wit: Isaac Bean, Henry Moore, David Patton. Proved by the oath of Isaac Bean 2 Dec 1796 before William McQuiston, J.P. Recorded 31 March 1797.

**F, 22-24**: 8 Sept 1795, Naomi Bean of Chester District to Isaac Bean of same, for £25 sterling, 150 acres granted 5 June 1786 adj. John Lea. Naomi Bean (mark) (Seal), Wit: James Young, Henry Moore. Proved by the oath of James Young 2 Dec 1796 before William McQuiston, J.P. Recorded 31 March 1797.

**F, 24-26**: 13 Sept 1791, Samuel Fulton of Pendleton County, SC, to Robert Thompson of Richland County, for £200 sterling, tract of 150 acres on waters of Little River in Chester County, adj. Gordon, Young, granted to Samuel Fulton. Samuel Fulton (wax seal), Wit: Thomas House, John House, Steward Cummons. Proved in Richland County by the oath of Steward Cummons 16 March 1793 before John Dickey, J.P. Recorded 31 March 1797.

**F, 26**: John Pratt of Chester County for $30 to James Gore, 50 acres, part of 200 acres granted to Daniel Price and conveyed to John Pratt, on a fork of Sandy River called Stoney fork, 1 April 1797. John Pratt (LS), Wit: William Boyd, Robert Walker (R). Proved by the oath of William Boyd 1 April 1797 before Saml Lacey, Clk. Recorded 1 April 1797.

**F, 27**: Charles Boyd of Chester County for £60 sterling to Doctor Charles McCrea of same, tract granted 9 Feb 1796 on waters of Sandy River, 123 acres adj. land surveyed for Richard Waring, Mary Evans, John Evans, 23 March 1797. Charles Boyd (Seal), Wit: Thomas Neely, Clem Fennell, Robert White.

Proved by the oath of Thomas Neely 23 March 1797 before James Crafford, J.P. Recorded 10 April 1797.

**F, 27-28:** George Lewis of Chester County for £60 sterling to Samuel Bradley of same, 998 acres, part of tract of 200 acres granted to William McFadden 24 Jan 1770 on waters of Fishing Creek, plat certified 31 Jan 1797, deed dated 9 Feb 1797. George Lewis (Seal), Wit: William Wiley, John Wiley, Robert Boyd. Sarah Lewis (X), wife of George Lewis, relinquished dower 9 Feb 1797 before Wm. Gaston, J. C. C. Proved by the oath of William Wiley 9 Feb 1797 before Wm. Gaston, J. C. C. Recorded 24 April 1797.

**F, 29-30:** 15 March 1779, Leaird Burns of Parish of St. Marks, Camden District, planter, to John Combest of same, planter, for five shillings, tract granted 9 Nov 1774 to said Leaird Burns, 150 acres on Rockey Creek adj. John Combest, Matthew Neely. Leard Burns (Seal), Wit: John Burns, Daniel Oaks (O). Proved by the oath of Daniel Oaks 16 March 1779 before Philip Walker, J.P. Recorded 24 April 1797.

**F, 30-31:** 13 March 1797, Cornelious Dorsey of Chester County, planter, to James Bradford of same, for £30 sterling, 74 acres surveyed for him 15 May 1793 on waters of Rockey Creek adj. Mary Bradford, James Crafford, Alexander Henry. Cornelious Dorsey (wax seal), Wit: William Bradford, Kimbral Bannon (X). Proved by the oath of William Bradford 17 April 1797 before Hugh Knox, J.P. Recorded 24 April 1797.

**F, 31-32:** 13 March 1797, Cornelious Dorsey of Chester County, planter, to James Bradford of same, for £30 sterling, 80 acres on NW side of Rockey Creek adj. James Wylie, James Crafford. Cornelious Dorsey (wax seal), Wit: William Bradford, Kimbral Bannon (X). Proved by the oath of William Bradford 17 April 1797 before Hugh Knox, J.P. Recorded 24 April 1797.

**F, 32:** Joshua Gore of Chester County for £3 s17 sterling to James Green Tims, one loom, one mans saddle, one woman's saddle, 17 head o hogs, three feather beds, bestead & furniture, two spinning wheels, one table, one chest, 17 April 1797. Joshua Gore (Seal), Wit: William Boyd, George Brown. Proved by the oath of William Boyd 17 April 1797 before Saml Lacey, C. C. C. Recorded 24 April 1797.

**F, 33:** James Loveing of Chester county for $30 to Amos Timms, son of James Timms, in Chester County, land granted to Ephraim Mitchell 16 Oct 1785, and conveyed to said James Timms, and from James Timms to James Loving, 17 April 1797. James Loving (X) (Seal), Wit: William Boyd, George Brown, Joshua Gore. Proved by the oath of William Boyd 17 April 1797 before Saml Lacey, C. C. C. Recorded 24 April 1797.

**F, 33-34:** James Donald of Chester county for $20 to Amos Timms, son of James Timms, tract of 12 acres, part of tract granted to John Donald in Chester County on waters of Sandy River adj. John Carter, Daniel Rogers, 8

Nov 1796. James Donald (Seal), Wit: William Boyd, James Timms. Proved by the oath of William Boyd 17 April 1797 before Saml Lacey, C. C. C. Recorded 26 April 1797.

**F, 34-35**: James Bankhead & Elizabeth his wife of Chester County for £60 sterling to James McFadden, 200 acres adj. John Cooper, Sarah Knox, Patrick McGarrity, 200 acres granted to John Morriss and conveyed to James Bankhead. James Bankhead (Seal), Elizabeth Bankhead (Seal), Wit: Edward McFadden, William Smith, John Bankhead. Proved by the oath of Edward McFadden 17 April 1797 before Saml Lacey Clk. Recorded 26 April 1797.

**F, 35**: Robert Walker of Chester County to James Green Timms, seven head of cattle of a reddish colour, marked with an over half crop int he right ear & a smooth crop & underbit in the left ear, for $14, 17 April 1797. Robert Walker (R) (Seal), Wit: Will Boyd, George Brown. Proved by the oath of William Boyd 17 April 1797 before Saml Lacey, C. C. C. Recorded 26 April 1797.

**F, 35-36**: 15 March 1797, Nathan Jaggers of Chester County to John and Leonard Crosby, sons of John Crosby deceased, for £20 sterling, tract on Saludy Road, part of tract of 465 acres granted to John Jaggers 1 Jan 1785 and conveyed from him to Nathan Jaggers. Nathan Jaggers (Seal), Wit: Wm Embry, Richard Odum (RO), Jeremiah Jaggars. Proved by the oath of William Embry & Richard Odum 17 April 1797 before Hugh Knox, J.P. Recorded 26 April 1797.

**F, 37**: 7 Jan 1797, Randolph Wright of Chester County, to John Grant Junior of same, for £12 sterling, 50 acres on waters of Rockey Creek and known by being the NW part of 250 acres granted to a certain Randolph Wright 3 Dec 1790. Randolph Wright (Seal), Wit: Edmund Strange, William Strange. Proved in Fairfield County by the oath of Edmund Strange before M. Pickett, J.P.

**F, 38**: Matthew McClurkin of Chester County for £60 sterling, to Mary Donoley, widow & Executrix of Hugh Donoley deceased of same, 100 acres on a branch of little rockey creek, granted to said Matthew McClurkin 1 Jan 1787. Matthew McClurkin (Seal), Wit: Thomas Ewart, Alexander Buoyz, John Ready. Proved by the oath of Alexander Buoyes 18 Feb 1797 before William McQuiston, J.P. Recorded 26 April 1797.

**F, 39-40**: 21 March 1797, Samuel Fariss of Chester County to Elijah Bankston of same, for £40 sterling, 122 acres on waters of Rockey Creek adj. John Winn Junr, Hugh Montgomery, John Ellis, granted to Jacob Brown but surveyed for John Winn Junr & Relapsed by said Jacob Brown and by said Jacob Brown conveyed to John Winn Junr and by John Winn Junr to John Polley and by John Polley to Samuel Fariss 3 May 1794, recorded in Book D, page 163. Samuel Feres (Seal), Wit: Andw Hemphill, John Morriss (X). Proved by the oath of John Morriss 3 April 1797 before John McCreary, J.P. Recorded 26 April 1797.

**F, 40-41**: 22 April 1797, John Quinton of Chester County, farmer, to Mary Watson Quinton, neice to the said John Quinton, for natural love and affection and $1, one black mare about nine years old about 13½ hands high, branded on the near should & Buttock, also one horse colt two years old with a star in his forehead. John Quenton (wax seal), Wit: Thomas Hoyle, George Conn (mark). Proved by the oath of Thomas Hoyle and George Conn 24 April 1797 before Reuben Lacey, J.P. Recorded 3 May 1797.

**F, 41**: 22 April 1797, Thomas Hoyle of Chester County to Mary Watson Quinton, for natural love and affection, one pied cow & calf, the cow about seven years old marked with a crop in the left ear and a slit in the right one, brindled, two iron potts. Thomas Hoyle (wax seal), Wit: John Quenton, George Conn (mark). Proved by the oath of John Quenton and George Conn 24 April 1797 before Reuben Lacey, J.P. Recorded 3 May 1797.

**F, 42**: 21 March 1797, James Quinton of Chester County, planter, to Mary Watson Quinton, for natural love and affection, one woman's saddle, a spinning wheel, one pair of cotton cards, one bed & Furniture, one chest full of waring apparel, one dutch oven, one washing tub. James Quenton (Seal), Wit: Thomas Hoyle, George Conn (mark). Proved by the oath of Thomas Hoyle and George Conn 24 April 1797 before Reuben Lacey, J.P.

**F, 42-43**: South Carolina, Chester County. Catherine Brakefield of county aforesaid to Christopher Brakefield of same, for $40, one bed & furniture & bedstead, four gowns, six petticoats, one flax wheel, three aprons and $7 which William Murrey owes, 20 Feb 1797. Catherine Brakefield (X) (Seal), Wit: Sarah Brakefield (X), George Brakefield. Proved by the oath of Sarah Brakefield 15 July 1797 before Saml Lacey, Clk. Recorded 15 May 1797.

**F, 43**: 2nd Dec 1796. Mark Eaves of Chester County to John Edwards, one negro boy named David of the age of nine years for £30 sterling. Mark Eaves (Seal), Wit: H. Harrison, Charlotte Harrison. Proved by the oath of Henry Harrison 8 May 1797 before James Crafford, J.P. Recorded 24 May 1797.

**F, 44**: David Weir of Chester County for £40 sterling to Revd. John Hemphill of same, 53 acres on a small branch of Rockey Creek adj. David Bell, Arch'd Coulter, David Wier, granted to Thomas Baker Franklin 5 Feb 1787 and by him conveyed to David Wier 13 Aug 1787, dated 26 Feb 1796. David Wier (Seal), Wit: James Strong, James McDill. Jane Weir (mark), the late wife of David Weir, relinquished dower 24 Jan 1797 before Edward Lacey, J. C. C. Proved by the oath of James Strong 22 Aug 1797 before Saml Lacey, Clk. Recorded 23 Aug 1797.

**F, 45**: David Weir of Chester County for £40 sterling to Revd. John Hemphill of same, 100 acres on a small branch of Rockey Creek adj. David Bell, Arch'd Coulter, David Wier, granted to Thomas Daniel 16 June 1768, dated 26 Feb 1796. David Wier (Seal), Wit: James Strong, James McDill. Jane Weir (mark), the late wife of David Weir, relinquished dower 24 Jan 1797 before Edward

Lacey, J. C. C. Proved by the oath of James Strong 22 Aug 1797 before Saml Lacey, Clk. Recorded 23 Aug 1797.

**F, 46-47**: 25 Feb 1775, John Lee of Camden District, SC, on the waters of the Wateree River to John McClurkin of same place, planter, for £100, tract granted 14 March 1762 to Isaac Ellidg, 150 acres on Rockey Creek adj. John Lee, which said Lee purchased of said Ellidge. John Lee (IL (wax seal), Mary Lee (mark) (wax seal), Wit: Wilson Thompson, John McClurkin. Proved by the oath of John McClurkin 27 May 1797 before William McQuiston, J.P. Recorded 1 June 1797.

**F, 48-49**: 18 Feb 1783, John McClurkin of Camden District, Parish of St. Mark, waters of Wateree River, for £100, to Thomas McClurkin of same, tract granted 14 March 1762 to Isaac Ellidg, 150 acres on Rockey Creek adj. John Lee, which said Lee purchased of said Ellidge, and said Lee sold to John McClurkin 25 March 1775. John McClurkin (mark) (seal), Wit: Ephraim McCully, Andrew Graham. Proved by the oath of Andrew Graham 27 May 1797 before William McQuiston, J.P. Recorded 1 June 1797.

**F, 50-51**: 25 April 1785, Jonathan Dunhan of Camden District to Archibald Coulter of same, for £27 s2 d10, tract granted 13 March 1772 to Jonathan Dunhan, 300 acres on the south fork of Rockey Creek adj. John Lee, Archibald Coulter. Jonathan Dungan (X) (wax seal), Elinor Dungan (mark) (wax seal), Wit: Andrew Graham, John Neel (mark). Proved by the oath of Andrew Graham 27 May 1797 before William McQuiston, J.P. Recorded 2 June 1797.

**F, 51-52**: Josiah Hill of Chester County for $130 to William Estes of same, 210 acres on a branch called Jewels fork, waters of Sandy River, 10 June 1797. Josiah Hill (seal), Wit: Samuel Lacey, William Lacey. Proved by the oath of Samuel Lacey 10 June 1797 before Saml Lacey, Clk. Recorded 12 June 1797.

**F, 52-53**: Plat of 60 acres adj. David Hunter, Edward Henderson, Matthew Gaston, Alexander Rosborough.

Abraham Wright of Chester County for $70 to Thomas Wright of same, 60 acres in Chester county adj. Edward Henderson, Mathew Gaston, Alexander Rosborough, part of tract of 100 acres granted to Mathew Gaston, and conveyed by said Matthew Gaston to David Porter and by him to said Abraham Wright. Abraham Wright (Seal), Wit: John Simpson, John Cowen. Proved by the oath of John Simpson 12 March 1796 before Hugh Knox ,J.PO. Recorded 26 June 1797.

**F, 53-54**: Abraham Wright for $18 to Thomas Wright, planter, one black mare, four milk cows, four heifers, mark'd with a crop & split in the left era and a split in the right, a weavers loom, two beds & furniture, 6 Jan 1797. Abraham Wright (Seal), Wit: Sails Miller, Henry Wright (X). Proved by the oath of Silas Miler 9 June 1797 before Hugh McCluer, J.P. Recorded 26 June 1797.

**F, 54-55**: Elisabeth Nance of Chester county for £82 s10 sterling to James Martin, 275 acres, part of tract granted to Peter Nance in Feb 1773 for 400 acres, on a branch above the court house road ford near the house of Philip Walker deceased, adj. McCulley, Francis Henderson, Samuel McKinney, James McCluer, 6 March 1797. Elisabeth Nance (Seal), Wit: Richard Nance, Thomas C. Land, Samuel Kell. Proved by the oath of James Kell 17 June 1797 before Hugh Knox, J.P. Recorded 3 July 1797.

**F, 55-56**: Joseph Wier of Chester County for £60 sterling to James Wier of same, 100 acres being the NW end of a tract run for Richard Kerr for 200 acres granted to him 17 May 1774 on waters of Rockey Creek adj. Jacob Culp, Benjamin Harriss, Samuel Maxwell, Gasper Sleeker, 2 March 1797. Joseph Wier (Seal), Wit: James Lowrie, William Chesnut, Richard Kerr (R). Proved by the oath of Richard Carr 1 May 1797 before James Peden, J.P. Recorded 3 July 1797.

**F, 57-58**: 22 Dec 1795, Ferdinand Hopkins of Chester County to William Hill of same, for £20 sterling, tract on waters of Wilsons Creek in Chester County, 100 acres part of a larger tract. Ferd'd Hopkins (Seal),Wit: William Hill Junr (X), Major Hill (X). Proved by the oath of Major Hill 14 April 1796 before E. Nunn, J. P. Recorded 10 July 1797.

**F, 58**: John Hunter of Chester County manumits Jenny, a negro wench, who has served me now about 13 years and is not given to any vice. She was brought over from Africa when very young and not capable of having been guilty of any crime to occasion her being sold and from all probability stolen or carried away unjustly & sold into slavery. Although I purchased her in a legal way, according to the laws of the state, I do not see how she can be justly kept in slavery according to the Law of God, 7 July 1797. John Hunter (wax seal), Wit: John Hunter Junr, Archd Kell. Proved by the oath of John Hunter Junr 11 July 1797 before Saml Lacey, Clk.

**F, 59-60**: Plat of 150 acres adj. Paul Ferguson, James Adair.

William Jones of Chester County for $86 to William Hoyle of same, planter, 150 acres on the waters of Sandy River, part of a tract granted to Jonathan Jones Senr, 2 Oct 1786 for 485 acres, 4 July 1797. William Jones (wax seal), Wit: Leonard Jones, Joseph Hinkle. Elizabeth Jones (E), wife of William Jones, relinquished dower 4 July 1797 before Edward Lacey, Judge of C. C. C. Proved by the oath of Joseph Hinkle 4 July 1797 before R. Owen, J.P. Recorded 12 July 1797.

**F, 60-62**: 18 Aug 1790, Alexander Gordon and wife Sarah of Fairfield County, Camden District, for £50 sterling, to Matthew McClurkin of Chester County, tract granted 20 Dec 1762 to Francis Pinson, 50 acres on a branch of Rockey [Creek]. Alexander Gordon (Seal), Sarah Gordon (Seal), Wit: Andrew Graham, Thomas McClurkin. Proved by the oath of Andrew Graham 1 July 1797 before William McQuiston, J.P. Recorded 13 July 1797.

**F, 62-64**: 18 Aug 1790, Alexander Gordon and wife Sarah of Fairfield County, Camden District, for £100 sterling, to Matthew McClurkin of Chester County, tract granted 2 Jan 1754 to George Taylor, 400 acres on a branch of Rockey Creek, and said George Taylor did sell to John Lee and John Lee did bequeath to Alexander Gordon and his wife Sarah by his will.. Alexander Gordon (Seal), Sarah Gordon (Seal), Wit: Andrew Graham, Thomas McClurkin. Proved by the oath of Andrew Graham 1 July 1797 before William McQuiston, J.P. Recorded 14 July 1797.

**F, 64-65**: 26 July 1796, Hugh Knox, late Sheriff of Chester County, to Daniel Cook of same, taylor, whereas Patrick Hamilton in Chester county Court did implead Philip Sharkey on an attachment for £5 s16 sterling, sheriff sells, tract on west side Cattawba River, granted to said Philip Sharkey 10 April 1770, attachment returned in July Term 1789, now sells for £8 s13 d4 sterling. Hugh Knox (wax seal), Wit: Robert Tort, Patrick Hamilton (O). Recorded 28 July 1797.

**F, 66-67**: Daniel Cook of SC, taylor, for $100 to John Bristol of Chester County, 100 acres in Chester County granted to Philip Sharkey and sold by Hugh Knox, sheriff, 28 July 1796. Daniel Cook (wax seal), Wit: Hugh Whiteside, Caleb Feries, Alexander Thompson. Proved by the oath of Caleb Faries 20 Aug 1796 before Hugh Whiteside. Recorded 21 July 1797.

**F, 67-68**: William Fairiss of York County, planter, for £60 sterling to Daniel Davis of Chester County, 150 acres between the south and north forks of Fishing Creek, near Samuel McCance, Samuel Neeley, near Elliott, 25 Nov 1796. William Faries (wax seal), Wit: Hugh Whiteside, Samuel Neeley, Thomas Neeley. Proved by the oath of Thomas Neeley 4 July 1797 before R. Owen, J.P. Recorded 21 July 1797.

**F, 68-69**: Thomas McCulley of Chester County for $100 to John McCulley of same, 100 acres on waters of Rockey Creek granted to Thomas Larry adj. Philip Walker, Francis Henderson, William McGarrity, 25 July 1797. Thomas McCulley (Seal), Wit: William Boyd, Thomas Gillespy. Agness McCulley (X), wife of Thomas McCulley, relinquished dower 20 July 1797 before Joseph Brown, J. C. C. Proved by the oath of William Boyd 25 July 1797. Recorded 2 Aug 1797.

**F, 69-70**: South Carolina, Chester County. Peter Sealey of county aforesaid, planter, for one shilling, 174½ acres, half of tract granted to Peter Sealey 17 March 1796, adj. Abner Willis, 25 July 1797. Peter Sealey (Seal), Wit: Thomas Estis, Asia Darby, Benjamin Trusty (X). Proved by the oath of Thomas Estis 25 July 1797 before Thomas Jinkins, J.P. Sarah Seely, wife of Peter Seely, relinquished dower 25 July 1797 before Jo. Brown, J. C. C. Recorded 2 Aug 1797.

**F, 70-71**: William Martin of Camden District, Craven County, bound to Abraham Henderson of same, in the sum of £10,000, 25 Feb 1780, to make over to Abraham Henderson a tract of 200 acres on waters of Rockey Creek adj. Benjamin Mitchell, Francis Henderson Junr. William Martin (wax seal), Wit: William Boyd, Joseph Henderson. Abraham Henderson assigned bond to Jacob Huffman 4 Aug 1787. Jacob Huffman (X) assigned bond to Hugh Donaldy 4 Sept 1787. Hugh Donley (X) assigned bond to James McLonam 15 Feb 1788. Test; Laird Burns, Forsithe McLonam. William Boyd proved the bond of William Martin 25 July 1797 before William McQuiston, J.P. Recorded 2 Aug 1797.

**F, 71-72:** John Green of Chester County for $225 to John Boyd of same, 54½ acres, part of tract granted to David Morrow, 100 acres granted 3 June 1768 on the south fork of Fishing Creek, and conveyed from David Morrow to John Green, 6 Feb 1780, recorded in Chester county, deed dated 4 Feb 1797. John Green (wax seal), Wit: William Boyd, Charles Boyd, Paul Ferguson. Proved by the oath of William Boyd 25 July 1797. Recorded 3 Aug 1797.

**F, 72:** Robert Coulter of Chester County for £15 to Edward McDaniel of same, tract whereon the said Edward McDaniel now lives, 200 acres, dated 24 July 1797. Robert Coulter (Seal), Wit: Samuel McCaw, William McCaw. Proved by the oath of William McCaw 25 July 1 797 before William McQuiston, J.P. Recorded 3 Aug 1797.

**F, 72-73:** John McGuire of Chester County for £32 sterling to Thomas Gillaspey of same, 100 acres on waters of Rockey Creek, being part of a tract granted to James Bigham for 450 acres 31 Aug 1774 adj. William McGarrity, Thomas Gillaspey, 12 July 1797. John McGuire (wax seal), Wit: William M. Davison, Margaret McCreary, John McCreary. Proved by the oath of William M. Davison 12 July 1797 before John McCreary, J.P. Jane McGuire, wife of John McGuire, relinquished dower ____ 1797 before Jo Brown, J. C. C. Recorded 14 Aug 1797.

**F, 74:** Paul Ferguson of Chester County for $300 to John Green of same, 200 acres granted to Agness Hannah 8 Dec 1775 on a branch of Rockey Creek adj. James McClure, Elizabeth White, conveyed from Agness Hannah to Paul Ferguson 21 Jan 1785, recorded in Chester county Book F, pages 11-13. Paul Ferguson (wax seal), Wit: Jesse Hinkle, William Wylie, James Ferguson. Proved by the oath of William Wylie 25 July 1797 before Hugh McCluer, J.P. Recorded 14 Aug 1797.

**F, 74-75:** John & Thomas Steel of Chester County for £15 sterling to Thomas Findley of same, 20 acres, part of 400 acres granted to Catherine Steel 8 Nov 1771, dated 30 March 1797. John Steel (Seal), Thomas Steel (Seal), Wit: John McKown, David Fullerton. Proved by the oath of Capt. John McKown & David Fullerton 30 March 1797 before John McCreary, J,.P. Recorded 14 Aug 1797.

**F, 75-76:** Nicodemus Barns of Chester County for £8 sterling to James Ratteree of same, 97 acres adj. Lylius Sheols's line, part of tract granted to said Nicodeemus Barns 5 May 1788 on the dry branch waters of the Beaver dam or north fork of Rockey creek, 146 acres. Nichodeemus Barns (wax seal), Wit: John McCreary, David Fullerton, Peter Brown (X). Proved by the oath of David Fullerton 13 May 1797 before John McCreary, J.P. Recorded 14 Aug 1797.

**F, 76-77:** South Carolina, Chester County. Richard Jones & Sarah his wife of county aforesaid to Agness Cowsert (during her life or widowhood), and then to John Cowsert, Elinor Cowsert, James Cowsert, Agness Cowsert Junr, Thomas Cowsert, & Grissey Cowsert, tract on waters of Little Turkey Creek adj. William Worthy, David Hopkins, Mark Robinson, part of tract granted to David Hopkins 2331 acres 15 July 1785, dated 26 July 1797. Richard Jones (X) (Seal), Wit: John Colwell, James Johnston. Proved by the oath of James Johnston 25 July 1797 before Saml Lacey, Clk. Sarah Jones (X), wife of Richard Jones, relinquished dower 26 July 1797 before W. Gaston, J.C.C.

**F, 77-78:** John Barker of Chester County for one shilling sterling to Wilson Henderson of same, tract on waters of Sandy River adj.land surveyed for James Timms, 86 acres being a survey made by James Timms admr. on the estate of William Barker deceased, and by virtue of a bounty warrant granted to said Barker deceased for service done in defence of said state in the late war between the United States & Great Britain passing into a grant 6 Feb 1797, dated 26 July 1797. John Barker (X) (Seal), Wit: Thomas Oneal, Noah Bennett, Adam Henderson. Proved by the oath of Thomas Oneel 26 July 1797 before John Pratt, J.P. Recorded 16 Aug 1797.

**F, 78:** James McQuiston of Chester County for £25 sterling to Archibald McQuiston of Fairfield County, 200 acres in Chester County on waters of Rockey Creek adj. James Stuart, Michael Dickson, granted to William McQuiston and by succession of title now vested in said James McQuiston, 25 July 1797. James McQuiston (Seal), Wit: James Blair, John Douglass. July Term 1797, this deed was acknowledged in open court. Recorded 16 Aug 1797.

**F, 79:** James McQuiston of Chester County for £200 sterling to Hugh McQuiston of same, 400 acres in Chester County on a branch of Rockey Creek adj. John Fleming, Mary Conters, John Knox, Robert Knox, Robert & John Walker, 25 July 1797. James McQuiston (Seal), Wit: Archibald McQuiston, James Blair. July Term 1797, this deed was acknowledged in open court. Recorded 17 Aug 1797.

**F, 79:** Sarah Wilson of Chester county for £50 sterling to John Roden, one negro woman named Chloe about 36 years old & one negro boy named Jim about 18 months old, 7 Dec 1790. Sarah Wilson (X) (Seal),wit: Elijah Nunn, Greenberry Roden. Proved by the oath of Greenbury Roden 26 July 1797 before Saml Lacey, Clk. Recorded 17 Aug 1797.

**F, 79-80**: Mark Eaves of Chester County for £70 sterling to Joseph Edwards of same, 200 acres adj. lands of said Mark Eaves, Jacob Cooper, Solomon Crook, William Crook, dated 10 Feb 1797. Mark Eaves (wax seal), Wit: Chas Boyd, Susannah Crook (X), H. Harrison.

**F, 80-81**: South Carolina, Chester County. Johannah Thomas, widow of William Thomas deceased, for $500 to Hugh Thomas, all my right, title, and dower in the husband William Thomas's estate, both personal & real, to my son Hugh Thomas, 20 April 1797. Johannah Thomas (X) (Seal), Wit: Jarrot Young (X), William Linton Thomas. Proved by the oath of Jarrott Young 24 July 1797 before E. Nunn, J.P. Recorded 17 Aug 1797.

**F, 81**: David Hunter & Agness his wife of Chester county, planter, for £50 sterling to George Allen of York County, SC, planter, one half of a tract granted to said David Hunter on waters of Fishing Creek, 378 acres, the one half being 185 acres, 10 Nov 1796. David Hunter (wax seal) , Agness Hunter (mark) (wax seal), Wit: Hugh Whiteside, Samuel Whiteside, Margaret Whiteside (M). Proved by the oath of Samuel Whiteside 18 July 1797 before Hugh Whiteside. Recorded 17 Aug 1797.

**F, 81-82**: John Leonard of Washington County, Georgia, to John Edwards of Chester County, tract granted to Abraham Rush in 1765, 100 acres on Fishing Creek, 17 March 1797. John Leonard (Seal), Wit: William Dunnavant, Charles M. Boyd, H. Harrison. Proved by the oath of William Dunnavant 24 July 1797 before John McCreary, J.P. Recorded 17 Aug 1797.

**F, 82-83**: 2 Jan 1797, Jonathan Hemphill of Washington County, Georgia, to Thomas Thorn of Chester county, for £84 sterling, 250 acres, part of tract of 400 acres granted to Joseph Thomason adj. Blackley Shoemake, Henry Dye, recorded in Grant Book DDDD, page 67, and said Joseph Thomson conveyed to James Hemphill 13 Dec 1785, the said 250 acres. Jonathan Hemphill (Seal), Wit: Arthur Bowdon, Andw Hemphill. Proved by the oath of Andrew Hemphill 29 April 1797 before John McCreary, J.P. Recorded 17 Aug 1797.

**F, 83-84**: 2 Nov 1788, James Hemphill Senr., planter, of Chester County to Jonathan Hemphill of same, for £200 sterling, 400 acres adj. Blackley Shoemake, Aaron Alexander. James Hemphill (Seal), Wit: William Scott, Robert Hemphill, Andw Hemphill. Proved by the oath of William Scott 24 July 1789 before Andw Hemphill, J.P. Recorded 18 Aug 1797.

**F, 84-85**: 18 May 1797, George Kennedy of Chester County to Abraham Ross of same, for $300, 200 acres on waters of Rockey Creek adj. Hugh Bonner, originally granted to Henry Smith 11 Aug 1774, recorded in Grant Book RRR, and George Kennedy, husband to Mary Kennedy, being lawful heir to said land, the only surviving daughter or child of Henry Smith deceased. George Kennedy (Seal), Mary Kennedy (O) (Seal), Wit: John Douglass, Hugh Ross, Francis Ross. Proved by the oath of Hugh Ross 26 July 1797 before Hugh

Knox, J.P. Mary Kennedy (O), wife of George Kennedy relinquished dower 25 July 1797 before Edward Lacey, J.C.C. Recorded 18 Aug 1797.

**F, 85-86**: 1 Jan 1787, Michael Atterbery in Chester County to Josiah Cook of same, for £50 sterling, 100 acres on waters of Brushey Fork, granted to Michael Atteberry 9 Jan 1785. Michael Atterberry (M), Elisabeth Atterberry (X) (wax seal), Wit: Thomas Atterberry (X), John Atterberry (X), Thomas Mitchell (X). Proved by the oath of Thomas Mitchell 24 July 1797 before Saml Lacey, Clk. Recorded 18 Aug 1797.

**F, 86**: Elijah Nunn of Chester County for $50 to Samuel Harmon of Union County, SC, tract on waters of Brushey Fork Creek, 26 acres, part of a tract granted to Elijah Nunn, deed dated 16 July 1797. E. Nunn (wax seal), Wit: James Anderson, James Harmon. Recorded 18 Aug 1797.

**F, 87**: James Young of Chester County on waters of Turkey Creek for $20 to John Anderson of said county, 95 acres adj. William Gaston, 19 July 1797. James Young (wax seal), Wit: James Anderson, James Hermon. Proved by the oath of James Hermon 25 July 1797 before E. Nunn, J.P. Recorded 21 Aug 1797.

**F, 87-88**: William Anderson of state of Georgia, blacksmith, for $200 to John Anderson of Turkey Creek, Chester County, to hold in trust for John Anderson, son of the land John Anderson, deceased, tract on Susey Bowls branch of Turkey Creek, 250 acres, part of tract of 350 acres granted to William Anderson 21 Jan 1785, dated 8 April 1797. William Anderson (wax seal), Wit: Reuben Lacey, Thomas Robins. Proved by the oath of Reuben Lacey 25 July 1797 before E. Nunn. J.P. Recorded 21 Aug 1797.

**F, 88**: Plat of 218 acres "Mr. Atteberry's plantation." Recorded 21 Aug 1797.

**F, 89-90**: 6 July 1790, Peter Jones, Esqr., Sheriff of Chester county, to Thomas Brandon, Esqr., of Union County, whereas James Johnston of Chester County did on the third day of June 1789 obtain a writ against Adam McCool which was returned before the justices of the county court of Chester on first Monday in October and continued till 8 April 1790, when said James Johnston obtained a judgment, to levy of the goods and chattles, lands, and tenements of Adam McCool £14 s5 d8 and £5 s15 costs, sheriff sells tract on the north side of Broad River known by the name of the Round Elbow adj. John McCool, Adam McCool Junr, sold 6 July 1790 for £26 s1 d4 sterling. Peter Jones Sheriff (Seal), Wit: Zachariah Bell Junior, Christopher Streight, Thomas McElhenny Junior. Proved by the oath of Christopher Streight 25 July 1797 before Saml Lacey, Clk. Recorded 21 Aug 1797.

**F, 90-91**: 23 June 1795, Ferdinand Hopkins of Chester County to James Atterberry of same, for £50 SC currency, 152 acres granted 15 Oct 1784 on waters of Brushy fork of Sandy River adj. Jonathan Mayfield, certified 19 Oct 1784. Ferd'd Hopkins (seal), Wit: D'd Hopkins, Abraham Myers. Proved by the oath of Abraham Myers 25 July 1797 before Saml Lacey, Clk. Recorded 21 Aug 1797.

**F, 91-93**: 12 Sept 1796, John McDonald of Chester County for £50 to Asia Darby of same, 100 acres, part of tract granted to Thomas Morris 2 May 1785, and conveyed from Thomas Morriss by a will to Richard Morriss & Conveyed from said Richard Morriss to John McDonald, on Sternes's branch, waters of Brushy Fork of Sandy River. John McDonald (Seal), Elisabeth McDonald (E) (Seal), Wit: Peter Seely, J. Wallis. Elisabeth McDonald assigned her right to Asia Darby 12 Sept 1796. Proved by the oath of Peter Seely 25 July 1797 before Thomas Jinkins, J.P. Recorded 21 Aug 1797.

**F, 93**: South Carolina, Chester County. James Timms of county aforesaid for £5 to Richard Anderson, 34½ acres granted to James Timms 2 March 1795, James Timms (Seal), Wit: William McGriff, Thomas Oneel, Joseph Bennett. Proved by the oath of Thomas Oneel 22 July 1797 before Reuben Lacey, J.P. Recorded 23 Aug 1797.

**F, 93-95**: William Jones of Chester County for $300 to Joseph Jones of same, 143 acres on Sandy River the east side of Broad River granted to Jonathan Jones Senior 2 Oct 1786, recorded in Grant Book OOOO, page 111, and conveyed by said Jonathan Jones Senior to said William Jones 28 March 1791, recorded in Book B, page 366, dated 27 March 1797. William Jones (LS), Wit: Jonathan Jones, Daniel Atkins (mark). Proved by the oath of Jonathan Jones 27 March 1797 before Saml Lacey, Clk. Elizabeth Jones (E), wife of William Jones, relinquished dower 17 June 1797 before Edward Lacey, J. C. C. Recorded 23 Aug 1797.

**F, 95-96**: South Carolina, Chester County. 28 Feb 1797, Peter Corbell of county aforesaid with consent of his wife Judith Nutt to General Edward Lacey for making provision for their present and future issue to become a sole and separate trader or dealer, for £5. Peter Corbell (Seal), Edwd Lacey (Seal), Wit: Saml Lacey Junr, Samuel Lacey. Proved by the oath of Samuel Lacey 19 Aug 1797 before Saml Lacey, Clk. Recorded 23 Aug 1797.

**F, 96-97**: South Carolina, Chester County. Thomas Jinkins of county aforesaid for £50 to Peter Seely, 100 acres, part of tract of 378 acres granted to Allen Burton 21 Jan 1785 on waters of Sandy River, 11 March 1797. Thomas Jenkins (Seal), Wit: Thomas Estes, Wm. Jenkins. Proved by the oath of Thos Estes 25 July 1797 before John Pratt, J.P. Agness Jinkins, wife of Thomas Jinkins, relinquished dower 25 July 1797 before Jo Brown, J. C. C. Recorded 23 Aug 1797.

**F, 97-98**: South Carolina, Chester County. Peter Seely of county aforesaid, planter, for one shilling sterling, to Samuel Seely Junr, 175½ acres on the long branch of Sealy's Creek, being half of a tract granted to Peter Seely 17 March 1796, adj. Abner Walker, Robert Frost, 25 July 1797. Peter Seely (Seal), Wit: Thomas Estes, Asa Darby, Benjamin Trusty (X). Proved by the oath of

Thomas Estes 28 July 1797 before Thomas Jinkins, J.P. Sarah Seely, wife of Peter Seely, relinquished dower 25 July 1797 before Jo Brown, J. C. C. Recorded 24 Aug 1797.

**F, 98-99**: 24 July 1797, John Service of Chester County to Ann Kennedy of same, for £20 sterling, tract on a branch of Rockey Creek adj. land surveyed for Jane McCartney, granted to Margaret Wylie, 100 acres 1 Feb 1768 and transferred unto William Boyd & sold to said John Service by William Boyd 4 Nov 1786, recorded in the clerks office of said county. John Service (mark) (Seal), Wit: John Combest, Samuel Combest, Saml Moore. Recorded 24 Aug 1797.

**F, 99-100**: Plat of 164 acres. 9 Jan 1796, Stephen Ditshaw & Nancey his wife of Chester County to William Knox of same, for £459 s3 sterling, 164 acres, part of two grants, one granted to Robert Gaston 4 Nov 1772 & Conveyed to above mentioned Stephen Ditshaw on a branch of Rockey Creek, the other granted to Thomas McElhany 7 May 1792 and conveyed to said Ditshaw 14 Nov 1795, said tract adj. James McCluer, Robert Walker, Robert Walker, Montgomery, William Colwell, William Miller, William Knox. Johann Stephen Ditshau [signed in German] (Seal), Nancey Ditshaw (mark) (Seal), Wit: Thomas Porter, William Morton, James Ferguson. Proved by the oath of William Morton 28 Feb 1797 before Hugh McClure. Recorded 24 Aug 1797.

**F, 100-101**: Fairfield County. Alexander McEwen & Andrew McDowell, both of county aforesaid, for £100 sterling to Samuel McKinney of Chester County, three tracts of 100 acres each, two of said tracts being leased to Alexander McEwen by the commissioners John Berwick, Thomas Waring Senr, & John Ewing Calhoun, who were commissioners appended to dispose of & make sale of all the confiscated lands at publick auction, the two different tracts of land which were sold as the confiscated property of William Ballentine & John Downey, 30 June 1783, and the third tract granted to Andr Mcdowell & Alexander McEwen 5 Dec 1781 on Rockey Creek, Chester County adj. John Adams, Andr McDowell, Alexander McEwen, John McEwen, 2 May 1797. Alexander McKown (Seal), Andr McDowell (Seal), Wit: John McEwen Junr, I. Hudson, Robert Forsyth. Proved by the oath of Isaac Hudson in Chester county 1 July 1797 before John McCreary. Camden District. Mary McKewn, wife of Alexander McKewn, and Mary McDowel, wife of Andrew McDowel, relinquished dower 2 May 1797 before John Turner, Justice Fairfield County. Recorded 25 Aug 1797.

**F, 101-103**: 1 April 1785, David Morrow, late of Camden District, yeoman, to John Boyd of same, yeoman, for £50 sterling, tract granted 13 May 1768 to William Fairiss, 150 acres in the Parish of Saint Marks, near Fishing Creek adj. David Morrow, Stephen Terry, Richard Carrell, conveyed to said David Morrow by said William Farriss 11 March 1771, recorded in Book Y No. 3, page 27, 13 Dec 1771. David Morrow (mark) (wax seal), Wit: Samuel Morrow, Alexander Elder. Proved in Spartanburgh County by the oath of Samuel Morrow 17 Feb 1786 before H. White, J. P. Recorded 26 Aug 1797.

**F, 103-103**: Plat (rectangle) showing Saluda Road. William Lacey of Chester County, yeoman, for $40 to James McNeal of York County, planter, lot at Chester Court House on the north side of the Saluda Road, the third lott form the present court house, along said road towards the Fishdam Ford on Broad River, part of tract of 736 acres granted to James Stuart 1 Dec 1788, conveyed by James Stuart & the other half on the opposite side of said road to William Stuart. William Lacey (Seal), William Stuart (Seal), Wit: Edwd Lacey, Saml Lacey Junior. Proved by the oath of Edward Lacey 25 Aug 1797 before Saml Lacey, Clk. Recorded 26 Aug 1797.

**F, 104-105**: John McKown & Jane McKown of Chester County appoint George McKown of Burbon County, Kentucky, our lawful attorney to ask, demand, sue for, recover & receive from John McKown or Alexander McKown formerly of the county of Lancaster, State of Pennsylvania, all such sums due unto said John McKown & Jane McKown from the estate of George McKown deceased, 5 Sept 1797. John McKown (Seal), Jane McCown (Seal), Wit: Alexander McKown, James McCown, George Morris. Proved by the oath of Alexander McKown, James McKown, and George Morris in Chester County 5 Sept 1797 before John McCreary, J. P. Certificate from Saml Lacey that John McCreary is a J.P. Certificate from Edward Lacey, on of the judges of the county court that Samuel Lacey is the clerk of court for Chester County, 8 Sept 1797. Recorded 8 Sept 1797.

**F, 105-106**: An Inventory of property mortgage to Ebenezer Elliott admr of the estates of William Elliott and Benjamin Elliott, late of Chester County, deceased, by Charles Orr, he being by note & otherwise indebted to the estate s of the deceased persons. 5 head of horse, 1 foal, 4 cows, 2 steers & 4 young ones, 10 sheep, a number of hogs, beds and household furniture.

25 July 1797. Charles Orr to Ebenezer Elliott, both of Chester County, for £36 sterling, mortgage of certain property. Charles Orr (wax seal), Wit: Joseph Gaston, James Elliott. Proved by the oath of Joseph Gaston 25 July 1797 before John McCreary, J.P.

**F, 106-107**: 13 Oct 1796, David Tomb, Sina Tomb, John McKelvey, Elisabeth McKelvey, Jane Kirkpatrick, Josiah Kirkpatrick, James Jamieson and Mary Jamieson, of Pinckney District, Chester County, for £50 sterling, to Elizabeth Tomb of same, 91 acres on waters of Turkey Creek on Wilsons branch. David Tomb, Sina Tomb, James Jamieson, Mary Jamieson, John McKelvey, Elisabeth McKelvey, Josiah Kirkpatrick, Jane Kirkpatrick (wax seal), Wit: Robert Love, Sarah Brown, I. Rogers. Proved by the oath of Isaac Rogers 22 Aug 1797 before Clayton Rogers, J.P. Recorded 22 Sept 1797.

**F, 107-108**: 13 Oct 1796, Elisabeth Tomb, David Tomb, Sina Tomb, Jane Kirkpatrick, Josiah Kirkpatrick, James Jamieson and Mary Jamieson, of Pinckney District, Chester County, for £50 sterling, to John McKelvey and Elisabeth McKelvey of same, 255 acres on waters of Turkey Creek on Wilsons branch. Elisabeth Tomb (O), David Tomb, Sina Tomb, Josiah Kirkpatrick,

Jane Kirkpatrick, James Jamieson, Mary Jamieson, (wax seal), Wit: Robert Love, Sarah Brown, I. Rogers. Proved by the oath of Isaac Rogers 22 Aug 1797 before Clayton Rogers, J.P. Recorded 22 Sept 1797.

**F, 108-109**: 13 Oct 1796, Elisabeth Tomb, David Tomb, Sina Tomb, John McKelvey, Elisabeth McKelvey, James Jamieson and Mary Jamieson, of Pinckney District, Chester County, for £50 sterling, to Josiah Kirkpatrick, and Jane Kirkpatrick, of same, 75 acres on waters of Turkey Creek on Wilsons branch. Elisabeth Tomb (O), David Tomb, Sina Tomb, John McKelvey, Elisabeth McKelvey, James Jamieson, Mary Jamieson, (wax seal), Wit: Robert Love, Sarah Brown, I. Rogers. Proved by the oath of Isaac Rogers 22 Aug 1797 before Clayton Rogers, J.P. Recorded 22 Sept 1797.

**F, 109-110**: John Carter of Chester County for $117 to Benjamin Carter of same, 135 acres on waters of Sandy River adj. Henry Cottrell, John Carter, Thomas Atterberry, part of 400 acres granted to Benjamin Carter 18 March 1773, and did will the said tract to his son John Carter, 26 Aug 1797. John Carter (Seal), Wit: William Boyd, Thomas Oneel, Henry Cotterell. Proved by the oath of Thomas Oneel 19 Sept 1797 before John Lacey, Clk. Recorded 27 Sept 1797.

**F, 110**: 6 Sept 1792, Thomas Roden of Chester County to Lewis Roberts of same, for ten shillings sterling, 153 acres, part of 182 acres on Welches Creek adj. James Daugherty, Solomon Peters, granted to Thomas Roden 2 Oct 1791. Thomas Roden (Seal), Wit: Enoch Butler, James Butler (X). Proved by the oath of Enoch Butler 9 Sept 1797 before John Pratt, J.P. Recorded 17 Sept 1797.

**F, 111**: 18 March 1784, Peter Noland of Camden District to Sampson Noland for £400 sterling money of SC, tract granted to Zachariah Isbell 10 April 1767, memorial entered in Book G No. 7, page 526, 10 Oct 1765, recorded in the Secretarys Office in Book ZZ, page 429, and since conveyed to Amos Timms and from him to said Peter Noland 9 Sept 1782, 100 acres. Peter Noland (wax seal), Wit: Nathl Abney M. D., Danl Duff, Isaac Stroud. Proved in 96 District by the oath of Capt. Daniel Duff 5 June 1784 before Wm Farr, J.P. Recorded 27 Sept 1797.

**F, 112**: 18 March 1784, Peter Noland of Camden District to Sampson Noland of the state of North Carolina for £500 sterling money of SC, tract granted 7 Aug 1767 to George Flinn, memorial entered in Book H No. 8, page 273, 12 Sept 1767, recorded in the Secretarys Office in Book BBB, page 150, and by said Flenn to Amos Timms 4 Dec 1767, recorded in Book L No. 3, page 498, 4 Nov 1768, and from said Amos Timms to Peter Noland 9 Sept 1782, 150 acres. Peter Noland (wax seal), Wit: Nathl Abney M. D., Danl Duff, Isaac Stroud. Proved in 96 District by the oath of Capt. Daniel Duff 5 June 1784 before Wm Farr, J.P. Recorded 27 Sept 1797.

**F, 113**: Sampson Noland & Elizabeth Noland of Chester County for £550 sterling to Patrick McGriff of same, tract of 100 acres on the main Sandy River surveyed & granted to Zachariah Isbell 3 April 1765 and conveyed from him to Amos Timms and from him to Peter Noland and from him to Sampson Noland, also 150 acres on Sandy River 150 acres granted adj. Zachariah Isbell, Thomas Roden, granted to George Flynn and conveyed to Zachariah Isbell and from him to Amos Timms and from him to Peter Noland and from him to Sampson Noland, 20 March 1797. Sampson Noland (wax seal), Elisabeth Noland (X) (wax seal), Wit: Peter Thomas, John McGriffin, Philip Noland. Proved by the oath of John McGriff 20 Sept 1797 before Saml Lacey, Clk. Recorded 28 Sept 1797.

**F, 114**: John Morriss of Abbeville County, SC, Bricklayer, for £20 sterling to Robert Harper of Chester County, tract on waters of dry fork of Fishing Creek on the Saluda Road that goes to the Fishdam ford on Broad River adj. Richard Kerrel, granted to John Finley 8 Dec 1775, recorded in Book III, page 686, dated 11 Sept 1797. John Morris (wax seal), Wit: A. C. Jones Junr, B. Jones. Proved 11 Oct 1797 by the oath of A. C. Jones Junr who stated that he and Benjn Jones were witnesses before Am. Cr. Jones, J. A. C. Breefy Morris, wife of John Morris, relinquished dower 11 Sept 1797 before Adam Crain Jones, Justice of Abbeville County. Recorded 28 Sept 1797.

**F, 115**: Plat of Thomas Neils plantation, 556 acres. Josiah Hill of Chester County, yeoman for $60 to Thomas Neil of same, yeoman, 56 acres on waters of Sealeys Creek, a fork of Sandy River, part of 12,700 acres granted to said Josiah Hill, dated 22 Aug 1797. Wit: Wm. Lacey, Samuel Lacey. Proved by the oath of Samuel Lacey 22 Aug 1797 before Edwd Lacey, J. C. C. Recorded 28 Sept 1797.

**F, 115-116**: Plat of David Woodside's 92½ acres showing adj. land owners Mr. Estes, Robert Ash, Kerman Culp. Josiah Hill of Chester County, yeoman for £20 to David Woodside of same, planter, 92½ acres on waters of Sandy River, part of 12,700 acres granted to said Josiah Hill, dated 18 Sept 1797. Wit: Joseph Bennett, James Bennett. Proved by the oath of Joseph Bennett Junr 18 Sept 1797 before Saml Lacey, C. C. C. Recorded 29 Sept 1797.

**F, 116**: Plat of 198 acres showing adj. land owners George Harden, Mr. Bennett, Thomas Neil, Edward Self. Josiah Hill of Chester County, yeoman for $200 to James Bennett & Joseph Bennett Junr of same, planters, 198 acres on waters of Sandy River, part of 12,700 acres granted to said Josiah Hill, dated 18 Sept 1797. Wit: Joseph Bennett, David Woodside. Proved by the oath of David Woodside 18 Sept 1797 before Saml Lacey, C. C. C. Recorded 29 Sept 1797.

**F, 117**: Plat of Christopher Breakfield's plantation of 150 acres. Josiah Hill of Chester County, yeoman for $200 to Christopher Breakfield of same, planter, 150 acres on waters of Sandy River, part of 12,700 acres granted to said Josiah

# CHESTER COUNTY SC DEED ABSTRACTS

Hill, dated 6 Oct 1797. Wit: Saml Lacey Junr, John Beaird. Proved by the oath of John Beaird 6 Oct 1797 before Saml Lacey, C. C. C. Recorded 27 Oct 1797.

**F, 118:** William Lacey of Chester County for $20 to Samuel Shaw of City of Charleston, lot of land at Chester Court House being the fifth lott from the present Court House along Fishdam Road on the north side of said Road & the second lott below the lott of James McNeal's, 5 Sept 1797. Wm Lacey (LS), Wit: Samuel Lacey, Edward Lacey Junr. Proved by the oath of Samuel Lacey, Sheriff, 3 Oct 1797 before Saml Lacey, C. C. C. Recorded 27 Oct 1797.

**F, 118-119, 120-122:** Lease and release 20 & 21 Oct 1788, William Williams of Lancaster County, SC, District of Camden, planter, to Benjamin Williams of Chester County, planter, for £40 sterling, tract on south side of Turkey Creek on Susey Bowls branch, 200 acres adj. John Walker, heirs of Reed, plat dated 14 Oct 1788, recorded in Book TTTT, page 251. William Williams (Seal), Lucey Williams (Seal), Wit: Harburd Horton, Aaron Williams. Proved by the oath of Harburt Horton in Chester County 23 Jan 1794 before Jo Brown, J. C. C. Recorded 4 Nov 1797.

**F, 119-120:** South Carolina, Chester County. 24 Jan 1792, James Adare to George Conn, tract on waters of Turkey Creek on Susey Boles branch, part of tract granted by patent to John Walker 200 acres. James Adare (wax seal), Anne Adare, Wit: Hamilton Brown, Robert Robinson. Proved by the oath of Hamilton Brown 31 Oct 1797 before Jo Brown, Judge. Recorded 4 Nov 1797.

**F, 122-124:** 21 Oct 1788, 22 Sept 1790, Benjamin Williams of Chester County, planter, to Moses Williams, son of said Benjamin, for natural love and affection, tract granted 3 April 1786 to William Williams, 100 acres, part of 200 acres on Bowles Branch of Turkey Creek, sold by William Williams to Benjamin Williams 20 Oct 1788. Benja. Williams (wax seal), Wit: John Brown, David Reid, John Nicholas Bell (X). Recorded 8 Nov 1797. Proved by the oath of David Reid 3 May 1792 before Jo. Brown, J. C. C.

**F, 124:** 13 Oct 1796, James Jamieson and Mary Jamieson of York County, John McKelvey, Elisabeth McKelvey, Elisabeth Tomb, Josiah Kirkpatrick and Jane Kirkpatrick, of Pinckney District, Chester County, for £50 sterling, to David Tomb of same, 106 acres on waters of Turkey Creek on Wilsons branch. Elisabeth Tomb (O), James Jamieson, Mary Jamieson, John McKelvey, Elizabeth McKelvey, Josiah Kirkpatrick, Jane Kirkpatrick (wax seal), Wit: Robert Love, Sarah Brown, I. Rogers. Proved by the oath of Isaac Rogers 22 Aug 1797 before Clayton Rogers, J.P. Recorded 9 Nov 1797.

**F, 125:** Moses Cantzon of Lancaster county for £300 sterling to Mark Eaves of Chester County, tract in Chester County on west side of the Cattawba River, part of tract of 800 acres granted by NC to 6 April 1753 to Jacob Cooper, on said river, 440 acres, dated 31 July 1797. Moses Cantzon (wax seal), Wit: William McDonald, Robt Barkley, Danl Wade. Proved in Chester

County by the oath of Wm McDonald 29 Aug 1797 before John McCreary, J.P. Recorded 10 Nov 1797.

**F, 125-126**: South Carolina, Chester County. George Conn of county aforesaid for $300 to Thomas Eakin Junr of same, one bay mare 9 years old 14½ hands high branded on the near cheek C, also one sorrel mare 3 years old, 14 hands high, 16 head of cattle, 21 head of hogs, 8 head of sheep, three beds & furniture, one loom & Tacklings, two pots & an oven, two saddles, two wheels, six chairs, one cupboard and furniture, 24 Oct 1797. George Conn (mark) (Seal), Wit: Robert Cowley (X), John Conn (C). Proved by the oath of Robert Cowley 28 Oct 1797 before Saml Lacey Clk. Recorded 10 Nov 1797.

**F, 126-127**: 27 Oct 1797, Samuel Lacey, Sheriff of Chester County, to Amos Timms Senr of same, whereas Richard Evans did in the county court implead James Timms on an action of debt in 1796 and obtained judgment for his debt & Cost of suit to be levied on the goods & chattles lands & tenements of said James Timms, by writ of fieri facias to levy £9 s19 d3 sterling, sold on 4 March 1797, 125 acres granted to James Timms admr. of James Hawkins 28 March 1778, adj. Col. Patrick McGriff, James Timms, Edward Henderson, Churchwell Charter, on waters of Sandy River, sold for $25. Samuel Lacey sheriff of Chester County (LS), Wit: Saml Lacey Junr, Hollis Timms. Proved by the oath of Hollis Tims 27 Oct 1797 before Saml Lacey, Clk. Recorded 15 Nov 1797.

**F, 127**: South Carolina, Chester County. John Service for £21 sterling sells to Nancy Kennedy (widow of George Kennedy) all my right & title to the within named property for which I have received full satisfaction, 13 Oct 1797. John Service Sen'r (O), Wit: Wm Kenney, John Combest. Recorded 15 Nov 1797.

**F, 127-128**: David Eakins of Chester county for $100 to Agness Livingston of same, 300 acres except 125 acres which said David Eakins made over to John Quinton, originally granted to David Eakins 2 July 1787, 6 Nov 1797. David Akins, Margaret Eakins (X) (wax seal), Wit: John Anderson, Thomas Anderson. Proved by the oath of John Anderson 11 Nov 1797 before E. Nunn, J.P. Recorded 15 Nov 1797.

**F, 128**: South Carolina, Chester County. Jeremiah Thomas & Polley his wife of county aforesaid for £100 sterling, to Jesse T. Wallis, 125 acres, part of tract conveyed from Edmund Lee & wife to said Jeremiah Thomas 19 Oct 1793, recorded in Chester County 24 June 1794, Book D, page 196, dated 6 June 1797. Jeremiah Thomas (LS), Polley Thomas (X) (LS), Wit: Thomas Fletchall, Elisabeth Thomas (X). Proved by the oath of Thomas Fletchall 2 Dec 1797 before Saml Lacey, Clk.

**F, 129**: James Adare of Chester County, Sadler, for $100 to John Lockhart of same, farmer, 117 acres on waters of Suseys Creek, adj. widow Brown, James Adare, John Walker, Daniel Travis, said tract originally granted to James Adare 3 Oct 1796, dated 24 Oct 1797. James Adare (Seal), Wit: Aaron

Lockart, James Tyner, John Tyner. Proved by the oath of James Tyner 25 Oct 1797 before E. Nunn, J.P. Recorded 4 Dec 1797.

F, 129-130: Samuel Combest of Chester County for $10 to William Combest of same, 100 acres on Rockey Creek adj. Mathew Neeley, being a tract of 100 acres granted by Gov. William Bull of SC, dated 24 Dec 1797. Samuel Combest (Seal), Anne Kennedy (mark), Wit: John Combest, John Service. Proved by the oath of John Combest 1 Jan 1798 before Saml Lacey, Clk. Recorded 4 Jan 1798.

F, 130-131: 9 Dec 1797, Samuel Combest of Chester County to John Combest of same, for $5, 100 acres on Rockey Creek originally granted to Matthew Neely 27 Aug 1765 and conveyed to John Combest Senr by said Nealy, released in the Genl Audrs Office in Book M No 9, page 1, 20 Sept 1774, said release dated 5 Nov 1767, said John Combest Senr deceased & dying intestate and Samuel Combest his eldest son then heir in law to said land. Samuel Combest (Seal), Anne Kennedy (mark), Wit: John Service, William Combest. Proved by the oath of William Combest 1 Jan 1798 before Saml Lacey, C. C. C. Recorded 5 Jan 1798.

F, 131-132: South Carolina, Chester County. James Timms of county aforesaid for £10 sterling, to James Timms Junr, 23 acres on waters of Sandy River granted to me 9 Sept 1794, dated 15 Dec 1797. James Timms (Seal), Wit: Joseph Timms, William Estes, Hollis Timms. Proved by the oath of Hollis Timms 30 Dec 1797 before Saml Lacey, Clk. Recorded 5 Jan 1798.

F, 132: South Carolina, Chester County. James Timms of county aforesaid for £50 sterling, to Walter Timms, 100 acres on waters of Sandy River, part of tract granted, dated 15 Dec 1797. James Timms (Seal), Wit: Blaky Carter, William Estes, Hollis Timms. Proved by the oath of Hollis Timms 30 Dec 1797 before Saml Lacey, Clk. Recorded Jan 1798.

F, 132-133: 11 May 1791, Robert Miller & Mary Miller, planter & spinster, to James McCluer of Chester County for £19 sterling, 1540 acres on a branch of Rockey Creek adj. Robert Walker, John McKown, Agnes Henry, granted to said Robert Miller 6 Feb 1773. Robert Miller (Seal), Mary Miller (mark) (Seal), Wit: Robert Walker, Andrew Miller. Proved by the oath of Robert Walker 14 Dec 1792 before Philip Walker, J.P. Recorded 4 Jan 1798.

F, 133-134: Andrew Hemphill of Chester County for $340 to Alexander English of same, one negro man slave named Cuffe about 30 or 31 years of age, 10 Feb 1797. And'w Hemphill (Seal), Wit: Jenet Morrow (X), Andrew Gardner. Proved by the oath of Jennet Morrow 14 Sept 1797 before Hugh Knox, J.P. Recorded 6 Jan 1798.

F, 134: David Eakins & Margaret his wife of Chester County for $50 to Jane McCalla of same, 146 acres, part of tract granted to said David Eakins 3 Sept 1787, dated 15 Dec 1797. David Eakins (wax seal), Margaret Eakins (wax seal), Wit: James Hermon, Margaret Eakins. Proved by the oath of Margaret Eakins 30 Dec 1797 before E. Nunn, J.P.

**F, 134-135**: James Johnston Senr of Chester County, planter, for £1 sterling to James Montgomery of same, part of tract of 182 acres granted to said Johnston 4 March 1787, dated 12 May 1796. James Johnston (wax seal), Wit: Alex'dr Bryce, James Johnston Junr. Proved by the oath of James Johnston Junr 4 Dec 1797 before E. Nunn, J.P. Recorded 8 Jan 1798.

**F, 135-136**: James Johnston & wife Martha of Chester County for $170 to John Cubit of same, tract on waters of little Turkey Creek, 200 acres, part of tract granted to said James Johnston 5 March 1787, dated ____ 1797. James Johnston (Seal), Martha Johnston (mark) (Seal), Wit: John Nougher, John Cousert. Proved by the oath of John Nougher 29 Nov 1797 before E. Nunn, J.P. Recorded 8 Jan 1797.

**F, 136**: 18 Sept 1797, Mathew Rogers of York County, SC, to Stuart Brown of Chester County, for £1, tract on waters of Turkey Creek adj. James Wright, John Brown, part of tract granted to Matthew Rogers 8 July 1774. Matthew Rogers (wax seal), Wit: James McNees, John Armstrong. Proved by the oath of James McNees 28 Dec 1797 before Wm. Gaston, J.C.C.

**F, 136-137**: Andrew Walker of Fairfield County, SC, for £60 sterling to Mary Lowrie of Chester County, 100 acres, part of a tract granted to John McClurkin for 518 acres on the waters of the south fork of Rockey Creek and said John McClurkin & Margret his wife did convey to said Andrew Walker 259 acres in 1792 adj. William Boyles, dated 27 Jan 179997. Andrew Walker (Seal), Wit: James Strong, Drury Walker, Robert Neal. Plat included showing adj. Wilson, Samuel Hamilton. Deed proved by the oath of James Strong 4 Dec 1797 before James Peden, J.P. Recorded 10 Jan 1798.

**F, 137-138**: David Eakins & Margaret his wife of Chester County for $50 to Margaret Eakins of same, 148 acres on waters of Turkey Creek, part of tract granted to said David Eakins 13 Sept 1787. David Eakins (wax seal), Margaret Eakins (mark) (wax seal), Wit: Samuel McCalley, Jas Hermon. Proved by the oath of Samuel McCalley 30 Dec 1797 before E. Nunn, J.P. Recorded 10 Jan 1798.

**F, 138-139**: Randolph Carter of Fairfield County & Samuel Carter, late of Chester County, but now of Rutherford County, North Carolina, for £60 sterling, to Archibald Wilson of Chester County, 107 acres in Chester county on waters of Sandy River, part of tract granted to Samuel Carter 17 March 1785 but transferred from said Samuel Carter to said Randolph Carter 15 May 1787, adj. Samuel Carter, dated 9 May 1796. Randolph Carter (Seal), Samuel Carter (Seal), Wit: Wm McQuiston, John Carter, Robt Lemonds. Proved by the oath of Robert Lemonds 1 Jan 1798 before Saml Lacey, Clk. Recorded 10 Jan 1798.

**F, 139-140:** 27 Nov 1795, Joseph Boyd, planter, of Chester county to Adam Mills, planter, of same, for £20, 92 acres, part of tract granted 19 Feb 1791 to Joseph Boyd, 482 acres on waters of Sandy River adj. James Wylie, Charles Boyd. Jos. Boyd (wax seal), Wit: Andrew Graham, John Kennedy, Alex'dr Boyd. Proved by the oath of Andrew Graham 1 Jan 1798 before John McCreary, J.P. Recorded 10 Jan 1798.

**F, 140-142:** 1 June 1792, John McClurkin of Fairfield County to Agnes Bean of Chester County, for £40 sterling, 259 acres, part of 518 acres granted to said John McClurkin 1 Oct 1787 on waters of south fork of Rockey Creek adj. John Burns, Elisabeth Chambers. John McClurkin (wax seal), Wit: Isaac Bean, Henry Moore, James McClurken (X). Proved by the oath of Isaac Bean 16 Nov 1796 before Willm McQuiston, J.P. Recorded 11 Jan 1798.

**F, 141-144:** 22 Nov 1792, Matthew McClurkin & his wife Jenny of Chester County to John McKee of same, for £100 sterling, tract granted 20 Dec 1762 to Francis Pinson, 50 acres in Craven County, now Chester, on a branch of Rockey Creek adj. John Lee. Matthew McClurken (Seal), Jannet McClurken (mark) (Seal), Wit: Andrew Graham, Robert Caskey. Proved by the oath of Andrew Graham 25 March 1793 before John Bell, J.P. Recorded 11 Jan 1798.

**F, 143-146:** 22 Nov 1792, Matthew McClurkin & his wife Jenny of Chester County, to John McKee of same, for £60 sterling, 49½ acres, part of tract granted 2 Jan 1754 to George Taylor, 400 acres in Craven County, now Chester, on a branch of Rockey Creek and said Taylor did convey to John Lee and John Lee did bequeath 200 acres of said tract to Alexander Gordon & his wife Sarah Gordon by his will, and said Alexander Gordon and his wife did sell to Matthew McClurken, 18 Aug 1790. Matthew McClurken (Seal), Jannet McClurken (mark) (Seal), Wit: Andrew Graham, Robert Caskey. Proved by the oath of Andrew Graham 25 March 1793 before John Bell, J.P. Recorded 11 Jan 1798.

**F, 146:** Plat of James Kirkpatrick's plantation, 146 acres adj. William Good, Thomas Pugh.

Josiah Hill of Chester County, yeoman, for $100 to James Kirkpatrick, 146 acres, part of 12,700 acres grantd to said Josiah Hill, deed dated 8 Jan 1798. Josiah Hill (seal),wit: Samuel Lacey, Samuel Lacey Junr. Proved by the oath of Samuel Lacey Senr 8 Jan 1798 before Saml Lacey, Clk. Recorded 12 Jan 1798.

**F, 147:** 5 Oct 1793, William Watson of Chester County to Allen deGranffen-ried for £10 sterling, part of tract granted to William head on SAndy River, 220 acres. William Watson (W), Bethiah Watson, Wit: W. Embry, Absalom Littlefield (X), John Davis (X). Proved by the oath of W. Embry 8 Dec 1797 before Thomas Jenkins, J.P. Recorded 12 Jan 1798.

**F, 147-148**: James Timms of Chester County for $100 to James Gillchrist of same, 100 acres on waters of Sandy River adj. John McCombs, Alexander Rosborough, William Rainey, Hardwick, granted to James Timms admr. of John Watts decd, dated 12 Jan 1797. James Timms (Seal), Wit: James Loving (X), Will Boyd, William Loving. Proved by the oath of William Loving 4 Dec 1797 before E. Nunn, J.P. Recorded 12 Jan 1798.

**F, 148**: Robert Wilson of York County, SC, for $8 to Amos Timms senr of same, 5½ acres on waters of Sandy River, granted to me 6 Feb 1797, deed dated 3 Nov 1797. Robert Wilson (Seal), Wit: William Loving, Thomas Fletchall, Joseph Loving. Proved by the oath of William Loving 4 Dec 1797 before E. Nunn, J.P. Recorded 12 Jan 1798.

**F, 148-149**: Plat of 50 acres "John Fergusons Land" adj.to John Ferguson, James Dugan, Widow Ferguson.

John Ray of Chester County for $100 to Henry Smith, 50 acres on waters of Sandy River, part of 250 acres granted to John Ferguson 7 May 1787, conveyed to said John Ray 8 Dec 1793, recorded in Chester County Deed Book D, page 82, dated 22 Feb 1797. John Ray (mark) (wax seal), Wit: Daniel Adkins (mark), James Loving (X), Bart. Griffin. Proved by the oath of Bartholomew Griffin 24 Feb 1797 before Robert Owen, J.P. Recorded 15 Jan 1798.

**F, 149-150**: 14 July 1797, Henry Culp & Elisabeth his wife to Robert White of Chester County, for £90 sterling, 100 acres on Tinkers Creek originally granted to William Taylor and conveyed by him to Peter Culp & by his will to said Henry Culp. Henry Culp (seal), Elisabeth Culp (X) (Seal), Wit: Thos Neely, James Hamilton, William White. Proved by the oath of James Hamilton 12 Jan 1798 before John McCreary, J.P. Recorded 15 Jan 1798.

**F, 150**: Anne Brown alias Anne Wallace & John Wallace of Chester county for $2 to Polly Gordon daughter apparent of James Gordon & also for natural love & affection, one negro man slave named Stephen about 19 years of age, 8 Jan 1798. Anna Wallace (LS), John Wallace (mark) (LS), Wit: Saml Lacey Junr, Robert Lacey. Proved by the oath of Robert Lacey 12 Jan 1798 before Saml Lacey, Clk. Recorded 15 Jan 1798.

**F, 150-151**: John Wallace & Anna his wife (late widow of James Brown decd), for ten shillings sterling to Polley Gordon (daughter apparent of James Gordon) and for love and affection, a steer horse colt two years old last spring, a bright bay with a black main & tail, has a small star in his forehead & trots natural, also one seventh part of the estate of James Brown deceased, 8 Jan 1798. John Wallace (mark) (LS), Anne Wallace (LS), Wit:Robert Lacey, Josiah Hill. Proved by the oath of Robert Lacey 12 Jan 1798 before Saml Lacey, Clk. Recorded 15 Jan 1798.

**F, 151**: South Carolina, Chester County. James [*sic*, for Amos?] Timms Senr of county aforesaid for $50 to Thomas Bennett of same, 50 acres, part of tract granted to James Timms 7 Jan 1794 on waters of Sandy River adj. James Timms, 25 Nov 1797. James [stricken] Amos Timms (Seal), Wit: Thomas Gore, Joseph Bennett (X), Alex'dr Wilson (mark). Proved by the oath of Joseph Bennett 16 Jan 1798 before Saml Lacey, Clk. Recorded 16 Jan 1798.

**F, 151-152**: South Carolina, Chester County. James Timms of county aforesaid to Thomas Bennett for $50, 81 acres on waters of Sandy River granted 6 Feb 1797, surveyed 7 Jan 1797, dated 15 Dec 1797. James Timms (Seal), Wit: Amos Timms Senr, J. Wallis, W. Watts. Proved by the oath of Jesse Wallis 16 Jan 1798 before Saml Lacey, Clk. Recorded 16 Jan 1798.

**F, 152**: South Carolina, Chester County. James Timms of county aforesaid for $40 to Thomas Fletchall of same, 31½ acres on waters of Sandy River on my spring branch, 22 Dec 1797. James Timms (Seal), Wit: J. Wallis, James Loving (X). Proved by the oath of Jesse Wallis 16 Jan 1798 before Saml Lacey, Clk.

**F, 153**: Plat of 368 "William Stuart's land" showing adj. land owners William Rainey, William Morrow, Charles Miller, General Lacey.

22 Sept 1794, James Stuart & wife Elizabeth of Chester County to William Stewart of same, for £100 sterling, 368 acres, being the south half of 736 acres granted to said James Stuart 1 Dec 1788, recorded in Book YYYY, page 205. James Stuart (wax seal), Bettey Stuart (X) (wax seal), Wit: John Jaggers, Francis Grisham (X), Major Grisham (mark). Proved by the oath of John Jaggers 25 Jan 1798 before Robt Owen, J.P. Recorded 3 Feb 1798.

**F, 154**: Plat of "Mr. Mitchell's plantation, 100 acres" showing adj. land owners William Miles, Robert Gorrell.

Josiah Hill of Chester County, yeoman, to Henry Mitchell of same, taylor, for $100, 100 acres on waters of Sandy River, part of 12,700 granted to said Josiah Hill, deed dated 18 Nov 1797. Josiah Hill (seal), Wit: James McGriff (X), Robert Lacey. Proved by the oath of Robert Lacey 10 Feb 1798 before Saml Lacey, Clk. Recorded 5 Feb 1798.

**F, 154-155**: 16 Dec 1797, John Love of Chester county to Robert Love of same, for £5 sterling, tract on Turkey Creek, part of three tracts of land granted to John Love 4 Dec 1774, 5 June 1786, 9 April 1768, 131 acres adj. James Love. John Love (wax seal), Wit: Richard Hughes, Isham Saffold Fannen, Joseph Love. Proved by the oath of Joseph Love 22 Jan 1798 before Clayton Rogers, J.P. Recorded 5 Feb 1798.

**F, 155**: James Douglas of Chester County for $100 to Enoch Edwards of same, planter, 100 acres on the dividing ridge between Rockey Creek & Sandy River granted to Elisabeth Crawford 21 March 1768 conveyed to me from James Crawford, 20 Jan 1798. James Douglas (Seal), Wit: John Douglass, John

McClorkan, John Ramsey. Proved by the oath of John Ramsey 25 Jan 1798 before Robt Owen, J.P. Recorded 5 Feb 1798.

**F, 155-156:** Ferdinand Hopkins of Chester County, for £35 to Joel Triplet of same, 128 acres including the plantation whereon the said Joel Triplet now lives, 28 Dec 1797. Fred Hopkins (Seal), Wit: Sherw'd Nance, Wm Worthy (X). Proved by the oath of Sherwood Nance 29 Dec 1797 before E. Nunn, J.P. Recorded 4 Feb 1798.

**F, 156-157:** 5 Feb 1798, Samuel Lacey, Sheriff of Chester County, to James Elliott of same, whereas Mary Ferguson admx. of James Ferguson decd did in the county aforesaid implead Charles Orr & James Elliott admrs. of william Higgans deceased on an action of debt and in 1796 did obtain judgment, in the sum of £5 s10 d3 sterling, sheriff on 7 Jan 1797 sold 150 acres which were of said William Hagans in his lifetime adj. lands of said Charles Orr, Thomas Stroud, John Harbison, on a branch of Rocky Creek known by the name of the Bever Dam, sold to James Elliott for $104. Saml Lacey Sheriff (Seal), Wit: Peter Corbell, Thomas B. Franklin. Proved by the oath of Thomas B. Franklin 6 Feb 1798 before Saml Lacey, Clk. Plat included showing 200 acres granted to Wm Higgins 15 Sept 1774. by John McCreary. Recorded 6 Feb 1798.

**F, 157-158:** Plat of 301½ acres. Josiah Hill of Chester County, yeoman, to Thomas Pugh of same, planter, for £60 sterling, 301½ acres on waters of Sandy River & Mill Creek, part of 12,700 granted to said Josiah Hill, deed dated 30 Sept 1797. Josiah Hill (Seal), Wit: James Fowler, Thomas Cabeen. Proved by the oath of Thomas Cabeen 15 Jan 1798 before Saml Lacey, Clk. Recorded 10 Feb 1798.

**F, 158:** Plat of James McCalla's plantation containing 330 acres showing adj. land owners James Adams, Samuel Givens, Valentine Bell.

Josiah Hill of Chester County, yeoman, to James McCalla of same, planter, for $200, 330 acres on waters of Turkey Creek, part of 12,700 granted to said Josiah Hill, deed dated 3 Oct 1797. Josiah Hill (Seal), Wit: Reuben Lacey, Samuel Lacey. Proved by the oath of Samuel Lacey Senr 12 Feb 1798 before Saml Lacey, Clk. Recorded 12 Feb 1798.

**F, 158-159:** John McCreary of Chester County for $20 to Robert Brown, 56 acres on waters of Fishing Creek granted to me the said John McCreary 4 Dec 1797, dated 12 Jan 1798. John McCreary (Seal), Wit: Walter Brown (W), Austin Culp. Acknowledged in open court January Term 1798. Recorded 12 Feb 1798.

**F, 159:** John Service Senr of Chester County for $150 to John Service Junr of same, tract of land of 100 cres surveyed for Richard Taliaferro and granted to Jacob Dansby 1 Sept 1794, on the north fork of Rocky Creek adj. John Martin, 9 Jan 1798. John Service Senr (mark), Wit: Henry Moore, Samuel

Johnston, Geo Kennedy. Acknowledged in open court 26 Jan 1798. Recorded 12 Feb 1798.

F, 160: William Boyd of Chester County for £25 sterling to Thomas Latta of same, 50 acres on both sides of Fishing Creek adj. Isaac Smith, John Latta, granted to William Boyd 27 Sept 1772, dated 26 Jan 1798. Will: Boyd (wax seal), Wit: Samuel Lowrie, John Brown. Ann Boyd, wife of William Boyd, relinquished dower 26 Jan 1798 before Jo. Brown, J. C. C. Proved by the oath of John Brown 26 Jan 1798 before Joseph Gaston, J.P.

F, 160-161: William Smith of Chester County for £45 sterling to William Wier of same, 162 acres on Fishing [Creek] adj. John McKinney, White, Kirkpatrick, William McCammon, Robert Gaston, James Knox deceased, granted to William Smith 3 Oct 1796 for 194 acres, dated 4 Oct 1797. William Smith (wax seal), Wit: David Fullerton, James Fullerton, John McCreary. Proved by the oath of David Fullerton 16 Nov 1797 before John McCreary, J.P. Recorded 12 Feb 1798.

F, 161-162: Hubbard Stevens of Chester county for natural affection and five shillings to my four children Robert Stevens, William Stevens, Nancy Stevens & Mary Stevens, one negro man slave named Jimm, one negro woman slave named Lid, one bay coloured hose about 14 hands high, one sorrel coloured mare about 14 hands high, two feather beds and the furniture, 20 head of neet cattle, 30 head of hogs, 15 Aug 1797. Hubbard Stevens (H) (wax seal), Wit: James McKown, William Morris (X). Proved by the oath of James McCown & William Morris 145 Aug 1797 before John McCreary, J.P. Recorded 12 Feb 1798.

F, 162-163: 10 Nov 1797, John Dodd and Rebekkah his wife, formerly Rebekkah Hartness, of Fairfield County, Camden District, to Samuel Ferguson of Chester County, Pinckney District, for £30 sterling, 82 acres, part of a grant to Matthew Hartness for 325 acres on waters of big rockey creek adj. said Matthew Hartness, Charles Kitchens, James Norton, Andrew Hannon. John Dods (Seal), Rebekkah Dods (Seal), Wit: Andw Hemphill, Robert McCullough, John Park. Proved by the oath of Andrew Hemphill 25 Jan 1798. Recorded 12 Feb 1798.

F, 163-164: Middleton McDonald of Lancaster County for £100 to William Scogin of Chester county, 200 acres on the SW side of the Cattawba River in Chester county adj. Jas McKown, originally granted to Benj. Ford 13 Aug 1762 and conveyed by said Benjamin Ford to William Ford & from William Ford to said Middleton McDonald, 11 Feb 1797. Middleton McDonald (Seal), Wit: Joseph John Wade, Betsey Stokes, Middleton McDonald Junr. Elizabeth McDonald (X), wife of Middleton McDonald, relinquished dower 11 Feb 1797 in Lancaster County before Danl Wade, J. L. C. Proved by the oath of Elisabeth Stokes 11 Feb 1797 before Danl Wade, J. L. C. Recorded 15 Feb 1798.

**F, 164**: Ferdinand Hopkins of Chester County, for £30 to Elisha Mayfield of same, tract on north side of Johns Creek originally granted to Ephraim Mitchell, Esqr., & by succession of title now vested in said Ferdinand Hopkins, 100 acres, 23 Jan 1798. Ferd. Hopkins (Seal), Wit: John White, Allen Mayfield. Proved by the oaths of both witnesses 23 Jan 1798 before E. Nunn, J.P. Recorded 15 Feb 1798.

**F, 164-165**: John McClurkin of Chester County for £36 sterling to William Smith of same, 100 acres adj. Thomas Stone, 100 acres granted to Robert McClurkin and conveyed by said McClurkin to his son by birth right, John McClurkin, 25 Nov 1797. John McClurkin (wax seal), Wit: Edward McFadden, Thomas Morrison (TM), John Cherry. Proved by the oath of Edward McFadden 25 Jan 1798 before Hugh McClure, J.P. Recorded 15 Feb 1798.

**F, 165**: George Wier of Chester County for $50 to James Kennedy of same, part of a certain tract surveyed between the said Wier & Kennedy, the original grant being in said Wier's name, 27 acres on waters of Sandy River & Rockey Creek adj. Hugh Wier, John Wilson, James Wilkings, 14 Nov 1797. George Weer (Seal), Wit: John Wilson, Hugh Weir. Proved by the oath of John Wilson 25 Jan 1798 before Hugh McClure, J.P. Recorded 15 Feb 1798.

**F, 165-167**: 26 Oct 1779, Thomas Kelsey of the Parish of St. Marks, planter, to Hugh Kelsey of same, planter, for £300, tract granted 14 Aug 1774 to Samuel Kelsey, 100 acres on a branch of Sandy River adj. Benjamin Ellis, John Mills, and said Samuel Kelsey died intestate and without issue and Thomas Kelsey being his eldest brother. Thomas Kelsey (wax seal), Wit: John Morrow, Samuel Kelsey, Robt Kelsey. Proved by the oath of Samuel Kelsey 25 Jan 1798 before John McCreary. Recorded 15 Feb 1798.

**F, 167-168**: 22 Jan 1798, Samuel Ferguson & Isbel his wife of Chester County to Josiah Allen of same, for £40 sterling, 126 acres, part of tract of 300 acres granted to John Reynolds on Hogues branch, and by said John Reynolds to Edmund Strange 10 Sept 1769 and by said Edmund Strange to Samuel Ferguson 16 Dec 1791, recorded in Chester Deed Book D, page 338, 120 acres. Samuel Ferguson (Seal), Isbel Ferguson (X) (Seal), Wit: John Morris, And'w Hemphill, And'w Dunn Senr. Proved by the oath of John Morris 23 Jan 1798 before John McCreary, J.P. Recorded 16 Feb 1798.

**F, 168-169**: 8 Jan 1798, Samuel Faires of Chester County to Elijah Bankston of same, for £40 sterling, 122 acres originally granted to Jacob Brown deceased 5 March 1787 on waters of Rockey Creek adj. John Winn Junr, Hugh Montgomery, John Ellis, originally surveyed for John Winn Junr & relapsed by the said Jacob Brown in the Location Office and by Daniel Brown, exr. of the will of Jacob Brown deceased, by indenture dated 717 June 1792 and recorded 13 June 1794 in Book D, page 159 to John Polley, and by said John Polley to Samuel Fairy 3 May 1794, recorded 13 June 1794 in Book D page 168. Samuel Ferres (Seal), Wit: John Morris (X), Andw Hemphill. Proved by the oath of John Morris (X) before John McCreary, J.P. Recorded 16 Feb 1798.

219

**F, 169**: Owen Lea of Chester County for £100 sterling to William Estes of same, 95 acres on waters of Sandy River granted 2 March 1789 to William Britain, dated 17 Aug 1797. Owen Lea (Seal), Wit: Jesse Wallis, John Wright, William Wilks. Proved by the oath of Wm Wilkes before Robert Owen, J.P. Recorded 16 Feb 1798.

**F, 169-170**: South Carolina, Chester County. Reuben Lacey, Esqr., of county aforesaid for $225 to William Robison of York County, SC, one negro slave girl named Mariah about 16 years old, has no thumb of the left hand & one crooked finger ont he same hand, 18 Dec 1797. Reuben Lacey (Seal), Wit: Catlett Conner, Joshua Lacey. Proved in Chester County by the oath of Catlett Conner 25 Jan 1798 before Robt Owen, J.P. Recorded 19 Feb 1798.

**F, 170**: 8 Dec 1794, Thomas Franklin of Pinckney District, SC, to Robert Nix of same, for £10 sterling, tract of 100 acres, part of a tract granted to said Archibald Roberts 18 Oct 1784, on waters of Sandy River between said Archibald Robert's field and Robert nix's field. Thomas Franklin, Mary Franklin (X) (Seal), Wit: John Parks, Archibald Roberts, William Parks. Proved by the oath of John Parks 5 March 1795 before John Pratt, J.P. Recorded 19 Feb 1798.

**F, 171**: 30 Jan 1794, John Carter of Fairfield County to Jacob Barker of Chester County, for £100, tract of 200 acres granted to William Carter 7 May 1774 on Martin's branch, a branch of Sandy River adj. Charles Nix. John Carter (Seal), Wit: Thomas Franklin (X), Jesse Obriant (J). Proved by the oath of Thomas Franklin 30 July 1795 before John Pratt, J.P. Recorded 19 Feb 1798.

**F, 171-172**: 24 Nov 1797, Samuel Lacey, Sheriff of Chester County to Archibald Gill of same, whereas the executors of John Gill deceased in Chester County did implead Peter Jones on an action of debt in the sum of £26 s17 d6 sterling, sheriff sold on 2 Jan 1796, 173 acres on waters of Cattawba River adj. Jonathan Hemphill, Charles Wall, Donald McDonald, James Cloud, granted to Thomas Morris 6 Feb 1792, sold for £15 sterling. Samuel Lacey sheriff of Chester County (Seal), Wit: Saml Lacey Junr, James Anderson, Geo Dale. Proved by the oath of James Anderson 24 Nov 1797 before Saml Lacey, Clk. Recorded 19 Feb 1798.

**F, 172-173**: 27 Feb 1795, Moses Smith & Mary his wife of Chester County to Abner Smith of Fairfield County, for £50 sterling, 116 acres on both sides of big Rockey Creek adj. William Willson, James Hemphill, Walker, John Rennolds, granted 7 Jan 1793. Moses Smith (Seal), Mary Smith (Seal), Wit: Joshua Smith, George Bready, Mary Smith. Proved by the oath of Joshua Smith 28 Feb 1795 before And'w Hemphill, J.P. Recorded 26 Feb 1798.

**F, 173-174**: 27 Feb 1795, Moses Smith & Mary his wife of Chester County to Abner Smith of Fairfield County, for £50 sterling, 100 acres originally granted to John McFadden 7 Oct 1762 and by said John McFadden and wife Mary conveyed to said Moses Smith for £100 sterling, recorded in Chester Book B, page 433 on big Rockey Creek adj. said Moses Smith, William Boyd, Andrew Hemphill. Moses Smith (Seal), Mary Smith (Seal), Wit: Joshua Smith, George Bready, Mary Smith. Proved by the oath of Joshua Smith 28 Feb 1795 before And'w Hemphill, J.P. Recorded 26 Feb 1798.

**F, 174-175**: South Carolina, Chester County. Abner Smith of state aforesaid for $500 to George Tucker of State of North Carolina, one tract of 100 acres known by a dividing line made by & between Moses Smith & Andrew Hemphill originally granted to John McFadden on Big Rocky Creek 7 Oct 1752 and by said john McFadden conveyed to Moses Smith 4 Sept 1789 and by him to Abner Smith 26 Feb 1795, also another tract of 116 acres on both sides big Rockey Creek adj. the aforesaid tract originally granted to Moses Smith 7 Feb 1795. Abner Smith (Seal), Wit: And'w Hemphill, Benj'a Clifton, James Clifton. Proved by the oath of Andrew Hemphill, Esqr., 17 Feb 1798 before John McCreary, J.P. Recorded 28 Feb 1798.

**F, 175-176**: James Adair and Mary his wife of Chester County for £85 sterling to John Carter Junr of same, 132 acres, being part of a tract of 200 acres granted to Moses Bond 19 Feb 1767 and by several conveyances have now become vested in Mary Adair late Mary Simms except 68 acres which was conveyed to John Carter Senr, on a small branch of Sandy River, 29 Aug 1797. James Adair (Seal), Mary Adair (Seal), Wit: Jo Brown, James Tyner. Mary Adair, wife of James Adair, relinquished dower 24 Feb 1798 before Wm Gaston, J.C.C. Proved by the oath of Joseph Brown 24 Feb 1798 before Wm. Gaston, J.C.C.

**F, 176**: Josiah Hill of Chester County for $100 to Reuben Lacey of same, 164 acres on waters of Turkey Creek, part of 12,700 acres granted to Josiah Hill, dated 2 Feb 1798. Josiah Hill (Seal), Wit: Saml Lacey Junr, Robert Lacey. Proved by the oath of Robert Lacey before Saml Lacey, Clk, 2 Feb 1798. Recorded 28 Feb 1798.

**F, 176-177**: Joseph Crawford of Abeville County, SC, planter, for £30 sterling, to Mark Eaves of Chester County, tract in Chester County bounded by lands surveyed for Frederick Imen, John Cantzon, William Cook, 100 acres granted to James Dorman 12 Aug 1768, dated 8 Sept 1797. Joseph Crawford (wax seal), Agness Crawford (mark) (wax seal), Wit: John Caldwell, Robert Harper, Zachariah Strickland (X). Proved by the oath of Robert Harper 5 March 1798 before Saml Lacey, Clk. Recorded 6 March 1798.

**F, 177-178**: James Kanmour of York County, SC, for $200 to Philip Cline, formerly of the county of Chester, 200 acres on waters of Fishing Creek, adj. a north survey granted to Casper Sleeker (now belonging to Henry Culp) adj. Greer[?], James Harbison, John Culp, James Kanmour, being part of tract granted to said James Kanmour for 350 acres, 22 Aug 1797. James Kenmour (O) (Seal), Wit: Jesse Horton, John Kenmour, John McCreary. Proved by the oath of Jesse Horton and John Kenmour 22 Aug 1797 before John McCreary, J.P. Recorded 6 March 1798.

**F, 178-179**: 27 June 1797, Moses Cantzon of Lancaster County, SC, planter, to William Hopkins of Richland County, SC, planter, for £50 sterling, 400 acres on the south branch of Sandy River adj. John Land, granted to James Moffet 6 Dec 1768, recorded in Book EEE, page 126, conveyed 26 Jan 1791 to Moses Cantzon. Moses Cantzon (wax seal), Wit: Abigail Yancey, John Cantzon, Richard Graves. Proved in Lancaster County by the oath of Richard Graves 27 June 1797 before Jos'h Lee, J.P. Recorded 7 March 1798.

**F, 180-181**: 2 Sept 1779, William Penney and Elisabeth his wife of Macklinburgh County, North Carolina, to John McAlilla and Elisabeth his wife of Camden District, SC, planter, for £1000 current money of SC, tract granted 2 June 1759 to Joseph Earley, 250 acres in Craven County now Camden District on the head of Bullskin Creek. William Penney (Seal), Elisabeth Penney (mark) (Seal), Wit: Arthur McCree, James Humphrey, William Martin. Proved in Camden District by the oath of William Martin 7 June 1781 before John McCaw, J.P. Recorded 7 March 1798.

**F, 181-182**: 17 Dec 1770, Joseph Early and Nancey his wife of Camden District, Craven County, planter, to William Penney and Elisabeth his wife of the state of North Carolina, for ten shillings 250 acres in on the head of Bullskin Creek. Joseph Earley (X) (was seal), Nancy Earley (mark) (wax seal), Wit: Will: Boyd, Michael Blair, Hugh Stuart. Proved by the oath of Hugh Stuart 2 May 1778 before Amos Tims, J.P. Recorded 7 March 1798.

**F, 182**: Jacob Densby of Chester County for $110 to George clark of same, 200 acres surveyed for Richard Taliaferro and granted to said Jacob Dansby 1 Sept 1794 on the north fork of Rockey Creek, dated 7 Oct 1797. J. Dansby (Seal), Wit: Geo Kennedy, John Burns, Arch'd Martin. Proved by the oath of George Kennedy 10 March 1798 before Saml Lacey, Clk.

**F, 182-183**: South Carolina, Chester County. John Conn of county aforesaid for $200 to Simon Dunn of same, one sorrel horse about five years old about 13½ hands high, has a white spot on the right buttock & one other bay horse 2 years old, neither dock'd nor branded... 7 Oct 1797. John Conn (C), Wit: George Conn (mark), Thomas Stevenson. Proved by the oath of George Conn 24 Jan 1798 before Saml Lacey, Clk. Recorded 9 April 1798.

**F, 183-184**: South Carolina, Pinckney District. 4 Sept 1797, William Bratton, Sheriff of District aforesaid to Joseph Sadler of York County, whereas Jonathan Jones late of Chester County was seized of a plantation containing 200 acres on the waters of Sandy River and being indebted to Mary Howard, admx of John Howard of state aforesaid, and said Mary did exhibit her petition to the judges of the court of common please of the state aforesaid and a summary process was issued at a court held at Pinckneyville in April Term 1795, and said Mary should recover £8 s1 d7½ and costs, and by a decree issued by John Martin, clerk of said court, sheriff sells 200 acres on waters of Sandy River for $7 paid by Joseph Sadler. W. Bratton (Seal), Wit: J. Simpson, David Sadler. Proved by the oath of David Sadler 4 April 1798 before Saml Lacey, Clk. Recorded 10 April 1798.

**F, 184-185**: 26 Aug 1777, Thomas Heany of Parish of St. Marks, weaver, to John Morrow of same, yeoman, for £300 tract granted 9 Dec 1773 to Thomas Heany & Jane his wife, 150 acres in Craven County on a small branch of Sandy River. Thomas Heany (wax seal), Jane Heany (mark) (wax seal), Wit: William Morrow, Robert Kelsey (R), Samuel Woodsides (mark). Proved in Camden District by the oath of Samuel Woodside 2 Sept 1777 before Michael Dickson, J.P. Recorded 19 April 1798.

**F, 185**: John Walker of Chester County, yeoman, for 80 to Joseph Morrow, wheel wright, 100 acres on Rocky Creek adj. John Burns, granted to said John Walker 25 April 1765 by SC, dated 1 Nov 1797. John Walker (J) (wax seal), Wit: Geo Gill, Alex'dr Pagan, William Nelson. Proved by the oath of George Gill 18 April 1798 before Joseph Gaston, J.P. Recorded 19 April 1798.

**F, 185-186**: William Bradford and Sarah his wife, William Nelson and Mary his wife, Hugh Ross and Margaret his wife, and Elisabeth Wylie, all of Chester County, planters, for $350 to Joseph Morrow of same, wheelwright, 350 acres on the head branches of Rockey Creek adj. William Wylie, Michael Dickson, John Burns, John Gill, granted to William Wylie which William Wylie is now deceased & the said land descending to the above named Sarah wife of William Bradford and Mary wife of William Nelson and Margaret wife of Hugh Ross and Elisabeth Wylie, 1 Nov 1797. William Bradford (wax seal), Sarah Bradford (X) (wax seal), William Nelson (wax seal), Mary Nelson (X) (wax seal), Hugh Ross (wax seal), Margaret Ross (X) (wax seal), Elisabeth Wylie (X) (wax seal), Wit: George Gill, Hugh Whiteside, Alex'dr Walker. Proved by the oath of Hugh Whiteside, Esqr., 16 April 1798 before Joseph Gaston, J.P. Recorded 19 April 1798.

**F, 186-187**: Chester County, South Carolina, Pinckney District. 12 Jan 1797, Jacob and Agness Sutton of county aforesaid for £38 s10 sterling to Alexander Morton of same, 150 acres on Beaverdam creek adj. Mr. Martin's old line, being 150 acres granted to said Sutton 7 May 1787. Jacob Sutton, Agness Sutton (seal), Wit: Jonathan Ferguson, James Gaston, Jacob Ferguson. Proved by the oath of Jonathan Ferguson 23 March 1797 before John McCreary, J.,P. Recorded 19 April 1798.

**F, 187**: 27 Feb 1798, Joshua Gore and wife Fanny of Chester County to Allen DeGraffenreidt of same, for £10 sterling, 227 acres adj. John McCalpen, granted to Joshua Gore 5 Dec 1785. Joshua Gore (wax seal), Fanny Gore (X) (wax seal), Wit: Wm. Hobson, Michael Gore, John Gore (X). Proved by the oath of William Hobson 1 March 1798 before John Pratt, J.P. Recorded 19 April 1798.

**F, 187-188**: Eli Kitchens and Agness his wife of Chester County for £20 sterling to Richard Wylie of same, 100 acres in Chester county adj. Widow Harkness, George Wier, Thomas Gather, Andrew Harmond, granted from Charles Kitchens to his son Eli Kitchens by birth right, 27 Nov 1797. Eli Kitchens (wax seal), Wit: Edward McFadden, Martha Norton, Robert Boyd. Proved by the oath of Robert Boyd 11 April 1798 before John McCreary, J.P. Recorded 2 May 1798.

**F, 188-189**: 26 Dec 1797, Samuel Davis of Surrey County, North Carolina, to John Ray of Chester County, SC, for £214.28, 200 acres, part of tract granted to John Ferguson 7 May 1787 for 256 acres on a branch of Sandy River adj. Widow Ferguson, James Douglass, James Biggam, James Pagan, Peter Coonrod, conveyed from said John Ferguson to John Ray by deed 18 Dec 1793 and from John Ray to said Samuel Davis (exclusive of 50 acres granted to Henry Smith by said John Ray). Samuel Davis (Seal), Wit: Enoch Edwards, John Owen. Proved by the oath of John Owen 28 March 1798 before Hugh Knox, J.P. Recorded 7 May 1798.

**F, 189-190**: William Murrey of Chester County for £200 sterling to Thomas Rainey of same, 229 acres, 25 Jan 1797. William Murrey (X) (Seal), Wit: Jeremiah Kingsley, Robert Hadlock. Proved by the oath of Jeremiah Kingsley 27 May 1797 before Edward Lacey, J. C. C. Recorded 7 May 1798.

**F, 190**: David Boyd of Chester County for $300 to Davis Gore of Chester county, 41 acres part of tract granted to David Boyd on waters of Sandy River adj. David Boyd, Col. Patrick McGriff, Eleazer Gore, 24 Feb 1798. David Boyd (Seal), Wit: Philip Noland, Thomas McGriff. Proved by the oath of Philip Noland 24 Feb 1798 before E. Nunn, J.P. Recorded 7 May 1798.

**F, 190-191**: James Jamison and Joseph Jamison of York County, SC, for £60 sterling to Stephen Kirk of Chester County, tract on east side of Broad River granted 29 April 1768 by North Carolina to James Jamison adj. Wilson, including the plantation whereon the said Stephen Kirk now lives, a memorial of which grant was entered in the Auditor Genls Office in SC in Book L No. 11, page 480, 24 Oct 1772, 100 acres. James Jamison (Seal), Joseph Jamison (Seal), Wit: Thomas Gilham, Ralph Rogers, Hugh Sherer. Proved by the oath of Thomas Gilham 3 April 1798 before Clayton Rogers, J.P. Plat included. Recorded 7 May 1798.

**F, 191-192**: Thomas Blair of Hancock County, Georgia, for £30 sterling to Patrick Fenney of Chester County, 163 acres on waters of Rocky Creek, part of a tract granted to Thomas Blair adj. Thomas Blair Senr, Philip Walker, Esqr, 27 Nov 1797. Thomas Blair (Seal), Polley Blair (X) (Seal), Wit: William Crawford, Alexander Morrison, Jas McDill. Recorded 9 May 1798. Proved by the oath of Alexander Morrison 24 Aug 1811 before J. Rosborough, J. Q.

**F, 192**: South Carolina, Chester County. James Timms of county aforesaid for £15 sterling, 19 acres on waters of Sandy River granted 6 Feb 1797. James

Timms (Seal), Wit: J. Wallis, Blaky Carter, William Estes. Proved by the oath of Blaky Carter 212 April 1798 before Saml Lacey, Clk. Recorded 9 May 1798.

**F, 192-193**: South Carolina, Chester County. James Timms of county aforesaid for £40 sterling to James Loving, 46 acres on waters of Sandy River adj. John Wright, Wilson Henderson, and said James Loving, 16 Dec 1797. James Timms (Seal), Wit: J. Wallis, Blaky Carter, William Estis. Proved by the oath of Blaky Carter 21 April 1798 before Saml Lacey, Clk. Recorded 9 May 1798.

**F, 193**: South Carolina, Chester County. James Timms of county aforesaid for £80 sterling to James Loving, 86 acres granted 6 Feb 1797, dated 16 Dec 1797. James Timms (Seal), Wit: J. Wallis, Blaky Carter, William Estis. Proved by the oath of Blaky Carter 21 April 1798 before Saml Lacey, Clk. Recorded 9 May 1798.

**F, 194-195**: 18 Dec 1797, Walter Timms of Chester County for £50 sterling to Amos Timms Jr of same, 100 acres on waters of Sandy River adj. Frazier, Col. P. McGriff, Bonds, said Amos Timms to pay to the five daughters of James Timms £50 sterling by installments that is to say to his daughter Elisabeth Timms on 25 Dec 1800 £10, to her sister Tamy on 25 Dec 1800, £10, to his daughter Polly on 25 Dec 1802 £10, to his daughter Patsey on 25 Dec 1803 £10, to his daughter Sally on 25 Dec 1803 £10. Walter Timms (X) (wax seal), Wit: Hollis Timms, Joseph Timms, Adams Henderson. Proved by the oath of Joseph Timms 16 April 1798 before John Pratt, J.P. Recorded 10 May 1798.

**F, 195-196**: John Weir of Chester County for 150 silver dollars to Benjamin Wham of same, 102 acres on waters of Sandy River adj. Major Grisham, James Trussell, Thomas B. Franklin, William Nunn, David Pruit, granted to Samuel Lowrie 1 Dec 1788, and said Samuel Lowrie did make over said plantation by deed 21 March 1795 to John Trussell and John Trussell by deed 1 Dec 1759 to John Wier, dated 4 April 1798. John Wier (Seal), Wit: William Rainey, James Woodburn, And'w Crawford. Mary Wier, wife of John Weir, relinquished dower 16 April 1798 before Jo. Brown, J.C. Acknowledged in open court by John Wier, September Court 1798. Recorded 10 May 1798.

**F, 196-197**: 5 Aug 1795, Alexander Walker, planter, to William Milling, planter, all of Chester County, SC, for £51 s10 sterling, 100 acres on a small branch of Rockey Creek adj. land formerly belonging to Michael Dickson. Alexander Walker (X) (wax seal), Wit: John McElroy, William Murray. Proved by the oath of William Murrow/Murray 10 April 1798 before Saml Lacey, Clk. Recorded 10 May 1798.

**F, 197**: Plat of 100 acres. Pursuant to a precept dated 2 Dec 1766, I have surv'd and laid out unto Jean Miller, 100 acres on N side of Broad River on a branch of Sandy Creek, it being 10 feet wide and three inches deep, adj. Jeremiah Potts, Zachariah Isbell, certified 16 Dec 1766. Jno Winn, Depty Surv. Surveyor Genls Office, Columbia, June 8th 1792 a true copy.

F, 197-198: John Owen of Chester County to Hezekiah Donald of same, for $100, tract of land granted to George Miller 20 Aug 1767 for 100 acres per the annexed plat, conveyed from said George Miler to William Saunders and from said Saunders to Francis Jenkins and by deed of conveyance and then mortgaged by said Francis Jenkins to John Rice 16 Dec 1774, then sold by virtue of said mortgage to me, deed dated 16 Oct 1797. John Owen (Seal), Wit: John Clark, Joseph McElhenny. Acknowledged in open court by John Owen Senr, April Court 1798. Recorded 10 May 1798.

F, 198-199: James Kennedy of Fairfield County for $176 to Adam Trout of Chester County, 276 acres, part of tract granted to said Kennedy 3 April 1786 for 405 acres on waters of Beaver Dam, a branch of Rockey Creek, dated 10 Jan 1798. James Kennedy (wax seal), Wit: David Fullerton, John Jones, John McCreary. Proved by the oath of John Jones 24 Jan 1798 before John McCreary, J.P. Recorded 10 May 1798.

F, 199: Francis Henderson of Chester County for £50 sterling to Alexander Walker of same, 146 acres on Rockey Creek surveyed for said Francis Henderson 21 Feb 1797 adj. Peter Nance, David Hunter, McCown, Ballentine, 29 Aug 1797. Francis Henderson (Seal), Wit: John McCulley, James Willson, Thomas McCulley. Proved by the oath of Thomas McCulley 2 Sept 1797 before John McCreary, J.P. Recorded 20 May 1798.

F, 199-200: 8 June 1797, John Park and Sarah his wife of Chester county for £110 sterling to William Steenson of same, 90 acres on little Rockey Creek adj. Francis Adams, Daniel Cottney, Colonel Middleton, part of a grant of 200 acres to Grisel Mayben and sold to Samuel Erwin 15 Feb 1787 for £15 sterling and by Samuel Erwin to John Park for £10 sterling 16 April 1789. John Park (wax seal), Sarah Park (X) (wax seal), Wit: And'w Hemphill, George Eggnew (J), Joshua Smith. Proved by the oath of Andrew Hemphill 25 Jan 1798 before John McCreary, J.P. Recorded 11 May 1798.

F, 200-201: Asa Tindall & Martha Tindall of State of Georgia, planter, for £30 sterling to William Love McCool of Chester County, 100 acres granted to John Long 6 June 1785 and by said John Long conveyed to Drewry Going by deed 1 July 1788 and by said Drewry Going conveyed to Asa Tindall 11 Oct 1791 on a branch of Turkey Creek adj. James Kirkpatrick, Clayton Rogers, 18 July 1797. Asa Tindall (wax seal), Martha Tindall (wax seal), Wit: J.Rogers, Rachel Rogers. Proved by the oath of J. Rogers 22 Jan 1798 before Clayton Rogers, J. P. Recorded 11 May 1798.

F, 201-202: 30 Aug 1792, Francis Kirkpatrick of Chester County to John Thomas McCool of same, for £70 sterling, 220 acres on north side Broad River part of tract of 790 acres granted to James Kirkpatrick Senior by NC adj. corner of the antient tract granted to James Kirkpatrick Junior. Francis Kirkpatrick (wax seal), Margaret Kirkpatrick (mark) (wax seal), Wit: Wm. Love, Richard Love,James Wallace. Proved by the oath of Richard Love before William Gaston, J.P., 24 Jan 1798. Recorded 11 May 1798.

**F, 202**: 17 Nov 1789, John McCool of Ninety Six District, Union County to James Love Senr of Camden District, Chester County, for £500 sterling, 850 acres granted 3 Dec 1787 on waters of Turkey Creek adj. Moses Williams, James Wilson, Hugh Wilson, James Kirkpatrick, William Chapman. John McCool (Seal), Wit: And'w Torrance, Wm Gaston, Wm. Dalrymple. Proved by the oath of Wm Gaston __ Jan 1798 before Jo. Brown, J. C. Recorded 11 May 1798.

**F, 202-203**: 13 April 1792, William Gaston, Esquire of Chester County, to James Love of same, for £50 sterling, 200 acres on waters of Turkey Creek. Wm Gaston (wax seal), Wit: William Love, Richard Love, James Love. Proved by the oath of Richard Love 24 Jan 1798 before Wm Gaston, J. C. C. Recorded 11 May 1798.

**F, 203**: 3 Aug 1795, John White and his wife Sarah of Chester County to Thomas Mitchell of same, for £100 sterling, 103 acres granted to said White certified 4 Jan 1790. John White (wax seal), Sarah White (X) (wax seal), Wit: Ferd'd Hopkins, Geo W. Hopkins. Proved by the oath of Ferdinand hopkins 9 Feb 1796 before E. Nunn, J.P. Recorded 11 May 1798.

**F, 204**: 3 Aug 1795, John White and his wife Sarah of Chester County to Thomas Mitchell of same, for £25 sterling, tract on dreans of Brushey fork of Sandy River including the plantation whereon William King now lives, adj. Triplet's field, Thomas Moore, Josias Cook, 108¼ acres. John White (wax seal), Sarah White (X) (wax seal), Wit: Ferd'd Hopkins, Geo W. Hopkins. Proved by the oath of Ferdinand Hopkins 9 Feb 1796 before E. Nunn, J.P. Recorded 14 May 1798.

**F, 204-205**: William Stuart of Chester County for $800 to George Kennedy of same, a house and lot of 11 acres at Chester Court House or in Chesterville granted to James Stuart 1 Dec 1788, part of 368 acres conveyed 22 Sept 1795, recorded in Book F, page 153, 3 Feb 1798, dated 5 Feb 1798. William Stuart (Seal), Wit: John Willson, Peter Petree (mark). Plat included showing Charleston Road. Proved by the oath of John Willson 12 May 1798 before Saml Lacey, Clk. Recorded 14 May 1798.

**F, 205-206**: 3 Aug 1795, Thomas Mitchell of Chester County to John White of same, for £100 sterling, part of tract granted to James Oneal 26 Aug 1774 & since conveyed by Oneal to Ferdinand Hopkins and by him to said Thomas Mitchell, on north side Broad River, first below Wilcoxes landing, William Boyd, 199 acres. Thomas Mitchell (X) (wax seal), Hepsabeth Mitchell (X) (wax seal), Wit: Ferd'd Hopkins, Geo W. Hopkins. Proved by the oath of Ferdinand Hopkins 23 Jan 1798 before E. Nunn, J.P. Recorded 14 May 1798.

**F, 206-207**: 14 April 1796, Ferdinand Hopkins of Chester County to John White of same, for £50 sterling, part of tract granted to James Oneal 20 Aug 1774 and by him conveyed to Ferdinand Hopkins, 118 acres below Wilcoxes boat landing. Ferd'd Hopkins (seal), Wit: Sherwood Nance, Major Hill (X).

Proved by the oath of both wit 14 April 1796 before E. Nunn, J.P. Recorded 14 May 1798.

**F, 207-208**: Lease and release. 15 April 1790, Samuel Irwin and wife Jennit to Andrew Dunn for £40 sterling, 52 acres on a branch of little Rockey creek granted to said Samuel Irwin 5 Sept 1785. Samuel Erwin (Seal), Jennit Erwin (X) (Seal), Wit: William Dunn, William Ingram. Proved by the oath of Wm Dunn 23 Dec 1794 before Andrew Hemphill, J.P. Recorded 14 May 1798.

**F, 209**: South Carolina, Chester County, Pinckney District. Richard Thomson of county aforesaid for £20 to William Steenson of same, 350 acres granted to Benjamin Standley 13 July 1770 adj. William Alexander, plat recorded 13 July 1770, Book FFF, page 23, dated 4 Jan 1798. Richard Thomson (wax seal), Wit: And'w Hemphill, John McDonald, James Nesbitt. Proved by the oath of Andrew Hemphill 25 Jan 1798 before John McCreary, J.P. Recorded 15 May 1798.

**F, 209**: John Prentice, schoolmaster, of Chester County, appoint trusty friend Robert Steenson eldest son of William Steenson of same county,planter, attorney to recover from such as are indebted to me as per my Book left with him, also the care of my plantation upon Fishing Creek commonly known as Rieve's old place, to receive rent for two years, dated 12 June 1797. John Prentice (wax seal), Wit: John Brownlee, Wm. Andrew, Danl Green. Proved by the oath of Daniel Green 25 Jan 1798 before John McCreary, J.P. Recorded 15 May 1798.

**F, 210-212**: 15 Nov 1791, David Hunter of Kershaw County, planter, to George Ross of same, planter, for £1 sterling, for natural love affection & good will which said David has towards his wife Agness Hunter & his two sons Samuel Gealy Hunter & William Cochran Hunter, confirms to said George Ross, several tracts of land, one tract of 300 acres on Flag Reed, waters of Little River in Abbeville County, originally granted to the said David ____, a tract in Chester County on Fishing Creek settlement adj. the lands of the Catabaw Nation of Indians granted to said David for 370 acres, a tract in Kershaw County on Green Swamp, waters of Saunders Creek, 360 acres granted to said David, also plantation whereon I now live at Flat Rock Creek, waters of Grannys Quarter, 200 acres granted to William McDowell 86 acres, and the remaining part of said David, said McDowall's grant dated 4 Aug 1788, said Davis grant dated 5 March 1787, also a tract on waters of Granneys Quarter Creek adj. Rugeleys old mill, granted to William McDowall for 64 acres 4 Feb 1788, also the plantation whereon Nathaniel Rogers now lives, 100 acres adj. Rugeleys old mill place, which I lately purchased from Elijah Rogers. David Hunter (wax seal), Wit: Andrew Hoves, Ambros Neilson, Esther Hunter (X). Proved in Chester County by the oath of Ambrose Nelson 22 Nov 1792 before Francis Boykin, J.P. A schedule annexed to this indenture of two negroes, goods & chattles, household furniture, 15 Nov 1792, cattle. Proved in Kershaw County by the oath of Ambrose Nelson 7 Dec 1792 before Francis Boykin, J.P. Recorded 15 May 1798.

**F, 212**: John Ray of Chester County for $428.15 to Samuel Davis of Surry County, North Carolina, 256 acres (except 50 acres already conveyed to Henry Smith adj.the said Henry Smith's land), granted to John Ferguson 7 May 1787 on waters of Sandy River adj. James Douglass, James Biggam, James Pagan, Peter Coonrod, 26 Dec 1797. John Ray (O) (Seal), Wit: Enoch Edwards, John Owen. Proved by the oath of Enoch Edwards 26 Dec 1797 before R. Owen, J.P. Recorded 1 June 1798.

**F, 213**: Plat of Captain Peter Corbell's Lott. William Lacey of Chester County for $30 to Judith Nutt Corbell of same, a part of a tract of land that was granted to James Stuart, and from thence conveyed to William Lacey, which said lott is on the Saluda Road, it being whereon the Chester Court house (viz) the former now stands which said court house were sold by the Judges to Peter Corbell, 30 Sept 1797. Wm Lacey (Seal), Wit: John McCreary, William Shaw. Proved by the oath of William Shaw 31 May 1798 before Saml Lacey, Clk. Recorded 1 June 1798.

**F, 213-214**: Plat of Captain Peter Corbell's Lott containing one quarter of an acre adj. Jas Stuart, and public land. William Lacey of Chester County for $30 to Judith Nutt Corbell of same, lot adj. to the court house, ¼ acre, 30 Sept 1797. Wm Lacey (Seal), Wit: John McCreary, William Shaw. Proved by the oath of William Shaw 31 May 1798 before Saml Lacey, Clk. Recorded 1 June 1798.

**F, 214**: Judith Nutt Corbell of Chester County, Free-dealer, & Peter Corbell my husband, for $300 to William Barnett of same, a house and lot of ¼ acre whereon the first court house of said county was built on the Saluda road or Main Street in said Village, also another lot of ¼ acre adj. to it adj. William Lacey, Thomas Anderson, _____ 1798. Judith N. Corbell (Seal), Peter Corbell (Seal), Wit: Hugh Gaston, Thomas B. Franklin. Proved by the oath of Thomas B. Franklin 30 May 1798 before Saml Lacey, Clk. Recorded 1 June 1798.

**F, 215**: Whereas Mr. Hugh Gaston of Chester County hath lent me the sum of $100, I mortgage to said Hugh Gaston, one house & lot at Chester Court House, being the old court house & the lot whereon it stands, 29 May 1798. William Barnett (Seal), Wit: saml Lacey Junr, Thos. B. Franklin. Proved by the oath of Thomas B. Franklin 30 May 1798 before Saml Lacey, Clk. Recorded 1 June 1798. Mortgage satisfied 28 May 1799.

**F, 215**: South Carolina, Chester County. Reuben Lacey of county aforesaid for $50 to James Kirkpatrick, a bay mare about 14 years of age about 15 hands high branded on the near jaw G, trots natural, also two feather beds & furniture, 18 Dec 1797. Reuben Lacey (Seal), Wit: Wm Robison, Catlett Conner. Proved by the oath of Catlett Conner 2 June 1798 before Saml Lacey, C.C.C. Recorded 4 June 1798.

**F, 216**: James Barron of Union County for £20 to John R. Love of Chester County, tract of 100 acres granted to Zachariah Bell 4 April 1785 on waters of Bells Creek adj. lands belonging to the corporation of Bullocks Creek Meeting House, conveyed by Zacheriah Bell to James Barron 23 Sept 1785, dated 13 Jan 1798. James Barron (Seal), Wit: John McCool, Richard Love, James Love Junr. Proved by the oath of Richard Love 13 Jan 1798 before Wm. Gaston, J. C. C. Martha Barron, wife of James Barron, relinquished dower 13 Jan 1798 before Wm. Gaston, J. C. C. Recorded 4 June 1798.

**F, 216-217**: Francis Rea of Chester County for £30 to William Paul of same, 200 acres on the waters of Rockey Creek, part of tract granted to Francis Rea adj. Thomas Blair, Alexander Walker, Widow Steel, Alexander Hendry, Thomas Huston, 29 Dec 1797. Francis Rea (M) (wax seal), Wit: Wm Nunn, Robert Sanderson, Loftin Nunn. Proved by the oath of William Nunn 16 June 1798 before Saml Lacey, Clk. Recorded 20 June 1798.

**F, 217**: William Blair of Chester County for £5 to William Paul of same, 22 acres on the waters of Rockey Creek in Chester county, part of a tract granted to Thomas Blair and transferred by William Blair, heir at law of said Thomas Blair, 28 July 1797. William Blair (Seal), Wit: Joseph Wright, William Crawford, Wm. McCaw. Proved by the oath of William Crawford 13 June 1798 before H. McCluer, J.P. Recorded 20 June 1798.

**F, 218**: South Carolina, Camden District. 4 Dec 1783, Catharine Brown to Hambleton Brown for £10 sterling, 116 acres on a branch of Turkey Creek granted to said Catharine Brown by patent 20 July 1772. Catharine Brown (O) (wax seal), Wit: James Fowler, James Brown, Turner Kendrick. Proved by the oath of James Brown ___ July 1785 before Edw'd Lacey, J.P.

**F, 218-219**: Elisabeth Elliott, William Wilson & John Thomson, admors of the estate of Wm. Elliott decd, of Chester county for £150 current money to William Lewis of Chester county, two negro slaves one named Sambo & the other Molley, 22 Nov 1796. Elisabeth Elliott (l), William Wilson, John Thomson; Test: Geo. Gill. Proved by the oath of Col. Geo Gill 16 June 1798 before Saml Lacey, Clk. Recorded 21 June 1798.

**F, 219-220**: 7 June 1793, Elijah Brown of Pendleton County, SC, to William Walker of Chester County, tract on waters of Fishing Creek adj. lands of Richard Kerrell, William Griffin, granted to William Brown, Esqr., deceased, 27 Nov 1770, memorial entered in Book K, No 10, page 292, 3 Jan 1770, which land become the sole property of said E. Brown as highest bidder at a sale made 28 Sept 1784 by Edward Lacey & Elijah Brown exors of the will of said deceased William Brown, 137 acres adj. the former 300 acres and land surveyed for John Walker and granted to said Elijah Brown 5 June 1786, plat certified 17 Aug 1785. Elijah Brown (wax seal), Wit: John Beaird, Robert Smith, James McCurdy. Proved by the oath of John Beaird 16 July 1793 before Jno Mills, J.P. Recorded 21 June 1798.

**F, 220-221**: Samuel McKay of Chester county for £110 sterling to Alexander English of same, 100 acres on waters of Sandy River adj. to Chester County

Court House, originally granted to William Rainey 22 March 1775 and conveyed from said Rainey and Eleanor his wife by deed to William Robinson 16 Sept 1793. Saml McCay (Seal), Wit: Geo Kennedy, Jno Morrow. Proved by the oath of John Morrow 15 June 1798 before Joseph Brown, J. C. C. Elizabeth McCay, wife of Samuel McCay, relinquished dower 15 June 1798 before Joseph Brown, J. C. C. Recorded 21 June 1798.

**F, 221-222**: 22 Nov 1796, Michael Dickson of Pendleton County, SC, planter, to William Millen of Chester County, planter, for £15 sterling, 40 acres on waters of Rocky Creek in Chester County adj. Michael Dickson, part of 300 acres granted to Michael Dickson 16 April 1765. Michael Dickson (Seal), Wit: Hugh Dickson, John Hays, Charles Miller. Proved by the oath of Charles Miller 13 June 1798 before H. McCluer, J.P. Recorded 28 June 1798.

**F, 222-223**: 21 Nov 1796, Michael Dickson of Pendleton County, SC, planter, to William Millen of Chester County, planter, for £40 sterling, 100 acres on waters of Rocky Creek in Chester County adj. Michael Dickson, John Walker, granted to Michael Dickson 25 April 1764. Michael Dickson (Seal), Wit: Hugh Dickson, John Hays, Charles Miller. Proved by the oath of Charles Miller 13 June 1798 before H. McCluer, J.P. Recorded 28 June 1798.

**F, 223-224**: 22 Nov 1796, Michael Dickson of Pendleton County, SC, planter, to William Millen of Chester County, planter, for ten shillings sterling, 154 acres on waters of Rocky Creek in Chester County, part of 508 acres granted to Michael Dickson 5 Sept 1785. Michael Dickson (Seal), Wit: Hugh Dickson, John Hays, Charles Miller. Proved by the oath of Charles Miller 13 June 1798 before H. McCluer, J.P. Recorded 28 June 1798.

**F, 224-225**: 21 Nov 1796, Michael Dickson of Pendleton County, SC, planter, to William Millen of Chester County, planter, for £10 sterling, 48 acres on waters of Rocky Creek in Chester County, adj. land formerly Michael Dickson, Alexander Walker, John Walker, granted 24 Oct 1767. Michael Dickson (Seal), Wit: Hugh Dickson, John Hays, Charles Miller. Proved by the oath of Charles Miller 13 June 1798 before H. McCluer, J.P. Recorded 28 June 1798.

**F, 225-226**: 13 Aug 1789, Thomas Camron & Susannah his wife of Fairfield County for £25 sterling to William Milling of Chester County, 250 acres on waters of Rockey Creek adj. Michael Dickson, granted to John McClure 13 May 1768, and sold by said John McCluer to Thomas Camron. Thomas Camron (O) (Seal), Susannah Camron (O) (Seal), Wit: James Camron, John Camron, Charles Miller. Proved by the oath of Charles Miller 13 June 1798 before H. McCluer, J.P. Recorded 29 June 1798.

**F, 226-227**: 10 Aug 1789, Thomas Camron & Susannah his wife of Fairfield County for £25 sterling to Charles Miller of Chester County, 125 acres on waters of Rockey Creek adj. Michael Dickson, granted to John McClure 13 May 1768, and sold by said John McCluer to Thomas Camron. Thomas Camron (O) (Seal), Susannah Camron (O) (Seal), Wit: James Camron, John

Camron, Charles Miller. Proved by the oath of William Millen/Milling 13 June 1798 before H. McCluer, J.P. Recorded 29 June 1798.

**F, 227**: William Walker o Chester County, yeoman, for $50 to Joseph Morrow of same, wheel-wright, tract granted to William Walker of Fishing Creek 2 Jan 1797, 61 acres on waters of Rockey Creek adj. William Wylie, 1 Nov 1797. William Walker (wax seal), Wit: Charles Miller, John Murphey, Wm. Bohannan. Proved by the oath of John Murphy 13 June 1798 before H. McCluer, J.P.

**F, 227-228**: 27 Nov 1777, Manuel Powel of Camden District, SC, planter, to William Land of same, planter, for ten shillings, 50 acres on the branches of Rockey Creek, part of tract of 100 acres granted to Hugh Montgomery and made over by lease to David Powel deceased adj. Hugh Montgomery, Moses Reeves. Manuel Powel (X) (Seal), Elinor Powel (X) (Seal), Wit: Hugh Montgomery, George Morris. Proved by the oath of Hugh Montgomery 13 March 1778 before Philip Walker, J. P. Recorded 20 Aug 1798.

**F, 228-231**: 28 Nov 1777, Manuel Powel of Camden District, Craven County, SC, planter, to William Land of same, planter, for £130, 100 acres on the branches of Rockey Creek, part of tract of 200 acres granted to Hugh Montgomery 13 July 1770 and made over by lease to David Powel deceased adj. Benjamin Street, Benjamin Street, said Manuel Powel being heir at law to the said David Powell deceased. Manuel Powel (X) (Seal), Elinor Powel (X) (Seal), Wit: Hugh Montgomery, George Morris.

Proved by the oath of William Montgomery who saith that some years ago that he heard William Land buy a piece of land from Hugh Montgomery, 200 acres granted to said Hugh Montgomery on waters of Rockey Creek and on Houges branch, and deponent believes that said Land had titles to 15 acres and that he knew the said Wm Land to have it in his possession for about 6 years before his decease, 1 Nov 1793 before Andrew Hemphill, J. P.

Deposition of Agnes Morris that she knew Hugh Montgomery to sell the piece of land unto William Land and receive full pay, part of tract of 200 acres granted to said Hugh Montgomery adj. Manuel Powel, dated 1 Nov 1793, before Andw Hemphill, J.P.

Deposition of John Rennals that Hugh Montgomery did well to William Land some years ago a piece of land said land granted to Hugh Montgomery, on the old Rocky Mount road, 18 Jan 1797 before James Peden, J.P.

Case stated. Hugh Montgomery sold to William Land a tract of 15 acres more or less describing the natural boundaries in the house of Mary Land were burnt the titles unrecorded about the year 1776 William Land got possession of the land and kept possession by himself until this day. Since the death of the husband Mary has kept possession by the tenants. I conceive that the possession of Mary Jones will intitle her to the land before any other claim. J. Ellerbe[?] considered at Camden, Nov. 1793. Recorded 21 Aug 1798.

**F, 231-232**: 3 July 1795, William Moray of Chester County to William McKee of same, for £45 sterling, 100 acres bounding on land surveyed for Charles Miller & James Stuart, James Stuart and Samuel McMurrey, part of two plats of land originally granted to said William Morray and one to Charles Miller, reference to Grant Book LLLL, page 249 for William Morray and Grant Book TTT, page 238 to Charles Miller. William Morray (Seal), Susannah Morray (Seal), Wit: Wm Boyd, James Robinson. Proved by the oath of James Robinson 24 July 1798 before Saml Lacey, Clk. Recorded 21 Aug 1798.

**F, 233**: Joseph Davis for trust and confidence that I put in my two sons Richard and John Davis impower then to rent or sell a certain tract with a mill on it in the State of Georgia, Franklin County, on waters of Togoloo River, 49 acres, 12 Feb 1798, Joseph Davis. Wit: Mary Davis (X), Wm. Embry. Recorded 21 Aug 1798.

**F, 233-236**: Lease and release. 4 March 1791, William Carrell of Chester County to Francis Land of same, for £30 sterling, 122½ acres, part of grant to 800 acres on a branch of Broad River, adj. Ephraim Lyles, Nathan Atterberry, granted to Solomon Peters 7 May 1774 and transferred by said Solomon Peters to William Carrel 3 July 1789. Willis Carrell (seal), Esther Carrell (X) (Seal), Wit: Isaiah Coleman, Robert Lemonds, Saml Carter. Proved by the oath of Samuel Carter 25 March 1794 before John Bell, J.P. Recorded 21 Aug 1798.

**F, 236-237**: William Tannehill for $300 to William Cornwell, 50 acres, 16 April 1798. William Tanehill (Seal), Wit: John Pratt, Joseph Timms, Hugh Knox. Elizabeth Tannehill (X), wife of William Tannehill, relinquished dower 16 April 1798 before Jo Brown. Proved by the oath of John Pratt, esqr., 25 July 1798 before Hugh Knox, J.P. Recorded 22 Aug 1798.

**F, 237**: 28 May 1798, Abner Wilkes and his wife Patsey of Chester County for £60 sterling to Thomas Humphries, tract on waters of Rockey branch, a branch of Sandy River adj. Jesse Wall, Mannen Gore, 88 acres. Abner Wilkes (Seal), Patty Wilkes (Seal), Wit: Jeremiah Kingsley, Charles Humphries. Proved by the oath of Jeremiah Kingsley 25 July 1798 before E. Nunn, J.P. Recorded 22 Aug 1798.

**F, 237-238**: William Gyles of Chester County, planter, for $300 to Arthur Gyles of same, 106 acres on west side of Cattawba River adj. William McDonald, widow Harrison, part of tract granted to Casper Sleeker, dated 31 Jan 1798. William Gyles (X) (Seal), Catharine Gyles (X) (Seal), Wit: Robt Davison, Robt Gaston, Joshua Crook. Proved by the oath of Robt Davison 23 April 1798 before Jos Gaston, J.P. Recorded 22 Aug 1798.

**F, 238-239**: Edmund Lee and Nancey his wife of Chester County for £5 sterling to Thomas Estes of same, 82 acres, part of tract granted to Hazael Hardwick on waters of Sealeys Creek adj. William Shaw, 23 Nov 1797. Edmund Lea (Seal), Nancy Lea (X) (Seal), Wit: Jesse Wallis, John Wright. Proved by the oath of John Wright 25 July 1798 before Saml Lacey, Clk. Recorded 22 Aug 1798.

**F, 239-240**: 1 June 1796, Jonathan Hemphill & Esther his wife of Chester county to Francis Adams of same, for £27 sterling, 50 acres on a dividing line made by said Jonathan Hemphill and Thomas Land, part of tract of 400 acres granted to Joseph Thompson 4 April 1785 adj. Robert Robinson, Joseph Thompson, conveyed to James Hemphill by indenture 30 Dec 1785 and by James Hemphill to said Jonathan Hemphill 2 Nov 1788. Jon'n Hemphill (Seal), Esther Hemphill (X) (Seal), Wit: Andrew Hemphill, Saml Ferguson. Proved by the oath of Samuel Ferguson 11 July 1798 before John McCreary, J.P. Recorded 22 Aug 1798.

**F, 240-241**: 30 Jan 1793, James Dougherty & Mary his wife of Charleston District, SC, to Gabriel Holsey and Silus Holsey of Camden District, for £35 sterling, 200 acres on waters of Little River adj. land of Moses Hill originally granted to Richard Guin, Enoch Grubs, and said tract was granted to said James Dougherty 3 April 1786. Jas Dougharty (wax seal), Mary Dougharty (mark) (wax seal), Wit: Henry Head, Simon Butler, Leonard Taylor. Proved by the oath of Leonard Taylor 25 July 1798 before John Pratt, J.P. Recorded 22 Aug 1798.

**F, 241**: Edmund Lea and Nancey his wife of Chester County for £120 sterling to Thomas Estes of same, 100 acres on waters of Sealeys Creek part of tract on which William Shaw now lives, adj. James Timms, Hazael Hardwick, 23 Nov 1797. Edmund Lea (Seal), Nancy Lea (X) (Seal), Wit: Jesse Wallis, John Wright. Proved by the oath of John Wright 25 July 1798 before Saml Lacey, Clk. Recorded 22 Aug 1798.

**F, 242**: Moses McCown of Chester County for $100 to Alexander McCown Junr of same, 50 acres on Fishing Creek adj. Robert Swan, on the bank of Fishing Creek, surveyed for me about 1765, dated 9 Feb 1798. Moses McCown (wax seal), Wit: David Fullerton, John Jones, Sm. McCreary, John McCreary. Proved by the oath of David Fullerton and John Jones 21 July 1798 before John McCreary, J.P. Recorded 23 Aug 1798.

**F, 242-243**: William Hopkins of Richard [*sic*, for Richland] County, SC, for $300 to Eli Cornwell of Chester County, 200 acres in Craven County when granted on the dreans of Sandy River adj. land claimed by Daniel Rice, Edward Wilson, Randolph Wilson, land claimed by Daniel Price (now by Jas Gore), 21 March 1798. Wm Hopkins (Seal), Mary Hopkins (O) (Seal), Wit: James Gore, Isaac Tucker. Mary Hopkins, wife of William Hopkins, relinquished dower in Richland County 2 April 1798 before Isaac Tucker, J.

R. C. Proved in Chester County by the oath of James Gore Junior 27 July 1798 before John Pratt, J.P. Recorded 23 Aug 1798.

**F, 243-244:** Joseph Ferguson of Chester County for $40 to John Service Senior, a certain bay mare seven years old, about 13 hands high, a star in her face and snip on her nose, three cows, one a brown cow no ear mark, and one light brindled with a white face and one dark brown marked with a crop off the right ear, 23 June 1798. Joseph Ferguson (O) (Seal), Wit: Saml Lacey Junior, Geo Kennedy. Proved by the oath of George Kennedy 24 Aug 1798 before Saml Lacey, Clk. Recorded 27 Aug 1798.

**F, 244-245:** Aaron Lockart of Chester County for £100 sterling paid by John Lockart of same, 100 acres on Leighs branch on NE side of Broad River granted to said Aaron Lockart 21 April 1775 also part of another tract of 100 acres adj. Markley, supposed to be about 30 acres, 20 Aug 1798. Aaron Lockert (Seal), Wit: Chas Gillmore, Elijah Going. Proved by the oath of Chas Gillmore 21 Aug 1798 before Jo. Brown, J. C. C. Recorded 27 Aug 1798.

**F, 245-246:** South Carolina, Chester County. 2 Feb 1793, John McEwin Senior of Fairfield County to Stephen Keenan of Chester County, for £20 tract granted 23 June 1774 to John Harlowe, 200 acres conveyed to John McEwen by John Harlowe, on waters of Rockey Creek adj. Ann Hannah, John Downey. John McEwen (mark) (Seal), Wit: John McEwen Jr., Thomas Simpson. Proved by the oath of Thomas Simpson 10 July 1798 before Hugh McCluer, J.P. Recorded 5 Sept 1798.

**F, 246-247:** Isaac Hudson of Chester County for $100 to Stephen Keenan of same, 100 acres adj. said Hudson, lands granted to Ralph Baker, said Keenan, Stone, Alexander Rosborough, originally granted to David Hunter, originally granted to Agness Hannah, the said tract being part of two tracts one granted to David Hunter and the other to Agnes Hannah, 24 Jan 1798. Isaac Hudson (wax seal), Wit: Thomas Simpson. Nancy Hudson, wife off Isaac Hudson, relinquished dower 31 Jan 1798 before Hugh Whiteside, Judge of Chester Court. Proved by the oath of Thomas Simpson 10 July 1798 before Hugh McCluer, J.P. Recorded 4 Sept 1798.

**F, 247-248:** South Carolina, Pinckney District. 14 June 1792, James Adair to Thomas Stevenson, both of district aforesaid, for £50 sterling, tract of 200 acres on waters of Mill Creek, granted to James Adair 5 Feb 1787. James Adare (wax seal), Anne Adare, Wit: James L. Gaston, James Fowler, Obediah Roberts. Proved by the oath of Rev. James Fowler 1 Sept 1798 before Saml Lacey, Clk. Recorded 7 Sept 1798.

**F, 248-249:** Received Stewart's Town, September 4, 1798 of Saml Johnson, £17 s2 in full for a negro fellow named Daniel who was conveyed to me by my father by a deed of gift. Nancy Harrison, Wit: Geo Kennedy. Proved by the oath of George Kennedy 8 Sept 1798 before E. Nunn, J.P. Recorded 28 Sept 1798.

**F, 249**: Joshua Gore of Chester County, planter, for $6 to Thomas Baker Franklin, Inn-keeper, 40 acres granted to Robert wilson 6 Feb 1797 but by a resurvey found to be but 7.2 acres adj. William Morrow, 12 May 1798. Joshua Gore (wax seal), Wit: John Pratt, Thomas Davis. Proved by the oath of John Pratt 12 May 1798 before Hugh Knox, J.P.

**F, 250**: Jacob Morris of Chester County for $100 to Thomas B. Franklin of same, 100 acres on Sterns branch of Sandy River, being the third part of a tract of 300 acres granted to Thomas Morris deceased 2 May 1785 and bequeathed to said Jacob Morris by said Thomas Morris' last will and testament, 8 Sept 1798. Jacob Morris (Seal), Charles Boyd, James Morris. Proved by the oath of James Morris 2 Sept 1798 before Saml Lacey, Clk. Recorded 8 Sept 1798.

**F, 250-251**: Joseph Bennett of Chester county for £50 sterling to Thomas B. Franklin, 100 acres on waters of Sandy River,part of tract granted to Thomas Morris 2 May 1785, bequeathed to James Morris by Thomas Morris's last will and testament and conveyed by James Morris to John Humphreys and from John Humphreys by virtue of an executed of Sheriff sale to William Moore, Sheriff, in 1794, and conveyed to Jeremiah Roden, and by Jeremiah Roden to Joseph Bennett, 22 June 1798. Joseph Bennett (wax seal), Wit: Geo Kennedy, John Kennedy, James Neal. Proved by the oath of John Kennedy 8 Sept 1798 before Saml Lacey, Clk. Recorded 11 Sept 1798.

**F, 251-252**: Henry Sanders of Pendleton County appoint my friend Michael Gore to ask, demand, sue for, levy, recover and receive all such sums of money, debts, rents, goods, particularly the heirs of James Sanders' estate, 3 Aug 1796. Henry Sanders (X) (Seal), Wit: Pat McGriff, William McGriff. Proved by the oath of Col. Patrick McGriff 4 Feb 1797 before John Pratt, J.P. Saml Lacey certified that John Pratt was a lawful and acting magistrate for Chester County, 17 Sept 1798. Recorded 11 Sept 1798.

**F, 252-253**: Michael Gore of Chester County appoints Clement Gore of same, attorney, to ask for sue, demand, all that appears to be my right in a tract called the Resurvey or Gores Adventure, in Montgomery County, Maryland, 6 Sept 1798. Michael Gore (Seal), Wit: Wm. Jinkins, Michael Gore. Proved by the oath of William Jinkins 6 Sept 1798 before Thos Jinkins, J.P. Saml Lacey certified that Thomas Jinkins was a lawful and acting magistrate for Chester County, 17 Sept 1798. Recorded 11 Sept 1798.

**F, 253-254**: Michael Gore of Chester County appoints Clement Gore of same, attorney, to ask for sue, demand, whatever may be due to Henry Sanders from the heirs of James Sanders's estate, which I am impowered to receive by a letter of attorney dated 3 August 1796, also which may be detailed from Elias Plummer by the heirs of Ann Self which I have the power to collected by letter of attorney dated 11 Aug 1796 by the said Elias Plummer, 6 Sept 1798. Michael Gore (Seal), Wit: Wm. Jinkins, Michael Gore. Proved by the oath of William Jinkins 6 Sept 1798 before Thos Jinkins, J.P. Saml Lacey certified that Thomas Jinkins was a lawful and acting magistrate for Chester County, 17 Sept 1798. Recorded 12 Sept 1798.

**F, 254**: John Pratt of Chester County for $80 to Thomas B. Franklin, 53½ acres in Chester County on waters of Sandy River adj. David Grisham, 5 March 1798. John Pratt (Seal), Wit: Wm Wood, James Loveing (X). Proved by the oath of William Wood 8 Sept 1798 before Saml Lacey, Clk. Recorded 24 Sept 1798.

**F, 254-255**: James Hughey & Sarah my wife of Chester County for $1000 to Moses Smith of same, 100 acres on Flinthams Creek, a branch of Sandy River, adj. James Hughey, a tract originally granted to Minor Winn, granted to Edward Flintham, 18 July 1798. James Hughey (Seal), Wit: John Weir, Jacob Dungan, John Franklin. Proved by the oath of John Weir 25 July 1798 before John Pratt, J.P. Sarah Huey, wife of James Huey, relinquished dower 25 July 1798 before Jo. Brown. Recorded 24 Sept 1798.

**F, 256**: George Kelsey of Chester County for $50 to Thomas Gray of same, 56 acres in Craven County at the time of survey on west side of Fishing Creek, excepting out of said sale 2½ acres of land joining Christopher Strong's line including a meeting house, burial ground and retiring house, granted to said George Kelsey 7 May 1774, 6 Feb 1797. George Kelsey (wax seal), Wit: Hugh Whiteside, Wm. Whiteside, Archibald Morrow (X). Proved by the oath of William Whiteside 6 Feb 1797 before Hugh Whiteside. Recorded 24 Sept 1798.

**F, 256-257**: Thomas Gray of Chester County, planter, for $50 to Thomas Neeley of same, waggon maker, 56 acres in Chester County on west side of Fishing Creek (2½ acres excepted including a meeting house, burial ground and retiring house), granted to George Kelsey and by him conveyed to Thomas Gray 6 Feb 1797, dated 25 May 1798. Thomas Gray (wax seal), Wit: James Neely, William Neely. Proved by the oath of William Neely 25 May 1798 before Hugh Whiteside. Recorded 24 Sept 1798.

**F, 257-258**: William Blackstock of York County, SC, for $700 to Thomas Neely of Chester County, tract originally granted to sundry persons, first to Charles Strong now deceased, 200 acres supposed them to be in North Carolina, but now in Chester County between the main forks of Fishing Creek adj. Samuel McCance, conveyed by Christopher Strong, son and heir of Charles Strong deceased, to the Revd. William Blackstock; secondly 50 acres surveyed for Christopher Strong 9 June 1789 in the fork of Fishing Creek adj. land surveyed for William Boyd, Robert Glover, James Jack & John Boyd, Samuel Barnet; thirdly 100 acres being a part of two surveys one granted to Joseph Mitchell by Gov. Tryon of NC and conveyed to James Jack and by him conveyed to John Hays and by said Hays to Christopher Strong, the other originally granted to Robert Harper and by him conveyed to John Hays and by Hays to Christopher Strong; these tracts conveyed by said Christopher Strong unto Rev. William Blackstock 19 Oct 1793; dated 25 May 1798.

William Blackstock (wax seal), Wit: Thomas Gray, Hugh Whiteside, William Neely. Proved by the oath of William Neely 25 May 1798 before Hugh Whiteside. Recorded 24 Sept 1798.

**F, 258-259**: South Carolina, Chester County. Personally came George Kennedy before me (the subscribing Justice) and made oath that about 29 Dec 1796 he went in company with Samuel Johnston merchant to the house of Philip Sandifurr of York County and then & there heard some conversation take place between the said Johnston & Sandifurr respecting the sale of a certain negro woman called Rose made by William Sandifurr son of said Philip to the said Johnston & when Johnston made mention that he had purchased such a negro from said William, said Philip seemed surprised & said he did not know that William had any such negro. Johnston asked him now William came by the negro, said Philip told him William did not steal her, but he might well think so from what he was to give for her; but that the negro was his & if he would give him $300 for her he should have her & said Johnston told him he could give no such price, but if the negro belonged to him, send for her, for he would not be accountable for her any longer & said Philip said very well he should send for her as soon as the weather cleared up said Johnston told he would be give he would come or send soon for she was at his house & he did not know what might become of her if neglected & said Philip said he was not afraid she would run away, if she did he could find her, or if she was stole he find her, sworn 17 Sept 1798. Geo. Kennedy before Robt Owen, J.P. Recorded 24 Sept 1798.

**F, 259-260**: Plat of General Edward Lacey's plantation, 368 acres showing adj. land owners William Rainey, Paul Ferguson, Hitchcock, James Adair, Jonathan Jones.

22 Sept 1795, James Stuart & Elisabeth his wife of Chester County to William Lacey of same, for £100 sterling, 368 acres being the north half of a tract of 736 acres granted to said James Stuart 1 Dec 1788, recorded in grant book YYYY, page 205. James Stuart (wax seal), Betsey Stuart (X) (wax seal), Wit: John Jaggers, Frances Grisham (X), Major Grisham (mark). Proved by the oath of Major Grisham 17 Sept 1798 before R. Owen, J.P. Recorded 24 Sept 1798.

**F, 260-261**: William Tannehill of Chester County for $300 to William Cornwell of same, 100 acres on north side of Broad river on Sandy River adj. George Tannihill [not dated]. William Tanehill (LS), Wit: John Pratt, Joseph Timms, Hugh Knox. Proved by the oath of John Pratt 25 July 1798 before Hugh Knox, J.P. Elisabeth Tannihill, wife of William Tannihill, relinquished dower before Joseph Brown, 24 April 1798. Recorded 22 Oct 1798.

**F, 261-262**: 10 Jan 1793, Samuel Erwin, planter, of Chester County to Joseph Simpson, weaver, of same, for £30 sterling, 100 acres on waters of Rockey Creek adj. said Samuel Erwin, Henry Isbell, Widow Dunstith, recorded in Book XXX, page 144, memorial entered in the Aud Genls Office in Bok M

No 14, page 121, 26 Sept 1775, granted to Christopher Strong 4 May 1775. Wit: William Dunn, Andrew Dunn. Proved by the oath of William Dunn 26 Jan 1793 before Andw Hemphill, J.P.

**F, 262-263**: 2 Dec 1794, John Strong and Mary his wife of Chester County t Andrew Dunn Junior, planter, for £60 sterling, 100 acres on Rockey Creek granted to Samuel Erwin deceased 17 March 1775, made over to Jno Strong 12 Dec 1779[?]. John Strong (Seal), Mary Strong (mark) (seal), Wit: John Orr, James Gillespy. Proved by the oath of James Gillespie 15 Nov 1795 before Andw Hemphill, J. P. Recorded 23 Oct 1798.

**F, 264-265**: South Carolina, Chester County, Pinckney District. 23 May 1798, John Adair of said county to Andrew Dunn Junior of same, for £9 s10, 50 acres, part of 150 acres granted to Samuel Erwin on waters of little Rockey Creek. John Adair (Seal), Wit: John Coulter, Thomas Mayben, John Rodmont. Proved by the oath of John Redmond 6 Oct 1798 before James Peden, J.P. Recorded 23 Oct 1798.

**F, 265**: Isham Fielding & Elisabeth his wife, William Henderson & Drusiller his wife, Clem Fennel & Mary Fennel, legatees of Stith Fennel deceased of Chester County to John Letsinger of same, their parts of the land that formerly belonged to Stith Fennel deceased, part of grant to Casper Sleeker Senior, 17 April 1798. Isham Fielding (X) (Seal), Elisabeth Fielding (mark) (Seal), William Henderson (Seal), Drusiller Henderson (X) (Seal), Clem Fennell (Seal), Wit: David Ferral, Henry Jordan. Proved by the oath of David Ferral 15 Oct 1798 before James Crafford. Recorded 24 Oct 1798.

**F, 266**: William Lacey of Chester County for $50 to Samuel Johnston ½ acre in the village of Chester, 20 Oct 1798. William Lacey (Seal), Wit: William Jones, James Abernethy. Proved by the oath of James Abernethy 20 Oct 1798 before Saml Lacey, Clk. Recorded 20 Oct 1798.

**F, 266-267**: John Burns of Chester County for $100 to George Kennedy of same, 59 acres near Chester Court House adj. land surveyed for Charles Miller, Samuel Walker, James Stuart, part of 736 acres granted to James Stuart 1 Dec 1788, dated 19 Oct 1798. John Burns (Seal), Wit: Saml Lacey Junr, Jno Johnston. Proved by the oath of John Johnston 19 Oct 1798 before Saml Lacey, Clk., Recorded 23 Oct 1798.

**F, 267-269**: 6 June 1796, William Bratton, Esqr., Sheriff of Pinckney District, to Usley Bond of Chester County, tract of 211 acres on waters of Sandy River and whereas Moses Bond was indebted to William & George Tanehill, sons & Heirs of George Tanihill deceased, and said William & George Tanihill did exhibit their petition to the judges of the court of common pleas of said state in 1796 and Moses Bond deceased was in debt in the sum of £55 sterling, and by writ of fi fa from under the hand of John Martin, Esqr., Clerk of said court at Pinckney, 1 April 1796, sold for £17 s10 sterling. William Bratton Shff

(Seal), Wit: Andrew Egger, John Breiard. Proved by the oath of Andrew Egger 16 July 1798 before E. Nunn, J.P. Recorded 19 Nov 1798.

**F, 269**: Usly Bond of Chester County for £100 sterling to George Brown of same, land on Suseys Creek of Sandy River, 211 acres, part o tract granted to John Bond for 400 acres, granted 13 May 1768, and transferred from said John Bond by will to Moses Bond deceased, and sold by sheriff of Pinckney District to said Usley Bond, 25 July 1798. Usley Bond (X) (Seal), Wit: Peter Corbell, A. Egger. Proved by the oath of Andrew Egger 25 July 1798 before E. Nunn, J.P. Recorded 27 Nov 1798.

**F, 269-270**: 17 April 1797, Samuel Combess of Chester County to James Onail of same, for £20 sterling, 122 acres above said James Onail's land. Samuel Combess (Seal), Wit: Robt Owen, Thos B. Franklin, Thos Rollins (R). Proved by the oath of Thomas B. Franklin 18 Dec 1798 before Saml Lacey, Clk. Recorded 18 Dec 1798.

**F, 270-271**: John Cooper of Chester County for $79 to Charles Boyles, 29½ acres granted 6 Jan 1794 adj. David Morrow, Hugh Cooper, 13 Feb 1798. John Cooper (wax seal), Wit: Thos Davis, John Boyd, David Boyd. Proved by the oath of David Boyd 18 Dec 1798 before Hugh McClure, J.P. Recorded 28 Dec 1798.

**F, 271-272**: John Carter of Chester County for $60 to James Bishop of same, 100 acres in Craven County now Chester County on Rockey Creek granted to said John Carter 15 ____ 1784, dated 6 Oct 1798. John Carter (wax seal), Wit: William Millen, Wm Bohannan, Saml Combest. Proved by the oath of Wm Bohannon 27 Dec 1798 before Robt Owen, J.P. Recorded 2 Jan 1799.

**F, 272-273**: Hannah Carter (relict of Jacob Carter deceased) of Chester County for $200 to James Bishop & wife Martha, 100 acres on waters of Rockey Creek, left to me by the will of said Jacob Carter decd, 23 Dec 1779, dated 26 Dec 1798. Hannah Carter (mark) (Seal), Wit: William Morray, wm. Bohannan, Alex'dr Millen. Proved by the oath of Wm Bohannon 27 Dec 1798 before Robt Owen, J.P. Recorded 3 Jan 1799.

**F, 273**: South Carolina, Chester County. Thomas Oneal of aforesaid county for £100 sterling to Henry Cotterell of same, 101½ acres adj. Fairy's line, Thomas Atterberry's line, Thomas Atterberry Senior, 21 July 1797. Thomas Oneal (Seal), Wit: Jesse Wallis, Thomas Atteberry (X). Proved by the oath of Jesse Wallis 1 Jan 1799 before Hugh McCluer, J.P. Recorded 3 Jan 1799.

**F, 273-274**: John Carter of Chester County for £100 sterling to Henry Cotterell of same, 150 acres on waters of Sandy River on a branch called Kitts Creek, part of tract granted to Benjamin Carter, 15 Sept 1797. John Carter (seal), Wit: J.Wallis, Vincent Lee. Plat included showing adjacent land owners Henry Cotterell, Josiah Hill, John Carter, Benjamin Carter. Proved by the oath of Jesse Wallis 1 Jan 1799 before Hugh McCluer, J.P. Recorded 3 Jan 1799.

**F, 274-275**: Ferdinand Hopkins of Chester County for £41 s13 d6 sterling to Michael Gore of same, 416 3/4 acres originally granted to Anderson Thomas and by him conveyed to Ferdinand Hopkins on waters of Sandy River, 31 July 1798. Ferd'd Hopkins (Seal), Wit: Zacheriah Perkins, D. Gore. Proved by the oath of Davis Gore 17 Sept 1798 before John Pratt. Recorded 3 Jan 1799.

**F, 275-276**: Edward Lacey now of Chester County appoints Michael Gore of same his attorney to ask, demand, sue for, & recover of Benjamin Saxton Esqr. (attorney lat law), all lawful costs & damages in a certain action brought in Ninety Six District in my name as plaintiff against Thomas W. Waters defendant for a negro wench named Jude and her son, 4 Sept 1798. Edw'd Lacey (Seal), Wit: Wm. Barnett, Jeremiah Thomas. Proved by the oath of William Barnett 1 Jan 1799. Recorded 4 Jan 1799.

**F, 276-277**: Plat showing adjacent land owner Thomas Atterberry Senr. Benjamin Carter of Chester County for $100 to Thomas Atterberry of same, 31 acres on Kitts Creek, waters of Sandy River, part of tract granted to Benjamin Carter Senr and conveyed from John Carter to me, 17 May 1798. Benjamin Carter (Seal), Wit: Thomas Oneal, Nathan Cottrell. Proved by the oath of Thomas Oneal 28 July 1798. Recorded 4 Jan 1799.

**F, 277**: William Stuart of Chester County for $10 by the Justice sof Chester County Court House, lot on which Chester Court House stands, 8 Oct 1798. William Stuart (Seal), Wit: Jas L. Gaston, John Gaston, John Brown. Proved by the oath of James L. Gaston 8 Oct 1798 before John Pratt, J.P. Recorded 4 Jan 1799.

**F, 277-278**: 16 Oct 1784, Kemp Strother of Camden District to Woodlief Thomas of Amelia County, Virginia, for £650, 300 acres in Craven County on waters of Sandy Creek, a branch of Broad River, granted to Henry Middleton Esqr., 19 June 1772. Kemp T. Strother (wax seal), Wit: James Thomas, Susanna Thomas, Mary Herbin (X). Proved by the oath of Susanna Moorman formerly Thomas 28 Sept 1798 before Thomas Jinkins, J.P. Recorded 4 Jan 1799.

**F, 278-279**: James Grant of Chester County for $20 to Nancey Smith of same, 33 acres on waters of Sandy River, part of tract of 133 acres conveyed to said James Grant by Josiah Hill, on and about Loves road including the situation & improvement made by Jacob Brakefield & the spring adjacent thereto, 18 Dec 1798. James Grant (mark) (LS), Wit: Samuel Lacey, William Smith (X). Proved by the oath of Samuel Lacey 18 Dec 1798 before Saml Lacey, Clk. Recorded 5 Jan 1799.

**F, 279-280**: South Carolina, Chester County. 2 Jan 1799, Richard Allen of county aforesaid to John Allen of same, for £15 sterling, 100 acres, being part of a tract of land granted to Francis Bremar and signed over to Richard Allen on Sandy River adj. John Osburn, Charles Allen, Peter Seely, John Wood, Dorsey. Richard Allen (X) (Seal), Wit: Cornelious Dorsey, John Dorsey.

Proved by the oath of Cornelious Dorsey 5 Jan 1799 before Saml Lacey, Clk. Recorded 9 Jan 1799.

**F, 280-281**: South Carolina, Chester County. 1 Jan 1799, Richard Allen of county aforesaid to Cornelious Dorsey of same, for $20, 50 acres, part of tract granted to Francis Bremar & Signer over to Richard Allen adj. John Wood, near Cornelious Dorsey, John Osburn, John Allen. Richard Allen (Seal), John Allen, John Dorsey. Proved by the oath of John Allen 5 Jan 1799 before Saml Lacey, Clk. Recorded 9 Jan 1799.

**F, 281**: James Egger of Chester County for $124 to James L. Gaston of same, 100 acres on Mill Creek, part of 350 acres granted to James Adare 4 Feb 1787 and by said Adare conveyed to Thomas Stevenson 14 June 1792 and by said Stevenson conveyed to James Egger 7 Aug 1793, dated 8 Sept 1798. James Egger (Seal), Wit: John Gaston, John Winsor (X), Sarah Given. Proved by the oath of John Gaston 8 Sept 1798 before Wm. Gaston, J. C. C. Esther Egger (mark), wife of James Egger, relinquished dower 8 Sept 1798 before Wm. Gaston, J. C. C. Recorded 14 Jan 1799.

**F, 282**: 13 Sept 1789, John Hamilton for £20 north currency to John Hamilton, tract on a branch of Sandy River. John Hamilton (O) (Seal), Charles Hamilton, Wit: Wm Hamilton, John Carson. Proved in Lincoln County, North Carolina, by the oath of John Carson 16 Aug 1797 before J. Wilson, J.P. Recorded 3 Jan 1799.

## END OF DEED BOOK F

(Slave), Abram 23, 32, 177
(Slave), Aff 177
(Slave), Alse 116
(Slave), Amelia 59
(Slave), Amy 44
(Slave), Anaka 129
(Slave), Becca 105
(Slave), Beck 144, 152
(Slave), Ben 77
(Slave), Bett 112
(Slave), Betty 65
(Slave), Billey 59
(Slave), Billy 116
(Slave), Bob 122, 181
(Slave), Buster 50
(Slave), Cate 84, 152
(Slave), Cato 44, 87
(Slave), Ceasar 135
(Slave), Ceaser 58
(Slave), Charles 152
(Slave), Chloe 202
(Slave), Clare 121
(Slave), Cloe 65
(Slave), Commadore Bobb 44
(Slave), Cuffe 212
(Slave), Cupit 23
(Slave), Daniel 65, 235
(Slave), David 197
(Slave), Dawkins 163
(Slave), Derry 50
(Slave), Dick 8, 65
(Slave), Dina 50
(Slave), Dinah 72, 77
(Slave), Dinna 23
(Slave), Doll 38, 122
(Slave), Dolly 15
(Slave), Edde 105
(Slave), Eder 128
(Slave), Edy 44
(Slave), Eli 80
(Slave), Ephraim 189
(Slave), Ester 71
(Slave), Esther 121, 129
(Slave), Esther 77
(Slave), Fortune 23
(Slave), George 111, 159
(Slave), Grace 56, 62
(Slave), Guy 9, 107, 182
(Slave), Hagar 55
(Slave), Hall 97, 183
(Slave), Hanible 80
(Slave), Hannah 44, 56, 77, 116, 119, 144, 193
(Slave), Harriett 157
(Slave), Harry 65, 77, 120, 163
(Slave), Isaac 36, 65

(Slave), Jack 23, 44, 96, 135
(Slave), Jacob 65, 77, 113, 145
(Slave), Jemimah 91
(Slave), Jenney 65
(Slave), Jenny 199
(Slave), Jeremiah 94
(Slave), Jim 202
(Slave), Jimm 39, 218
(Slave), Joan 144
(Slave), Joseph 97
(Slave), Juda 176
(Slave), Jude 36, 58, 64, 140, 176, 241
(Slave), Judy 76
(Slave), Juness 77
(Slave), Let 176
(Slave), Lid 218
(Slave), Limbrick 160
(Slave), London 84
(Slave), Lucey 65
(Slave), Margaret 137, 138
(Slave), Mariah 220
(Slave), Mary 62
(Slave), Meriah 77
(Slave), Milley 65
(Slave), Mingo 65
(Slave), Molley 230
(Slave), Moriah 181
(Slave), Morris 65
(Slave), Morrow 65
(Slave), Moses 129
(Slave), Nan 122, 182
(Slave), Nancy 44
(Slave), Ned 182
(Slave), Nelly 96, 152
(Slave), Patt 86, 99, 138
(Slave), Patt/Patsey 109
(Slave), Patty 50
(Slave), Peter 91, 163, 182
(Slave), Phebe 44
(Slave), Phil 159
(Slave), Philis 76
(Slave), Phillis 13, 50, 65, 144
(Slave), Phoebe 135, 152
(Slave), Polly 62
(Slave), Prince 33
(Slave), Rachel 66, 80, 177
(Slave), Rebecca 152
(Slave), Robin 65
(Slave), Rose 76, 127, 238
(Slave), Sall 135
(Slave), Sam 139
(Slave), Sambo 230
(Slave), Sampson 148
(Slave), Samuel 56
(Slave), Sank 49, 114
(Slave), Sarah 44, 56, 77, 116, 187

# NAME INDEX

Brown, Agness 13
Brown, Alexander 3, 5, 9, 18, 19, 21, 30,
  34, 35, 46, 105, 108, 159
Brown, Ann/a 43, 176
Brown, Anne/a (Wallace) 215
Brown, Archibald 184
Brown, Catharine 25, 46, 108, 154, 230
Brown, Daniel 33, 126, 219
Brown, Eake 53
Brown, Elijah 9, 22, 230
Brown, Gabrial 64
Brown, George 195, 196, 240
Brown, Hambleton 92, 108, 230
Brown, Hamilton 210
Brown, Hugh 159
Brown, Jacob 9, 118, 126, 127, 196, 219
Brown, James 2, 43, 46, 93, 108, 110,
  161, 162, 164, 215, 230
Brown, Jean 43
Brown, Jo. 181, 201, 205, 206, 210, 218,
  225, 227, 233, 235, 237
Brown, John 12, 73, 93, 117, 141, 159,
  182, 210, 213, 218, 241
Brown, Joseph 2, 4-6, 23, 31, 33, 34, 37,
  42, 49, 52, 53, 61, 68, 69, 93, 108, 141,
  142, 161, 200, 221, 231, 238
Brown, Katharine 19, 24
Brown, Margrett 56
Brown, Mary 142
Brown, Moses 91
Brown, Peter 202
Brown, Robert 56, 58, 102, 103, 165, 217
Brown, Samuel 3, 9, 13, 18, 19, 33
Brown, Sarah 2, 207, 208, 210
Brown, Steward 64, 34
Brown, Stewart 133
Brown, Stuart 139, 213
Brown, Thomas 40
Brown, Walter 52, 99, 184, 217
Brown, widow 211
Brown, Willey S. 9, 19, 22, 26, 27
Brown, William 8, 19, 22, 24, 25, 35,
  123, 154, 230
Browne, Elijah 27
Brownlee, John 228
Bryce, Alex'dr 213
Bryson, Robert 157
Bull, William 17, 137, 212
Bunsley[?], James 68
Bunsly, James 125
Buoyes, Alexander 196
Buoyz, Alexander 196
Burcham, James 26
Burkel, Richard 95
Burkloe, Richard 95
Burnet, John 117
Burnet, Margaret 117

Burnett, Benjamin 161
Burnett, John 120
Burnett, Robt 72
Burns, James 16, 18, 94
Burns, Jane 105
Burns, Jennet 126
Burns, John 14, 16, 147, 156, 165, 166,
  195, 214, 222, 223, 239
Burns, Laird 94, 105, 126, 201
Burns, Lard 78
Burns, Lea(i)rd 195
Burns, Thomas 25
Burnsides 131
Burnsides, Alexander 193
Burnsly, James 81
Burress, William 7
Burton, Allen 12, 13, 122, 205
Burton, Allin 12
Burton, Benjamin 12, 13
Burton, Walthal 12, 152
Butler, Enoch 208
Butler, James 208
Butler, Simon 234
Buzeley, Peter 192
Cabane, Thomas 65
Cabean, Thomas 168, 172, 174
Cabeen, Thomas 65, 105, 109, 168, 217
Caldwel, Tom 54
Caldwell, Curtis 146
Caldwell, John 42, 100, 221
Caldwell, Margaret 45
Caldwell, Robert 81, 152
Caldwell, Samuel 45, 48, 104
Calhoun, John 38
Calhoun, John Ewing 206
Callaway, James 154, 155
Calligan, 140
Calvert, John 122
Cameron, John 177
Campbell, Alexander 16, 49, 77, 79, 107
Campbell, James 77, 79, 107
Campbell, Jane 120
Campbell, Janet (Morrison) 102
Campbell, John 1, 49, 77
Campbell, Margaret 35, 186
Campbell, Margret (Wright) 185
Campbell, Mary (Crawford) 128, 158
Campbell, Nat'n Greg 183
Campbell, Sarah (Wylie) 54
Camron, James 231
Camron, John 231, 232
Camron, Susannah 231
Camron, Thomas 22, 231
Cantzon, John 221, 222
Cantzon, Moses 75, 210, 222
Car, James 146
Carell, Dennis 91

Gilchrist, James 43, 189
Giles, William 147
Gilham, Thomas 224
Gill, Agness 32
Gill, Archibald 58, 59, 107, 220
Gill, George 8, 9, 18, 62, 107, 108, 126, 137, 179, 189, 223, 230
Gill, James 7, 21, 24, 29, 30, 104, 108, 109
Gill, John 7, 8, 32, 52, 109, 126, 171, 220, 223
Gill, Mary (Gaston) 104
Gill, Robert 3, 7, 8, 10, 17, 60, 79, 91
Gill, Sarah 7, 8, 109
Gillam, John 101, 171
Gillaspey, Thomas 201
Gillchrist, James 215
Gillespie, James 239
Gillespie, Thomas 193
Gillespy, James 239
Gillespy, Thomas 200
Gilliam, John 41, 171
Gillmore, Chas 235
Gillon, John 173
Gipson, John 12, 13
Given, Edward 181
Given, John 106
Given, Samuel 130, 181
Given, Sarah 242
Given, William 5, 46
Givens, Samuel 110, 217
Givin/s, William 6, 48
Gladden, William 172, 173
Gladney, Richard 21, 23, 98
Glascock, William 181
Glenn, Bernard 49
Glenn, Daniel 77
Glenn, James 17, 27, 49, 65, 156
Glenn, John 121
Glenn, Nathan 65
Glenn, Robert 92, 96, 129
Glenn, Thomas 27, 63
Glover, George 60, 108, 179
Glover, John 192, 193
Glover, Robert 2, 11, 60, 137, 169, 170, 237
Glover, Susanna/h 8, 16, 60
Goad, Mary 148
Goad, William 148
Goar, Mannin 23
Goen, Drewry 133
Goen, Sarah 133
Goin, Job 37
Going, Drewry 226
Going, Drury 37, 38, 74, 75, 77, 82
Going, Elijah 235
Going, Isaac 74, 75

Going, Job 74, 75
Golden, Salley 109
Golden, Sarah 109
Good, William 102, 214
Gorden, John 71, 75
Gorden, Ruth (Anderson) 75
Gordon, 194
Gordon, Alexander 128, 183, 187, 199, 200, 214
Gordon, David 136
Gordon, Hugh 176
Gordon, James 105, 175, 176, 215
Gordon, John 43, 75
Gordon, Poll(e)y 215
Gordon, Sarah 199, 200, 214
Gore, Clement 236
Gore, Davis 224, 241
Gore, Ele(a)zer 44, 62, 68, 224
Gore, Elisha 55, 85
Gore, Elizabeth 68
Gore, Fanny 223
Gore, Francis 87
Gore, James 13, 20, 35, 43, 54, 63, 64, 68, 70, 85, 90, 91, 99, 194, 234, 235
Gore, James Mannin 29
Gore, John 91, 223
Gore, John Ashford 62, 85, 87, 91
Gore, Joshua 52, 68, 165, 166, 195, 223, 236
Gore, Mannen 23, 233
Gore, Mannin 13, 53
Gore, Mannon 103
Gore, Mary 91
Gore, Michael 129, 223, 236, 241
Gore, Thomas 31, 32, 39, 62, 70, 145, 146, 216
Gorham, Wm 56
Gorrell, Agness 24
Gorrell, Ralph 38
Gorrell, Robert 24, 35, 38, 48, 216
Gorrell, Will 24
Gose, Aron 56
Goyen, Drewry 133
Goyen, Sarah 133
Graft 8
Graham, Andrew 78, 105, 110, 131, 148, 154, 173, 174, 187, 198, 199, 200, 214
Graham, George 120
Graham, James 46, 120, 148, 155, 181
Graham, John 143, 144, 159
Graham, Marg(a)ret 78, 187
Graham, Mary 146
Graham, William 65, 140, 159, 167, 170
Grant, James 167, 241
Grant, John 196
Grant, Peter 121, 172

Hamilton, Wm 242
Hampton, 44, 96
Hampton, Charles 61
Hampton, Wade 176
Hances, Thomas 160
Hand, Jonathan 16
Haney, Thomas 88
Hanna, Ann 81
Hanna, James 17, 95, 104, 109, 165, 192
Hanna, Thomas 109
Hannah, Agnes/s 20, 109, 184, 192, 201, 235
Hannah, Ann 235
Hannah, James 192
Hannah, Mary 20
Hannah, Thomas 192
Hannon, Andrew 218
Hanson, Richard 169
Harberson, Mary 89
Harberson, Robert 89
Harbin, Nathaniel 44, 96
Harbinson, Widow 17
Harbison, Alexander 186
Harbison, James 104, 105, 129, 143, 158, 186, 187, 221
Harbison, John 159, 217
Harbison, Margaret 158
Harbison, Matthew 104, 105
Harbison, Patrick 95, 143, 184
Harcum, Elisha 116
Harden, George 209
Harden, Henry 162, 163
Harden, Ralph 163
Hardin, John 42
Hardis, 102
Hardwick 215
Hardwick, Hasel 87, 92, 98, 101, 126, 160, 175
Hardwick, Haz(a)el 4, 11, 13, 45, 53, 63, 109, 234
Hardwick, James 34, 83, 90, 92, 126
Hardwick, Kasel 83
Hardwick, Mary 11
Harkness, Widow 224
Harlowe, John 81, 235
Harmon, Elisabeth 194
Harmon, James 204
Harmon, Samuel 204
Harmond, Andrew 224
Harp, James 39, 40
Harp, Tobias 39
Harper, Daniel 67, 78
Harper, James 81, 151, 163
Harper, John 17
Harper, Margaret 32
Harper, Rachel 151

Harper, Robert 32, 100, 105, 116, 138, 151, 158, 163, 209, 221, 237
Harper, William 59
Harper, Williamson 59, 124, 130, 141
Harris, John 27
Harrison, Charlotte 188, 197
Harrison, H. 203
Harrison, Henry 188, 190, 197
Harrison, Nancy 235
Harrison, widow 233
Harriss, Benjamin 199
Harriss, Samuel 94
Harshaw, Daniel 48
Hart, Ann (Miller) 5
Hart, Michael 33
Harth, John 57
Hartness, Matthew 218
Hartness, Rebekkah (Dodd) 218
Hasden, William 32
Hawkins, James 211
Hawkins, William 92
Hay, David 93
Hayes, John 32, 33, 36
Haynes, Thomas 12
Hays, David 81
Hays, James 31, 34
Hays, John 12, 26, 31, 32, 36, 100, 101, 116, 231, 237
Hays, Mary 100
Hays, Pennelope? 34
Hays, Penneso 34
Hays, William 184
Head, Ann 68
Head, Daniel 84
Head, George 12, 28, 91, 97
Head, Henry 91, 92, 97, 234
Head, James 91, 92, 97, 183
Head, John Stermatt 183
Head, Richard 96, 97, 113, 145, 146, 168
Head, Sarah 145, 146
Head, William 6, 12, 43, 51, 84, 124, 214
Heany, Jane 223
Heany, Thomas 223
Heares, Jane 27
Heares, John 27
Hearis, John 27
Heart, Ann 15
Hedgpeth, John 123, 124
Heges, George 67
Hemphill, Andrew 4, 23, 25, 28, 35, 45-47, 49-51, 53, 54, 58, 73, 78, 92-94, 100, 104, 112, 118, 126-130, 134-137, 140-142, 144, 146, 149-151, 157, 164, 169, 172, 177, 178, 192, 196, 203, 212, 218-221, 226, 228, 232, 234, 239
Hemphill, Charles 151

138, 140, 144, 149, 163, 176-178, 186, 187, 202, 204

Hopkins, Ferdinand 18, 21, 39, 49, 63, 65, 66, 92-94, 96, 114, 128, 129, 163, 176, 185, 199, 204, 217, 219, 227, 241

Hopkins, Ferd 54, 217, 185

Hopkins, Geo W. 227

Hopkins, John 43, 90, 134

Hopkins, Mary 21, 94, 114, 117, 163, 234

Hopkins, Newton 63, 65, 66

Hopkins, Washington 20, 63

Hopkins, William 222, 234

Horton, Harburd/Harburt 210

Horton, Jesse 221, 222

Hoskins, Jehu 154

House, John 194

House, Thomas 111, 178, 194

Housten, Elinor 94

Housten, William 94

Houston, James 4, 105, 109

Hoves, Andrew 228

Howard, John 222

Howard, Mary 222

Howell, Thos 38

Howell, W. 38

Hoyle, Thomas 197

Hoyle, William 199

Hudson, Allen 184

Hudson, David 94

Hudson, George 78

Hudson, Isaac 183, 206, 235

Hudson, Nancy 235

Hudson, William 78, 156

Huey, James 12, 20, 28, 31, 63, 96, 101, 107, 113, 118, 190, 237

Huey, Joseph 169

Huey, Sarah 31, 237

Huffman, Jacob 201

Huger, Daniel 48

Hughes, 179

Hughes, Cager 55

Hughes, Isaac 178

Hughes, Josiah 46, 66

Hughes, Rece 178

Hughes, Rees/e 46, 107, 121

Hughes, Rice 55, 66, 110

Hughes, Richard 41, 216

Hughes, Rua 49

Hughes, Thomas 41, 42, 52, 81

Hughes, W. 143

Hughes, William 42, 43, 77, 133

Hughey, James 90, 96, 97, 117, 237

Hughey, Joseph 63

Hughey, Samuel 27

Hughey, Sarah 90, 237

Hughey, Thomas 114

Hughs, Isaac 81

Hughs, James 133

Hughs, John 81

Hughs, Reece 79, 133, 149, 178

Hughs, Thomas 81, 122

Hughs, William 77, 81

Humphis, John 53

Humphres, Charles 75

Humphres, Elizabeth 75

Humphres, John 13, 75

Humphres, Lucy[?] 23

Humphres, Mary 20

Humphress, William 23

Humphrey, James 222

Humphrey, Thomas 20

Humphreys, Charles 175

Humphreys, Elizabeth 175

Humphreys, John 170, 175, 236

Humphreys, Thomas 20, 111

Humphries, Absalum/Absolum 161

Humphries, Alse 160

Humphries, Charles 69, 84, 160, 161, 233

Humphries, Elisabeth 175, 179

Humphries, Elizabeth 179

Humphries, John 63, 150, 172, 175, 179, 183

Humphries, Mary 20

Humphries, Richard 161

Humphries, Robert 103

Humphries, Thomas 20, 103, 160, 161, 179, 183, 233

Humphries, William 58

Humphris, Charles 13

Humphris, John 66

Humphris, Wm. 23

Humphry/s, Absalom 36

Humphry/s, Charles 175

Humphry/s, John 175

Humpres, Thos 5

Humpris, John 13

Hunt, William 40, 143

Hunter, Agness 203, 228

Hunter, Alexander 68

Hunter, David 5, 11, 21, 25, 27, 37, 39, 41, 45, 79, 121, 143, 164, 171, 178, 184, 187, 198, 203, 226, 228, 235

Hunter, Elisha 93

Hunter, Esther 228

Hunter, George 134

Hunter, Henry 69, 70

Hunter, John 61, 70, 199

Hunter, Samuel 75

Hunter, Samuel Gealy 228

Hunter, William Cochran 228

Hurst, Joseph 116

Huse, Richard 42

Kitchens, Ann 34
Kitchens, Charles 218, 224
Kitchens, Eli 224
Kitchens, Josiah 88, 171, 181
Kitchens, Zachariah 180
Kitchings, Ann 43
Kitchings, Charles 28
Knight, Jon'thn 140
Knowling, Philip 68, 89
Knowling, Samson 68
Knox, Catharine 170
Knox, Elizabeth 11
Knox, Hugh 8, 33, 51, 63, 67, 88-90, 95, 99, 103, 109, 144, 149, 150, 152, 157-159, 164, 165, 168, 170-174, 184, 186, 189, 190, 194-196, 198-200, 203, 204, 212, 224, 233, 236, 238
Knox, James 4, 11, 13, 44, 45, 50-52, 54, 56, 63, 67, 68, 70, 72, 73, 77, 78, 81, 84, 101, 108, 124, 125, 129, 130, 134, 135, 151, 156, 157, 161, 167, 187, 218
Knox, Jane 109, 189
Knox, Jax 132
Knox, Jeannet 122
Knox, Jiney 174
Knox, John 8, 60, 71, 74, 166, 168, 170, 202
Knox, Matthew 156
Knox, Patience 185
Knox, Robert 21, 202
Knox, Samuel 12, 101, 151, 169, 170, 180
Knox, Sarah 81, 92, 125, 159, 196
Knox, William 11, 125, 171, 185, 206
Kolb, Herman 62, 133
Koonrod, Peter 53
Kuykendall, Abraham 23
Lacey, Col. 48
Lacey, Edward 2, 8, 14, 19, 22, 24, 25, 28, 33-37, 41, 47, 49, 52, 53, 58, 61, 65, 76, 92, 96, 102, 105, 107, 136, 138, 143, 148, 154, 157, 166-168, 171, 172, 174, 176, 180-182, 185, 189, 191, 192, 197-199, 204, 205, 207, 209, 210, 224, 230, 238, 241
Lacey, General 216
Lacey, Jane 37, 136, 167
Lacey, John 208
Lacey, Joshua 220
Lacey, Reuben 24, 33, 140, 162, 181, 197, 204, 205, 217, 220, 221, 229
Lacey, Reubin 155
Lacey, Robert 172, 174, 215, 216, 221
Lacey, Rueben 175, 192
Lacey, S. 100
Lacey, Samuel 32, 40, 41, 84, 90, 111, 121, 125, 126, 129-131, 134, 136,
138, 140, 143-146, 148, 154-156, 159, 163, 165, 166, 168-172, 174-176, 179, 181-185, 191, 194-199, 202, 204, 205, 207, 209-217, 220-223, 225, 227, 229, 230, 233-237, 239-242
Lacey, William 145, 174, 198, 207, 209, 210, 229, 238, 239
Lackey, John 137, 178
Lacy, Edward 49
Lacy, Jane 2
Laird, Elizabeth 46
Laird, Lodowick 46
Laird, Messey 55
Laird, Robert 46, 66
Laird, William 46
Lamands, James 32
Lamands, Martha 32
Lamands, Robert 32
Lamonds, Robert 32
Lance, John 67, 115, 117
Land, Benjamin 53
Land, Charlotte 142
Land, Francis 233
Land, James 122, 134
Land, John 25, 45, 118, 135, 181, 222
Land, Mary 232
Land, Richard 134
Land, Thomas 49, 54, 116, 134, 234
Land, Thomas C. 199
Land, William 53, 232
Landers, Ezekiel 25
Lands, John 171
Landsbey, James 106
Lang, Thomas 71
Langbey, James 2
Langsbee, Elizabeth 11
Langsbee, James 11, 12
Langsbey, James 2, 11, 169, 179
Langsby, Elizabeth 11
Langsby, James 11, 12, 42, 137, 170
Lanse, John 142
Lard, Eliz'a 133
Lard, Saml 4
Lard, Sarah 16
Lard, William 16, 30, 180
Larry, Thomas 200
Latta, John 5, 6, 15, 39, 49, 79, 138, 218
Latta, Thomas 138, 175, 178, 218
Lay, James 18
Lay, John 183, 191
Lea, Edmond 31
Lea, Edmund 83, 234
Lea, James 155
Lea, John 181, 194
Lea, Nanc(e)y 83, 234
Lea, Nansey 83
Lea, Owen 220

McCalla, James 42, 117, 145, 148, 217
McCalla, Jane 212
McCalla, Matthew 117
McCalla, Rosa 145
McCalla, Thomas 78, 85
McCalley, Samuel 213
McCalpen, John 223
McCalpin, John 44
McCammon, James 121, 164
McCammon, William 121, 162, 218
McCance, Andrew 178, 191
McCance, Samuel 21, 38, 178, 191, 200, 237
McCannon, John 105, 129
McCarlney, Jane 6
McCarta, Moses 7
McCarter, James 14, 31
McCarter, Moses 148
McCartney, Jain 17
McCartney, Jane 206
McCary, Hervy 150
McCauley, Thomas 78
McCaw, Anne 18
McCaw, James 22, 148
McCaw, John 165, 222
McCaw, Samuel 150, 201
McCaw, William 18, 150, 201, 230
McCawley, James 149
McCawley, Thomas 81
McCay, Elizabeth 231
McCay, Samuel 231
McClanchan, Robert 116
McClary, Robert 1
McClehena, James 28
McClehena, John 28
McClehena, William 28
McCleland, John 103
McCleland, Robert 61, 103
McClelland, John 104
McClelland, Rebecca 104
McClelland, Robert 104
McClenahan, Jas 142
McClenahan, John 57, 113
McClenahan, Robert 142
McClihena, James 28
McClintock, J. 54
McClintock, James 59
McClintock, Matthew 168
McClintock, William 45
McClorkan, John 217
McCluer, H. 230-232
McCluer, Hugh 48, 99, 132, 137, 158, 166, 167, 171, 178, 180, 187-189, 192, 198, 201, 235, 240
McCluer, James 22, 109, 132, 134, 135, 137, 166, 167, 169, 170, 179, 192, 199, 206, 212

McCluer, Jane 132
McCluer, John 50, 123, 231
McCluer, Martha 123
McCluer, William 157
McClure, Charles 4, 9
McClure, Hu's 83
McClure, Hugh 44, 60, 99, 178, 206, 219, 240
McClure, James 2, 7, 8, 11, 21, 23, 48, 50, 187, 201
McClure, Jane 21
McClure, Jean 23
McClure, John 7, 8, 101, 231
McClure, Mary (Gaston) 50
McClure, William 7, 8
McClurken, James 214
McClurken, Jannet 214
McClurken, Matthew 214
McClurkin, Jenny 214
McClurkin, John 120, 147, 198, 213, 214, 219
McClurkin, Marg(a)ret 147, 213
McClurkin, Matthew 155, 177, 196, 199, 200, 214
McClurkin, Robert 219
McClurkin, Thomas 152, 155, 173, 198-200
McColla, David 14
McColla, Mary 14
McCollough, John 45, 125
McCollough, Robert 35
McCollum, Neuman 178
McColpin, Elizabeth 52
McColpin, John 53, 63, 64, 117, 118, 189
McColpin, Nancy 63
McCombs, Ann 96
McCombs, John 53, 96, 167, 215
McConnel, Margaret 78
McCool, Adam 9, 29, 39, 40, 81, 204
McCool, Jane/Jean 81
McCool, John 9, 34, 81, 139, 204, 227, 230
McCool, John Thomas 177, 226
McCool, Joseph 81
McCool, William Love 177, 226
McCorpin, John 125
McCoun, Alexdr 98
McCoun, John 98
McCoun, Moses 72
McCowen, Alexander 67
McCown-- see also McKown, etc.
McCown 226
McCown, Alexander 13, 40, 41, 47, 50, 73, 112, 192, 234
McCown, Elisabeth 50
McCown, Frank 41
McCown, Hannah 119

Fishdam Ford 5, 207, 209, 210
Fishing Creek 1-15, 17, 19-23, 26-30, 32, 33,
    35-43, 46, 47, 50-52, 54, 56, 57, 59, 60, 63,
    66, 67, 69, 70, 72, 73, 76, 78, 79, 82, 83,
    85, 87, 88, 91-93, 98-105, 108-110, 116,
    119-122, 124-126, 130, 136, 137, 139, 141,
    147, 156-160, 162-164, 169, 170, 175-181,
    184, 186, 188, 189, 191, 192, 194, 195, 200,
    201, 203, 206, 209, 217, 218, 221, 228, 230,
    232, 234, 237
Flag Reed 228
Flat Rock Creek 228
Flenthams branch 57
Flinthams/ems Creek 12, 4, 63, 89, 90, 96,
    113, 237
Flintons Creek 127
Floyds waggon road 148
Fort Lacey 66
Franklin County Ga. 233
Franklin County Pa. 82
Georges Run 67
Georgia 58, 136, 193, 204, 226
Gibeses path 22
Giles path 61
Gilford County NC. 4
Gores Adventure 236
Gorrells old field 24
Granby town 52
Grannys Quarter 228
Grannys Quarter Creek 228
Granville County NC. 4, 68, 69, 140
Great Britain 202
Green County Ga. 163
Green Swamp 228
Greene County Ga. 107
Greenville County 19
Greenville County Va. 102, 103
Guilford County NC. 38, 40
Hagues branch 100, 134, 135, 142
Hagues Creek 134
Hallifax County NC. 135, 142
Hampshire County Va. 67
Hancock County Ga. 224
Hardens corner 134
Harvey Cotrel's branch 60
Heages branch 118
Hedges branch 53
Henrys Run 56
Hickory Creek 1
Hogs branch 16
Hogues branch 92, 219
Hopewell Church 157
Houges branch 232
Hunters branch 171, 184
Jack Love's branch 42, 149
Jacob Culp's mill Branch 102
Jewels fork 192, 198
Jinkins Path 166
Johns Creek 219
Jones's Creek 29, 41
Kairney Run 37
Kentucky 63
Kershaw County 91, 94, 145, 192, 228
Kirkpatrick's branch 141

Kitts Creek 240, 241
Lancaster County 13, 16, 40, 45, 70, 75, 78,
    85, 98, 110, 111, 130, 139, 152, 155, 159,
    173, 184, 210, 173, 184, 186, 210, 218, 222
Lancaster District 184
Lancaster Pa. 207
Land's ford 54, 102, 103, 129, 186
Laurance County 71, 72, 76, 77
Leighs branch 235
Lewis's old place 88
Liber[ty] County, SC 91
Lick Branch 156, 180
Liles ford 65
Lincoln County NC. 33, 40, 166, 242
Lincoln County Va. 64
Little River 44, 96, 103, 106, 110, 115, 120,
    128, 146, 154, 174, 183, 194, 228, 234
Little Rocky Creek 27, 49, 55, 110, 134, 135,
    143, 150, 151, 157, 177, 196, 226, 228, 239
Little Sandy River 24, 163
Little Turkey Creek 39, 114, 117, 202, 213
Londonderry Ireland 38
long branch 187
Love's corner 40
Love's Creek 131
Love's ford 24, 98
Love's road 42, 136, 241
Lyles's ford 102, 103
Madison[?] County Ky. 71
Mahafies land 110
Main Fishing Creek 121, 138
Martin's Branch 37, 51, 123, 124, 147, 160,
    220
McClures branch 42
McCollister's old place 167
McCool road 40
McDonald's ford 184, 188
Mecklenburg County NC. 7, 8, 10, 15, 17,
    22, 28, 34, 35, 37, 38, 52, 82, 105, 119, 120,
    127, 122, 138, 148, 152, 156, 171, 172, 222
Mecklenburg NC. 26, 32, 173
Mercer County Ky. 110
Mill Creek 38, 40, 67, 107, 110, 114, 122,
    133, 155, 157, 168, 176, 181, 185, 191, 217,
    235, 242
Mill seat 40
Montgomery County Md. 236
Mreses seat 40
Nation ford 24
Neals Creek 57
Neely's branch 14
New Acquisition District, SC 77
new Great Road 42
Newberry County 39, 53, 62, 126
Ninety Six District 14, 24, 36, 40-42, 50, 81,
    84, 98, 106, 109, 192, 208, 227, 241
North Carolina 2, 4, 38, 46, 48, 58, 63, 67,
    75, 80, 81, 82, 88, 100, 121, 124, 144, 152,
    164, 172, 173, 208, 221, 224, 226, 237
Northampton County Pa. 116
Northumberland County Va. 116
old Cattawba Nation 128
Old Saluda Road 18, 122, 128
Orange County NC. 4, 63, 66

*Orangeburgh District, South Carolina, Estate Partitions
from the Court of Equity, 1824–1837*

*Parish Registers of Prince George Winyah Church,
Georgetown, South Carolina, 1815–1936*

*Petitions for Land from the South Carolina Council Journals
Volume I: 1734/5–1748
Volume II: 1748–1752
Volume III: 1752–1753
Volume IV: 1754–1756
Volume V: 1757–1765*

*South Carolina Deed Abstracts, 1773–1778, Books F-4 through X-4*

*South Carolina Deed Abstracts, 1776–1783, Books Y-4 through H-5*

*South Carolina Deed Abstracts, 1783–1788, Books I-5 through Z-5*

*South Carolina's Royal Grants,
Volume One: Books 1 through 9, 1731–1761
Volume Two: Books 10 through 17, 1760–1768
Volume Three: Books 18 through 24, 1768–1773
Volume Four: Books 25 through 31, 1772–1775
Volume Five: Books 32 through 37, 1735–1776
Volume Six: Books 38 through 41, 1670–1785
Volume Seven: Books 42, 43 and Other Grants, 1711–1775*

*South Carolina's State Grants
Volume I: Grant Books 1 through 6, 1784–1790
Volume II: Grant Books 7 through 11, 1785–1786
Volume III: Grant Books 12 through 15, 1786–1787
Volume IV: Grant Books 16 through 20, 1786–1787
Volume V: Grant Books 16 through 20, 1786–1787*

*Spartanburg County, South Carolina, Will Abstracts 1787–1840*

*The Bedenbaugh-Betenbaugh Family:
Descendants of Johann Michael Bidenbach
from Germany to South Carolina, 1752*

*Tryon County, North Carolina, Minutes of the Court of Pleas
and Quarter Sessions, 1769–1779*

*Union County, South Carolina Deed Abstracts,
Volume I: Deed Books A-F, 1785–1800 [1752–1800]
Volume II: Deed Books G-K, 1800–1811 [1769–1811]
Volume III: Deed Books L-P, 1811–1820 [1770–1820]
Volume IV: Deed Books, 1820–1828
Volume V: Deed Books T-W, 1828–1835 [1778–1835]*

*Union County, South Carolina, Will Abstracts, 1787–1849*

*Winton (Barnwell) County, South Carolina Minutes of
County Court and Will Book 1, 1785–1791*

*York County, South Carolina, Deed Abstracts:
Volume 1: Deed Books A-E, 1786–1801 [1772–1801]*

*York County, South Carolina, Will Abstracts, 1787–1862 [1770–1862]*

www.ingramcontent.com/pod-product-compliance
Lightning Source LLC
Chambersburg PA
CBHW071842270326
41929CB00013B/2077